WORDS AND THEIR WAYS
IN ENGLISH SPEECH

WORDS AND THEIR WAYS
IN ENGLISH SPEECH

BY

JAMES BRADSTREET GREENOUGH
PROFESSOR OF LATIN IN HARVARD UNIVERSITY

AND

GEORGE LYMAN KITTREDGE
PROFESSOR OF ENGLISH IN HARVARD UNIVERSITY

New York
THE MACMILLAN COMPANY
LONDON: MACMILLAN & CO., Ltd.
1920

All rights reserved

COPYRIGHT, 1901,
BY THE MACMILLAN COMPANY.

Set up and electrotyped July, 1901.

Norwood Press
J. S. Cushing & Co. — Berwick & Smith
Norwood Mass. U.S.A.

MEMORIAE

FRANCISCI IACOBI CHILD

MVLTOS ANNOS

VNIV. HARV. PROFESSORIS

DVO

DISCIPVLI EIVS ET AMICI

VT CVM EO ITA INTER SE CONIVNCTI

VTERQVE EIVSDEM VNIV. PROF.

SED LONGE DIVERS. AETATVM ET DIVERS. STVDIORVM

GRATI

HVNC LIBRVM

DEDICANT

PREFACE

THE practical man, who rides in electric cars, talks by the long-distance telephone, and dictates his letters to a stenographer, seldom has time to think that he is the heir of all the ages. Yet, however busy he may be, there are moments when the amazing phenomenon of articulate speech comes home to him as a kind of commonplace miracle. To answer some of the questions that occur to one at such moments is the main purpose of this book.

Chapters XIII and XIV are an essential part of the treatment, but have been so adjusted that the reader who finds them abstruse may skip them without scruple.

Obligations are thankfully acknowledged to a long line of etymologists, lexicographers, and philologists, whom it would be mere pedantry to call by name. The writers find themselves especially indebted to the great Oxford Dictionary, to the publications of Professor Skeat, and to the etymological work of Professor Sheldon in Webster's International Dictionary. Thanks are also due to A. C. Goodell, Esq., Albert Matthews, Esq., and Professor Sheldon for particular favors.

J. B. G.
G. L. K.

TABLE OF CONTENTS

CHAPTER		PAGE
I.	The Origin of Language	1
II.	Language is Poetry	7
III.	Learned Words and Popular Words	19
IV.	Learned Words become Popular	29
V.	Technical or Class Dialects	42
VI.	Slang and Legitimate Speech	55
VII.	The Literary Language	80
VIII.	The Latin in English	93
IX.	Fashion in Language	110
X.	Complexity of the English Vocabulary	128
XI.	Unity of the English Vocabulary	147
XII.	Cognates and Borrowed Words	159
XIII.	The Development of Words. I. Roots, Stems, Inflection	168
XIV.	The Development of Words. II. Derivation and Composition	185
XV.	Fossils	193
XVI.	The Conventional Character of Language	219
XVII.	Generalization and Specialization of Meaning	234
XVIII.	Special Processes in the Development of Meaning: Radiation, etc.	259
XIX.	Transference of Meaning	272

CHAPTER		PAGE
XX.	Degeneration of Meaning	284
XXI.	Euphemism	300
XXII.	Hyperbole or Exaggeration	309
XXIII.	Folk-Etymology	330
XXIV.	Doublets and Homonyms	345
XXV.	Words from the Names of Animals	361
XXVI.	Words from Places or Persons	372
Appendix		391
Index of Matters		397
Index of Words		411

WORDS AND THEIR WAYS
IN ENGLISH SPEECH

ABBREVIATIONS

A.N., Anglo-Norman.
A.S., Anglo-Saxon.
Fr., French.
Ger., German.
Gr., Greek.
Ital., Italian.

L., Latin.
L.L., Low Latin.
O. H. Ger., Old High German.
O.N., Old Norse.
Pg., Portuguese.
Sp., Spanish.

WORDS AND THEIR WAYS

CHAPTER I

THE ORIGIN OF LANGUAGE

THE expression of our thoughts by means of language is a practice of so long standing that we accept it almost as an instinctive performance. Nobody can remember when or how he learned to talk. Indeed, it is seldom possible to recall even those moments in later life when, after the art of speech had been acquired, we became familiar with particular words which, as we know well enough, must have been from time to time added to our personal vocabulary. We can, to be sure, remember when we were first introduced to the technical language of some particular science, as mathematics or medicine or political economy. We may even recollect the person from whom we first heard a new phrase which has since become a part of our habitual stock. And all of us are aware of specific additions to our vocabulary from that ephemeral element in everyday speech known as 'slang,' which is constantly providing us with strange terms that force themselves upon our attention because everybody employs them, and that rapidly die out only to be replaced by equally grotesque novelties. But the sum-total of our retrospect accounts for only the minutest fraction of our whole outfit of words and phrases. And were it not for our observation of infants, who cannot speak at all, and of young children, who are painfully learning the art of speech, we should inevitably believe that the expression of our thoughts in language was spontaneous action, quite independent of our own will and exertions, like breathing or the circulation of the blood.

Yet no phenomenon is more amazing than that of speech. Nor can any process be imagined more complicated than that by which the vocabulary of a highly developed language, like English, comes into existence and fits itself to the multifarious needs of civilized man in the utterance of thought and emotion. If to the process of oral speech we add the corollary processes of reading and writing, we have a series of phenomena which no thinking man can contemplate without a kind of awe.

Language is the expression of thought by means of words; that is, by means of signs of a peculiar sort made with the vocal organs. Since the tongue is one of the most important of these organs, and since we are habitually conscious of using it in articulation, we often call our language our 'tongue,' — and the word *language* itself is derived, through the French, from *lingua*, the Latin name for that organ.[1]

The origin of language is an unsolved problem. It was once supposed that man was created a talking animal; that is to say, that he could speak immediately on his creation, through a special faculty inherent in his very nature. Some scholars maintained that our first parents were instructed in the rudiments of speech by God himself, or that language *in esse* was a gift bestowed by the deity

---

[1] M.E. *langage*, from Fr. *langage*, from L. *lingua*.

immediately after Adam was created. Along with these opinions went, in former times, the opinion that Hebrew, the language of the Jewish Scriptures, was the primitive tongue of mankind. None of these views are now in favor, either with theologians or with philologists. However we conceive the first man to have come into existence, we are forced to believe that language as we know it was a human invention. Not language itself, but the inherent power to frame and develop a language was the birthright of man. This result, it will be seen, is purely negative. It defines what the origin of language was *not*, but it throws no light on the question what it *was*, and no satisfactory answer to the question has ever been proposed. Some scholars believe that human speech originated in man's attempt to imitate the sounds of nature, as if a child should call a dog 'bow-wow,' or a cow 'moo.' No doubt such imitation accounts for a certain number of words in our vocabulary, but there are great difficulties in carrying out the theory to its ultimate results. All that can be said is that the 'bow-wow theory,' as it is jocosely called, has never been driven from the field. Another view, which may be traced without any great difficulty to Herder's attempt to explain 'the speech of animals,' has found a warm defender in Max Müller. According to this view, which has a specious appearance of philosophical profundity, the utterances of primitive man were the spontaneous result, by reflex action, of impressions produced upon him by various external phenomena. Though the 'ding-dong theory,' as it is derisively called, is now discredited, and, in its entirety, is hardly susceptible of intelligible statement, it may, after all, contain a grain of truth.

Another partly discredited theory seeks the origin of

language in such involuntary exclamations as *oh! bah! pshaw!* and the like. Hence it is often called the 'pooh-pooh theory.'

The upshot of the whole discussion is a confession of ignorance. The impossibility of arriving at the truth is more and more evident, as the stupendous length of man's residence upon this planet before the dawn of history is more and more clearly recognized. We do not know, and we can never know, how language began. Yet we can study some of the processes of its development in form and in meaning for a period extending over several thousand years, and we find these processes essentially identical with those that we can imperfectly observe within the limits of our own lifetime.

Well-chosen words, arranged in a felicitous order, have a peculiar cadence which pleases the ear, irrespective of any meaning which they convey to the mind.[1] If the cadence is sufficiently measured, the result is verse or, to use the popular term, poetry. Now it is a familiar fact of literary history that good poetry always precedes good prose in the order of development. Indeed, the art of writing unmetrical language in a forcible and pleasing style is one of the latest achievements of any literature.

In the eighteenth century, when much attention was given to literary and linguistic origins, but when these were investigated on a basis rather of sentimental prepossession than of scientific reason, and when the body of material available for evidence was extremely scanty and had not been properly sifted, a peculiar theory of

---

[1] This is shown by the popularity of nursery rhymes and similar nonsensical jingles. Compare also 'The Hunting of the Snark,' and Aytoun's parody on Tennyson: 'Worship Mighty Mumbo Jumbo in the Mountains of the Moon.'

the connection between language and poetry gained very general favor. It was expressed in a taking form by Hamann, whose celebrated dictum, 'Poetry is the mother tongue of man,' was taken up and enforced by Herder in a way that gave it a commanding influence on contemporary thought, — an influence, indeed, which it has not altogether lost, even in the present age, whose tendencies are so different from those that prevailed a hundred years ago.

Primitive man was conceived by the romantic imagination of the eighteenth century as leading an ideal existence. Uncorrupted by contact with civilization, he lived near to nature, and all nature spoke to him in a voice more immediately intelligible than we can now conceive, even in the case of a poet like Wordsworth. Thus sympathetically impressed by natural phenomena, man gave utterance to the thoughts and feelings which they produced within him in melodious sounds, which instantly took shape as poetry. In short, according to this conception, language and song are inseparable, and our poetry is nothing but a survival, under more artificial conditions, of the primitive language which mankind uttered in the Golden Age.

Such theories are now known to be based on a false conception of the history of mankind as well as of the nature of articulate speech. Yet, like all theories that have at any time commanded the assent of thinking men, they must embody, in an imperfect expression, some quantum of truth. Primitive man may not have sung like the birds, but there is certainly a natural rhythm in language to which the mind and feelings immediately respond, just as there is a natural rhythm in the beating of the heart, the drawing of the breath, and even in many movements of the body which we call 'voluntary' and regard as arbitrarily controlled by the individual will. Language, that is to say, may not be poetry *in esse*, but it is always potential verse. From another point of view, too, the saying of Hamann may be justified if we interpret it with the license that all oracles demand. There is no process of figurative language, no device of grammar or rhetoric, no whim even of pedantic theorizers on eloquence, which does not find its parallel over and over again in the unstudied processes of our ordinary speech. It is profoundly true that 'all language is poetry.'[1]

[1] For further remarks on the origin of language see p. 391.

CHAPTER II

LANGUAGE IS POETRY

WHEN we examine the dictionary of any highly developed language like English, we are impressed not only with the enormous extent of the vocabulary, but with its infinite variety. There are plain words for common things (as *bread, stone, house, child, horse*) and simple physical acts (as *eat, drink, run, climb*); there are formal or dignified or poetical words for equally simple conceptions (like *residence, progeny, quaff, masticate*); there are vague words (like *thing, affair, matter, act, do*) and scientific terms of rigid exactness (like *oxygen, atmosphere, chloride, carbon, inoculate*); there are abstract terms for mental and moral qualities (as *sagacity, carelessness, probity, honor*) and adjectives describing persons who exemplify these qualities (as *sagacious, careless, honest, honorable*); there are words of a distinctly undignified character (like *chum, crank, bamboozle, blubber, bawl, fizzle*), others so dignified as to be uncommon in familiar talk (as *remunerative, emolument, eleemosynary, recalcitrant*) or so high-sounding as hardly to be allowable even in elaborate writing (as *exacerbate, cachinnation, adumbrate*); there are words which have poetical associations (as *golden, roseate, silver-tongued, gambol, soaring, eterne*), and others so prosaic that every poet avoids them (as *fry, exchequer, discount, cross-question, extra, medium, miscellaneous*); there are words so technical as to be understood by specialists only (as *elec-*

trolysis, cotyledon, ontology, quaternions), and others so childish as to be confined to the dialect of the nursery (as *naughty, mammy, dad, dolly*).

Frequently, too, we find a number of different words ('synonyms,' we call them) for what is essentially the same idea:[1] *ask, request, beseech, pray, beg, petition, supplicate, entreat, implore, solicit, crave, importune; angry, wrathful, incensed, irritated, vexed, resentful, enraged, furious, indignant, exasperated, irate, hot, infuriated; join, unite, associate, unify, link, connect, couple, combine.*[2]

The same marvellous variety shows itself when we study the different meanings of a single word. Thus *figure* may be equally well applied to a person's form, a polygon, a numerical sign, an elaborate drawing or picture in a book, a metaphor or simile; *energy* may be used in a general sense or in the technical language of science ('the conservation of *energy*'); *property* may be a quality, one's possessions, or (in theatrical language) a thing or utensil used in setting the stage; *character* may refer to one's personal qualities, or it may denote a mark or sign in writing or printing, or it may be colloquially used for an eccentric person.

The question is immediately suggested: Whence does a nation provide itself with this enormous mass of words, with their multifarious meanings so aptly differentiated as to express all the aspects of any conception that can occur to the mind of civilized man?

In the first place, no people is perfectly homogeneous,

---

[1] So-called synonyms almost always differ from each other in some shade of meaning, or in emphasis, or at all events in their connotations.

[2] The reader may easily multiply examples by collecting, for instance, the synonyms for *awkward, beautiful, healthy, strange, throw, go, law, sin, people, custom.*

and this is strikingly true of the English nation, which is
'Saxon and Norman and Dane,' as Tennyson wrote, and
Celtic as well. Each component part of the population
contributes its proportion of words, — small or large, but
always characteristic, and distinct in many particulars from
the contributions of all the rest. Then, too, all cultivated
languages have borrowed much from outside nations with
whom they have come in contact in war or trade or literature. Our own language, as we shall see, has enriched
itself in this way from every quarter of the globe.

The varied materials thus brought together are constantly subjected to what may be called mechanical processes of growth.[1] Every language has its machinery of
prefixes and suffixes and compounds, by means of which a
single word may become the centre of a considerable group
of related terms : as, *true, tru-th, tru-ly, un-true, un-tru-ly,
tru-th-ful, tru-th-ful-ness,* etc.

But these causes are not sufficient to explain the richness
and complexity of our speech. Such a result was achieved
only when this great mass of variously derived material
had been subjected for centuries to the language-making
instinct; that is, to the poetic faculty of man. The dictum
that 'all language is poetry,' then, if properly understood,
goes far toward answering the question with which we
are concerned.

The essentially poetical or figurative character of language may easily be seen by comparing a number of
passages from the poets with ordinary prosaic expressions.

When Wordsworth writes, in Laodamia, —

> The gods approve,
> The *depth*, and not the tumult of the soul,

---

[1] These processes will be studied in Chapters XIII, XIV.

the imaginative power of his phrasing at once appeals to us. If, however, we compare such common expressions as 'He was *deeply* moved,' '*profoundly* affected,' 'from the *bottom* of my heart,' we recognize the same figure of speech. In other words, the poetical history of Wordsworth's line goes back to that unknown time when some primitive poet, without knowing that he was talking poetry, first applied to the emotions words which in their literal sense were only applicable to the physical conception of *depth*. As time has passed, the primitive metaphor has grown so familiar that it has ceased to be a metaphor. It has become merely an ordinary meaning of a group of common words. The modern poet, perceiving the imaginative significance of this usage, elaborated the figure it embodied, phrased it anew with conscious literary art, and thus, in an instant, restored it to its full poetic rights. Similarly, we may compare with 'the *tumult* of the soul,' such prose expressions as 'his mind was *disturbed*,' 'his *agitation* was painful to witness,' 'the *violence* of his *emotion*,' — each of which, though no longer felt as figurative, embodies a metaphor precisely similar to Wordsworth's.[1] We are not at this moment concerned with the ethical or philosophical contents of Wordsworth's line, for these might have been stated, with perfect accuracy, in the plainest terms, but merely with the poetical language in which he clothed his thought.

When Banquo says to Macbeth that the witches' salutation 'might yet *enkindle* him unto the crown,' we perceive

---

[1] *Disturb* is to 'drive asunder in disorder,' from L. *dis-*, 'apart,' and *turba*, 'disorder,' 'a riotous crowd.' *Agitation* comes from L. *agito*, 'to drive to and fro.' *Violence* is from *vis*, 'force.' *Emotion* is the 'act of moving (one) away,' 'disturbance (of mind).'

that *enkindle* is used metaphorically. So, also, when Macbeth declares

> 'I have no *spur*
> To *prick* the sides of my intent.'

But we feel the figure less vividly in such a phrase as '*fired* with ambition,' and in the terms *instigation* and *incentive* we are not conscious of any metaphor whatever. Yet *instigation* comes from a root which means 'to goad,' and *incentive* means literally 'that which sets the tune' (from L. *in* and *canere*, 'to sing'); so that both these words were, in their first application to 'motives' or 'promptings,' quite as poetical as either *enkindle* or *spur*.

The ordinary processes by which words change their meanings are, then, essentially the same as the devices of poetry; or, to express the fact more accurately, the figurative language of poetry differs from the speech of common life mainly in employing fresher figures, or in revivifying those which have lost their freshness from age and constant use.

Language is fossil poetry which is constantly being worked over for the uses of speech. Our commonest words are worn-out metaphors.

Thus, *depend* is literally 'to hang from' (L. *dependo*); *egregious* means 'selected from the [common] herd' (L. *e*, 'from,' and *grex, gregis*, 'herd'); *spoil* means 'to strip,' i.e. 'to strip off the armor, etc., of a slain or defeated enemy'; *front* means 'forehead' (L. *frons, frontis*); *to fret* is originally 'to eat up,' 'to devour' (A.S. *fretan, for-*, 'away,' and *etan*, 'eat'), — compare 'gnawing anxiety'; *precocious* means 'too early ripe' (L. *praecox*, from *prae-*, 'before,' and *coquo*, 'to cook,' 'to ripen'); *to thrill* is literally 'to bore,' 'to pierce,' and is related to *drill* (the same word is seen in *nostril*, formerly *nosethril*); *sullen* means at first 'solitary' and comes (through the French) from L *solus*, 'alone' (whence our adjective *sole*).

Such illustrations might be multiplied indefinitely. Indeed, almost every word that we shall have occasion to study will serve as an example, for the processes that we are considering go on incessantly so long as a language is alive. We shall find that there is no device which we are accustomed to call poetical, no similitude so slight, no metaphor so strained or so commonplace, that language has not seized upon it to make new forms of expression as the needs of advancing thought required them. Even when the resultant words appear intensely prosaic, the processes that created them are identical with those of artistic poetry.

This important truth may be further illustrated in the growth of words from a single root.

The Indo-European family of languages (to which belong Sanskrit, Greek, Latin, English, and many other tongues) had a simple linguistic form (a 'root') PET, which signified 'rapid motion across the field of vision.'[1] This root is clearly seen in the Latin verb *peto*. Since such motion is produced either by *falling* or by *flying*, words with these meanings have been formed from the root PET in various languages of our family.[2] But such motion may include also the idea of 'intentional direction.' Hence other words from the same root have acquired the sense of 'aim,' and, by the transference from actual to figurative aim, the meanings (originally metaphorical) of 'seek' and 'ask.' All three senses, 'aim,'

---

[1] For the nature of roots and stems see Chapter XIII.
[2] Thus, Gr. πίπτω, πιτνέω, 'I fall'; πέτομαι, 'I fly.'

LANGUAGE IS POETRY

'seek,' and 'ask,' are found in the Latin verb *peto*. Thus from this one root PET, we have, by various differentiations of meaning, such words [1] as the following: —

Latin *penna*, 'a means of flying,' 'a wing,' 'a feather,' — whence, through the French, the English *pen*, originally applied to a quill used for writing, but now extended to other devices (steel pen, gold pen, stylographic pen, etc.).

Greek πτῶσις (*ptôsis*), 'a falling,' — then, figuratively, 'a case' in grammar (since the genitive, dative, and other so-called 'oblique' cases were conceived as *falling away from* the nominative, which was fancifully called the 'upright case').

im-petus, 'a force of forward movement,' — first literal, then figurative.

ap-petite, 'a craving' (of body or mind).

re-peat, 'to go back *to get* something,' 'to take up a thing a second time.'

petition, 'a seeking,' 'a request.'

com-petition, 'a seeking together,' — then, especially, 'rivalry' (in modern times applied especially to commercial rivalry).

petulant, 'butting' (as goats do), 'attacking,' — then figuratively, for 'ill-humored,' 'irritable.'

Another root, PU, meant 'clean,' and thence came the Latin adjectives *putus*, 'clean,' and *purus*, 'clear.' From *putus* arose a verb *puto*, 'to clean.' In a vine-bearing country, *cleaning* is particularly 'pruning,' and from that idea, specially applied in surgery, we get *amputation*. In mercantile language 'to clean up accounts' (*putare rationes*) became a common expression for 'reckoning,' and finally 'accounts' (*rationes*) was dropped, and *puto* was used for 'reckon' in general (as in *computation*). From 'reckon' we pass easily to 'think,' [2] and this becomes the

---

[1] These words are built up by the mechanical means of word-formations developed in the various languages. Such formative mechanics will be treated later (see Chapters XIII, XIV).

[2] Compare the provincial use of *I reckon* for 'I think,' in both England and America.

ruling sense of *puto* (as in the adjective *putative*). From the same mercantile dialect comes *imputo*, 'reckon in,' 'credit or charge to the account of,' whence we get *imputation*. From 'considering' or 'turning back to observe' (cf. *re-gard*, *re-spect*, both meaning originally 'to look back') we get the word *reputation;* and *deputation* is derived from another idea of 'consideration carried out in *resolve*.' Thus from a root signifying originally 'clean,' the imagination of the race, utilizing the mechanical means which the laws of derivation and composition afford, has gradually formed a group of words of the most varied meaning. Vine-dressing, surgery, mathematics, commerce, and politics are all included within this circle, and one word (*reputation*) is general enough to apply to all men.

Finally we may establish the poetical character of language by a striking and conclusive test. Literature has been attentively studied, *as literature*, for hundreds and even thousands of years. Hence there has grown up among scholars a set of technical terms, — the names of the so-called 'figures of speech,' — which designate what are commonly regarded as the ornaments or devices that characterize the poetical style as opposed to the speech of everyday life. Yet it is easy to see that all of these 'figures' are perfectly familiar in our ordinary talk. *Metaphor*, the most important of all figures, we have already considered. It occurs everywhere, and one can hardly utter a sentence without employing it. Every occupation of mankind, every subject (however remote) that engages man's attention, has furnished us with metaphorical expressions.[1] We shall have occasion to return to this point again and again. For the present we may

[1] The particular sources of the English vocabulary will be discussed in later chapters.

pass to other figures, making a selection from those comprised in the list commonly printed in works on grammar or rhetoric.

Simile is involved in the great class of English adjectives that end in *-ly*, which is an abraded form of *like*.[1] Thus a '*manly* boy' is a boy who is '*like* a man' in certain traits of character. So *cowardly*, *ruffianly*, *saintly*, *homely* ('like home,' and so 'ordinary,' 'commonplace,' with a further development of meaning in America to 'hard-featured,' 'plain'). Still clearer cases of simile are the more recent adjectives compounded with *like:* as, *childlike*, *lionlike*, *birdlike*, *homelike*, etc.

Metonymy is the figure by which a thing is designated, not by its own name, but by the name of something that resembles or suggests it, — as in Tennyson's 'the bright death' for 'the keen fatal knife,' or Horace's *Pontica pinus* for 'ship of wood from Pontus.' This 'figure' is so common in ordinary speech that it seldom attracts our attention. Thus we say *irons* for 'fetters,' *glasses* for 'spectacles,' or 'drinking-glasses,' *the knife* for 'surgery,' *canvas* for 'sails,' *style* (from L. *stilus*, a writing implement) for 'manner of writing,' *bilboes* for 'shackles' (from *Bilbao*, in Spain, famous for its iron and steel), and so on. Many of the words thus treated are perfectly prosaic, but the process is the same as that of poetry. A man's *linen* or *flannels* are just as much metonymy as Milton's 'nodding horror' for the branches of a thick and dismal forest.

Synecdoche (the part for the whole, the genus for the species, or *vice versa*) is seen in 'sixty *head*' (of cattle), 'fifty *sail*' (of ships), 'a *bottomry* bond,' 'a *poll* tax,' a *rumshop*, a *gin-palace*, a *cutthroat* for a 'murderer,' a *hangman* for an 'executioner.'

[1] See pp. 185–6 for details.

Antonomasia, or the use of a person's name for any one who resembles him, is very common : a *Solomon*, a *Shylock*, 'a *Daniel* come to judgment,' a *Mæcenas*, 'a regular *Nero*,' 'a *Roland* for an *Oliver*.'

Hyperbole is natural in unstudied speech: 'I beg a *thousand* pardons,' 'scared to *death*,' 'I'd give the *world* to see him.' Expressions of approval and disapproval are especially affected by hyperbole ('good for nothing,' 'a magnificent idea'), and the language of schoolgirls is proverbially made up of it: 'thanks awfully,' 'extravagantly fond,' 'tremendously angry,' 'immensely obliged.'

Antithesis is frequent in the commonest expressions: as, 'up and down,' 'hither and yon,' 'this way and that.' So, 'Napoleon the Little,' 'Prince and Peasant.'

Alliteration, a favorite poetic fancy, is found in such phrases as, 'tit for tat,' 'blind as a bat,' 'spick and span,' 'the seven senses,' 'neck or nothing,' 'rough and ready.'

Onomatopœia has given rise to such words as *whiz*, *buzz*, *chickadee*, *bobolink*, and countless others. Many of them are humorous, and not a few are slangy.

Irony appears in 'a *pretty* how-d'ye-do!' 'Here's richness!' and other colloquialisms. Horace's 'splendide mendax' is called a poetical *oxymoron*, but such phrases as 'a magnificent failure,' 'a beautiful imbroglio,' 'to swim like a stone,' show the same figure, — the joining of two inconsistent words to produce a peculiar rhetorical effect.

Catachresis, as it is called by the pedantic grammarians, — that is, an 'abuse' of language consisting in the employment of a harsh metaphor, — is not peculiar to the poets. A well-known writer has ventured 'He *spasmed* to him,' to express the act of a boy making signs to another by contortion of the face. This is not likely to become good English, but it might easily become slang, and 'mis-

LANGUAGE IS POETRY

uses of language' quite as extraordinary have often made their way into our vocabulary. 'To *jockey* a confiding partner' is an example. A *chaush* is a Turkish official interpreter; in 1609, a particular *chaush* is said to have distinguished himself by swindling a number of merchants in London; hence *chouse* for 'defraud,'—a sufficiently good instance of *catachresis* in its origin.

Litotes, or understatement, is found in all languages, but is heard particularly in New England provincialisms, as well as in slang. It comes partly from euphemism, and partly from caution or hesitation. Thus we have 'the late unpleasantness' for the Civil War, 'no conjuror' for a stupid person, 'pretty well' and 'so-so' for 'in good health.' The sarcastic *rather!* may be compared.

Periphrasis, like litotes, is a favorite means of avoiding plain language: 'he came to grief,' 'I hope nothing will happen to him,' 'I am inclined to think your accounts are not very accurate,' will serve as examples.

Pleonasm, or the practice of saying the same thing twice over in the same expression, is a universal characteristic of speech: as, 'go back again,' 'reared up,' 'go away from here,' 'he fell down and jumped up again.' Excessive pleonasm is of course objectionable, but it is idle for the purist to object to such idiomatic phrases as those which we have just cited. They are of the very fibre of language. As well complain of 'John! John!' or 'no! no!' on the ground that one *John* or one *no* would suffice. The double comparative ('*most unkindest* cut of all'), formerly in good use, is an excellent example of pleonasm.[1] The same tendency may be seen in such compounds as *inexsuperabilis*.

---

[1] Many forms which appear to be units are really instances of 'double comparison.' Thus *nearer* is *near* (comparative of *nigh*) with a comparative suffix -*er* added. Similarly *farther*, *nethermost*, *uppermost*, and so

Thus we have subjected the principle that 'language is poetry' to a variety of tests. We have compared specific passages of poetry with ordinary phraseology, and have found a similarly metaphorical character in both. We have observed the imaginative nature of the development of many meanings from a simple root-idea. We have recognized the existence of many so-called 'figures of speech' in the commonest locutions of everyday life. We may feel certain, therefore, that the principle is a sound one, and may utilize it whenever it appears to be useful in our further study of English words.

on. Compare the incorrect *furtherer* and *furtherest*, which are simply examples of the same tendency that have not had the fortune to gain admittance to good linguistic society. Cf. p. 200.

CHAPTER III

LEARNED WORDS AND POPULAR WORDS

In every cultivated language there are two great classes of words which, taken together, comprise the whole vocabulary. First, there are those words with which we become acquainted in ordinary conversation, — which we learn, that is to say, from the members of our own family and from our familiar associates, and which we should know and use even if we could not read or write. They concern the common things of life, and are the stock in trade of all who speak the language. Such words may be called 'popular,' since they belong to the people at large and are not the exclusive possession of a limited class.

On the other hand, our language includes a multitude of words which are comparatively seldom used in ordinary conversation. Their meanings are known to every educated person, but there is little occasion to employ them at home or in the market-place. Our first acquaintance with them comes not from our mother's lips or from the talk of our schoolmates, but from books that we read, lectures that we hear, or the more formal conversation of highly educated speakers, who are discussing some particular topic in a style appropriately elevated above the habitual level of everyday life. Such words are called 'learned,' and the distinction between them and 'popular' words is of great importance to a right understanding of linguistic process.

The difference between popular and learned words may be easily seen in a few examples. We may describe a girl as 'lively' or as 'vivacious.' In the first case, we are using a native English formation from the familiar noun *life*. In the latter, we are using a Latin derivative which has precisely the same meaning. Yet the atmosphere of the two words is quite different. No one ever got the adjective *lively* out of a book. It is a part of everybody's vocabulary. We cannot remember a time when we did not know it, and we feel sure that we learned it long before we were able to read. On the other hand, we must have passed several years of our lives before learning the word *vivacious*. We may even remember the first time that we saw it in print or heard it from some grown-up friend who was talking over our childish heads. Both *lively* and *vivacious* are good English words, but *lively* is 'popular' and *vivacious* is 'learned.'

From the same point of view we may contrast the following pairs of synonyms:[1] *the same, identical; speech, oration; fire, conflagration; choose, select; brave, valorous; swallowing, deglutition; striking, percussion; building, edifice; shady, umbrageous; puckery, astringent; learned, erudite; secret, cryptic; destroy, annihilate; stiff, rigid; flabby, flaccid; queer, eccentric; behead, decapitate; round, circular; thin, emaciated; fat, corpulent; truthful, veracious; try, endeavor; bit, modicum; piece, fragment; sharp, acute; crazy, maniacal; king, sovereign; book, volume; lying, mendacious; beggar, mendicant; teacher, instructor; play, drama; air, atmosphere; paint, pigment.*

The terms 'popular' and 'learned,' as applied to words, are not absolute definitions. No two persons have the

[1] Not all the words are exact synonyms, but that is of no importance in the present discussion.

same stock of words, and the same word may be 'popular' in one man's vocabulary and 'learned' in another's.[1] There are also different grades of 'popularity'; indeed there is in reality a continuous gradation from infantile words like *mamma* and *papa* to such erudite derivatives as *concatenation* and *cataclysm*. Still, the division into 'learned' and 'popular' is convenient and sound. Disputes may arise as to the classification of any particular word, but there can be no difference of opinion about the general principle. We must be careful, however, to avoid misconception. When we call a word 'popular,' we do not mean that it is a favorite word, but simply that it belongs to the people as a whole, — that is, it is everybody's word, not the possession of a limited number. When we call a word 'learned,' we do not mean that it is used by scholars alone, but simply that its presence in the English vocabulary is due to books and the cultivation of literature rather than to the actual needs of ordinary conversation.

Here is one of the main differences between a cultivated and an uncultivated language. Both possess a large stock of 'popular' words; but the cultivated language is also rich in 'learned' words, with which the ruder tongue has not provided itself, simply because it has never felt the need of them.

In English it will usually be found that the so-called learned words are of foreign origin. Most of them are derived from French or Latin, and a considerable number from Greek. The reason is obvious. The development

---

[1] It is instructive to study one's own vocabulary from this point of view, — making a list of (1) those words which we feel sure we learned in childhood, (2) those which we have learned in later life, but not from books, (3) those which have entered our vocabulary from books. We shall also find it useful to consider the difference between our reading vocabulary and our speaking vocabulary.

of English literature has not been isolated, but has taken place in close connection with the earnest study of foreign literatures. Thus, in the fourteenth century, when our language was assuming substantially the shape which it now bears, the literary exponent of English life and thought, Geoffrey Chaucer, the first of our great poets, was profoundly influenced by Latin literature as well as by that of France and Italy. In the sixteenth and seventeenth centuries, the Greek and Latin classics were vigorously studied by almost every English writer of any consequence, and the great authors of antiquity were regarded as models, not merely of general literary form, but of expression in all its details. These foreign influences have varied much in character and intensity. But it is safe to say that there has been no time since 1350 when English writers of the highest class have not looked to Latin, French, and Italian authors for guidance and inspiration. From 1600 to the present day the direct influence of Greek literature and philosophy has also been enormous, — affecting as it has the finest spirits in a peculiarly pervasive way, — and its indirect influence is quite beyond calculation. Greek civilization, we should remember, has acted upon us, not merely through Greek literature and art, but also through the medium of Latin, since the Romans borrowed their higher culture from Greece.

Now certain facts in the history of our language have made it peculiarly inclined to borrow from French and Latin. The Norman Conquest in the eleventh century made French the language of polite society in England; and, long after the contact between Norman-French and English had ceased to be of direct significance in our linguistic development, the reading and speaking of French and the study of French literature formed an important part of the education of English-speaking men and women. When literary English was in process of formation in the fourteenth and fifteenth centuries, the authors whose works determined the cultivated vocabulary were almost as familiar with French as with their mother tongue, and it was therefore natural that they should borrow a good many French words. But these same authors were also familiar with Latin, which, though called a dead language, has always been the professional dialect of ecclesiastics and a *lingua franca* for educated men. Thus the borrowing from French and from Latin went on side by side, and it is often impossible to say from which of the two languages a particular English word is taken. The practice of naturalizing French and Latin words was, then, firmly established in the fourteenth century, and when, in the sixteenth century, there was a great revival of Greek studies in England, the close literary relations between Greece and Rome facilitated the adoption of a considerable number of words from the Greek. Linguistic processes are cumulative: one does not stop when another begins. Hence we find all of these influences active in increasing the modern vocabulary. In particular, the language of science has looked to Greece for its terms, as the language of abstract thought has drawn its nomenclature from Latin.

It would, however, be a great mistake to suppose that all our 'popular' terms are of native origin, and that all foreign derivatives are 'learned.' The younger and less cultivated members of a community are naturally inclined to imitate the speech of the older and more cultivated. Hence, as time has passed, a great number of French and Latin words, and even some that are derived from the

Greek, have made themselves quite at home in ordinary conversation. Such words, whatever their origin, are as truly popular as if they had been a part of our language from the earliest period.

Examples of such popular[1] words of foreign derivation are the following: —

From French: *army, arrest, bay, card, catch, city, chase, chimney, conveyance, deceive, entry, engine, forge, hour, letter, mantle, mason, merchant, manner, mountain, map, move, navy, prince, pen, pencil, parlor, river, rage, soldier, second, table, veil, village.*

From Latin: *accommodate, act, add, adopt, animal, anxious, applause, arbitrate, auction, agent, calculate, cancer, circus, collapse, collision, column, congress, connect, consequence, contract, contradict, correct, creation, cucumber, curve, centennial, decorate, delicate, dentist, describe, diary, diffident, different, digest, direct, discuss, divide, educate, elect, emigrant, equal, erect, expect, extra, fact, genius, genuine, graduate, gratis, horrid, imitate, item, joke, junction, junior, major, magnificent, medicine, medium, miser, obstinate, omit, pagan, pastor, pauper, pedal, pendulum, permit, picture, plague, postpone, premium, prevent, prospect, protect, quiet, recess, recipe, reduce, regular, salute, secure, series, single, species, specimen, splendid, strict, student, subscribe, subtract, suburb, suffocate, suggest, tedious, timid, urge, vaccinate, various, ventilation, vest, veto, victor, vim, vote.*

From Greek: *anthracite, apathy, arsenic, aster, athlete, atlas, attic, barometer, biography, calomel, catarrh, catholic, catastrophe, catechism, caustic, chemist, crisis, dialogue, diphtheria, elastic, encyclopedia, hector, homeopathy, iodine, lexicon, microscope, monotonous, myth, neuralgia, panic,*

---

[1] The **exact grade of** 'popularity' differs in these examples (see p. 21).

panorama, photograph, skeleton, strychnine, tactics, telegraph, tonic, zoölogy.

No language can borrow extensively from foreign sources without losing a good many words of its own. Hence, if we compare the oldest form of English (Anglo-Saxon) with our modern speech, we shall discover that many words that were common in Anglo-Saxon have gone quite out of use, being replaced by their foreign equivalents. The 'learned' word has driven out the 'popular' word, and has thereupon, in many cases, become 'popular' itself. Thus instead of A.S. *herë* we use the French word *army;* instead of *thegn* or *thēow*, the French word *servant;* instead of *sciphere* (a compound of the Anglo-Saxon word for *ship* and that for *army*), we use *navy;* instead of *micel*, we say *large;* instead of *sigë*, *victory;* instead of *swīthë*, *very;* instead of *lāf*, we say *remainder* or *remnant*, — and so on.

Curiously enough, it sometimes happens that when both the native and the foreign word still have a place in our language, the latter has become the more popular, — the former being relegated to the higher or poetical style. Thus it is more natural for us to say *divide* (from L. *divido*) than *cleave* (from A.S. *cleōfan*); *travel* than *fare;* [1] *river* than *stream; castle* than *burg; residence* than *dwelling; remain* than *abide; expect* than *ween; pupil* or *scholar* than *learner; destruction* than *bale; protect* or *defend* than *shield; immediately* than *straightway; encourage* than *hearten; present* than *bestow; firm* than *steadfast; direct* than *forthright; impetuous* than *heady; modest* than *shamefaced; prince* than *atheling; noise* or *tumult* or *disturbance* than *din; people* than *folk;* [2] *prophet* than *soothsayer; fate*

---

[1] *Fare* is still common as a noun and in figurative senses.
[2] But the irregular plural *folks* is a common colloquialism.

than *weird;* lancer than *spearman;* I intend than I am minded; excavate than *delve;* resist than *withstand;* beautiful than *goodly;* gracious than *kindly.* The very fact that the native words belong to the older stock has made them poetical; for the language of poetry is always more archaic than that of prose.

Frequently we have kept both the native and the foreign word, but in different senses, thus increasing our vocabulary to good purpose. The foreign word may be more emphatic than the native: as in *brilliant, bright; scintillate, sparkle; astonishment, wonder; a conflagration, a fire; devour, eat up; labor, work.* Or the native word may be more emphatic than the foreign: as in *stench, odor; straightforward, direct; dead, deceased; murder, homicide.* Often, however, there is a wide distinction in meaning. Thus *driver* differs from *propellor; child* from *infant; history* from *tale; book* from *volume; forehead* from *front; length* from *longitude; moony* from *lunar; sunny* from *solar; nightly* from *nocturnal; churl* from *villain; wretch* from *miser; poor man* from *pauper; run across* from *occur; run into* from *incur; fight* from *debate.*

From time to time attempts have been made to oust foreign words from our vocabulary and to replace them by native words that have become either obsolete or less usual (that is to say, less popular). Whimsical theorists have even set up the principle that no word of foreign origin should be employed when a native word of the same meaning exists. In English, however, all such efforts are predestined to failure. They result, not in a simpler and more natural style, but in something unfamiliar, fantastic, and affected. Foreign words that have long been in common use are just as much English as if they had been a part of our language from the beginning. There is no rational theory on which they should be shunned. It would be just as reasonable for an Englishman whose ancestors had lived in the island ever since the time of King Alfred, to disown as his countrymen the descendants of a Frenchman or a German who settled there three hundred years ago. The test of the learned or the popular character of a word is not its etymology, but the facts relating to its habitual employment by plain speakers. Nor is there any principle on which, of two expressions, that which is popular should be preferred to that which is learned or less familiar. The sole criterion of choice consists in the appropriateness of one's language to the subject or the occasion. It would be ridiculous to address a crowd of soldiers in the same language that one would employ in a council of war. It would be no less ridiculous to harangue an assembly of generals as if they were a regiment on the eve of battle. The reaction against the excessive Latinization of English is a wholesome tendency, but it becomes a mere 'fad' when it is carried out in a *doctrinaire* manner. As Chaucer declares:—

> Ek Plato seith, whoso that can him rede,
> 'The wordes mot be cosin to the dede.'

Every educated person has at least two ways of speaking his mother tongue. The first is that which he employs in his family, among his familiar friends, and on ordinary occasions. The second is that which he uses in discoursing on more complicated subjects, and in addressing persons with whom he is less intimately acquainted. It is, in short, the language which he employs when he is 'on his dignity,' as he puts on evening dress when he is going to dine. The difference between these two forms of language consists, in great measure, in a difference of vocabulary.

The basis of familiar words must be the same in both, but the vocabulary appropriate to the more formal occasion will include many terms which would be stilted or affected in ordinary talk. There is also considerable difference between familiar and dignified language in the manner of utterance. Contrast the rapid utterance of our everyday dialect, full of contractions and clipped forms, with the more distinct enunciation of the pulpit or the platform. Thus, in conversation, we habitually employ such contractions as *I'll, don't, won't, it's, we'd, he'd,* and the like, which we should never use in public speaking, unless of set purpose, to give a markedly colloquial tinge to what we have to say.

CHAPTER IV

LEARNED WORDS BECOME POPULAR

THE true distinction between a 'learned' and a 'popular' word depends, as we have seen, not upon etymology but upon usage. It makes no difference how or where a word originated: it is popular if it is in common use among plain speakers and is not felt by them as a 'big word.' Thus *contradict*, *arbitrate*, and *photograph* were all three learned words in their origin, yet are now distinctly popular. *Contradict* (L. *contradictus*, from *contra-*, 'against,' and *dicere*, 'to say') has forced out of common use two native words *withsay* and *gainsay*, both of them originally popular, so that *withsay* has become obsolete and *gainsay* is learned. The reason for this extraordinary shift is apparently the use of the learned word in giving instructions to young children: 'You mustn't *contradict* people' is a very early lesson in manners. With *arbitrate* the case is different. This word has gained such currency in the labor discussions of the last few years that it is as familiar to every workman as *wages* or *strike*. Hence it is a popular word, though, like *contradict*, it had a learned origin (L. *arbitratus*, participle of *arbitror*, from *arbiter*, 'judge'). Observe that *arbiter* is still learned, though *arbitrate* and *arbitration* are popular.[1] The third example, *photograph*, differs from the other two in its origin. At the outset, it was, if possible, even more learned than *contradict* and *arbitrate*,

---

[1] The practice of international arbitration has also helped to make the words familiar.

being a term deliberately manufactured from the Greek to describe a highly technical process. It is put together from *photo-* (supposed stem of φῶς, *phōs*, the Greek for 'light,' seen in *phos-phorus*, 'light-bearer') and *-graph*, a clipped form of the Greek verb γράφειν (*gráphein*), 'to write.' If the process had remained a matter of scientific curiosity, the word *photograph* would have remained as learned as, for example, *cryptograph*,—but it became the commonest way of 'taking one's picture,' and hence the word is known to every child.[1]

These three examples show how varied are the causes which bring learned terms into the popular category. Scientific or technical words afford the clearest illustration of the process, since they are obviously learned in origin and often become, as knowledge spreads, the common property of all but the most ignorant speakers. If the progress of science makes the terms in question obsolete as a part of the technical vocabulary, their learned origin may be utterly forgotten, and they may become popular in the strictest sense. This is strikingly exemplified in a number of words whose history is so interesting that it must be given in some detail.

Ancient physiology divided the human body into solids, liquids, and what may be called aëriform substances. Of liquids there were thought to be four: *blood*, *phlegm*, *bile*, and *black bile* or *melancholy*. Three of these we recognize as matters of fact; but the fourth, the 'black bile,' was purely imaginary. These four liquids were known as *humors* (*humor* being the Latin word for 'liquid'), and good health was thought to depend on the maintenance of

---

[1] Compare *telegraph* (Gr. τῆλε, 'far'), a similarly learned formation that has become almost equally popular. *Phonograph* (Gr. φωνή 'sound') is pretty well known. *Telephone* (τῆλε and φωνή) is entirely popular.

a just proportion among them. This balance or commixture of the humors was known as a man's *temperament*, that is, his 'mixture' (L. *tempero*, 'to mix'), or as his *complexion* (from a Latin word meaning 'combination,' derived from *com-*, 'together,' and *plecto*, 'to weave'). Thus if a man had more blood than any other humor in his system, he was said to be of a *sanguine* temperament or complexion (L. *sanguis*, 'blood'); if more bile, of a *bilious* temperament or complexion; if more phlegm, of a *phlegmatic* temperament; if more melancholy (or black bile), of a *melancholy* temperament. If the temperament, or balance of the humors, was greatly disturbed, the result was *distemper*, that is, a 'variance from the proper mixture.' *Saturnine*, *jovial* (from *Jove*), and *mercurial*, as names for different temperaments or moods, preserve a faint echo of the old belief that the planets govern our physical and moral constitutions. We may compare *lunatic*, 'influenced by the moon (*luna*),' hence 'insane.'

All this science is dead and buried, *as science*, but it still survives in popular language, in which we constantly use the old terms to describe different kinds of men or different states of the mind or body. Thus a man may still be 'good-humored' or 'in bad humor,' and we still speak of his mental or bodily disposition as his 'temperament.' When we call a person 'sanguine,' we revert, without knowing it, to the old medical theory that a preponderance of blood in the temperament made one hopeful. Similarly, we call a man 'melancholy' or 'phlegmatic,' though we do not remember that the ideas which we attach to these words go back to obsolete physiology.[1]

[1] *Melancholy*, the imaginary fourth humor, has kept its name alive in medical science in *melancholia*, a kind of madness once thought to come from an excess of 'black bile' in the system.

Complexion has a particularly curious history. Originally, as we have seen, it was a medical term synonymous with *temperament*. Since, however, the preponderance of one or another humor was supposed to manifest itself in the color and texture of one's face, *complexion* soon received the meaning[1] which we now attach to it. Thus a learned and strictly technical term, of Latin origin, has been rejected from the vocabulary of science and become purely 'popular.' We have also preserved *distemper*, specializing it to diseases of animals, — as in 'the cattle distemper.'

Temper, however, which was a synonym of *temperament*, has taken a different course. We use it vaguely for 'disposition,' but commonly associate it in some way with 'irascibility.' 'Keep your *temper*,' 'he lost his *temper*,' 'ill-*tempered*,' show a trace of the old meaning; but the colloquial 'What a *temper*[2] he has,' 'He is in such a *temper!*' would never be referred to physiological science by one who did not know the history of the word.

But we are not yet done with the history of the word *humor*. A diseased condition of any one of the four humors might manifest itself as an eruption on the skin; hence such an eruption is still called a *humor* in common language. Again, an excess of one of the humors might make a man odd or fantastic in his speech and actions. Thus *humorous* took the meaning 'eccentric,'[3] and a

---

[1] By a process of specialization (see p. 265).

[2] That is, 'what a *bad* temper,' the modifying adjective idea remaining, though no adjective is used. This kind of quasi-ellipsis is a common cause of specialization of meaning in words (see pp. 252–3).

[3] *Eccentric* means literally 'deviating from the centre' or 'having a different centre' (G. ἐκ, 'from' and κέντρον, whence L. *centrum*, 'centre').

'*humorous* man' was what we call, in modern slang, 'a *crank*.' The 'comedy of humors,' of which Ben Jonson is the best exponent, found material in caricaturing such eccentric persons. From this sense, *humor* had an easy development to that of 'a keen perception of the odd or incongruous,' and we thus arrive at the regular modern meaning of the word. It is certainly a long way from *humor* in the literal sense of 'liquid' or 'moisture' to *humor* in the sense in which that quality is so often associated with wit.

Finally, the old physiology, as we have seen, ascribed to the human system certain volatile or aëriform substances, which were believed to pass through the arteries and to be of primary importance in all the processes of life. These were called *spirits*[1] (L. *spiritus*, 'breath' or 'air'), and they fell into three classes, the *natural*, the *vital*, and the *animal* spirits. It is in unconscious obedience to this superannuated science that we use such words and phrases as 'in high (low, good, bad) *spirits*,' *high-spirited*, *low-spirited*, 'a *spirited* horse,' 'a *spiritless* performance,' and that we speak of one who is spontaneously merry as having 'a great flow of *animal spirits*.'

The dead science of astrology has also bequeathed to us a number of interesting terms,—once severely technical, now for the most part commonplace enough. *Disaster* is 'bad star' (L. *dis-*, 'away from,' 'contrary,' and *astrum*, 'star'; cf. *aster*, 'the star-flower,' *asteroid*, 'little star,' and *astro-logy* itself). 'This business has an evil *aspect*' is a similar figure. The *aspect* of the heavens is the way in which the planets *look at* each other and at the earth (L. *aspectus*, 'looking at,' 'glance'). *Influence* is the

[1] Not to be confounded with the religious and theological senses of *spirit*, which are many.

'in-flowing' (L. *fluo*, 'flow') of planetary power upon the fortunes of men. Other astrological terms are *predominant* (said of a planet more powerful than the rest at a given moment), 'his star is in the *ascendant*,' and *horoscope;* but these are less familiar, and the last-mentioned is still technical. Compare also 'born under a lucky *star*,' and the trivial oath 'my *stars!*' which has been humorously extended to 'my stars and garters!' as if the allusion were to the insignia of the Order of the Garter, which include an eight-pointed star encircling the figure of St. George.[1]

In the same way, even the most abstruse philosophy has contributed familiar words to our common stock. About the middle of the fourth century before Christ, when the world had been inundated with a flood of new ideas for some three hundred years, — a period of such intellectual activity as mankind had never seen, — it occurred to Aristotle, in his matchless peripatetic lectures, to want short words for the general philosophic ideas of the 'nature' and 'magnitude' of any individual thing. He found in the Greek language the words ποῖος and πόσος (*poîos* and *pósos*), 'of what sort?' and 'how great?' ready to his hand, but no one had ever before needed abstract terms for these ideas.[2] So, by means of derivative endings existing in our family of languages, he boldly formed ποιότης (*poiótēs*), and ποσότης (*posótēs*), which must have appeared to the Greek purist of his time as strange and uncouth as *of-what-sort-ness* and *how-much-ness* would seem

[1] Such elaboration is common in oaths, its object being to disguise their profanity (see p. 304). Justice Shallow's 'by cock and pie' is a good example. 'By cock' is (like *by gad*, *by gosh*, etc.) a mere corruption to make the oath innocuous, and *pie* (magpie) is added to carry out the suggestion that *cock* refers to a bird. The suggestion that *pie* in this oath is the 'mass-book' is unfounded. [2] Except Plato, Theæt., 182 **A.**

LEARNED WORDS BECOME POPULAR

to us to-day.[1] But they served his turn, and took their place in the technical dialect of the Greek philosophers. Two hundred years later, when Cicero interpreted these ideas to his countrymen, he imitated the boldness of Aristotle, and ventured *qualitas* (from *qualis*, 'of what sort?'), a Latin word of equivalent meaning to ποιότης (*poiótēs*) and similar formation. Still later, *quantitas* (from *quantus*, 'how much?') was manufactured as a translation of ποσότης (*posótēs*).

So, in the course of linguistic history, these two Greek terms for 'how-much-ness' and 'of-what-sort-ness,' invented to supply a refined philosophic need, have in the forms *quantity* and *quality* become the common possession of every shopman, and are two of the most familiar words in the English language.

Quiddity (L. *quidditas*), coined by the mediæval schoolmen when *qualitas* had lost some of its scientific exactness, has had less currency. It is formed from the interrogative Latin *quid*, 'what?' and means 'what-ness,' 'characteristic quality.' Since the schoolmen were proverbial hair-splitters, *quiddity* has taken on the sense of a 'quibble.'[2] We may barely mention the colloquial ' He knows *what's what!*' which seems to be derived from the arguments of these same philosophers, who, having asked themselves ' What is this and that?' until they had exhausted the list of available subtleties, achieved the famous question 'quid

---

[1] Some years ago a New England philosopher was much ridiculed for using 'the thing-ness of the here' for 'the actuality of the present.' There was nothing absurd in his coinage: it was simply minted 'an age too late.'

[2] Compare *quillet* (from L. *quid-libet*, 'what you please'), and *quip* from *quipproquo* (for *quid pro quo*), 'repartee.' *Quibble* is thought to be a contamination of *quip* and *quillet* (or *quiddity*). The words all echo the jargon of the schools.

est *quid?*' 'What is this *what* that we use so glibly? Butler's Hudibras puts the matter in a nutshell:—

> He knew what's what! and that's as high
> As metaphysic wit can fly.

About a century before Aristotle's time, Empedocles had conceived the universe as composed of four substances,—fire (conceived as material), air, earth, and water, to which, inasmuch as things were regarded as made up of these as component parts, just as letters are variously combined into words, was given the name στοιχεῖα (*stoicheia*), 'letters of the alphabet.' This was afterward translated into Latin by the word *elementa*, which also meant 'letters,' and a singular form *elementum* was made to fit it. The subsequent history of this word has been most curious. In English, *element* has retained all of its meanings. In the original sense of 'letters of the alphabet' we use *elements* for 'the rudiments of learning' (the a-b-c of knowledge), and have the adjective *elementary*. But the word is also applied to the four elements, fire, air, water, and earth, or to any of them (particularly the first three): as, 'the fury of the elements,' for a storm, 'the fiery elements,' 'out of its element' (as of a fish out of water), 'the fiery element,' 'the watery element.' In older English 'the element' often meant 'the heaven,' 'the sky,'—as in 'the cinders of the element'[1] for the 'stars,'—and this use still survives among the negroes in the Southern states. Finally, though the doctrine involved has long ceased to be consistent with modern thought, the word also retains the sense of 'elements generally,' 'constituent materials,' and the like, and has

[1] Shakspere, Henry IV, Part I, act iv, scene 3, l. 58.

given such words as *elemental*, in the same generalized sense.

Now Aristotle, feeling the want of some more subtle material for the heavens, suspected the existence of a fifth substance (*aether*), to which his successors gave the name πέμπτη οὐσία (*pémptē ousía*), 'fifth being' or 'form of existence,' utilizing the abstract noun οὐσία (*ousía*), 'being,' formed from ὤν (*ón*), the present particle of εἶναι (*eînai*), 'to be.' The Romans, not having the participle of *esse*, nor this abstract from it, got along without the word. Cicero calls the aether *quintum genus*, 'fifth kind,' and *quinta natura*, 'fifth nature'; and Horace loosely uses *quinta pars*, 'fifth part,' in alluding to the doctrine. But the later Latin devised a rude abstract form *essentia* (as if from *esse*) to represent the idea, and this in English became *essence*, a word which, as well as *quintessence* (*quinta essentia*, 'fifth essence') as a kind of superlative, has had the widest currency in the language for the most subtle component part of anything, or that which makes it what it is, — as it were, the 'soul' of a thing.

Thus language picks out with almost a chemical certainty what is suitable for it, and any language at any moment is a naturally selected residuum of all which the human mind has thought or conceived ever since that line of civilization began.

In the fifth century B.C., there came to Athens from Cilicia, the native country, it will be remembered, of Paul the Apostle, a remarkable man, Zeno, and established a school of philosophers, who, from their habit of teaching in one of the great colonnades of Athens, were called *Stoics*, or 'philosophers of the Porch.'[1] This sect influenced the thought of the world for more than five hundred years,

---

[1] Gr. στωικός, from στοά, 'roofed colonnade.'

and counted among its devotees many of the grandest souls of pagan times. They developed a marvellous scheme of the universe, in which everything visible and invisible was organically connected into a stupendous unit of which 'the Body Nature is and God the Soul,' or rather into a living sentient organism, the soul of which was the only God.[1]

The speculations of the Stoics profoundly affected all subsequent thought, so that it is almost impossible to state their doctrines without using words that bear the Stoic imprint. It is, however, in the realm of ethics that we find language most vividly impressed by their conceptions. The aim of all the philosophers of that age was a selfish one, — the superiority of the soul of the *sapiens*, or 'sage,' to all the chances or changes of the universe, his complete serenity, 'equanimity' (*aequanimitas*) or 'composure' (*securitas*, p. 278) amid the whirl of things about him. This the sect sought to find in the perfect mental and moral conformity of the *sapiens* to the scheme of the universe and its governing soul, Providence, or what we should call 'the divine will.' *Sequi naturam* was their motto. Though the controlling motive of such conformity was selfishness, yet, since the *sapiens* too was but a part of the whole organism, his scheme of conduct necessarily included acting for the good of the universe as well, though he acted primarily for himself.

The serenity above mentioned was incompatible with the existence in the sage of any ruffling emotions, such as love, hate, desire, or fear, which, from their disturbing nature, the Stoics called πάθη (*páthē*, plural of πάθος,

[1] In accordance with this idea, even human speech, being divinely constituted, had within it the true nature of all things; for was not language a part of the same stupendous organism? Hence the search for the 'etymon' in the endeavor to ascertain the truths of nature (pp. 229 ff.).

páthos), 'diseases,' a word that was derived from a root meaning originally 'suffer,' though it had long been specialized to 'suffering from disease.'[1] Hence this philosophic serenity was called ἀπάθεια (*apátheia*) or 'freedom from disease.' But since the Stoics identified emotions with diseases, this *apátheia* was 'freedom from *emotions*' (πάθη), whence *apathy*, its English representative, means 'absence of feeling,' as in 'the *apathy* of despair.' Thus we have abandoned the idea of 'disease,' but we still keep the term denoting 'freedom from it' to express 'want of feeling,' the idea that the word acquired through the conceptions of the Stoics. Compare also *stoical* and *stoicism* in a similar sense.

Now when the Stoic ethics were expounded in Latin, Gr. *páthos* was literally translated,[2] not by any Latin term thus used in the same meaning, but by *passio*, a word that meant simply 'suffering,' from *patior*, 'to suffer,' which is rightly or wrongly supposed to be from the same root.

In English we have retained the natural meaning of *passio*, that is, 'suffering,' in a few phrases (such as 'the *passion* of our Lord '), just as we have *patient*, 'suffering,' 'sufferer,' 'a patient,' and *passive*, all from *patior* in its common acceptation. But since the Latin *passio* was used to translate πάθος (*páthos*) in the Stoic sense, it came more and more to be applied to those 'emotions' which the Stoics called by that name. Borrowed by us in this meaning also, and variously specialized as referring to particular emotions, it came to be used in English as we almost always use it to-day, for 'a passion,' or 'the passions.' This likewise accounts for our adjective *impassive*,

[1] Thus, when Cicero wished to represent it in Latin, he used *morbi* (the word which we have in *morbid*).

[2] Probably under the influence of the idea of the Stoic etymon.

in which we have the curious phenomenon of a word that is practically synonymous with its contradictory, *passive*. Both adjectives come from *patior*, but *passive* is derived from the verb in its proper sense of 'suffer,' while *impassive*, its contrary, involves the special Stoic idea of *apátheia*, and means 'showing no emotion,' which is, in effect, the same as *passive*, 'suffering, but doing nothing.' So *impassibility* (of countenance, for instance) would have no meaning but for the Stoic ideas that were attached to various derivatives of *patior* entirely apart from their original meaning.

With the English *pathos*, which is simply the Greek πάθος borrowed without change of form, the Stoics have nothing to do; but it is worth while to mention it to complete our account of this extraordinary word. The Greek word easily became specialized, and, changing its relations, came to mean, among other things, 'suffering' from the point of view not of the sufferer, but of one who looks on (at a tragedy, for instance). In this sense it was adopted as an English word, and, with its adjective *pathetic*,[1] is much used in literary criticism to describe a quality of style with reference to the feelings of the spectator or reporter. By its side, and serving in a manner as its opposite, stands the jocose word *bathos*. This is simply the Greek βάθος, 'depth,' which was borrowed by Pope in the eighteenth century to signify what he called 'the art of sinking in poetry,' that is, a descent from the sublime to the ridiculous. *Bathos* has maintained its place chiefly through its combined similarity and antagonism to *pathos*. It is probable that without this resemblance and

[1] Strictly speaking, *pathetic* is not derived form πάθος but from the Greek adjective παθητικός, which comes from the same root; but the adjective and the noun are closely associated in English.

antithesis it could not have lasted long enough to become a part of the language.

Of all the technical terms of the Stoic philosophy, only *passion* has become completely popular; but the history of this word is not intelligible apart from the others, and the whole group illustrates, in the most striking way, both the continuity of civilization and the scope and significance of etymological study.

CHAPTER V

TECHNICAL OR CLASS DIALECTS

IN Chapters III and IV we have distinguished between popular and learned words, and have seen how learned words may pass into the popular category, drawing some of our most striking examples from the language of science and philosophy. This matter of technical language, however, requires some further discussion.

Every profession or trade, every art, and every science has its technical vocabulary, the function of which is partly to designate things or processes which have no names in ordinary English, and partly to secure greater exactness in nomenclature. Such special dialects, or jargons, are necessary in technical discussion of any kind. Being universally understood by the devotees of the particular science or art, they have the precision of a mathematical formula. Besides, they save time, for it is much more economical to name a process than to describe it. Thousands of these technical terms are very properly included in every large dictionary, yet, as a whole, they are rather on the outskirts of the English language than actually within its borders.

Different occupations, however, differ widely in the character of their special vocabularies. In trades and handicrafts, and other vocations, like farming and fishery, that have occupied great numbers of men from remote times, the technical vocabulary is very old. It consists largely of native words, or of borrowed words that have worked themselves into the very fibre of our language. Hence, though highly technical in many particulars, these vocabularies are more familiar in sound, and more generally understood, than most other technicalities. The special dialects of law, medicine, divinity, and philosophy have also, in their older strata, become pretty familiar to cultivated persons, and have contributed much to the popular vocabulary. Yet every vocation still possesses a large body of technical terms that remain essentially foreign, even to educated speech. And the proportion has been much increased in the last fifty years, particularly in the various departments of natural and political science and in the mechanic arts. Here new terms are coined with the greatest freedom, and abandoned with indifference when they have served their turn. Most of the new coinages are confined to special discussions, and seldom get into general literature or conversation. Yet no profession is nowadays, as all professions once were, a close guild. The lawyer, the physician, the man of science, the divine, associates freely with his fellow-creatures, and does not meet them in a merely professional way. Furthermore, what is called 'popular science' makes everybody acquainted with modern views and recent discoveries. Any important experiment, though made in a remote or provincial laboratory, is at once reported in the newspapers, and everybody is soon talking about it, — as in the case of the Röntgen rays and wireless telegraphy. Thus our common speech is always taking up new technical terms and making them commonplace. The process began with the conversion of the Anglo-Saxons, soon after their settlement in Britain. Ecclesiastical words from the Latin (mostly of Greek origin) were the first to come in. Among these were: —

abbot: A.S. *abbod*, from L. *abbas, abbatis*, which comes, through the Greek, from the Syriac *abba*, 'father.'

alb: A.S. *albe*, from L. *albus*, 'white.'

bishop: A.S. *biscop*, from L. *episcopus* (Gr. ἐπίσκοπος, *epískopos*, literally 'overseer'). *Episcopal* is a later borrowing from the Latin.

cowl: A.S. *cugle*, from L. *cucullus*, 'hood.'

monk: A.S. *munuc*, from L. *monachus*, 'one who lives alone' (from Gr. μόνος, *mónos*, 'alone,' seen in *monologue, monotone, monarchy*, etc.).

minster: A.S. *mynster*, from L. *monasterium* (also from Gr. μόνος). *Monastery* is a later borrowing, like *episcopal*.

noon: A.S. *nōn*, from L. *nona* (*hora*), 'ninth hour' (three o'clock in the afternoon; the shift in meaning coincided with a change in the time of the service called *nones*).

nun: A.S. *nonne*, from L. *nonna* (from a Greek word of uncertain origin).

pope: A.S. *pāpa*, from L. *papa*, 'father,' originally a childish word. It is the same as our *papa*, which we have independently adopted from the French *papa*, which is the same Latin word.

A.S. *prēost*, from L. *presbyter* (Gr. πρεσβύτερος, *presbúteros*, 'elder'). The Latin *presbyter* was afterward borrowed without change, and gives its name to the Presbyterian Church, in which the ministers are not called 'priests.'

school: A.S. *scōl*, from L. *schola*, which is from the Gr. σχολή (*scholḗ*), 'leisure.'[1]

verse: A.S. *vers, fers*, from L. *versus*, 'a turning,' 'a line of verse.'

clerk: A.S. *clerc*. *Clerk, clergy*, and *clerical* well illustrate the variety of our vocabulary. They all come ultimately from Greek κληρικός (*klērikós*), 'clerical' (literally, 'pertaining to the lot,' from κλῆρος, *klêros*, 'lot,' later 'orders' in the ecclesiastical sense[2]). *Clerk*, however, was borrowed from L. *clericus* by the Anglo-Saxons, as *cleric, clerc*, and has maintained itself in the latter form. The same Latin word gave *clerc* in Old French, and thence come O. Fr. *clergie*

---

[1] The shift of meaning, which seems so peculiar to our schoolboys, is simple enough. War and politics were the business of the Greek and Roman gentleman. He gave to literature (with good effect!) what leisure he had from these more serious pursuits. Similarly we have *ludus* in Latin, and *ludi magister* ('a master of sport') meant 'schoolmaster.' *Pedagogue*, however, was originally the slave who led (Gr. ἄγω) the boy (παῖς, παιδός) to school.

[2] See Deuteronomy xviii. 2.

and our *clergy* (which also shows the influence of another O. Fr. word, *clergié*, from L.L. *clericatus*). *Clerical* comes directly from L.L. *clericalis*, a derivative of *clericus*. *Clergy* and *clerk* doubtless became popular almost immediately, and the latter (through its sense of 'scholar') has received a wide extension of meaning. But *clerical* is comparatively a learned word.

From the beginning of our language to the present day, Latin has been, in large part, the language of scholars and of the learned professions; hence, a multitude of technical terms are of Latin origin. Medicine has also brought in a great many Greek terms, since the ancient physicians were largely Greeks. In the Middle Ages there were a succession of distinguished Arabian physicians who had become saturated with Greek culture, and from them we have a number of words, some Arabic, some Greek in an Arabic form (see p. 108).

The law, from the time of the Norman Conquest, had two technical languages, Latin and Norman French. The latter gradually developed into what is still known as Law French,—a curious jargon containing a large admixture of English words. Hence, the law-terms which have made their way into our ordinary vocabulary, show now a French and now a Latin derivation, and in many instances are out-and-out Latin, with no change in form. Thus we have, for example:—

From French: *mortgage*, from *mort*, 'dead,' and *gage*, 'pledge' (the same word seen in our *wager* and *wages*).

champerty, from *champart* (L. *campi pars*).

mortmain, from *mort*, and *main*, 'hand.'

convey, from O. Fr. *conveier* (L.L. *conviare*, from L. *con-* and *via*, 'way'); *convoy* is from the modern Fr. *convoyer*, of the same derivation. Technical derivatives of *convey* are *conveyance* and *conveyancer*.

entail, from O. Fr. *entailler*, 'cut off,' 'curtail' (from L. *talea*, 'a rod,' 'a cutting'; cf. *tally*, *tailor*).

tort, from O. Fr. *tort*, L. *tortum*, 'twisted' (cf. *con-tort*, *distort*, *torture*, *torsion*).

From Latin: *justiciar*, *justiciary*, and *justicer*, from L.L. *justiciarius*.
abalienate, from L. *alienus*, 'another's.'
divorce, from L.L. *divorcium* (for *divortium*), from *di-*, 'separate,' and *vortere*, 'turn.'
injunction, from L. *in-jungere*, 'join into,' 'enjoin.
Latin without change: *subpoena* (literally 'under penalty,' — from the beginning of the writ).
affidavit, L.L. 'he has pledged his faith,' from *ad-*, and *fides*, 'faith,' 'pledge.'
alibi, Latin adverb, 'elsewhere.'
alias, Latin adverb, 'otherwise.'
habeas corpus, etc., etc. See p. 102.

The language of philosophy is mostly of Latin origin. It includes also many Greek words, but most of these have passed through the Latin before reaching their English form. Thus *logic* is from L. *logica*, but this in turn is a mere transliteration of the Gr. λογική (*logikḗ*), from λόγος (*lógos*), 'discourse,' 'reason.'

So *metaphysics* is the Low Latin *metaphysica*, which has a curious history. In the manuscripts of Aristotle, the *physica*, that is, the works relating to 'nature '(Gr. φύσις, *phúsis*), were followed by those which dealt with abstract philosophy; hence, the latter were called, by his disciples, the works 'after (Gr. *metá*) the physics' (τὰ μετὰ τὰ φυσικά). But the phrase was capable of meaning also 'things beyond, or above, the natural,' and it was so understood by the scholastic philosophers, whose interpretation has prevailed. Hence, also, the sense of 'supernatural' which the word *metaphysical* frequently bore in Elizabethan English, as when Lady Macbeth speaks of 'metaphysical aid.'

In countless instances, the Greek philosophical term

was not adopted into Latin, but actually translated, as πάθος (*páthos*) was by *passio* (see pp. 39–40). In such cases the English has the Latin word, but with the meaning of the original Greek, often considerably modified in the course of centuries (as in *passion*).

Predicament is another example. Aristotle divided conceptions into certain general classes which he called *categories*, that is, literally, 'assertions,'[1] because they were meant to include everything that could be asserted of an object (as quality, quantity, etc.). The Greek word was translated literally by the Latin *praedicamentum* (from *praedico*, 'to predicate'), which gave us *predicament*. Both *predicament* and *category* came gradually to have a vaguer sense, — 'class,' 'condition,' — which *category* has kept, remaining always a learned word. *Predicament*, however, has become perfectly popular in the phrase 'in a bad predicament,' for 'in a bad situation,' whence *predicament*, without the adjective, in the sense of a 'fix,'— as 'What a *predicament!*'

The same is true of Latin theological language. But here a special influence was at work. Religious instruction has been the most pervasive form of education. Preaching, the confessional, and private exhortation have therefore made the greater number of theological terms pretty familiar to everybody, and many of them have become popular in the fullest sense.

Such are the Latin words *salvation, damnation, trinity, convert, vicar, curate, penitent, repent, reprobate, confess, absolve, absolution, doctrine* (sound, false), *altar, infidel, perverse, confession, purgatory;* and (Latin from Greek) *sceptic, heretic;* and (French from Latin) *assoil, penance,* 'day of *judgment*,' *aisle, friar, pilgrim, clergy, parson, repent,*

[1] Gr. κατηγορία, from κατηγορέω, 'assert,' from ἀγορά, 'assembly.'

grace, mercy, pity, etc. Others have remained more or less learned, but are not exclusively applied to theological ideas: as, 'works of *supererogation*,' *excommunicate, sanctify, justify, carnal, venial, obdurate, mediator, pastoral;* and (Latin from Greek) *dogma, heterodox, ascetic, evangelist, cathedral, orthodox, parochial, dogmatic.*

Further, since it was necessary to explain the doctrines of the church in simple language, a very large number of technical terms have been translated into English, and thus new meanings have been added to many popular words. Examples are: *hell, shrift, ghostly, flock, shepherd, sheep, the world, the flesh, righteous, unclean, love, doomsday, gospel, brother, deadly sin, evil, godly, godhead, son, kingdom, meekness, forgive, froward, hard heart.* The reading of the Bible in the vernacular has had the same effect, since the language of divinity is largely drawn from the Scriptures. No other technical dialect has contributed so many words or meanings to the ordinary vocabulary.

Observe that all the words cited above, or most of them, may be applied familiarly, in a figurative or jocose way, to matters in no way connected with law or divinity. Thus a man may *mortgage* his reputation; he may be a *heretic* in his medical theories, or *orthodox* in his political views. He may be socially *excommunicated* for his *sins* against propriety, or *acquitted* of a charge of prosiness by the *verdict* of a drawing-room.

Nautical terms often show great picturesqueness and humor. Some of them originated in slang, but have become quite technical. *Lazaret* is properly 'a hospital for lepers,' and comes from the parable of Lazarus in the sixteenth chapter of St. Luke. Its extension to hospitals in general, and its specialization to 'a hospital ship,' or 'a place of quarantine,' are not necessarily slangy in their origin. The sense of 'ship's storeroom,' however, certainly crosses the line. The application of *cockpit* to the place to which the wounded are carried during a sea fight, is clearly a bit of jocose and partly euphemistic slang. *Sick bay* is an easy nautical figure.

Holystones, for the 'stones with which the decks are scrubbed,' must also have had its origin in jest. Sailors go down on their knees to scrub. If *holy* is for *holey* (porous sandstone being the proper material), there is none the less a joke (as in the case of the Australian *holy dollar*).[1]

Dead-eye, or *deadman's eye*, for a kind of block with three holes in it, is grimly picturesque. The monocular *Dick Deadeye* in 'H. M. S. Pinafore' is either a pun or a misapprehension.

Sea-terms in common figurative use are *headway, leeway, under way, coast, steer clear of, clear the decks, on deck, lee shore, head-flaw, anchor, take the helm, to ship, to unship, cargo, to lighten ship, to weather the storm, a safe harbor, to run aground, to founder, to suffer shipwreck, a castaway, piratical, to scuttle, taken aback, aboard*, and many others.

Modern science has found it necessary to manufacture great numbers of words, and for this purpose has had recourse, not only to Latin, but to the rich storehouse of the Greek, which affords peculiar facilities for making compounds. These new words, however, have been treated as if they were Latin, since most of the Greek words already in our language had come through that language. Thus the name of the 'duck-mole' is a compound of the Greek πλατύς (*platús*), 'broad,' and πούς (*poús*), 'foot'; but the form used in English is not *platúpous* (which

[1] A dollar in which a hole has been punched (see p. 141).

would be Greek), but *platypus*, which is the form that *platúpous* takes when it is transferred into Latin. Sometimes the Latin form is used without change as an English word. Often, however, the new term takes an English form which makes it look as if it came from the French. For the Latin words which we had already borrowed through that language had set the fashion. Thus *telegraph*, which means 'the far-writer,' was formed from Greek τῆλε (*tēle*), 'far' and γράφω (*gráphō*), 'write.' The Greek form would be *tēlegráphos;* the Latin, *telegraphus.* But the French drops the final *-us* of Latin words (L. *morbidus*, Fr. *morbide*), and the English form is therefore *telegraph* (as if from Fr. *télégraphe*).

The coinage of naturalists and other scientific men varies greatly in its linguistic purity. Some of the words which they have manufactured from the Greek are as good as if they had been made in Athens, or Alexandria. Others would 'make Quintilian stare and gasp.' This is not strange, for the tendency of modern science has been to discourage classical study, but at the same time to ransack the classical vocabulary. In the case of foreign-sounding terms, however, our language swallows camels with avidity, and digests them without a qualm. The most clumsily manufactured term will become popular if the thing becomes familiar and if there is no other name for it. A striking instance is *ephthianura*, used in Australia as the vernacular name of a genus of small birds with 'diminished tails.' It is, of course, a bit of naturalists' Latin, and looks and sounds well enough. But it appears actually to have been made up by giving a Latin termination to a Greek phrase, ἔφθιεν οὐρά (*éphthien ourá*), which means 'its tail wasted away' (ἔφθιεν, *éphthien*, being the past tense of a verb related to our word *phthisis*, which is also borrowed from the Greek). No Greek or Roman could possibly have made such a noun, but our language accepts it with the same complacency with which it has accepted *nincompoop*, a corruption of *non compos mentis*, or *hoax* from *hocus pocus* (itself a piece of dog-Latin). *Gas*, a word devised by the Dutch chemist von Helmont in the seventeenth century, has had a veritably triumphant career. It was suggested to its inventor by the Greek χάος (*cháos*), but cannot be called anything but an out-and-out invention.

The classifying habit of the natural sciences reacts on many unscientific terms in a curious way. It is convenient for the naturalist to have the vernacular or 'trivial' names of plants and animals coincide in their scope, so far as possible, with the orders and families and genera of his system. Hence we are bidden to limit the name *fly* to dipterous insects, *bug* to the *hemiptera*, *worm* to the order *vermes*, and are rebuked if we speak of a whale as a 'big fish.' This is all very well for the purposes of science, but we must not allow ourselves to be browbeaten. The whale was a 'fish' when the 'order *cetacea*' had never been heard of, and will remain a 'Wal-*fisch*' in German long after some future zoölogist has reclassified the animal kingdom. The loose popular designations are quite as well established, and therefore as 'correct,' as the more limited terminology of science. Less 'accurate' they may be, but language is not always bound to scientific accuracy. It has its inalienable right to vague terms when there is no question of system at stake.

The technical vocabulary of art and music contains many Italian words. Some of these are unchanged in form (like *stanza*, *allegro*, *piano*, *falsetto*, *soprano*, *andante*, *concerto*, *trio*, *torso*, *terra cotta*, 'articles of *virtù*,' *piccolo*, *opera, operetta, finale*), others are clipped (like *violin* for *violino, duet* for *duetto, quartet* or *quartette* for *quartetto, madrigal* for *madrigale*) or otherwise changed. The clipping, as before, is after the French model, from which language other terms of the same kind have been taken (like *flageolet; hautboy* or *oboe,* from Fr. *hautbois,* 'high wood'; *figurine,* diminutive of *figure*).

The position of technical dialects or jargons with respect to our language is this: so long as the terms in question are used in technical discussions only, they scarcely belong to the English vocabulary at all. If they wander out of their narrow circle and are occasionally heard in current speech, they become a part of our vocabulary, though they are still a very special or technical part of it. But the process may go much farther: the objects or conceptions for which the terms stand may become very common, or the words may lose their strictly scientific sense and be applied vaguely or metaphorically. When this happens, the word has become fully naturalized, and its technical origin is pretty sure to be forgotten in the long run.

The propriety of using technical terms in speaking or writing depends on a common-sense principle. A remark should be intelligible, not merely to the speaker, who is presumed to know what he wishes to say, but also to the person addressed. Otherwise, it can hardly be called language in any proper sense. To be very technical in conversation not only savors of pedantry but makes the speaker unintelligible; and the same is true of a book addressed 'to the great variety of readers.' Among specialists, however, one can hardly go too far in the employment of technicalities, provided the terms belong to the accepted vocabulary of the science or art in question. That form of pedantry which consists in changing well-established designations for others that seem to the writer more appropriate is extremely common, and, indeed, may be called one of the weaknesses of the scientific temperament.

The lay reader is often tempted to laugh at the 'sesquipedalian monstrosities' of the scientific vocabulary. If such words are, as is frequently the case, formed with unnecessary grotesqueness, laughter is justifiable enough; but the mere fact that they are long and cumbrous, and that a good many of them are used, is no proper subject for jesting. The longest scientific term is really shorthand, as we shall soon find if we try to express, in ordinary language, what the single word conveys to those who understand it. It would be quite as reasonable to make fun of the x's and y's of the algebraist. But, on the other hand, until these words have actually made their way into the general vocabulary, they have scarcely more right to be rated as English than mathematical formulæ themselves.

The arts, science, philosophy, and religion are not alone in the necessity which they feel for a special vocabulary. Any limited circle having common interests is sure to develop a kind of 'class dialect,' — such as that of schoolboys, of university men, of travelling salesmen, of government clerks (or civil servants). For many persons, however, the centre of the universe is 'society.' Now 'society' is ever in search of novelty, — and it is a limited body of well-to-do women and men of leisure. From the almost exclusive association of these persons with each other, there arises a kind of special vocabulary, which is constantly changing with the changing fashions, yet maintains a measure of consistency, despite its unstable character. This society jargon is disseminated like the technical language of the philosopher or the man of science, by the same means and with even greater rapidity. Most of the words soon disappear, but a considerable number make good their place in ordinary speech. We shall study some of these coinages in the next chapter.

The two great classes of mankind are, of course, men and women. The occupations and interests of these classes are distinct in many particulars. As we should expect, the distinction manifests itself in the phenomena of language, for language is the most perfect mirror of all mental operations. Every one knows that the vocabulary of women differs considerably from that of men. In some countries, indeed, where women spend most of their time in retirement, and converse chiefly with each other, a specific 'women's dialect' has grown up. Even among English-speaking nations, where association between the sexes is but very slightly restricted, such differences are discernible. The use of *common*, for example, in the sense of 'vulgar' is distinctly a feminine peculiarity. It would sound effeminate in the speech of a man. So, in a less degree, with *person* for 'woman,' in contrast to 'lady.' *Nice* for 'fine' must have originated in the same way. The women's dialect is often more conservative than that of men,[1] and is likely to be marked by greater precision of utterance, as well as by differences in vocabulary.

[1] Pliny the Younger remarks, with admiration, that in certain letters written by a friend's wife he 'thought he was reading Plautus or Terence in prose' (Ep. i. 16).

CHAPTER VI

SLANG AND LEGITIMATE SPEECH

A PECULIAR kind of vagabond language, always hanging on the outskirts of legitimate speech, but continually straying or forcing its way into the most respectable company, is what we call *slang*. The prejudice against this form of speech is to be encouraged, though it usually rests on a misconception. There is nothing abnormal about slang. In making it, men proceed in precisely the same manner as in making language, and under the same natural laws. The motive, however, is somewhat different, for slang is not meant simply to express one's thoughts. Its coinage and circulation come rather from the wish of the individual to distinguish himself by oddity or grotesque humor.[1] Hence slang is seldom controlled by any regard for propriety, and it bids deliberate defiance to all considerations of good taste.

Slang is commonly made by the use of harsh, violent, or ludicrous metaphors, obscure analogies, meaningless words, and expressions derived from the less known or less esteemed vocations or customs. But the processes involved

[1] 'Thieves' slang' or 'peddlers' French' (*argot*, *Rothwälsch*) stands in a somewhat different position. It is, in fact, the professional jargon of a particular class of society, and is comparable, therefore, to other technical vocabularies, though the art or profession which it represents lies outside the bounds of respectable occupations. It has also the special object of concealment, and belongs therefore to the class of 'secret languages.'

are strikingly linguistic. In fact, slang may almost be called the only living language, the only language in which these processes can be seen in full activity. Take, for example, the expression *start in* for 'begin.' It is only a metaphor derived from lumbering operations, when men start into the woods in late autumn to begin the winter's work. 'Break ground,' which is in good use, is a figure of precisely the same kind, from the more respectable profession of building. So 'to pack up one's traps,'[1] from the vocation of trapping, is similar to the Latin *vasa colligere*, 'gather your pots and kettles,' which, originally soldiers' slang, came at last to be the regular expression for 'breaking camp.' 'On the stocks' for 'in preparation,' a metaphor from ship-building, is in good colloquial use. 'Down to bed rock' and 'peter out' are natural expressions among miners, but they become slang when transferred to other circumstances and used as figures of speech. So with the poker terms 'ante up' and 'it is up to you,' with 'come a cropper,' 'to be in at the death,' 'come to the scratch,' 'toe the mark,' 'well-groomed,' 'knock-out blow,' 'below the belt,' 'cock of the walk,' 'mass play,' 'get on to his curves,' and a thousand other expressions that have passed into slang from various fields of sport. None of these phrases is accepted at present, though they differ much in their degree of slanginess, but it is impossible to predict their standing a hundred years hence. For the sport of former days has made many contributions to our legitimate vocabulary. Thus *bias* (from bowling) is a dignified word, though *bowl over* is still colloquial. So 'to *parry* a thrust,' 'to *fence*' (in an argument), 'to *cross swords* with the opposing counsel,' 'to *bandy* words' (literally, 'to bat them to and fro' as in

---

[1] The Elizabethans said 'truss up your trinkets' in the same sense.

bandy-ball), 'to *wrestle* with a problem,'[1] 'to *trip* one *up* in a discussion,' 'to *track* or *trace* a quotation' or 'to *lose track of* a subject,' 'to run *counter*' (literally, of dogs who follow the scent in the wrong direction), 'to *hit* (or *miss*) the mark,' 'within an *ace* of,' are all good English expressions, though most of them were formerly slang and passed through the intermediate stage of colloquialism before they secured admission to the literary language. The now disreputable amusement of cockfighting (which was once respectable enough to divide with scholarship and archery the attention of Roger Ascham) has provided the language with *crestfallen*, 'in high *feather*,' and Shakspere's *overcrow* (cf. *to crow over*). 'To show the *white feather*' is from the same source, since white feathers in a gamecock's tail are a sign of impure breeding. Often the origin of such words or phrases has been quite forgotten, but, when traced, discloses their true character at once. *Fair play* is still recognized as a figure from gambling; but *foul play*, now specialized to 'murder,' is hardly felt as a metaphor at all. Only the etymologist knows that *hazard* may be the Arabic *al zār*, 'the die,' and that *chance* means 'the fall of the dice' (L.L. *cadentia*,[2] from *cado*). Yet both words still have gaming associations: *hazard* is a particular kind of dice-play, and 'to take one's chances,' 'a good or bad chance,' 'the chances are against it' are transparent metaphors.

Many examples might be cited from sports that have the dignified associations of antiquity. Thus, 'to tilt at' (cf.

[1] Cf. St. Paul's famous figure in Ephesians vi. 12: 'For we wrestle not against flesh and blood, but against principalities,' etc.

[2] Whence also *cadence*, which has no connection with gaming, but comes from another specialization of the word.

full tilt), 'to break a lance,' 'in the lists,' 'to run one's course,' 'to reach the goal,' 'to win the palm.' Slang is no novelty, as many persons imagine. It is only new slang that is novel. 'The ancients did not know that they were ancients.'

Provincialisms or dialect words are often adopted into slang, exactly as they are adopted into literary language. When Sir Thomas Lipton spoke of 'lifting the cup,' he was merely using a provincialism,[1] but when the people of the United States took up the expression in good-natured mockery it became slang. Burns's *croon* was also a dialect term, but it almost immediately commended itself to the poets, and is now in good use. So *vamos* is a proper Mexican word (Sp. 'let us go'), but when it is quoted and used by Americans for 'depart' (*vamoose*), as many words have been borrowed from other languages, it becomes slang. So *savvy* (Sp. *sabe usted*, 'do you know?') is a slang word for 'comprehension'; but *ignoramus* (L. 'we do not know,' used as a law term) is excellent English. A *fiasco* is properly a theatrical failure. The Italian say *far fiasco* ('to make a bottle') for 'to break down or fail in a theatrical performance.' The origin of the phrase is unknown,[2] but *fiasco* is now sufficiently reputable English, though it is of recent introduction. Many other foreign words, now thoroughly naturalized, seem to have had slangy associations at some period of their history. This is especially likely in the case of those that may have been introduced by soldiers who have served in foreign parts. *Bravado* (Sp. *bravada*) looks like a word of this kind. *Bizarre* (which we take from French) has never been slangy in English.

---

[1] Compare 'to *lift* cattle' and *shoplifter*.
[2] But cf. ληκυθίζω and *ampullor* (p. 67, note).

SLANG AND LEGITIMATE SPEECH

In French, however, it formerly meant 'soldierly,' and if it is actually from the Basque *bizarra*, 'beard,' we may conjecture that it was not a dignified borrowing. The '*sack* of a city' (from Fr. *sac*, 'pack,' 'plunder') betrays its own origin; compare also *loot*, from the Hindoo word for 'booty.'

A few additional examples may be cited to illustrate these points, and in particular to show how near slang lies to legitimate speech. We may say with propriety a *carnival* or a *Saturnalia* of crime, but not a *perfect circus*. A man may well be *recalcitrant*,[1] but only in colloquial style can he be a *kicker*. We cannot with dignity allude to the *curves* of base-ball, but a *bias*, from the game of bowls, is proper enough. *A 1* is hardly out of the region of slang, but *probity* and *improbity*, similar mercantile expressions, have cleared their skirts of commercial associations, and are in good use.[2] You can hardly *jump on* a man, nor can you *go at* him, but you can readily *assail* or *assault*[3] him, and the Romans used *adire* for 'go to' in all senses. *Insult* means literally 'to jump at or upon.' *Apprehendo* is merely Latin for 'catch on.' So *attend to* is domestic language for 'punish,' but the Romans used *animadvertere*[4] not only for 'attend to' in the literal sense, but for 'punish' as well, and *animadversion* is in good literary use.

[1] L. *re-*, 'back,' and *calcitro*, 'kick,' from *calx*, *calcis*, 'heel.'

[2] The L. *improbus* must have meant originally 'not first-class,' and its use by Plautus of two girls in the sense of a 'bad lot' clearly shows its slangy character. Yet this word, with its opposite, *probus*, has become one of the most respectable in the Latin language, and in English has lost all trace of its origin.

[3] *Assail* is French from L. *ad*, 'to,' 'at,' and *salio*, 'jump'; *assault* is also French from *ad* and *saltus*, 'a jumping,' which comes from the same verb *salio*.

[4] From *animum advertere*, 'to turn the attention to.'

Our *desire* is a product of soldiers' slang. It evidently comes (through the French) from *desidero*, 'to miss' a soldier who is 'out of his place' at roll-call. Once transferred, on account of its familiarity, to a more general meaning, *desidero* finally became the usual word for 'long for.' Thus, a word belonging, if not to slang, at least to a special vocation, becomes universal.[1] Doubtless *fire over one's head, on guard, enrolled* (in a body or sect), *in marching order, expedite, expedition*, and many others come from the same source.

Salary affords a good instance of ancient slang. The L. *salarium* meant, among other things, 'salt-money,' an allowance which a soldier received to buy salt with (L. *sal*, 'salt'), but it was soon extended to the present meaning of 'salary.' Such an extension was clearly slang in the first instance. Compare our colloquial 'earn his *salt*,' and '*pin*-money.' *Sardonic* also looks like venerable slang. It is certainly so if it comes from the name of a *Sardinian* (Gr. *Sardô*, 'Sardinia') plant which puckered up the eater's face into a sardonic smile. A *solecism* is so called from the bad Greek of the colonists of *Soli* in Asia Minor. Doubtless it was at first a slang designation. Compare the 'Stratford French' of Chaucer's Prioress, who was ignorant of the 'French of Paris,' and the old phrase 'French of Norfolk' for the Norfolk dialect of English.

A kind of slang occurs in various languages which has great influence on common speech. The tendency to use diminutives for the names of familiar objects or customary tools has been often remarked, and there are diminutives in Greek, Latin, and other languages, which must have

[1] See Greenough, in Harvard Studies in Classical Philology, I, 96.

had this origin.[1] The use of *his* with familiar words, as 'He knew *his* Homer from beginning to end,' is purified slang of the same kind, and it is common to use *little* of anything familiar, in a kind of baby-talk, prompted by the same feeling: as, 'Eat your little dinner,' 'his little horse.' The writer was once in Greece, talking in this style with an intimate friend, and observed that he was really translating the Homeric φίλος (*phílos*). The suspicion was not far off that this too had been slang, but was afterward adopted by the literary language. In some languages, as the Lithuanian, almost any noun may thus take a diminutive form,—in other words, this kind of slang has become the ordinary speech.

Slang is fond of clipped words: as, *monk* for *monkey*, *exam* for *examination*, *loony* for *lunatic*, *middy* for *midshipman*, *auto* for *automobile*, *biz* for *business*, *leg* for *blackleg*, *'varsity* for *university*.[2] Many such formations have passed into the accepted vocabulary. Thus *cab* is short for *cabriolet*, *van* for *vanguard* (for *avant-guard*), *fence* for *defence*, *miss* for *mistress*, *pert* for *apert*, *mob* for *mobile vulgus*, *'bus* for *omnibus* (itself originally a slang term), *cad* for *cadet*, *gin* for *Geneva*, *rum* for *rumbullion*, *pad* for *footpad*, *piano* for *pianoforte*, *cit* for *citizen*, *kilo* for *kilogram*, *hack* for *hackney*, *zoo* for *zoölogical garden*, *loo* for *lanterloo*,[3] *gill* ('a girl,' 'a flirt') for *Gillian* (i.e. *Juliana*), *wag* for *waghalter*,[4] *per cent* for *per centum*, *pros*

---

[1] See Cooper, Word-Formation in the Sermo Plebeius, p. 167. English examples are *jimmy* (*jemmy*) and *betty* for burglars' tools, *jack* (as in *bootjack*), a *spinning jenny*, *billy* for a 'club' or (in Australia) for a 'bushman's kettle.' Cf. p. 386.

[2] Cf. the provincial English *varsal* for *universal* (England) and the Yankee *tarnal* for *eternal* (now nearly obsolete).

[3] Itself originally slang, being the refrain of a comic song.

[4] That is, 'one fit to be hanged,' 'a rogue.' The sense of 'droll fellow,' 'humorist' is more recent: see the disquisition on 'the insipid

and *cons* for *pros* and *contras*, *consols* for *consolidated annuities*, *sweets* for *sweetmeats*, *sport* for *disport*, *cat* for *cat-o'-nine-tails*.

Recognized colloquialisms are *hypo* for *hypochondria*, or *sodium hypophosphite*, *pyro* for *pyrogallic acid*, *typo* for *typographer*, *phiz* for *physiognomy* (already shortened by the Elizabethans to *fisnomy* or *visnamy*), *coon* for *raccoon* (from Fr. *raton*, 'rat'), *possum* for *opossum*, *cute* for *acute*, *pub* for *public house*, *cycle* for *bicycle*, *fib* probably from *fibble-fabble* (a reduplicated form of *fable*), *specs* for *spectacles*, *smalls* for *smallclothes*, *phone* for *telephone*, *sport* for *sportsman*, *whip* for *whipper-in*, *confab* for *confabulation*, *on tick* from *ticket*, *non con* for *non content*[1] (one voting in the negative in the House of Lords), *blue* for *bluestocking*, the *blues* for *blue devils*, *pike* for *turnpike*, *chap* for *chapman* ('merchant,' then 'fellow'),[2] *rickshaw* for *jinrickshaw*.

In 1710, Swift, in the Tatler (No. 230), complained of the 'continual corruption of the English tongue' in an amusing article of some historical importance. He inveighs against such colloquial clippings as *I'd*, *can't*, *he's*, *shan't*, which he calls 'abbreviations and elisions, by which consonants of most obdurate sound are joined together, without one softening vowel to intervene.' And he is particularly severe on 'the refinement which consists in pronouncing the first syllable in a word that has many, and dismissing the rest, such as *phizz*, *hipps*, *mobb*, *pozz*, *rep*, and many more, when we are already overloaded with monosyllables, which are the disgrace of

mirth of certain animals we usually call *wags*' in the Tatler, No. 184 (June 13, 1710).

[1] Also, formerly, for *Non-conformist*.
[2] See p. 287.

our language.' 'Thus,' continues the critic, 'we cram one syllable, and cut off the rest, as the owl fattened her mice after she had bit off their legs to prevent them from running away.' *Incog* and *plenipo* he fears will suffer still further mutilation to *inc* and *plen*. Another 'refinement' is 'the choice of certain words invented by some pretty fellows, such as *banter*, *bamboozle*, *country put*, and *kidney*,[1] some of which are now struggling for the vogue, and others are in possession of it.' 'I have done my utmost,' he adds, 'for some years past, to stop the progress of *mobb* and *banter*, but have been plainly borne down by numbers, and betrayed by those who promised to assist me.' And finally he is worried by certain young clergymen who 'in their sermons use all the modern terms of art, *sham*, *banter*, *mob*, *bubble*, *bully*, *cutting*, *shuffling*, and *palming*.' The reader will be interested to see that about half of the terms at which the essayist is so indignant have made good their position as respectable colloquialisms, and that several of them are quite at home in dignified composition.[2]

The clipping process is a natural tendency of language. It often implies familiarity, and has given us, for example, a multitude of pet names, like *Will* and *Tom* and *Moll*. Compare *doc* for *doctor*, *prof* for *professor*, and other jocose or vulgar appellatives, and the childish *fess* for *confess*. The so-called 'aphetic' forms, like *squire* for *esquire*, *bate* for *abate*, *scape* for *escape*, *pall* for *appall*, should also be considered. A very curious example of these is our common adverb *down*. This is for *adown*, which is a

[1] In such phrases as a 'man of that *kidney*,' *i.e.* 'kind' or 'disposition.'
[2] In the same paper Swift stigmatizes 'speculations, operations, preliminaries, ambassadors, pallisadoes, communication, circumvallation, battalions' as neologisms brought into common use by the war.

corruption of the Anglo-Saxon phrase *of dūne*, 'from the *down* or hill,' used of descending motion (cf. Ger. *bergab*). Thus we have in English the noun *down*, meaning 'a hill,' and an adverb *down*, derived from this same noun, but suggesting the opposite idea. 'Down in the valley' is a striking instance of the capabilities of language. *Size* is a clipped form of *assize*, which means literally 'a sitting' (of judges), as in *assizes*, and comes (through the French) from L. *assidere*, 'to sit by.' From 'judgment' or 'determination' to 'allotment,' 'allotted portion,' and thence to 'dimension,' is an easy passage. *Size* is a Cambridge University term for an 'allowance' from the buttery. Goldsmith was a *sizar* at Dublin, *i.e.* a 'charity-student' (such as formerly waited on the Fellows' table). *Size*, 'glue,' is also from *assideo* (through Italian *sisa*), being that which makes anything 'sit close' or 'stick' to another. A much-docked word is *drake*, 'male duck.' The history of *drake* is far from clear, but it is connected with A.S. *ened*, 'duck' (cognate with L. *anas, anatis*), of which, however, it preserves only the single letter *d* (cf. Ger. *Enterich*). *Wayward* is shortened from *awayward*, *back* (the adverb) from *aback*, *vails* from *avails*, *quinsy* from *squinancy*.[1] *Pose* is from *appose* (for *oppose*), 'to raise objections,' 'to interrogate' or 'examine' (in a discussion); a *poser* was an 'examiner'; *puzzle* is corrupted from *opposal*.

Slang delights in fantastic coinages and in grotesque combinations or distortions of existing words. When a whimsicality of this kind establishes itself as a permanent colloquialism, or gets into the accepted vocabulary, the etymologist has a hard nut to crack. Unless the early

[1] Fr. *esquinancie* from Gr. κυνάγχη, from κύων, κυνός, 'dog,' and ἄγχω, 'choke.'

history of the word is known, or at least the circumstances under which it came into use, the derivation is often an insoluble problem. And if the word is at all old, its history is likely to be obscure, for slang seldom gets into print until it has been in circulation for some time.

A few examples of such linguistic chimeras will now be given.

Bamboozle was a new slang word in 1710. It has been thought to be from *bam*, 'to hoax,' a slang word of about the same date; but *bam* is quite as likely to be an abbreviation of the longer form, and *boozle* remains unexplained. *Banter* is another unsolved puzzle. It was at least forty years old when Swift attacked it in the Tatler, in 1710. *Sham* is thought to be an affected pronunciation of *shame*. *Doggerel* is first found in Chaucer. The host objects to 'Sir Thopas' as 'rym dogerel,' using the term, however, as a kind of quotation: 'This may wel be rym dogerel,' *i.e.* 'This must be the rhyme doggerel that I have heard tell of.' The etymology is quite unknown, but it is hard to reject *dog*, in view of *dog-Latin*, *dog-logic*, and the like.

Cockney is almost certainly 'cock-egg' (M.E. *ey*, 'egg'). The word meant at first an unusually small egg (such as are termed in New England *litter-eggs*, since the hen is thought to lay one at the end of her litter). Thence developed the meaning of a 'cockered child,' a 'pet,' a 'mother's baby,' or, in a wider sense, a 'milksop,' and, next, 'a [pampered] citizen' (a feeble 'cit' as opposed to a hardy rustic). Specifically, it meant 'one ignorant of country matters,' as a *greenhorn* is one who knows nothing of city life. Its particular application to a Londoner was then natural, and was made as early as the sixteenth century.[1] All such jocose or abusive names for the inhabitants of particular places or countries are akin to slang, if not of out-and-out slang origin. So *Yankee* for 'New Englander,' often applied by Englishmen to all inhabitants of the United States;[2] *Dago* for Italian ; *Paddy* for Irishman; *Sawney* for Scotchman ; *Gothamite* for New Yorker, and the like. *Dago* is a queer misnomer. It must come from the Spanish *Diego*, yet it is usually applied to Italians; but slang does not make nice distinctions of blood : witness the contemptuous use of *nigger* for many dark-skinned races who have no similarity to the negro (so *blackamoor*, 'black Moor,' for Ethiopian). *Yankee* is still a puzzle. The suggestion that it is for *Yengees* or the like, and came from the attempt of the North American Indians to pronounce *English* has no foundation in the history of the word, and no inherent probability.

Chouse perhaps goes back to the Sultan's *chaush*, or official interpreter, who swindled certain Turkish merchants in London. *Blackguard* in the sixteenth and seventeenth centuries was a term for the scullions and other similar menials in a great household, as well as for the camp-followers in an army. *Blackleg* was slang for a swindling 'frequenter of the turf' in the eighteenth century. *Bully* was once a term of endearment, and has been connected with German *Buhle*, 'lover,' but this is very doubtful. *Coxcomb*, first 'fool,' then 'fop,'[3] comes from the imitation

[1] For the history of *cockney* see the Oxford Dictionary as corrected and supplemented by Dr. C. P. G. Scott, Trans. Amer. Philol. Assoc., XXIII, 206 ff. The form *ney* for *ey*, 'egg,' owes its *n* to the indefinite article *an* (*an ey* becoming *a ney*) ; see pp. 197-8.

[2] Cf. *Yankees* for 'American securities' in English financial cant, like *Kaffirs* and *Jungles* for South African and Indian stocks, respectively.

[3] *Fop* also meant 'fool' in general, but was afterward specialized to a particular kind of folly; and *sot* has a similar history, though here the specialization is different.

'cock's comb' which adorned the cap of the professional jester in Elizabethan times. *Ragamuffin* has something to do with *rag*, beyond a doubt. It occurs (in the form *Ragamofin*) as the name of a devil in the miracle-plays, — and devils were often described as 'ragged,' that is, 'shaggy,' in appearance. The word *rag* is related to *rug*. *Nincompoop* is a distortion of *non compos mentis*. To *wheedle* is literally 'to fawn,' 'to wag the tail,' from Ger. *wedeln*. *Chum* was defined in 1690 as 'chamberfellow,' and is usually regarded as a corruption of this term, but evidence is lacking. It has been university slang since the latter part of the seventeenth century, — and in 1684 Creech dedicated his translation of Lucretius 'to my chum, Mr. Hody of Wadham College.'

Bombast is 'cotton-wadding' (from Gr. βόμβυξ, *bómbux*, 'silk,' through Latin and French). So Prince Hal calls Falstaff 'my sweet creature of bombast.' Its application to an inflated style is an obvious jest, and is first found in Nashe (1589): 'the swelling bumbast of a bragging blank verse.'[1] It is not likely to be much older than his time. *Fustian*, in a similar sense, is of about the same age, and is a similarly jocose application of the name of the coarse stuff so called. The word is supposed to be derived from *Fustāt*, *i.e.* Cairo.[2]

Cozen has usually been referred to *cousin*, and the French *cousiner* favors this view. Cotgrave, in 1611, defined the French verb as 'to claim kindred for advantage . . . ; as he who, to save charges in travelling, goes from house to house, as cousin to the owner of every one.' This ety-

[1] For *bathos*, see p. 40.
[2] So the Greeks used λήκυθος (*lékuthos*), 'an oil-jar' (swelling in the body) for a 'bombastic style,' whence they made a verb, ληκυθίζω (*lēkuthízō*), 'to write fustian.' Horace translated the former by the Latin *ampulla*, and coined a verb, *ampullor*, to correspond.

mology has been doubted, but it is supported by a fact which has escaped even the editors of the Oxford Dictionary. 'To go a-cousining' is an old-fashioned New England phrase applied to one who quarters himself on his distant relatives.[1]

Cabal for an 'intrigue' or an 'intriguing clique' comes (through the French and mediæval Latin) from the Hebrew word for 'tradition' (*quabbālāh*), applied especially to a mystical interpretation of the Scriptures (which we have borrowed in the form *cabbala*). Its sense of 'political machination' was strengthened and perpetuated by its special application to Charles II's 'Committee for Foreign Affairs,' and in particular to five members of that 'cabinet council' whose names made the acrostic *cabal*: *C*lifford, *A*rlington, *B*uckingham, *A*shley (Shaftesbury), *L*auderdale.

Gerrymander (with hard *g*) is a capital instance of the license which the maker of slang allows himself. It is an established political term in the United States and Canada[2] for the 'redistricting' of a state in such a manner as to give a particular party an unfair advantage at an election. Such a measure was carried in Massachusetts in 1812, when Elbridge Gerry was governor of the Commonwealth. Some clever person observed that one of the newly laid-out districts that was expected to insure the success of the governor's party took, with a little imagination, the shape of a fantastic monster. A map of the district was published, in which this was indicated, and the monster was dubbed *gerrymander*, a word made up from *Gerry*

---

[1] This is the only use of *cozen* that is really vernacular in this country, where the habit of visiting country cousins is a common subject for satirical jest.

[2] In Canada and the West the hard *g* has been softened in pronunciation.

and *salamander*.[1] Usually such devices hardly survive the campaign that produces them, — but the gerrymander tickled the fancy of the American people, and the word is still in common use, both as a noun and as a verb. *Slantindicular*, a jocose amalgam of *slantin'* and *perpendicular* has not fared quite so well.

Even such lawless coinages as *gerrymander* and *slantindicular* are not essentially different from many forms produced by the ordinary processes of language (see Chapter XXIII, Folk-Etymology, for examples).

It is a favorite device of slang to replace a common word by a figurative expression or by some word that is well known as a synonym (or partial synonym) for the first, but in another sense. Thus 'He had the *face* to tell me' becomes 'the *cheek* to tell me'; *effrontery* becomes *brass* (from the figurative use of *brazen*); *handcuffs* are *bracelets*; a *preacher* is a *sky-pilot*; *hands* are *pickers and stealers*.[2] A man's *card* is his *pasteboard*; to *be hanged* is to *swing*; a *pocket flask* is a *pocket pistol*;[3] a *town* is a *burgh*; *money* is *cash* or *change*; *dinner table* is *mahogany*, and so on. The same process takes place with slang words themselves, in the eager desire for novelty. The old English *grit*, 'sand,' 'gravel,' came to be applied to the special grain or texture of grinding stones, on which, in fact, their efficacy depends. Thence it was transferred, in American slang, to the personal qualities of courage, firmness, and endurance. The expressiveness of the figure

[1] See an article on 'The Machinery of Politics and Proportional Representation' by W. R. Ware, in The American Law Review, VI, 282–6 (with a facsimile of the original gerrymander, from a broadside, p. 284).

[2] From the phrase in the catechism, 'to keep my hands from picking and stealing.'

[3] From Falstaff's jest in the First Part of Henry IV, where he pulls out a bottle instead of a pistol.

won general acceptance for the new sense both in the
'country of its origin' and in England. *Grit* seemed
lost to the slang vocabulary. At all events, it ceased to
be novel as soon as it became respectable. A new term
was straightway introduced to replace it, — *sand*, which
is actually a synonym of *grit* in another sense, and for a
time 'He has plenty of *sand*' was a common expression
among speakers of the slang dialect.

It is needless to remark that the same desire for novelty
is constantly at work in the figurative expressions and
new coinages of legitimate speech. It operates more
rapidly in slang, and with less regard for the proprieties,
but the general law is the same in both.

Artistic literature, apart from the mere conveyance of
thought, aims to charm and attract the reader by means
of an agreeable style; to stimulate his attention by clever
novelty, and even sometimes to shock him into thought
by grotesque or startling language. Thus arise a host of
new words, most of which soon die, but some of which
are sure to find their place in the general vocabulary.
And thus in particular, by the constant striving after
more delicate and subtle effects, there come into existence
new distinctions in the meanings of familiar terms which,
if they serve any good purpose, are pretty sure to become
permanent.

Phrase-composition, which we have already studied, is
alike active in slang and in law-abiding speech. *Nincompoop* (for *non compos mentis*), *carouse* (for *gar aus!*), and
hoax (from *hocus pocus*)[1] were all slang phrases. *Alarm*
(for *all' arme!*) and *jeopardy* (for *jeu parti*) are of dignified origin. Frequently the fag-end of a phrase or quotation obtains currency as a single word in some special

[1] See p. 189 for details.

sense. Here again slang and propriety join hands. *Propaganda* is abbreviated from 'Congregatio de propaganda fide,' a 'committee (of cardinals) for propagating the (Christian) faith.' *Præmunire*, a kind of writ, is a corruption of *praemoneri facias*, 'you shall cause to be forewarned.' The *Porte* is short for *Sublime Porte*. *Parole*, for 'solemn promise,' is a clipped form of *parole d'honneur*. The associations of these terms are irreproachable. In formation, however, they do not differ from many slangy or colloquial expressions. Thus *factotum* is for *Johannes factotum*, 'John do-all' (cf. jack-of-all-trades). *Amphitryon*, 'host,' is from Molière's 'l'Amphitryon où l'on dîne.'[1] To *chivy* or *chevy* is doubtless *Chevy Chace*; the full phrase is dialectic as both noun and verb. *Straw*, for 'slight but significant indication' (common in American political cant), is from the proverb, 'Straws show which way the wind blows.' So *chaff*, 'banter,' suggests 'An old bird is not caught with chaff.' *Box*, 'a bad predicament,' is from 'in the wrong box.' *Buncombe* is the name of a county in North Carolina. The sense of '*ad captandum* remarks' or 'showy verbiage,' is said to have come from the reply of a certain congressman, who insisted that he must 'make a speech for Buncombe' (*i.e.* for his constituents to hear of) on an occasion when the House of Representatives was eager to take a vote. A *jingo*, for 'one who favors an aggressive foreign policy,' comes from the burlesque oath *by jingo*, which occurred in the refrain of a boisterous political song current in England during the Turko-Russian War of 1877–8. The word has recently been transplanted from England to America, where it is applied (by their opponents) to those who are also styled 'impe-

[1] In the comedy of Amphitryon, act iii, scene 5.

rialists,' — a word of inevitably bad odor in a republic,[1] though inoffensive in an empire. We may leave the subject with an example from the sixteenth century. The Greek *Kyrie eleïson*, 'Lord, have mercy upon us,' was often abbreviated to *Kyrie*, and this (as well as the full phrase) was once a familiar vulgarism for a 'good scolding.'[2]

It appears, then, that there is no real difference in kind between the processes of slang and those of legitimate speech. Slang is only the rude luxuriance of the uncared-for soil, knowing not the hand of the gardener.

Yet it by no means follows that the products of slang are at once to be adopted, without further question. In the first place, all human speech, even the most intimate, is intended for the ears of others, and must therefore have a certain dignity, a certain courtesy, out of respect to one's hearers if not to one's self. Now slang, from the very fact that it *is* slang, that it is not the accepted medium of communication, has a taint of impropriety about it which makes it offensive. Again, the very currency of slang depends on its allusions to things which are not supposed to be universally familiar or generally respectable; and hence it is vulgar, since it brings in associations with what is for the moment regarded as unknown or in bad repute.

It is true that words have no character in themselves, being only conventional signs for the ideas which they express. Even bad grammar is essentially just as good as good grammar; it becomes bad merely because it is associated with persons that we dislike or look down on.

---

[1] Compare the Roman dislike to *rex*.

[2] See Tyndale's list of slang phrases from church terms and the like, in his Obedience of a Christian Man (Works of Tyndale and Frith, ed. Russell, I, 340).

And bad language is only such because it is not the accepted form of speech. Yet the recognized connotations of particular words are an integral part of expression, and when these are such as to shock or offend our associates, the words themselves should be avoided.

Furthermore, the accepted means of communication in any widespread language has a certain constant and enduring nature. Though language is ever changing, yet the permanent elements far outweigh the variable, so that it remains continuously intelligible through long periods of time. Slang words, on the contrary, are evanescent, counting their duration by days instead of decades, and becoming obsolete even while one is speaking them. Hence slang is ill-adapted to serve as a medium of intercourse and therefore is unsuitable for adoption into legitimate speech.

Finally, the unchecked and habitual use of slang (even polite slang) is deleterious to the mind. Not only is slang evanescent, — it also has no fixed meaning. Its terms are vague and ill-defined, and they grow more and more uncertain from day to day. Thus the use of slang tends to level all those nice distinctions of meaning, all those differentiations between word and word, which the consensus of the language has been at so much pains to build up. Everything is 'fine!' or 'immense!' or 'stunning!' or 'just gay!' from an appetizing breakfast to an epic poem, from Alpine scenery to the cut of a friend's coat. Slang has been called the 'lazy man's dialect,' and if the sign of cultivation is an enriched vocabulary, the constant use of vague and unselected terms for every shade of meaning must gradually reduce one's thought to the same ignorant level from which most slang proceeds. When such a word becomes definite in its meaning, it has almost ceased to be slang. If it happens to fill a real gap in our means of expression, language will take care of it, as we have already seen in numerous examples. In fact, anything that is good in slang is almost sure to be picked up and adopted in legitimate speech.

Of course, all slang is not on the same level. There are many grades, from that which is innocent and almost refined in its associations, to the odious coinages of a debased stage. It is often humorous, sometimes witty, and not seldom picturesque. The objections just urged hold good against its habitual employment as an extensive part of one's vocabulary. The discriminating use of a slang term, now and then, on occasion, is a different matter. As we have already seen, every educated person speaks his mother tongue in at least two ways, and the difference between the dignified and the colloquial style is considerable. Slang words frequently rise to the rank of colloquialisms, and thus in time gain admission to the more formal language. 'To hit straight from the shoulder,' 'I feel rather below par,' 'the new woman,' 'a boodle alderman,' 'to floor a man,' 'I was flabbergasted,' have crossed the line and are admissible colloquialisms. 'Hit or miss,' 'nip and tuck,' 'tooth and nail,' 'by hook or crook,' 'sink or swim,' 'rough-and-ready,' 'higgledy-piggledy,' have passed through the colloquial stage and are recognized idioms, though their form or sound, or something of their old associations, tends to exclude them from serious contexts.

One further distinction is necessary. A word or phrase which is slangy in general conversation stands in quite a different position when it is used in a limited circle, or under special circumstances. 'Horsey' words are not slang when one is 'talking horse,' nor hunting terms in

SLANG AND LEGITIMATE SPEECH 75

the hunting field, nor the cant phrases of politics on the hustings or on the stump. They belong rather to the category of jargons, or technical dialects, and are comparable to the special vocabularies of commerce, or medicine, or the law. It is only when they leave the technical circle, and are applied in a general way, that they become out-and-out slang, and this would be just as true of scientific or legal terms under similar circumstances. Here again there are grades of slanginess, in inverse proportion to the dignity of the associations which the words suggest. 'To *mortgage* one's reputation' is as essentially a slang phrase as 'to be *knocked out* in an examination,' but there is a considerable difference in the vulgarity of the expressions. 'To come a cropper' may be said to stand midway between the two. 'At fault' (from a dog that loses the scent) is a dignified idiom.

Again, an expression that is unquestionably slang may be so apt and necessary in the discussion of a particular subject, and so often quoted by the best writers, that it loses its taint and becomes a part of our common stock of quotations. Then the presence or absence of quotation marks is only a matter of greater or less familiarity, and eventually all feeling of quotation may disappear. The readiest admission to legitimate speech lies through our freedom in quoting from any source, good or bad. For when an expression is found in respectable company, the public seldom cares to ask how it got there. Not long ago the very vulgar slang phrase 'rush the growler' was quoted in a dignified and irreproachable article in a daily newspaper. It was used in a kind of technical sense, and, more than that, it had exactly the connotations that the writer desired. A score of such references might make the reader forget that this most objectionable expression ever was slang, or had any offensive associations. In this manner many words have made their way into the literary language. The Elizabethan drama, for instance, has preserved and propagated many such expressions, for in a play every speech is, in a manner, a quotation.

The slang of the United States differs in many particulars from that of Great Britain, and India and Australia show a multitude of peculiar coinages that differ from both. Yet the lively intercourse of trade and travel, the newspapers, the theatrical 'tour,' and the 'dialect sketch' have kept the different English-speaking peoples tolerably familiar with one another's latest coinages. For universal hospitality is the guiding principle of slang.

The bewildering variety of our language, and in particular the lawless and fantastic coinages which we have just been studying, may well suggest the question, 'Is there any criterion of good English? What principle of selection is one to follow who wishes to speak and write his mother tongue with purity and without affectation?' It is the business of grammar, rhetoric, and lexicography to answer this question.

As soon as a literary language is thoroughly developed, it becomes a subject of earnest study. Literature, like painting or music, has a technique, and it is the province of critics and rhetoricians to describe this technique, and to reduce its principles and its details to a form in which they may be conveniently acquired. Such principles are inferred, in the main, from the works of men of genius, but they soon become, so far as they are correct, fundamental conventions of expression, which must be followed by everybody who would make himself immediately intelligible. So long as a language is alive, it is, however, constantly changing, so that the grammar and rhetoric of

SLANG AND LEGITIMATE SPEECH 77

a living language can never be absolutely fixed. It is only when the language has ceased to be spoken, — has become, as we say, a dead language, — that fixed rules can be framed which every one who undertakes to write it must observe. The very statement that a language is dead implies that henceforward no individual or body of persons has power to change it in any particular.

Now all rules of grammar and rhetoric must be based on usage, for there is no other standard in linguistic matters; and in order that they may be capable of intelligible statement, the usage from which they are derived must be limited in time. Yet at the very moment when the rules are committed to writing, usage is shifting; for language never stands still until it ceases to move altogether. Hence the codified principles of literary expression will always be slightly behind the actual usage of one's contemporaries. In other words, we are here dealing with conservative forces which tend to retard the naturally rapid changes of speech. Conservatism always implies distrust of that which is new, however good it may be; and teaching implies not only docility on the part of the learner, but some dogmatism on the part of the instructor. Unless a man thinks he knows something, it is useless for him to teach it, just as it is idle for a boy to go to school who thinks he has nothing to learn. When dogmatic conservatism in language goes farther than is reasonable, we call it 'purism,' and stigmatize its disciples as 'purists.' Everybody, however, who speaks or writes with any care must be a purist in some degree, for we all have our pet aversions in matters of vocabulary and construction. Both the purist and the innovator are necessary factors in the development of a cultivated tongue. Without the purist our language would change with extravagant rapidity; our vocabulary, for example, would give daily hospitality to hosts of new words which have nothing but whim to justify them, and which would be soon superseded by equally lawless formations. Without the innovator our language would come to a dead stop, so far as literary expression is concerned, and in a short time the speech of books would have lagged so far behind the speech of conversation that the two would form different dialects. The history of any literary language is, then, a record of successive compromises and readjustments between the old and the new.

A novel word or phrase which has not yet secured unquestioned admission into the standard dialect is called a *neologism*, which is simply a Greek term for a 'new form of speech.' There is no test but time. If a neologism seems to most speakers to supply a lack in the language, or to be peculiarly fit for the expression of some special idea, it is sure to maintain itself against the protests of the literary and scholastic guild.

On the other hand, nothing can force a new term into any language against the inclination of a large majority of those who speak it. The field of language is strewn with the dry bones of adventurous words which once started out with the paternal blessing to make their fortune, but which have met with an untimely end, and serve only, when collected, to fill the shelves of a lexicographical museum. Some years ago, when the annexation of a large tract of territory to the United States was discussed, Charles Sumner endeavored to revive the obsolete word *annexion* in place of this somewhat cumbrous term. Sumner's position as an orator, a man of culture, and a statesman seemed to insure the favorable reception of this convenient form, but all these influences were of no avail.

For a year or two *annexion* was seen in the newspapers occasionally, but to most of the present generation it is as unknown as the eccentric ink-horn terms of the Elizabethan age.[1]

[1] See Sumner's speech on the Cession of Russian America (1867), and also that on the Proposed Annexion of the Island of San Domingo, 1870.

CHAPTER VII

THE LITERARY LANGUAGE

THE language which all educated users of English speak and write is in one sense an artificial tongue. It is what is called a 'literary language' as distinguished from the unstudied speech of peoples whose mother tongue comes to them without the influence of literature or the schools. This 'literary language' is not confined to cultivated speakers. It is the common property of all but the absolutely illiterate, the regular medium of communication throughout the English-speaking world. Different persons speak and write this standard English with different degrees of correctness and elegance, and there are local and national varieties in idiom and pronunciation which distinguish the English of England from that of America or of Australia. But such differences bear no proportion to the substantial uniformity of English speech. What is the origin of standard or literary English, which most of us take for granted as if it had existed from the beginning? The question is complicated, but the clew is easy to catch and to follow: it consists in the single word 'dialect.'

It is natural for a person whose knowledge of English conforms in the main to the literary or standard type to regard the dialect of Yorkshire or of Dorset as a degraded form of his own speech. Such an impression, however, is quite erroneous. The Yorkshireman's dialect is not a debased form of standard English. On the contrary, standard

English is merely a cultivated form of a dialect which originally had no more claim to be regarded as the general language of all England than the dialect of Yorkshire has to-day. In other words, — a dialect is not a degraded literary language; a literary language is an elevated dialect.

The piratical marauders who in the fifth and sixth centuries effected the Anglo-Saxon Conquest of Britain belonged to three or four different tribes and spoke as many dialects. These dialects, however, were very similar, and their variety did not interfere with mutual understanding. We may call them collectively 'Anglo-Saxon,' but we must remember that at this period there was no standard Anglo-Saxon language in the sense in which there is to-day a standard French or German. Each of our predatory ancestors spoke his own dialect with great satisfaction to himself and without considering whether it was better or worse than that of a shipmate who belonged to a neighboring tribe. Taken collectively, Anglo-Saxon was most nearly related to Old Frisian, the ancestor of the dialects still spoken in the Frisian Islands. It was also near akin to the Old Saxon, the ancestor of Modern *Plattdeutsch;* and to Old Frankish, the ancestor of Dutch and Flemish. Its relation to the Scandinavian languages and to the High German dialects was more remote.[1]

Of the three tribes who played important parts in the Anglo-Saxon Conquest, the Angles occupied the northern and central part of England and extended their conquest to the lowlands of Scotland. The southern part of Britain fell into the hands of the Saxons. The small but rich domain of Kent remained the possession of the Jutes. The seventh century finds the conquest completed, and

[1] Cf. pp. 159, 163.

the new lords of the soil settled substantially in accordance with these boundaries. They had no written language. Yet we must not infer that their several dialects had received no literary cultivation. Oral literature always precedes writing, so that, when the art of writing is finally introduced, there awaits it a considerable body of poetry, ready to be taken down and perpetuated. Thus the Angles and Saxons had a great quantity of heroic song, for which they had developed an elaborate metre and a peculiarly complicated style, quite different from that of their habitual language. Observe, however, that at the time of which we are speaking, no one of the various dialects spoken in Britain had a title to preëminence.

We have no written documents in these dialects until the eighth century, when Britain had been in the hands of its new masters for two or three hundred years. Presumably, the various dialects had grown apart during this time; for Angles, Saxons, and Jutes were more widely separated in their new home than they had been on the continent, and their little kingdoms were always at war. Yet in the eighth century the differences had not yet become great enough to make the dialects mutually unintelligible. They may be divided into (1) Northumbrian, the language of the kingdom of Northumbria, including the north of England and the south of Scotland; (2) Saxon, spoken throughout the south of England; (3) Mercian, spoken in the kingdom of Mercia, corresponding to the midland counties of the present day; (4) Kentish, spoken by the Jutes of Kent. The Northumbrian and the Mercian were Anglian dialects. The men of Kent spoke Jutish, and the Saxon was, as its name implies, the language of the Saxon contingent of the original invaders. Within each of the territories thus defined there was considerable divergency of speech, but this may be neglected in a general survey.

The first dialect that could lay claim to literary precedence was the Northumbrian (the language of Cædmon and the Venerable Bede), which, in the eighth century, seemed in a fair way to set the standard for the English tongue. But the fall of Northumbria from its political supremacy and the rise of the southern kingdom of Wessex completely changed the situation. Northumbrian sank once more to the position of a provincial dialect, and under King Alfred, in the ninth century, the West Saxon dialect put in a strong claim to be regarded as the literary language. Meantime, however, the name *English*, that is, 'Anglian,'[1] had associated itself inseparably with the idea of *any* literary form of the vernacular. The Northumbrians had called their tongue 'English' because it *was* English, — that is, Anglian. The Saxons of Wessex applied the same term to their own non-Anglian literary tongue.

From King Alfred to the Battle of Hastings is about two hundred years. In this time literary English (the West Saxon dialect) had made great strides and seemed far more likely to become the universal speech of Englishmen than Northumbrian had seemed three centuries before. If this development had not been violently interrupted, we should nowadays be speaking, in all probability, a language very similar to the Dutch. It was interrupted, as everybody knows, by the Norman Conquest.

The effect of the Norman Conquest on the history of our language is frequently misunderstood. The Normans

---

[1] *Engle* means 'Angles,' and *Englisc* 'Anglian.' The initial *e* shows 'umlaut' of an older *a*. *England* is *Engla* (genitive plural) *land*, 'the country of the Angles.'

were superior to the English in chivalric manners; but the English surpassed them in learning and in literary culture of the vernacular. The English of the year 1050 was not a rude, harsh-sounding jargon, but a highly developed language, with a copious vocabulary and an abundant literature in prose and verse. There is no evidence that the Normans despised the English language, and they certainly made no attempt to crush it. They talked a dialect of French, and no doubt they had no expectation of giving up their *patois;* but they had no wish to impose it on any one else. A far-seeing philosophical historian might, indeed, have foretold that either French or English would have to prevail in the long run. But such a philosopher would have had no doubt which of the two languages would survive. The Normans had already given up their native Scandinavian in favor of French, and they were heavily outnumbered by the English. The result was inevitable. It cannot have occurred to any Norman that his language was to become the vernacular tongue in Great Britain. It certainly never occurred to any Englishman that his own language was likely to become extinct.

What the Norman Conquest did was not to break up or confuse our language by coming into direct conflict with it, but simply to interrupt the literary tradition of the English tongue. At the time of the Battle of Hastings, the West Saxon dialect was the accepted literary language, and, although it was not yet in general use throughout the island, it was nevertheless in a strong position with reference to such an extension of its influence. With the coming of the Normans, this dialect fell from its pinnacle. French became the language of the court and of high society, not because the court despised

English, but because the court consisted of French-speaking Normans. There was no longer any encouragement for the cultivation of the special West Saxon form of English at the hands of scholars and poets. Hence when any Englishman wrote in the vernacular after the Norman dominion became established, he used his own local dialect, without regard to the standards of West Saxon that had existed before the Conquest. In other words, the Norman Conquest put the dialects of England once more on their mettle. West Saxon was reduced to the rank which it had occupied before the days of Alfred, and it was again an open question which of the three great dialects (Northumbrian, Mercian, and Saxon) should become the literary language of the English race.[1]

No doubt the speech of Normandy (the Norman French) exerted a certain amount of direct influence on the grammar and vocabulary of our language, but this influence was much smaller than is generally supposed. The decay of inflections, which is one of the distinguishing marks of modern English, had begun before the Normans came. It was accelerated by the Conquest, but only in an indirect way, through the break in literary tradition already referred to. A similar decay has taken place in Dutch and in Danish, which were never subjected to a Norman Conquest, and it must be regarded as a natural tendency of our language. Some words were borrowed from Norman French, but not enough to color the vocabulary to a perceptible degree. In short, the two languages lived amicably side by side for about two hundred years, neither affecting the other essentially. Indeed, every

[1] Of course, the conditions of the problem were not appreciated in the Middle Ages. Such movements as we are studying can be surveyed only from the vantage-ground of centuries.

student of Anglo-Norman knows that the French of the invaders suffered almost as much as the English of the conquered. In 1154 the Count of Anjou became king of England. At the beginning of the thirteenth century Normandy was lost to the English crown. This loss had important results. Henceforth the specific influence of Norman French upon the English language was very slight indeed, — hardly appreciable. In the latter part of the thirteenth century and throughout the fourteenth, Englishmen were vigorously engaged in translating and adapting French literature. Their models, however, were not Norman French, in the main, nor was their activity connected with the Conquest or with the fact that the ruling class was of Norman descent. The same translation and adaptation took place in Germany, and even to some extent in Norway. Central or Parisian French was now the recognized standard on the Continent, and the French of the English court was not Norman, but as good Parisian French as the nobility could muster. Moreover, by the first quarter of the fourteenth century, many of the descendants of the Normans had lost their French and were speaking English like their Saxon neighbors.

Everybody knows that modern English contains thousands of French words. We can hardly utter a sentence without using one. Yet comparatively few of these are derived from Norman French. Wholesale borrowing began about 1300 and continued for two hundred years, and the same process has gone on ever since, but in a more limited way. But most of our French words, from 1300 to 1900, have come not from the dialect of the Normans, but from Central or Parisian French, — the recognized literary standard.

All this borrowing, however, signified not the victory

of French, but the triumph of English as the vernacular language of Great Britain. Normans were Normans no longer, but Englishmen. The Normans were greatly outnumbered by the Saxons. They had long ceased to speak the Norman dialect; though many of them still regarded French as their mother tongue, and talked the Parisian dialect as well as they could, as Englishmen still do. As for the Saxon element in the population, they had placidly gone on speaking English, in various dialects, and in the long run the aristocracy were obliged to follow their lead. There was no death-struggle between two hostile languages, as many writers have imagined. Everything proceeded in the simplest and most natural way. In the usual course of events, a man can have but one mother tongue. The great majority of the population were content with English, which was therefore indispensable to the minority as well. A man might learn French if he liked, but he had to know English anyway. The result was that by 1400 the language of England was English, and French was what it is now, — the accomplishment of a limited class.

Meantime, what is to be said of the English 'literary language'? From shortly after the Norman Conquest up to the year 1300 there was no such thing. The English dialects were now so far apart that a Southerner could hardly understand a man from the Northern Counties. The Midlands occupied an intermediate position in language as well as geographically. The Northern dialect (the descendant of the old Northumbrian), some of the Southern dialects (the descendants of the Saxon), and at least two forms of the Midland dialect (the descendant of the Mercian) had gradually risen to the position of respectable literary tongues, but no one of them could claim precedence over any other. Everything pointed to the end of the fourteenth century as the time for the great decision. What was needed was a dialect that was widely intelligible and that was already the habitual language of certain powerful elements in the state. The East Midland seemed to meet the requirements. It was the dialect of London, of the court, — when the court spoke English, — of Oxford. It was the dialect in which Wyclif made his translation of the Bible, and, finally, it was the dialect in which Chaucer, the Londoner, naturally wrote.

There is an active revolt nowadays against the thesis that Chaucer 'made the English language.' Some of the most recent investigators of our linguistic history have even neglected to mention him at all in this connection. Yet there is much truth in the discredited old dictum, however absurdly it has sometimes been interpreted. To appreciate the facts, we must look for a moment at the posture of affairs in the latter half of the fourteenth century, — or, say, from 1340 to 1400, the accepted term of Chaucer's life. For it was within these sixty years that the East Midland dialect attained the rank of the English literary language, — a position which it has never lost.

It was an age of intense activity, — a singularly 'modern' time. One is tempted to say that all the problems that vex the world to-day either came into existence or manifested themselves with peculiar force within these sixty years. At all events, there is scarcely a political or social catchword of the present which cannot be applied to affairs in the fourteenth century. 'Labor' was giving trouble in a dozen ways. The Black Death had greatly reduced the number of farm-hands throughout the country. The survivors, once little better than serfs, asserted themselves in a manner that alarmed the landed proprietors and prompted some futile legislation. There was the *Jacquerie* or Peasants' Insurrection in France. In England there were the uprisings of Wat Tyler, John Ball, and Jack Straw, partly a revolt against unjust taxation and oppressive landlords, and partly, especially in London, an assault upon the Flemings, who had been imported by Edward III to establish the manufacture of cloth, and of whom native workmen were intensely jealous. The Eastern Question, too, was assuming a strangely modern appearance. In 1343 the Turk first got a foothold in Europe, and twenty years later began the meteoric career of Tamerlane, infinitely prophetic of barbarous possibilities from the Orient. The revolt against the Pope, which resulted in the complicated movement known as the Reformation, began in the fourteenth century with Wyclif in England and with John Huss in Bohemia. The Revival of Learning also falls in this century; Petrarch and Boccaccio were Chaucer's contemporaries. The interest in education was widespread. A whole chain of universities, from Cracow to Saint Andrews, were established between 1340 and 1410. The extension of the British empire was never a more vital question than at this time. The armed assertion of Edward's claims to the crown of France, the war of Richard II in Ireland, and the attempt of John of Gaunt to seize the kingdom of Castile, show how far-reaching this movement was. One can even see a forecast of the gold and silver question in the time of Edward III. The king's gold nobles became immediately famous. They were readily accepted by foreign merchants everywhere, as sovereigns pass current to-day. Many similar details might be enumerated, but enough has been said to indicate that Chaucer was born in a time of great religious and political and literary activity.

By station, and by the incidents of his career, Chaucer was peculiarly fitted to express the complicated life of this intensely 'modern' age. He belonged to the well-to-do burgher class, and his family stood in some kind of relation to the court. He was neither too high nor too low to be well acquainted with all varieties of English life. In his youth he became page to the Countess of Ulster, and from this time he always enjoyed some kind of official emolument within the royal gift. He was a Collector of the Customs, a Superintendent of Buildings, and an officer in charge of what we should now call the Thames Conservation. He was also a Member of Parliament for a short time. But his experiences were not merely insular. He visited France and Italy several times on business of state, and thus came into close relations with foreign life and letters as well as with diplomacy. As courtier, office-holder, legislator, soldier, diplomatist, burgher of London, he came into contact with every sort of person worth knowing, from king to apprentice. Probably no man had a broader and more intimate knowledge of the social life of the fourteenth century. Add to all this the splendid accident of genius, and you have a writer astonishingly well equipped to depict all sorts and conditions of men as they thought and acted in this interesting time.

Chaucer found his native East Midland dialect already a cultivated language. There had been much narrative poetry written in this dialect. It was, in the main, the English of commerce, of the court, and of the universities. Before he had written a line, the East Midland dialect seemed likely to become standard or literary English, and it doubtless would have achieved that position, even if he

THE LITERARY LANGUAGE

had never been born. Still, the process would have been more gradual and much less certain. What was needed at this juncture was a literary man, a poet of commanding genius, whose native dialect was that which stood ready to be stamped as literary English forever. Chaucer was such a poet; and after his death nobody doubted that the language as he had written it was the best English.

It must not be thought that Chaucer actually imported many new words into our language. Almost every word that he used can be found somewhere at any earlier date. Most of his French and Latin 'borrowings' had been made before. What he did for the Midland dialect was rather to write it with an ease, a polish, and a regularity which had not been hitherto attained, and to use it as the vehicle for first-rate poetry. This stamped the language of Chaucer at once as the literary standard. The excellence of his English is celebrated by his contemporaries and successors. By his side stood Gower, who wrote in the same dialect. Gower, though no genius, was a skilful versifier and the master of an extremely neat style. Fortunately, his influence on the language coincided with Chaucer's in almost every particular. Gower without Chaucer would not have sufficed. Chaucer without Gower would have been abundantly able to accomplish what was necessary. The coincidence of their efforts was fortunate for the English language. Chaucer died in 1400. His successors and feeble pupils, Hoccleve and Lydgate, though they contributed nothing of value to English poetry, did much to popularize the language of Chaucer, which they directly imitated in every possible way. There was no longer any doubt what was the English literary language: it was the East Midland dialect, and whoever wrote in any other dialect was not writing standard English, but a local or provincial *patois*. Since 1400 there has been a very slight shift, so that Modern English is a trifle more northerly than Chaucer's dialect, but this is of no importance in the present discussion.[1]

It is to be noticed that the dialect which finally became literary English, and which, therefore, all educated speakers of English use, however they may differ among themselves in details, is not the descendant of King Alfred's West Saxon, but of quite a different dialect, the Mercian. The West Saxon is now represented by the rustic dialects of Wilts and Dorset in the South of England.

The triumph of the Midland Dialect was complete by 1450, and soon caused most of the other dialects to fall into disuse as literary media. In the north, however, a variety of the Northumbrian was developed into the Scottish language, which was subjected to many special influences, and received much literary cultivation. The Scottish language could not maintain itself, however. It has been constrained to consort with the dialects once more, though it still maintains an exceptionally dignified position among them.

Thus every one of the three dialects of the Anglo-Saxons has had its chance. The Northumbrian became the first literary English. The West Saxon succeeded to that position, and held it until the Norman Conquest. In the fourteenth and fifteenth centuries the Mercian made good its claims and won a recognition which was final.

[1] The most striking evidence of this shift is seen in the use of *s* instead of *th* in the third person singular of verbs. Chaucer said *hath, doth, waileth*, for example, but we say *has, does, wails*.

CHAPTER VIII

THE LATIN IN ENGLISH

In sketching the development of the English language we have confined our attention to the native (Anglo-Saxon) element and to the influence exerted by Norman and Parisian French. We have yet to consider the indebtedness of our language to the Latin.

English began to borrow words from the Latin before there was any English. *Street* (L. *strata* [*via*], 'a paved road'), *wall* (L. *vallum*), *chalk* (L. *calx, calcis*, 'lime'), and a few other terms entered the West Germanic dialects before the Anglo-Saxon Conquest of Britain. A few others were learned by the invaders from the Britons, who had been Roman colonists for three or four hundred years. Among these were *port* (L. *portus*) and *-chester*, *-caster* (L. *castra*, 'camp'), as seen in the name of the County of *Chester*, and in *Silchester*, *Lancaster*, etc. The conversion of the invaders to Christianity immediately brought in a number of religious and ecclesiastical words, like *pope*, *bishop*, *monk*, *nun*, which we have already studied (p. 44). From this time to the present, the borrowing of Latin words has gone on incessantly. We have seen that this is true of the technical dialects of divinity, philosophy, law, and natural science. But the influence of Latin is not confined to the technical vocabulary. It is felt in almost every sentence that we utter. It pervades the whole system of English speech.

The relations between French and Latin on the one hand, and English and French on the other, make the influence of Latin on English extremely complex. In outline, however, the subject may be easily grasped.

One fact of cardinal importance should be kept constantly in mind. In the eighth century, when Anglo-Saxon was developing a written literature, every educated Englishman spoke and wrote Latin as easily as he spoke and wrote his mother tongue. Indeed, the ability to use Latin freely was, until a comparatively recent period, the chief distinguishing mark of an educated man. Hence in all the earlier periods of our language, anybody who was learned enough to borrow a Latin word at all, was sufficiently familiar with that language to borrow the word in conversation as well as from the written page. This significant fact is often lost sight of.

Before the Norman Conquest, then, a good many Latin words had been introduced into English, either orally or with the pen. Many of these disappeared when the literary West Saxon went to pieces, but a few have survived and are still in use.

After the Conquest, as we have seen, French words began to come into our language, — first from Norman French, and afterwards, in much larger numbers, from the Central dialect, the 'French of Paris' which Chaucer's Prioress had never learned. The Norman-French words which became English were mostly 'popular' from the outset. They include such simple terms as *peace*, *tower*, *castle*, *grief*, *prison*, *court*, *countess*, and the like, which are indistinguishable in the minds of all English-speaking persons from the commonest words of native origin. Later, from 1300 on, there took place a wholesale importation of words from Central French, and to this the large proportion of

French words in our language is chiefly due. This importation was made by Englishmen to whom French was almost a second mother tongue, and was therefore effected, to a considerable extent, through oral rather than written borrowing. Yet many French words came in through literary channels as well. Now, all literary Englishmen in the fourteenth and fifteenth centuries knew a good deal of Latin. Gower, for instance, wrote three long poems, — one in English, one in French, and one in Latin, — and handled the three languages with equal facility. Thus the same persons who were borrowing from French were at the same time borrowing from Latin, and, since French itself is only Latin in a corrupt form, it is often impossible to determine from which of the two languages a particular word was directly taken. The mere fact that the *form* of the English word is rather French than Latin does not settle the question. For the form which a Latin word assumed when it became English was frequently determined by the habits of the French language. Thus our word *figure* is ultimately derived from the Latin *figura*, of which the French *figure* is a clipped form. It is probable that we took the word directly from the French. Yet this is not certain. For any English writer who had wished to introduce the Latin *figura* into the vernacular would at once have modified the word after the French fashion. Thus, whether *figure* came from Latin directly or from French, it would inevitably have taken the same form in English : namely, *figure*. *Texture*, for example, is known to have come directly from the Latin *textura;* yet it has been remade, after the French model, as set by *figure* and other words already in the language, so that, so far as appears from its form, it might perfectly well have come from the French *texture*. So *flexure*, from the Latin *flexura*, has a similar form, as if it came from a French word *flexure*, though, in fact, no such word as *flexure* exists in the French language. How strong was this tendency to follow the French fashion in adapting words from the Latin may be seen in Chaucer's forms for proper names. The Old French form for *Cato* was *Catoun*, and this is regularly used by Chaucer and his contemporaries. So Chaucer writes *Achilles* and *Achille*, *Pandarus* and *Pandare*, indifferently. Indeed, when a word existed in both Latin and French, it must often have been impossible for the borrower himself to tell from which language he was taking it.

This state of things continued through the fourteenth and fifteenth centuries. A huge number of words came in from both Latin and French, and we are frequently at a loss to distinguish between them. In doubtful cases, however, the distinction is of almost no importance, since, even if the word passed through the French, it is none the less Latin, and was felt as quite as much Latin as French, whatever its immediate source may have been.

In many cases, however, it is easy to distinguish a word borrowed from the French. Thus we see at a glance that *deceive* does not come directly from the Latin *decipere*, but from its French form *décevoir*. So of *voyage* from Fr. *voyage* (L. *viaticum*), *poison* from Fr. *poison* (L. *potionem*), *venge* from Fr. *venger* (L. *vindicare*), *point* from Fr. *point* (L. *punctum*). In these examples, and many others, the French form has wandered so far from the Latin that doubt is impossible. This points to an important observation. French is, in the main, the vulgar Latin of the Gallic provincials in the shape in which centuries of decay have left it, just as Spanish is the Latin of the provincials of Spain, and Italian the remainder Latin of the Tuscans.

THE LATIN IN ENGLISH

By the ninth century this Gallic Latin had become so different from its prototype as to constitute a distinct language. There were, then, two kinds of Latin in Gaul at this time, the rustic and debased dialect, which we may, with a slight anticipation, call 'French,' and the educated Latin of the schools. Both had a continuous tradition from Roman times; but the former came from a vernacular and untutored tradition, the latter from the learned tradition of the church and the schools, identical with the scholar's dialect throughout the Western World. From the ninth to the twelfth century the vernacular changed rapidly. Recognized as a genuine language, not a mere *patois*, it received literary cultivation, which has ever since continued, until French has become the 'polite language' of Europe. With this cultivation, a multitude of words were borrowed from the classic Latin by educated men, exactly as was the case with English, and these 'learned' words are close to the Latin, whereas the 'popular' words that come from the rustic tradition usually bear a much less distinct resemblance to the Latin. Thus *sevrer* (our *sever*) and *séparer* both represent the Latin *separare*, but *sevrer* is the 'popular' or continuous vernacular form, and *séparer* a 'learned' or literary borrowing. Again, *sûreté* (older *seürté*) and *sécurité* both come from L. *securitatem*, but *sûreté* is 'popular' and *sécurité* is 'learned.' We could never hesitate to derive our *surety* from the French *sûreté*. *Security*, however, might come either from *sécurité*, or, as is more likely in this instance, directly from the Latin, the form which it takes being influenced by *surety* and other similar words which we have taken from the French.

These considerations not only serve to illustrate the difference between learned and popular words (to which we have already given some attention), but they suggest the complexity of the influences which Latin, both as a learned and as a popular tongue, has had upon the language which we speak, or, in other words, the continuity and complexity of the civilization which the English language expresses to the student of philology.[1]

If we pass on to the sixteenth century, we find the relation of French and Latin to our vocabulary quite different from that in the fourteenth and early fifteenth. The time of wholesale borrowing from the French has passed, but Latin borrowing is more active than ever. It is, however, distinctly *learned* borrowing. The Revival of Learning has sent men directly to the classics. Theological and philosophical studies are also pursued with vigor, and this means an immersal in Latin. Latin is still the scholar's language, but to speak French has become a mere accomplishment (as it is to-day) and the men who are adding words to our vocabulary no longer feel that French and Latin are equally near to them. These are 'learned times,' and a multitude of words are taken directly from the Latin, with no thought of their French relations. The fashion of reforming such words after the French model is still in force, for it has become a law of our speech, but we no longer hesitate to which language to refer an ambiguous form: we refer it to Latin without hesitation. In fact, the best test in all these doubtful cases is the age of the word in English. If it came in after 1500, the chances are overwhelmingly in favor of its having come directly from the Latin unless it bears an unmistakably French imprint. This learned

[1] We may remark, in passing, that nearly all the English words that are from Norman French are from popular forms, whereas the later borrowings include many learned terms.

borrowing from Latin went on vigorously till very recently, and is still common, as we have seen, in the technical vocabulary of the sciences. It brought in a multitude of useful words, and tended especially to enrich our language in its means of expressing shades of thought and securing variety of expression in general. But it was carried to pedantic lengths, and in the eighteenth and nineteenth centuries there was a revolt against it, which has restored the equilibrium between the several main components of the English language. The borrowings from French since 1500 have been scanty compared with those that preceded and with the borrowings from Latin. Yet a good many words have come in from that language, — especially military terms and society phrases. The latter have manifested themselves particularly in the times from the Restoration to the present day, during which French has been the language of diplomacy and polite society, as well as a general medium of communication for travellers of all nationalities.

In addition to the great stock of Latin words that have entered our language through the French, or under its influence, we have a huge mass of words and phrases taken directly from the Latin without change. Few persons realize the extent of this element in our vocabulary, and fewer still its significance.

A number of examples will bring out instantly some of the main points: *superior, minimum, vim, bonus, stimulus, animal, folio, item, nostrum, recipe, veto, vacuum, inertia, innuendo, dictum, alibi, errata, interim, memorandum, affidavit, via* (in 'via New York'). Here we have a score of words taken bodily from the Latin without change. Yet they are undoubtedly English and in common use. One of them (*vim*) is so very 'popular' as to be almost slangy.

Their diversity of form is also remarkable. They represent almost every turn and twist of Latin inflection. We find the first, second, and third declensions of nouns, all three genders, and both numbers. Three cases appear (nominative, accusative, and ablative), a verb, two perfect participles, a gerundive, a gerund in *o*. There are masculine and neuter adjectives, the comparative and superlative degrees, a possessive pronoun, three adverbs, the present and perfect indicative, and an imperative. In short, a boy who can explain all the Latin forms involved in this short list of thoroughly English words need fear no examination in Latin accidence.

This great diversity of form is highly significant. It suggests that we owe many words of this class, not to deliberate borrowing of a learned or literary character, but to the haphazard linguistic processes of conversation and daily life. Nor should we be surprised at this. Latin, as we have observed already, was a second vernacular to educated men for many centuries. Not only was it the language of the learned professions, but it long served as a means of communication among all but the positively illiterate. To learn to read was to learn to read Latin. Grammar was Latin grammar. Roger Ascham remarks in a matter-of-fact way that it would, of course, have been easier for him to write his Toxophilus in Latin than in English. Legal documents, even of the most ordinary kind, were indited in that language. So were records of every sort, not only those of the state, but the journals of guilds and trade-companies. All important accounts were also in Latin. Queen Elizabeth talked Latin with foreign ambassadors; Cromwell had Milton for his Latin secretary.

All this means that to a large fraction of the community Latin terms were, and always have been, actually the only familiar terms for certain ideas and certain things. This is still true in a measure, as with lawyers, for instance, and physicians; but it becomes more and more significant as we trace our history back to mediæval times. It was as natural for all persons who had occasion to mention such things, to use the Latin words for them when they were talking English as when they were talking Latin. Even to-day, when the doctors talk little Latin, and write it no more than they can help, it is far easier for them to speak of the *sequelae* of a disease than of its 'consequences,' and it would be mere affectation if they avoided such terms as *prophylaxis* and *diagnosis*, or tried to translate them into English. We have seen how easily learned words pass into the ordinary vocabulary and become popular. A man does not use vernacular words merely because they are vernacular, but because they are the words that he hears; and few Englishmen of any period have been so out of contact with the Church or the courts, with medicine or the arts, as not to be influenced by the language of those who are professionally identified with such pursuits. The habit, once established, propagated itself, as habits do, and became one of the regular tendencies of our language. The borrowings in question, then, are of all dates, remote and recent.

A moment's consideration of some of our examples will enforce what has just been said. *Recipe* is an imperative directing the apothecary to 'take' such and such drugs and compound them; it is the physician's formula in beginning a prescription, and has come to be the name of the document itself. *Nostrum* means 'our own' (or 'my own'), that is, 'a proprietary remedy,' unknown to the profession in general, — hence, a 'quack medicine.'

Innuendo is the gerund of *innuo*, 'to suggest,' used as a present participle to mean 'suggesting' or 'signifying.'; it has passed from the language of legal documents into its familiar use in ordinary speech. *Folio* is the ablative of *folium*, and means, literally, '*on* such and such a *leaf*' (in a written document); it is thus the common term in referring to a particular page, and, being constantly heard in the ablative, has become English in that case-form. *Memorandum* (often abbreviated to *mem.*) is the gerundive of *memoro*, 'remember,' and means '(that which) must be borne in mind.' *Item*, 'also,' is an old accountant's term. It was formerly prefixed to all the items in a bill or inventory except the first,[1] but gradually it lost its specific sense of 'also' and came to be used with them all; hence its meaning as an English word. *Bonus* is a recent addition to our vocabulary, and shows the persistence of the influences that we are studying. Perhaps it comes from the stock exchange. It means 'a good thing,' something 'to the good,' — and ought, strictly speaking, to be the neuter *bonum*. Its recent or jocose origin is indicated by this error in gender. Compare *premium*, which (being an older word in English) shows a correct form.

The genuinely vernacular nature of these words is emphasized when we pass to whole phrases, which have been taken into our language with the greatest freedom. No one when he says *ex parte*, or *post mortem*, or *bona fide*, is conscious of talking a foreign language; for these phrases and scores of others have become a part of the vernacular by inheritance and constant use, and although their home is Latin, they are as much English as if they had been translated, as they often are. No one can say that *dividers* is any more English than *divisor*.

---

[1] Which was *imprimis*, 'first.'

The only difference is that *divisor* is originally a technical term, Latin in form, which the progress of education has made known to every schoolboy, while *dividers* has been made over by means of an English termination and then specialized into a technicality. It is even doubtful which word is more vernacular to-day.

Subpoena has become an English noun and is used as a verb as well. It is merely the law term *sub poena*, 'under penalty.' Still more vernacular is the verb *to nonplus*. It is originally a term of scholastic disputation. A man was 'at a non plus' when he had 'no more' to say.

Sometimes such phrases are translated, but often the translation is more artificial — less English, indeed — than the Latin itself. An '*ex cathedra* opinion' is a perfectly natural phrase for one delivered authoritatively, but we should attach no such meaning to the English 'from the chair,' except by thinking of the Latin. 'In the article of death' is a mere slavish rendering of *in articulo mortis*. In itself, it means nothing, for *article* has no such sense in our language, but we understand the phrase by association with the Latin original. Similarly, *sine die* is occasionally made into pigeon-English as 'without day.' So with the French *mariage de convenance*, 'an arranged marriage.' We sometimes translate it by 'marriage of convenience,' which has no sense in English except as it has acquired one by virtue of the French. 'Cela va sans dire' has given us 'That goes without saying,' though '*goes*' does not mean 'is valid,' 'holds,' nor does *saying* mean 'statement.' The English phrase is not very well established, but it is always understood, for our language is so tolerant of foreign phrases that anything will pass muster that suggests one.

'Generally speaking' is an idiom that gives the strict

grammarian some trouble. For it is constantly used in apparent violation of the rule that the participle must have a noun to agree with: as, 'Generally speaking, bank notes are as good as gold.' But all difficulty vanishes when we observe that the phrase is merely the Late Latin *generaliter loquendo*, for nobody expects the gerund to agree with a noun.[1]

Inclusive, in such phrases as 'pages thirty to thirty-three *inclusive*,' is a curious instance of a Latin word made English. It is really the Latin adverb *inclusive*, 'inclusively,' and was felt as Latin in the sixteenth century (so also *exclusive*).[2] Probably it was first anglicized by a blunder, as we hear people pronounce *fide* as one syllable in *bona fide*. The possibility of the error, however, is strong evidence of the 'popularity' of such Latin phrases.

A remarkable bit of testimony consists in the habitual use of Latin abbreviations in English writing, and in the fact that these almost always suggest not the Latin words for which they stand, but the English equivalent. £, *s.*, *d.* mean to everybody 'pounds,' 'shillings,' and 'pence' — not *librae*, *solidi*, and *denarii*. Falstaff's tavern-bill showed *ob.* (*obolus*) among its entries, but Prince Hal read it 'half-penny.' *Pp.* (*paginae*) means 'pages,' and *LL. B.* (*Legum Baccalaureus*) 'bachelor of laws,' to most of us, though the doubling of the letter to indicate a plural is not an English, but a Latin habit, and though *laws* is not a legitimate translation of *leges* in the sense of 'two kinds

---

[1] *Considering*, *regarding*, and the like, are related to this use, but are commonly disposed of by calling them 'prepositions.' Similarly the 'preposition' *notwithstanding* is a mere translation of the Latin ablative absolute (*non obstante*). Cf. Bishop Andrewes (in 1620): "For either of these *non obstante*, nay notwithstanding both these, she had the happiness to see His Angels." Ninety-six Sermons, ed. 1841, III, 5.

[2] See Andrewes, Ninety-six Sermons, ed. 1841, I, 27.

of law'—civil and canon. So *i.e.* (*id est*) is read 'that is,' *e.g.* (*exempli gratia*), 'for example.' Now and then a foreigner in writing English uses *f.e.* or *f.i.*, but we find it hard to guess that he means 'for example' or 'for instance,' though the Latin *e.g.* occasions us no difficulty. *Viz.* is a curious example. It is *videlicet* ('you may know,' 'to wit'), the *z* being not a *z* at all, but an old sign of abbreviation resembling that letter in shape. We seldom say *videlicet* nowadays, preferring 'namely' or 'to wit' (a translation of *scilicet*, for *scire licet*), and even *viz* is sometimes heard.

Again we constantly use the Roman numerals without thinking of the Latin words for which they stand, or remembering that accounts were kept in Latin down to a pretty recent date. Most striking of all is the sign &, which, though merely a short way of writing *et*, is always called 'and,' and used to be annexed to the English alphabet under that designation. *Ampersand*, the name for the sign, is a corruption of '*and* per se *and*.' &c. and *etc.*, then, both stand for *et cetera*; yet we commonly read the former 'and so forth,' and reserve the Latin phrase for the latter.

It would require a special treatise to exhaust the subject of Latin words in English. Enough has been said to explain their presence and to indicate the main channels through which they entered the language. Few persons realize the extent of our indebtedness. Computations have often been made, but they have usually been based on the English vocabulary as a whole or on the vocabulary of a particular author. If the former course is adopted, the question rises 'What is the whole English vocabulary?' for every large dictionary contains a multitude of obsolete and technical terms that have no place in such a problem.

If the works of a single author are taken as a basis, there are equally great objections to the method, though of a different kind. A better method is to see what proportion of the Latin vocabulary has passed into English. With this in view, we have counted the words beginning with *A* in Harper's Latin Dictionary (Andrews-Freund, revised by Lewis), excluding proper names, doublets, parts of verbs, and adverbs in *-e* and *-ter*. Of the three thousand words there catalogued, one hundred and fifty-four (or about one in twenty) have been adopted bodily into our language in some Latin form, and a little over five hundred have some English representative taken, or supposed to be taken, through the French. Thus we have in the English vocabulary about one in four or five of all the words found in the Latin lexicon under *A*. There is no reason to suppose that this proportion would not hold good approximately for the whole alphabet. No doubt some words have been included in this computation that should have been omitted, but others have just as certainly been overlooked, and no account has been made of Low and Middle Latin. Roughly speaking, then, we are safe in asserting that our language has appropriated a full quarter of the Latin vocabulary, besides what it has gained by transferring Latin meanings to native words. Our indebtedness to Greek is chiefly in the way of learned or scientific terms which have been borrowed in very recent times.[1]

The extent of the French and Latin influence upon the English vocabulary makes our borrowings from other languages seem insignificant. The Celtic tongues have contributed very little, not because the Celts were exterminated, but partly because of the great dissimilarity

[1] See pp. 49–51.

between Celtic and Anglo-Saxon, partly because those Britons with whom the invaders had most intercourse had been Romanized to a considerable degree. *Bannock*, *bard*, *bog*, *brock* ('badger'), *brogue*, *down* ('hill'), *dun* ('dark-colored'), *glen*, *lad*, *loch*, *shamrock*, and *slogan* are specimens of the Celtic contingent in our language; but of these examples only *brock*, *dun*, and *down* go back to the Anglo-Saxon period.[1]

The Scandinavian influence is more important. It began as early as the ninth century, and was felt particularly in those northern and eastern districts in which there were Danish (or Norwegian) settlements. Many Scandinavian words did not survive the Middle English period, except dialectically. Most of our Old Norse contingent came into English in oral intercourse, but a few terms have been borrowed in recent times by literary men (as, *skald*, *edda*, *viking*, *valkyrie*, *Norn*). Among the old borrowings are *aloft* (O.N. *ā lopte*, 'up in the air,' from O.N. *loptr*, for *loftr*, cognate with A.S. *lyft*, Ger. *Luft*), *call*, *cast*, *sky*, *take*, *wrong*.

The influence of Italian and Spanish upon our literature has been very great, but upon our vocabulary these languages have had no appreciable effect. The reason is plain. Before the time when such an influence could have been exerted, our language was already fully formed, and had adopted from French or Latin nearly all those terms which it might conceivably have borrowed from related Romance languages. Art and music have brought in a number of Italian terms, however; and Spanish has contributed *flotilla*, *grandee*, *junta*, *pronunciamento*, *rene-*

---

[1] *Basket* and *cradle* are often cited as Celtic words, but there is no evidence for such a derivation. *Crock* is doubtful. *Mop* may be from the French. *Bodkin*, *mattock*, and *slough* are of uncertain origin.

gade, siesta, and a few others. A good many Spanish forms that were current in the sixteenth and seventeenth centuries have become obsolete.

Of the Semitic tongues, Hebrew and Arabic have made small contributions to our vocabulary. The Hebrew words are mostly biblical: as, — *cherub, seraph, shekel, hallelujah, mannah, Messiah.* Several of the Arabic words are connected with mathematics or chemistry, — sciences much cultivated by learned Arabs of the Middle Ages.[1] Thus we have *algebra* (from the Arabic article *al,* 'the,' and *jebr,* 'reduction' [by equations]); *alkali* (from *al* and *qalī,* 'ashes of the soda plant'); *alembic (anbīq,* from Gr. ἄμβιξ, *ámbix,* 'cup,' 'cap of a still'); *elixir* (from *al-iksīr,* 'the philosopher's stone,' from Greek ξηρός, *xērós,* 'dry,' since it was thought that this mysterious substance might be discovered in the form of a powder); *cipher* (from *çifr,* 'zero,' literally 'empty'). Other Arabic derivatives are *sofa, salaam* (literally 'peace'), *sherbet, admiral.* In *admiral* (formerly *amiral*), the final syllable is again the Arabic article, the word being a fragment of the phrase *amīr-al-bahr,* 'commander of the sea.'

The enterprising spirit of the English people and their fondness for travel and colonization, as well as the great development of their commerce, have brought in miscellaneous words from every quarter of the earth. No language is so hospitable as our own to these newcomers, perhaps because no other language already contains so many foreign elements. None of these borrowings, however, have affected the structure of our speech, since they have been for the most part simply the adoption of names for particular things. Thus we have *binnacle* and *dodo,* from Portuguese; *boor, brackish, hustle, isinglass, kink, knapsack,*

[1] See p. 45.

landscape, loiter, marline, slender, stove, yacht, from Dutch or Low German; *bazar* and *caravan,* from Persian; *polka,* from Polish; *hussar,* from Hungarian; *hominy, moccasin, tomahawk, squaw, wigwam,* from North American Indian; *tea, nankeen,* from Chinese; *taboo,* from Polynesian; *boomerang, kangaroo,* from native Australian, and so on. Such words enrich and diversify our vocabulary without essentially changing its character. We shall study many instances of this miscellaneous borrowing in subsequent chapters.

CHAPTER IX

FASHION IN LANGUAGE

A POWERFUL influence in bringing in new words or reviving old ones, as well as in changing the use and meaning of established expressions, is what may be called, in a broad way, 'fashion,'— a term under which we include not merely the fads and whimsicalities of the moment, but certain larger and more impressive movements and tendencies. The sway of fashion is easily detected both in literature and in our common talk. In the case of literature, we dignify such habits of expression by calling them stylistic tendencies. When they attract our attention in colloquial speech, we stigmatize them as slang or affectation. In the uncontrolled utterances of the street boy, these tendencies result in the rapid propagation of every new phrase that falls upon his ear, till there grows up a language so grotesquely vulgar as to acquire a kind of humorous right to existence. In the domain of letters, they result in those large differences of style which characterize particular schools of writing or even distinct 'epochs' or 'ages' in literary history. Yet the underlying principles are the same both in literature and in the individual, — fondness for novelty, the desire to be original, and finally, the wish of every man to be as wise as his neighbor, which results in a general imitation of whatever is striking or distinctive.

The effect of fashion in introducing new words into our vocabulary, in bringing certain words already existent into peculiar prominence for the time being, and in banishing some old words altogether, may be observed by contrasting the language of different individuals who, though frequenting much each other's society, are nevertheless brought under the control of different modes of expression. Thus, a law student, a medical student, and a young 'sport,' will be sure to have widely different vocabularies, even if they are personal friends. This is true not only when they are 'talking shop,' but when they are discussing subjects quite outside of their professional interests. The young lawyer will be sure to interlard his conversation with fragments of legal lore and with figures of speech derived from his text-books. The physician will find it difficult to avoid allusions to the clinic or the dissecting-room. The sporting man will speak a dialect compounded of the race-track, the prize-ring, and the foot-ball field. And all this may be quite without affectation. The words that we hear oftenest and that are associated with our dearest interests must come to our lips most readily. That a physician should speak of 'dissecting' a subject, a chemist of 'analyzing' it, a preacher of 'expounding' it, is as natural as that an ordinary man should speak of 'explaining' it or 'making it clear.' A calamity may be called 'a cropper' by the horsey man, 'a knock-out' by the amateur of pugilism, 'a lost case' by a lawyer. Such differences will be perceptible both in the colloquial dialect and in more dignified speech.

Another fashion is the knack of literary allusion. It is akin to the habit of quotation,— itself a fashion in language that comes and goes; but it shows itself in a less formal and tangible way. The use of scraps of French, much commoner fifty years ago than at present, and the trick of using big words on slight occasion, whether for humorous effect or for the sake of 'talking like a book,' are other examples of individual peculiarities which may at any moment become general.

But the sway of fashion may be observed not merely in the several vocabularies of speakers whose professions are different, but also in the changes that come over one's own vocabulary as it is subjected to successive influences in the course of a lifetime. School or the university produces a marked effect on the speech of a young man. Another immediate change comes about when he begins the study of his profession, or enters upon the business of his life. Even after one's vocabulary seems definitely established, current events of general interest will always modify it strongly for the time being. During the heat of a political campaign everybody talks political jargon, even when politics are not under discussion. The Spanish War filled American ears with hitherto unheard-of words of Spanish origin, and the war in South Africa has familiarized all of us with an odd corner of the Dutch vocabulary, hitherto known only to South African colonists. For a time it was easy to call any difficult barrier a *trocha*, and the policy of *reconcentration* often appeared in strange company. So every little hill was a *kopje*, a lodging-place of any kind was a *laager*, all sorts of things were *commandeered*, and the suggestion that this or that might 'stagger humanity' was on every lip. Similarly, intense religious excitement may charge the language of an individual or a community with biblical or theological terms or phrases. Within a century the progress of scientific discovery and invention, and the rise of the economic and social sciences, have profoundly affected our speech. 'Society' and 'social' have taken on new senses. The 'social problem' means much more than it ever did before. 'Unproductive consumer,' 'unearned increment,' 'the law of supply and demand,' 'medium of exchange,' 'standard of living,' 'wages fund,' 'pauper labor,' 'coöperative association,' are commonly heard, even from persons who have never read a chapter of political economy. 'Evolution,' 'the struggle for existence,' 'the survival of the fittest,' have become so vague in their common application that one hardly dares to employ them in serious discussion for fear of begging the question. *Force* is regularly used to explain everything, as if it were not in itself a word that assumes the very point which it attempts to prove. Indeed, it has become one of the vague terms which language requires to express indefinite and indefinable conceptions.

These are some of the fashions that every grown-up man can remember as having from time to time increased his vocabulary, and either enriched or impoverished his thought.

If we broaden our scope, we shall find that what happens to the individual in a single lifetime, applies also to a whole people in the lifetime of their language. New interests assert themselves from age to age, and induce new forms of expression. The fashion changes and language must 'follow the style.' Let us consider some of the movements that have affected the English language from time to time.

We may begin with a simple, but sufficiently curious, illustration. The style of the Anglo-Saxon translator of Bede's Ecclesiastical History is marked by a peculiar trick of repetition. Again and again he uses two synonymous nouns or verbs or adjectives, where one would suffice to convey his whole meaning. This may be called, then, an English literary habit of the ninth century. It came, perhaps, from an unskilful imitation of the Latin, or it may be due to some uncertainty as to the exact scope of the English words, then first applied to the finer shades of thought. At all events, the habit survived in English prose until the end of the eighteenth century. And, though out of favor at the moment, it has left a number of idiomatic or colloquial phrases in the language: as, 'end and aim,' 'lord and master,' 'without let or hindrance,' 'act and deed,' 'pure and simple,' 'in deed and truth,' 'really and truly,' 'bright and shining,' 'honest and true,' 'proud and haughty,' 'weak and feeble,' 'race and run,' 'grunt and groan,' 'pull and tug,' 'holla and bawl,' 'cry and scream,' 'clean and neat,' 'toil and delve.'[1]

Such double phrases occur very frequently in the Book of Common Prayer, where we find, for instance, 'sins and wickedness,' 'dissemble nor cloak,' 'assemble and meet together,' 'requisite and necessary,' 'erred and strayed,' 'declare and pronounce,' 'pardoneth and absolveth,' 'bless and sanctify,' 'offer and present,' 'rule and govern,' 'knowledge and understanding,' 'religiously and devoutly,' 'food and sustenance,' 'search and examine your consciences,' 'prayers and supplications,' 'to try and examine themselves,' 'confirm and strengthen.'

In several of these instances, one word is native and the other foreign. Hence many have supposed that the repe-

[1] It is not meant that these particular phrases came down from King Alfred's time, nor that they originated in tautology pure and simple, but merely that they owe their currency to a habit of the language which we may observe in full swing in the formal prose of the ninth century. On the whole matter see Emerson, Modern Language Notes, 1893, pp. 202 ff.; J. M. Hart, in An English Miscellany presented to Dr. Furnivall, pp. 150 ff.

tition came from a wish to be intelligible both to the Saxon and the Norman element in the population, or, at all events, both to the uneducated and to the educated classes. But this is pure assumption, and it is contradicted by the habits of English speech. Remembering the composite character of our vocabulary, we are not surprised that in a pair of synonyms one should be of native stock and the other borrowed. Besides, the examples from the prayer-book show every kind of combination: sometimes both words are native (as was of course always the case in Anglo-Saxon), sometimes both are foreign, and sometimes the pair includes one word of each kind. Most of our older writers illustrate the same stylistic habit. Lord Bacon, for instance, writes 'donatives and largesses,' 'pageants or gaudery,' 'amplitude and greatness,' 'to forsake or destitute a plantation,' 'he runs and is swift of foot,' 'good and fair dealing,' 'putrefy and corrupt,' 'the spreading or publishing of them,' 'to stay and arrest nature,' 'look sharply and attentively,' 'honored and respected.' The *rationale* of such phrases is evident enough. A single noun or verb seldom expresses the full scope of an idea. The pair of words covers the whole meaning intended by the writer, since the synonyms that he chooses have somewhat different senses. To be sure, some repetition is involved, since the second word repeats a large part of the meaning of the first, though adding some meaning of its own. Yet the author prefers to express his thought say one-and-a-quarter times to the opposite method of expressing three-quarters of it and leaving the rest to be inferred. In Modern English we take the latter course, though not uniformly. The older fashion conduces to dignity and copiousness of style, but easily betrays one into tiresome verbiage.

In the Middle Ages, the English language was a good deal affected by the allegorical treatment of love. This followed various conventions, drawing its figures especially from warfare, chivalry, the law, and religion. Thus the lady's heart was a castle to which the knight laid siege. The metaphor was elaborately developed and even acted, as a kind of pantomimic tableau. Hence our phrases, 'to take one's heart by storm,' 'to surrender at discretion.' Or the lover was the lady's vassal, her 'man,' bound to unquestioning obedience, her 'servant,' her 'thrall' or slave. Love was a monarch whose courtiers were Pity, Disdain, Fair Welcoming, False Semblant, and the like; he sat in judgment and heard the complaints of suitors against their hard-hearted mistresses. Strangest of all, to our thinking, is the religious convention. The lady was the 'saint' to whom one prayed. The God or Goddess of Love was addressed in terms appropriate to the Deity. Faithful lovers were Cupid's 'saints.' Dido and Phyllis, who died for Love, were Love's 'martyrs.' As the Church recognized seven deadly sins and seven principal virtues, so there were sins and virtues in the worship of Love. Hence came many figurative expressions which to us sound blasphemous or, at least, in very bad taste. But the religion of the Middle Ages was not remote from life. It was a matter of course, which nobody hesitated to talk about, and consequently such figures conveyed no hint of irreverence. One of the first and best effects of intelligent linguistic study is to emancipate us from that form of provincialism which erects the present fashions in language into eternal canons of criticism.

The Elizabethan age was marked rather by the prevalence of every possible kind of literary mannerism than by the predominance of any. Euphuism was only one of several fashions in speech and writing. The language of the Euphuist was not, as has often been thought, full of strange and affected words. So far as mere vocabulary is concerned, it was usually pure and dignified. But it resorted to excessive antithesis; it balanced itself so nicely from clause to clause as to make monotony into a fine art; and it heightened false point by puerile tricks of alliteration and jingle. Besides all this, it was overloaded with far-fetched similes from what passed for natural history. These peculiarities are all illustrated in the following passage from Lyly's Euphues, a kind of moral romance, from which the style in question takes its name:[1] —

It fareth with me, Psellus, as with the ostrich, who pricketh none but herself, which causeth her to run when she would rest; or as with the pelican, who striketh blood out of her own body to do others good; or with the wood-culver, who plucketh off her feathers in winter to keep others from the cold; or as with the stork, who, when she is least able, carrieth the greatest burthen. So I practise all things that may hurt me, to do her good that never regardeth my pains, so far is she from rewarding them.

The coinage of strange words, the borrowing of new terms from the classic languages, and excessive Latinization, were also characteristics of the Elizabethans. Hence the contemporary satire on 'ink-horn terms.' A rough-and-ready caricature is Rowlands' 'Signieur Word-Monger, the Ape of Eloquence' (1600): —

> As on the way I itinerated,
> A rural person I obviated,
> Interrogating time's transitation

[1] *Euphues* is the hero's name. It is Gr. εὐφυής, 'of an excellent nature,' from εὖ, 'well,' and φύω, 'to be born.' Εὖ is familiar to us in *eu-phony* (φωνή, 'sound'), and *euphemism* (φημί, 'to say'); φύω we have in *physics, physician, physiology,* and so on.

And of the passage demonstration.
My apprehension did ingenious scan
That he was merely a simplician;
So when I saw he was extravagant,
Unto the obscure vulgar consonant,
I bade him vanish most promiscuously,
And not contaminate my company.

Translated into plain English, this farrago means merely: 'As I was walking in the road, I met a countryman, who asked me the time and the way. When I saw he was a vagabond, and belonged to the common people, I told him to begone and not disgrace me by his company.'

Another trick of Elizabethan writers was to archaize. Chaucer was much read and 'Chaucerisms' were abundant. The most eminent of all archaizers is Spenser, only a small part of whose poetry is written in the language of his time. The influence of France, in which a remarkable literary movement was then in progress, has been traced in some of the Elizabethan whimsicalities.[1] Spain and Italy were also potent forces. Euphuism itself is commonly referred to Spanish influence, and certainly shows much likeness to the celebrated Guevara.

Sometimes sham antiques have slipped in. Spenser, the most distinguished of all our archaizers, made many mistakes, and his imitators in the eighteenth and nineteenth centuries were not better instructed. Thus the strange compound noun *derring-do*, which he introduced, and which has had some currency in the sense of 'courage,' 'valorous achievement,' is due to a headlong misunderstanding of a passage in Chaucer, 'in derring do that longeth to a knight,' *i.e.* 'in daring to do what belongs to a knight.'

[1] See J. B. Fletcher, Areopagus and Pleiade, in Journal of Germanic Philology, II, 429–53.

So *iwis*, an adverb meaning 'certainly' (cognate with Ger. *gewiss*), has usually been treated by archaizing writers as if it were a pronoun and a verb, — *I wis*, 'I know,' — though this is an impossible form, — the present tense being really *I wot*, and the preterite *I wistë* (cf. the biblical, 'he wist not what he said'). *Trow* really means 'to think,' but it has often been used as a synonym for 'I know.' *Gramarye* is set down in all the dictionaries as meaning 'magic' (like Fr. *grimoire*, which has the same origin), but the only old sense of this word that can be discovered in English is 'grammar,' — its original and proper meaning. It looks as if the sense of 'magic' were a coinage of Bishop Percy's, — a clever coinage, it must be admitted, or a happy blunder, for nothing ever had more the air of a fine old word.[1] The connection between the idea of 'grammar' (*i.e.* 'learning') and 'magic' is also close, and the Fr. *grimoire*, 'a conjuring book,' shows how natural the development is.

Finally, we may mention the universal Elizabethan habit of punning, which pervaded conversation and literature alike. Every kind of play on words was common, from the merest jingle in sound to the most elaborate calembour. Puns are now out of favor, probably because we think that the punster wishes us to laugh at them.[2] We should be careful, however, not to take the punning habit of the Elizabethans so seriously. Clearly the Elizabethans did not laugh at puns, unless they were peculiarly amusing.

---

[1] See Child, English and Scottish Popular Ballads, V, 340.

[2] *Pun* is of uncertain etymology, and was doubtless a slang word at the outset. It is commonly referred to *pound* (of which there is a clipped form *pun*, 'to beat,' occurring in Shakspere). An older word is *clench* or *clinch*, either from the twist in the meaning of the words punned on or from the sense of 'repartee,' — something that clinches the argument. *Quirk* (a 'turn' or 'flourish') and *quip* (from *quid pro quo*) are synonyms.

They got merely a certain intellectual titillation out of the grotesque association of ideas which punning induced. The pun became for the first and last time in our literary history a definite feature of the language. Some of the commonest puns became idiomatic, and attracted no attention whatever. Our own speech always seems familiar to us, however odd it may sound to our neighbors over the border, in space or in time.

In general, the Elizabethans handled the language with the greatest freedom. It was an age of novelty. The English people was at last awake to its importance as a power in the world at large. It was ceasing to be isolated, and was becoming conscious of a great political destiny. Discoveries, as of the New World, Utopian schemes, and phantom commonwealths were in the air. Men's minds were stimulated in the highest degree, and the mental temper was alert and ready. Fantastic imitation of foreign ways was inevitable. Each Elizabethan felt that he was an individual, and burned to distinguish himself, if only by the cut of his coat. It was the age of Pericles, without the restraints of Greek taste, — which, however, were not so binding on the actual Athenians as they have become in the tradition of retrospective critics. The stage reproduces for us almost every trick of Elizabethan speech and manners. The mere vocabulary of a single dramatist would wreck his reputation with the purists if he were a modern.

In the next age, thought, literature, and language were influenced by those complex causes which we sum up rather vaguely as 'Puritanism.' The most obvious effect on our language was to bring theology and biblical turns of phrase into the common speech to a degree unknown before. Yet it would be a serious mistake to suppose that any great number of the religious words that are now a part of our ordinary vocabulary are derived from this movement. Most of them had been in the language for a long time, and many had gone through a development which had obscured their origin, so that they were no longer felt as religious allusions. The religious vocabulary was not the invention of the Puritans, nor was its common use in everyday dialogue a specifically Puritan fashion. What the Puritans did was to carry the habit out to its ultimate limits in use. They also made constant appeal to the legislation of the Old Testament, and thus filled the language, for a time, with allusions to Hebrew law and ritual, as well as to the poets and prophets of the Old Dispensation. In short, they focussed their minds on biblical phraseology, with results that permanently affected our stock of words and idioms. In New England these forces worked with peculiar power. Congregationalism was long established by law, and all who refused to conform to that system were 'dissenters.'[1] The intellectual history of Massachusetts, for example, was practically unaffected by the Restoration.

The reaction from Puritanism in the life of the nation is mirrored in the language of the eighteenth century. Writers were in constant dread of 'enthusiasm' (which was a synonym for 'fanaticism') and 'the romantic' (by which was meant anything fanciful or imaginative or emotional that was not instantly reducible to common sense). Their ideal was the easy elegance of language which befits a cultivated man of fashion. Polish, wit, and epigram were the mode. Imagination was repressed. Warmth of feeling was not to be uttered without sus-

[1] See A. C. Goodell, in the Publications of the Colonial Society of Massachusetts, I, 140 ff.

picion of vulgarity. The good writer, it was held, should steer his course between exaltation, on the one hand, and dulness on the other. Above all, he should be clear and logical, or at all events, should have the semblance of being so. To preserve one's self-control under all circumstances, without appearing to be self-conscious, was to reach the acme of the kind of excellence then most admired. The model was France, the polite nation.

There can be no doubt that the eighteenth century had a beneficial effect on our language. In particular, it made for what we now call 'grammatical correctness.' The regularity of English syntax is mainly due to the tendencies which we have been describing. Many constructions, freely used in the Elizabethan age, were gradually discarded in the eighteenth century because they seemed to be irregular, or because they tended to ambiguity. Similarly, the meanings of words became more limited, with a manifest gain in exactness. And finally, our literary vocabulary was subjected to a purifying process. The Elizabethans, as we have seen, were very free in coining new words or in reviving old ones, and the learned times had brought in many sesquipedalian terms from the Latin. This gave a peculiar richness to Elizabethan phraseology, and a fine dignity to that of the seventeenth century; but such processes cannot go on indefinitely without removing the language of literature too far from that of common life. A period of rest has to intervene, that the language may, so to speak, take account of stock, or, to change the figure, may digest what it has somewhat indiscriminately devoured. The eighteenth century was such a period. No better standard can be found than the easy language of cultivated men who are neither specialists nor pedants, and this was the standard which the eighteenth century used in codifying 'good English.' Many blunders were made in matters of detail, but the general movement was sound, and its results were good. Of course, this schoolmastering tendency could not last forever. Long before the end of the century there were revolts against the repressive canons of what was called good taste, and the language began once more to go on in its free course of development. There is such a thing as pedantic dread of pedantry, and as soon as the eighteenth century reached that stage, its work had been done, and another readjustment began.

What is called the 'Romantic Revival,' toward the end of the eighteenth century, is the next great influence which our language felt. This is a vague term for a very complicated group of causes, and the literary historians find some trouble in defining it. The effect upon our language, however, is a much simpler matter to study. There was a revolt against French neatness and 'correctness' of style, a return to the older models of English, — to Spenser, and Shakspere, and Milton. Obsolete and half-obsolete words were revived, not always with an accurate knowledge of their sense. Variety and striking effects were sought after. Metaphor became bolder, and versification was freed from some of its more recent shackles. Poetry showed this first; and in the nineteenth century the reaction extended itself to prose. The easiest catchword for the revolt is 'individualism,' as opposed to the view that a man must conform his language to that of everybody else, or that all must follow some definite model or models, ancient or modern. We have a feeling that 'the style is the man,' and that every author is therefore entitled to use that form of language which best expresses his individuality. Thus it is impossible to say that there is any prevailing style that marks the nineteenth century. A hundred years hence, when the small men have sunk out of sight, and only a few great authors emerge from the level of forgotten medocrity, the future historian may be able to characterize nineteenth-century English, but it cannot be done by a contemporary. In one and the same author, we often find marked preciosity of phrase cheek by jowl with the baldest colloquialism. Affected brutality of diction associates itself on the same page with equally affected sentimental refinement. In some particulars, however, we can hardly go wrong. It is certain, as we have already remarked, that the progress of science and mechanics, and the widespread popular interest in discovery and invention, have profoundly modified our vocabulary. Another influence, of a widely different kind, has come from the almost passionate study of literature as a fine art, and from the consequent development of literary criticism. And, finally, there has never been a time in the history of our language when 'syntactical correctness' has ruled with so capricious and tyrannical a sway. The proof-reader has become a court of last resort for many of us.

We have now considered not only the great movements which brought the English language to pass, but some of the modifying influences or 'fashions' to which it has been subjected from age to age. Among the fashions, we have counted mere tricks of style, like the Anglo-Saxon tautology, and such far-reaching social and religious forces as Puritanism. Despite all these modifying influences, we observe that the English tongue is still the English tongue. It has changed much since the East Midland became the literary language five hundred years ago, yet all the changes have not essentially modified its character. The 'genius of the language' is still the same.

Such persistence of uniformity in the face of chance and change challenges our attention. Words, as we know, are but the signs of thought. They do nothing of themselves, and have only such senses as the mind of the speaker and the hearer gives them. Yet, when we observe their conduct in the presence of various forces that act upon them, they almost seem to have an independent life, apart from the mind of the man who uses them.

And, indeed, this is in a manner true. For no sooner has an idea been expressed in words than the form of expression reacts on the speaker and influences his subsequent thought. If this happens in the case of a casual utterance, phrased in a conventional way, how much more powerful must have been the reaction in the minds of those whose first acquaintance with that idea was associated with the particular form of language in which it was couched! Every one knows how a peculiar or striking phrase, embodying a certain thought, may recur to the memory whenever the thought comes back to us, and thus, by a kind of haunting persistence, make it difficult to phrase the thought otherwise. We all have our favorite catchwords, which, originating in this way, have become as much a part of our individuality as our tricks of gait or gesture or facial expression.

Now, in long lapses of time the continuance of similar impressions produces in one speaker a mode or habit of thought consonant with that of others. The several impressions in the mind as a particular word is constantly used act somewhat like objects in a composite photograph: all that is alike is constantly accumulating, while that which is individual or peculiar is as rapidly dissipated. Thus there arises a regular and persistent mode of thought, and consequently of expression, which more or less dominates the form of the language in the mouths of all its speakers, whether they mean to be guided by it or not. To this tendency the Germans have given the expressive name *Sprachgefühl*, or 'speech-feeling.' We have no settled term for it in English, — that is, no name which our *Sprachgefühl* has accepted, — so that we are more or less in the habit of employing the German word.

It is of course absurd to ascribe feeling to language, except in a metaphorical way. Fortunately, however, the vague syntax of composition (see p. 177) allows the German word to mean a 'feeling *for* speech' as well as 'feeling *of* speech,' and by-and-by we shall either adopt the term as an English word, or the *feeling* itself will accept some other suitable phrase to express the idea. For the *Sprachgefühl* is a very real thing in a long-cultivated language like our own. It affects every word that we utter, though we may think that we are speaking as the whim of the moment dictates; and thus it is the strongest and most pervasive of all conservative forces, and has kept our language true to itself through all the vicissitudes which we have been describing.

The writer has a thousand times had occasion to notice the difference in this *Sprachgefühl* in the use of Latin, French, and English, and has constantly been surprised at the way in which the language insisted upon writing itself almost in spite of him. Thus a monumental simplicity of style and a single point of view are almost inseparable from a Latin essay; French must make itself scintillating and epigrammatic; and it is almost impossible not to be copious and diffuse in writing English.

No author, however eminent, can disregard this subtle and pervasive law. Men of genius may take great liberties with their mother tongue without offence; but let them once run counter to its characteristic tendencies, let them violate the English *Sprachgefühl*, and their mannerism becomes, as it were, a foreign language. They are writing not English, but — say Carlylese.

CHAPTER X

COMPLEXITY OF THE ENGLISH VOCABULARY

No language has so complex and varied a vocabulary as English. Our everyday speech includes a multitude of words from all periods of history, and every quarter of the globe. All the great civilizations have contributed to our vocabulary. Indeed, the history of English words is the history of our civilization in all its aspects. A few examples will illustrate these truths in a striking way. Only familiar words have been chosen, but these have been made as miscellaneous as possible in order to bring out the complexity of the subject.

Candy comes from the Arabic *qand*, 'sugar'; the Arabs got their word from the Persian, and its ultimate source seems to be Indian, for it is connected in some manner with a Sanskrit verb which means 'break' ('fragments of crystallized sugar'). *Sugar* has a similar history, being derived from Arabic, and by Arabic from Sanskrit. *Molasses*, on the contrary, is from L. *mellaceus*, 'honeylike' (from *mel* 'honey,' whence *melli-fluous*, 'honey-flowing,' which we use of a sweet sound). *Rum*, the name of a third product of sugar-cane, seems to be of English origin; an older form is *rumbullion*, apparently a dialectic English word for 'disturbance,' or 'racket'; thus in its original application to a kind of liquor it was a mere bit of humorous slang. *Treacle* for 'sugar-syrup' (also for 'molasses') is ultimately derived from a Greek word signifying 'an an-

COMPLEXITY OF THE ENGLISH VOCABULARY 129

tidote for the bite of a wild beast.'[1] All of these words, except *rum*, reached our language through the French; *rum*, however, has been borrowed by French from English.

A scolding woman is a *scold*, *shrew*, *vixen*, *termagant*, or *virago*. The first three words are of native origin. *Scold* goes back to a root which means 'to shove or push'; *shrew* means 'cursed' (cf. *curst*, an old word for 'ill-tempered'), and it is connected with *shrewd*; *vixen* is the feminine form of *fox* (cf. Ger. *Fuchs*, *Füchsin*); *termagant* is a by-form of *Tervagant* (of unknown etymology), supposed in former times to be a savage god of the Saracens; *virago* is a Latin word, borrowed without change of form; its original sense is 'a manly woman' (*vir*, 'man'), 'a heroine,' 'an amazon.' The adjective *cross* is ultimately from L. *crux* ('a cross'),[2] and means first 'lying crosswise or athwart,' then 'contrary or perverse,' and finally 'ill-tempered.' *Ill-tempered* means literally 'ill-mixed,' and refers to the mixture of the humors in a person's system; a disturbance of the balance of this mixture puts one 'out of sorts.' *Ill* comes from the Scandinavian, *temper* from the Latin; so that the adjective last mentioned is a hybrid compound representing two widely separated civilizations which came into contact with each other in the British Islands. *Ill-humored* has the same source; it refers literally to one whose *humors* (see p. 30) are in bad order.

Pheasant comes through French and Latin from *Phasis*, the Greek name of a river in Asia. *Turkeys* were thought to have come from Turkey; hence the name; the word *Turk* itself is from the Persian, but is probably of Tartar origin. *Parrot* is 'little Peter,' from Fr. *Pierrot*, though no one knows why the bird was so called; *paroquet* has

[1] See p. 266 for details.
[2] For the history of the word see p. 349.

the same meaning, and so has *petrel* (Fr. *pétrel*). In the last instance there is perhaps an allusion to St. Peter's walking on the sea. *Robin* is of course a diminutive of *Robert*, which is an Old High German proper name (meaning 'bright in fame') that has reached us through the French to remind us that French civilization is partly of Teutonic origin. *Thrush*, *wren*, and *throstle* are native English words, and so is *dove;* but *pigeon* is French, from L. *pipio*, 'a peeper,' 'a chirper.' *Eagle* is French, from L. *aquila* (perhaps from *aquilus*, 'dark brown').

Car came to us from the Norman *carre*, used for almost any vehicle. *Carre* was from the late Latin *carra*, L. *carrus*. The Romans took the word from the Celts. In England *car* has become, in the main, a poetical word for 'chariot,' or the like, as in Milton's 'car of night.' In America, however, it is still in popular use in a special sense in connection with 'rapid transit' (see p. 271). We speak of 'steam cars,' 'railway cars,' 'passenger cars,' 'freight cars,' 'horse cars,' 'electric cars,' etc., and use the simple *car* as a generic term for them all. For Americans, then, its associations are distinctly prosaic. *Carriage* (also from Norman French) is properly an abstract or noun of action from the verb derived from *carre*. It is used both abstractly and concretely (for a single vehicle). *Vehicle* (still a rather literary or learned word) is borrowed directly from L. *vehiculum* (from *vehere*, to 'convey,' cognate with Eng. *way*). *Cart* is of uncertain etymology, but must be connected with A.S. *cræt*, 'cart.' It is perhaps akin to O. H. Ger. *cratto*, 'basket or hamper.' (*Crate*, from L. *crātis*, 'hurdle,' is a different word.) *Wagon*, or *waggon*, comes from Dutch or Low German. The native English term is *wain* (A.S. *wægn*, akin to *way*), a related word, which has become poetical. *Coach* is a much later word; it was introduced from the French *coche* in the sixteenth century (when coaches came into use). It was originally a Hungarian adjective, from the name of the town *Kocs* (pronounced *kotch*), so that *coach* is like *berlin, landau, hansom* (cf. *Concord wagon, Bath* or *Sedan chair*, etc.), and arises from the omission of the generic noun which the adjective limits.[1] *Dray* is the A.S. *drage*, 'dragnet,' from *dragan*, 'to draw.' It is connected with *dredge*, but *dredge* (though originally Teutonic) comes directly from Fr. *drège*. *Locomotive* is a learned formation (like Fr. *locomotif*), made as if from a Latin *locomotivus* (*loco-*, stem of *locus*, 'place,' + *motivus*, from *movere* 'move'). In the case of such learned words it is sometimes impossible to tell whether they were made up directly from the Latin or borrowed from the French, since the first user of them often had both languages in mind, and, even if he were imitating a French word, did so on the basis of Latin forms that were familiar to him. As we have already remarked, the Latin words that our language borrowed directly have usually been treated after the analogy of French formations, themselves taken from Latin.[2] The full form is *locomotive engine*. *Locomotive* has never become truly popular,— the commonest term being simply *engine*, an interesting case of successive specialization (see p. 248).

Cab was originally slang. It is shorthand for *cabriolet*, —a French diminutive of *cabriole*. The latter comes from the Italian *cabriola*, itself a diminutive of L. *capra*, 'she-goat.' The application of the name to a light vehicle is a manifest joke. *Calash* is merely an English pronunciation of Fr. *calèche*, which is of Slavonic origin. The original

---

[1] See pp. 253 ff. [2] See p. 95.

calashes had a removable top,— hence the word was also applied to a kind of hood. *Barouche* is the German *Barutsche*, respelled in the French fashion under the impression that it was a French word. The Germans took *Barutsche* from the Italian, its final source being the Latin *birōtus*, 'two-wheeled' (from *rota*, 'wheel'). *Chaise* is a much-worn form of the Greek καθέδρα (*kathédra*), 'a chair.' It has passed through L. *cathedra* (whence *cathedral*, from the bishop's throne), and Fr. *chaire*, 'pulpit,' the form *chaise* being an old Parisian dialectic pronunciation of *chaire*. The word *chaise* is older than the vehicle. When first borrowed in English it was applied to a litter (like a 'Sedan *chair*'). *Shay* (*chay*) is a seventeenth-century form (always regarded as vulgar), due to the idea that *chaise* was a plural (cf. *pea* from *pease;* vulgar *corp* from *corpse*).

Bicycle is an artificial modern formation from the Latin prefix *bi-*, which has long been freely used in English (especially in scientific terms), and *cycle*, itself a derivative (through the Latin and perhaps the French) from Gr. κύκλος (*kúklos*), 'wheel.' The English word is well formed,[1] and conveys an appropriate sense. The mere fact that it is a hybrid compound does not make it any the less acceptable English. Observe the rapid shortening of the word to plain *cycle*. A curious twist, *cicycle*, sometimes heard from the ignorant in England, illustrates both the tendency to assimilation of sounds and that to reduplication. In less educated times this form would have a good chance to prevail, since, like all such

[1] Unlike its predecessor *velocipede* (from L. *velox, velocis*, 'swift,' and *pes, pedis*, 'foot'), which was apparently intended to signify 'something rapidly propelled by the rider's feet.' If, however, *velocipede* meant simply 'swift-footed,' the word was legitimately made.

COMPLEXITY OF THE ENGLISH VOCABULARY 133

vulgar distortions, it obeys the dominating tendencies of linguistic change.

Spice is the same word as *species* and *specie*. It comes from the Latin *species* 'kind,' through O. Fr. *espice*, and in Middle English meant both 'kind' and 'spice.' The latter sense is a queer specialization and must have come through trade, — there were different *kinds* of these aromatic substances, and so *spices* came to be used for the substances themselves. *Species* was later borrowed directly from Latin without alteration. *Specie* is the ablative of *species*, and comes from the Latin phrase *in specie*, — used for payment in gold or silver (from the sense of 'treasure,' 'coin,' which *species* took in late Latin). Notice that from the noun *species*, a vulgar singular *specie* for 'kind' has been formed, *species* looking like a plural.[1]

Pepper is the Anglo-Saxon *pipor*, borrowed from L. *piper*, which came from the Greek; but the Greeks themselves took the word from the Orient. *Cinnamon* is the Hebrew *qinnāmōn*, which is borrowed from some other Eastern tongue. The older English form is *cinnamom*, from L. *cinnamomum*, itself from the Hebrew. But this English form was made over by scholars who were familiar with Hebrew and thought *cinnamom* erroneous. *Ginger* is also an Eastern word. Its earliest English form was *gingiver*, from O. Fr. *gengibre*, from L. *zingiber*, from Gr. ζιγγίβερις (*zingiberis*), from some Oriental language. The literal meaning is 'horn-shaped,' from the shape of the root. *Allspice* is so called from its supposed composite flavor of cloves, nutmegs, and cinnamon. *Nutmeg* (M.E. *notemuge*) is a hybrid compound of English *nut* (older *note*) and O. Fr. *muge*, 'musk.'

Grocer is literally one who sells at wholesale (*en gros*);

---

[1] See p. 139.

it is a comparatively modern word in its present application. *Doctor* (literally 'teacher,' as in 'Doctor of Divinity') is a title used as an appellative; its common application to physicians is due to the fact that 'doctors of medicine' outnumber all other kinds of doctors. *Carpenter* is from L.L. *carpentarius* (through the French), which meant formerly 'wagon-maker,' from L. *carpentum*, 'wagon,' related to *car* and, like *car*, of Celtic origin. *Cordwainer*, 'shoemaker,' has nothing to do with *cord;* it is the Old French *cordoanier*, a worker in *cordouan* or *Cordovan* leather (whence Eng. *cordwain*).

Shop is the Anglo-Saxon *sceoppa*, 'storehouse,' 'booth.' *Store*, from O. Fr. *estor*, 'provisions' (which is from L. *(in)staurare*, 'to restore'), meant in older English 'a collection' or 'accumulation,' especially of goods; hence it came to mean 'a storehouse' or 'depot.' In the United States and the British Colonies any shop where goods are sold, large or small, is often called a *store*. This is not mere provincial grandiloquence, as is often supposed, but results from the fact that, when the use grew up, the places in question were really storehouses, — as every 'shop' in a new country must necessarily be. *Emporium*, as often used, is deliberate and half-humorous magniloquence. The word means properly a market-town or centre of trade, and is a mere Latinization of the Greek ἐμπόριον (*empórion*), 'trading post' or 'factory.' *Factory* is from *factor*, 'agent.' A *factory* was formerly a trading post or establishment for the agents of a foreign trading company, — as 'the *factories* of the East India Company.' Later it was transferred to its present meaning of 'manufactory' (L. *manus*, 'hand'), being in a manner rederived from L. *factorium*,[1] 'a place where things are made.'

[1] In classical Latin, *factorium* has taken the special sense of 'oil-press.'

Pretty is the Anglo-Saxon *prættig*, 'sly,' which may come in a roundabout way (possibly through the Celtic) from L.L. *practica*, 'practice,' 'plot' (which is from Gr. πράττω, *práttō*, 'do,' 'make'). The transition in meaning from 'sly' to the present sense of *pretty* is doubtless through the notion of 'cleverness.' Compare the American nursery term *cunning* of a bright or amusing little child (*cunning* means literally 'knowing,' and had at first no bad sense).[1] So *handsome* is literally 'dexterous,' 'handy' (*-some* being the suffix seen in *winsome*, *gladsome*, etc.). *Beautiful* is a French word, *beauté*, with an English suffix. *Beauty* itself is from L.L. *bellitas*, from L. *bellus*, 'pretty.' *Lovely* is of course from *love*. Observe that all these adjectives, especially *pretty*, the oldest of them in English, show traces of being used as pet names or endearing adjectives. This is, indeed, enough to account for what seems at first the strange change of sense which *pretty* has undergone. The fantastical language of affection often makes pet names out of abusive ones. So Othello calls Desdemona 'excellent *wretch*,' and King Lear speaks of Cordelia as 'my poor *fool*.' *Rascal*, *worm*, *villain*, *tyke* ('cur'), *goose*, and even *snake*, have all been used in this way; cf. the L. *asellus*, 'little donkey.' We should remember Helena's list of

> Pretty, fond, adoptious christendoms
> That blinking Cupid gossips,

in All's Well That Ends Well.

Corn is a native word (akin to L. *granum*, whence *grain* is derived); its original sense is 'a single grain,' as in the biblical 'a corn of wheat,' and *kernel* is its diminu-

[1] On the change of meaning in *sly*, *cunning*, and *knowing*, see p. 289.

tive.[1] Collectively *corn* is used in England for any kind of grain. In the United States, however, the word (when used without an adjective) regularly means 'maize' or 'Indian corn,' and is never applied to wheat, rye, barley, or oats. *Maize* (a term seldom heard in the United States) is a Haytian word, *mahiz* (or *mahis*), which came into our language through the Spanish *maiz*.

Ink comes (O. Fr. *enque*, modern *encre*) from *encaustum*, a Latinization of Gr. ἔγκαυστον (*énkauston*), 'something burnt in,' connected with *caustic* and *holocaust*. *Pen* is simply 'feather' (Fr. *penne* from L. *penna*). *Paper* is the *papyrus* plant (French, from Latin, from Greek). *Parchment* comes (through the French) from L. *Pergamenus*, an adjective from *Pergamum*, a city in Asia. *Write* is a native word which meant originally 'to scratch.' *Book* is also native, but it meant originally 'beech,' for our ancestors used to cut runic letters on wooden staves or rods; cf. Ger. *Buchstaben*, 'letters of the alphabet' (literally 'beech-staves'). *Alphabet* is from the Greek letters *alpha* and *beta* (our A and B).

For 'precious stone' the Anglo-Saxons had a mysterious word *eorcnan-stān*. They also borrowed *gemma* from the Latin, in the form *gim*, and this survived as a native word till the fourteenth century. In that century, however, in which the influence of French and Latin was particularly strong, the word was remade and brought nearer to its Latin original, taking the form *gemmë*. This remaking is usually said to have been under the influence of the French *gemme* (itself from the Latin),—but this is not so certain; for it is not possible to separate Latin and

[1] Anglo-Saxon *cyrnel* is a regular diminutive of *corn*, showing the diminutive ending -*el* (related to the Latin ending in *filio-lus*, 'little son') and 'umlaut' or vowel-mutation (as in *gold*, *gylden*, 'golden').

French influence in a case like this. *Jewel* is certainly from the French. It is a diminutive of L. *jocus* (whence Fr. *jeu*), and meant originally 'plaything.'[1] The names of different precious stones are of very various origin. *Diamond* is the same word as *adamant;* it comes through the French and the Latin from the Greek ἄδαμας (*ádamas*), 'untamed,'—and was so called from its hardness; L. *domare* (whence our *indomitable*) and English *tame* belong to the same root. *Emerald* is from the Greek σμάραγδος (*smáragdos*), through Latin and French. *Sapphire* has a similar derivation; but the Greeks must have got it from some Oriental people, for the word is not Indo-European and resembles the Hebrew *sappīr*. *Ruby* is connected with L. *ruber*, 'red.' *Pearl* means 'little pear' (Fr. from L. *pirum*, 'pear'). *Jet* is O. Fr. *jet*, from L. *gagates*, a Greek word derived from *Gagas*, the name of a town in Asia Minor. *Agate* is French, from Gr. ἀχάτης (*achátēs*), through Latin. *Jade* is French from Spanish. In its oldest form it is connected with L. *ilia*, 'flanks,' because jade was thought to cure side-ache, in accordance with the old view that ascribed all kinds of mysterious 'virtues' to gems. Most of these gem-names came, it will be remarked, from the East, and reached England through Greece, Rome, and France successively. This correctly represents the history of civilization in the matter of gems, except in one respect. We should make a mistake if we inferred that the English owed their knowledge of such things to the French. Anglo-Saxon had names for many gems, derived directly from the Latin (as in the case of the word *gem* itself), but these words went out of use after the Norman Conquest, when the persons who continued to speak English had little occasion to talk of precious stones; and

---

[1] See Sheldon, in Studies and Notes in Philology and Literature, I, 123.

the words passed into the language again later, through the French.

Apple and *berry* are native words of unknown origin, though the latter is perhaps associated with a root meaning 'to eat.' *Pear* and *plum* were adapted from the Latin *pirum* and *prunum* by Anglo-Saxons (*piru*, *plūm*). So *beet* (A.S. *bēte*, from L. *beta*), — and a good many other names of plants. *Peach* comes through the French from L. *Persicum* (*malum*), 'Persian apple.' *Grape* is an old French word (Fr. *grappe*) from an Old High German word for 'hook,' and is related to *grab*, *grapple*, *cramp*; the French applied the term to a 'bunch of grapes,' the connection of ideas coming through the relation between 'clutching' and 'a handful.' *Potato* is the native Haytian name slightly altered by the Spaniards (Haytian *batata*, Spanish *patata*); the word, like the tuber, was borrowed in the sixteenth century. The American 'sweet potato' is a plant of quite a different family, but it has the best of rights to its name, — for it was called *potato* before this name was given to the white tuber that is now regarded as the true potato.

Parsley has had a strange history. It is a Greek compound πετροσέλινον (*petrosélinon*), 'rock parsley,' from πέτρος (*pétros*), 'rock' (whence the name *Peter*, — see Matthew xvi. 18) and σέλινον (*sélinon*), 'parsley.' The Romans borrowed the word as *petroselinum*, and it was taken into Anglo-Saxon as *petersilie*.[1] In French the Latin word wore down to *persil*, and this was taken bodily into English in the same form *persil*. Side by side with *persil*, however, the English made a form *persely*, which is a kind of compromise between the Anglo-Saxon and the French, and this form has survived in our modern *parsley*.

---

[1] This is also the German word for 'parsley.'

COMPLEXITY OF THE ENGLISH VOCABULARY 139

Squash means one thing in England, another in America, —and the two senses come from languages as widely separated as it is possible for languages to be. The English *squash* means an 'unripe peapod' (or 'peascod'), and is connected with the verb *squash*, 'to crush'; the latter probably coming (through the Old French *esquachier*, modern, *écacher*) from a Low Latin *excoacticare*, from *ex* and *cogere, coactum*, 'to drive together,' 'to compel.' The American squash is a kind of gourd (something like the English vegetable marrow), the word coming from the Massachusetts Indian *asquash* (plural of *asq*), 'raw,' 'green,' *i.e.* 'green vegetables.' It is an odd coincidence that two such different languages as Latin and North American Indian should independently bestow upon our speech two different words identical in form and sound. But every cultivated modern tongue, being the record of a long and complicated civilization, is full of such anomalies (cf. p. 360).

Pea is the result of a common error. The Latin *pisum* gave A.S. *pisë*, which became *pesë* in Middle English. Then the *-ë* disappeared, leaving *pes* (whence *pease*). The *s*, though really a part of the word itself, was taken as the plural ending, and hence a singular *pea* was made, — as if *corp* had been made from *corps(e)*.[1]

Mint and *money* are really the same word. Both come from L. *moneta* (which had both meanings) from *Juno Moneta*, whose temple was the Roman mint. The surname *Moneta* is from the verb *monere*, 'to warn' or 'advise' (which we have in *monitor, admonish*), and has nothing to do with coining. The Anglo-Saxons borrowed *moneta*

---

[1] Indeed, this form *corp* is known in vulgar English, and was once in good use. For other cases of a singular made in this way cf. *burial*, and see pp. 132–3.

as *mynet* (whence *mint*), and in French the Latin word became *moneie* (modern *monnaie*), whence our *money*.

We still have two old phrases 'pay the *shot*' and 'pay the *scot*,' for 'pay your reckoning (at a tavern),' as well as *scot-free*, literally 'free of expense.' In this use, *shot* is the Anglo-Saxon *scot*, 'a share,' connected with *scēotan* 'to shoot' (A.S. *sc* becoming *sh* in modern English); *scot*, however, comes from O. Fr. *escot* (modern *écot*),[1] itself a loan word from the Germanic, so that *scot* and *shot* are really identical in etymology. *Penny* is Anglo-Saxon, but the abbreviation *d.* is the Latin *denarius*. *Farthing* is from *fourth* (A.S. *fēorthung* from *fēortha*). *Shilling* (A.S. *scilling*) means perhaps 'the clinking coin' (cf. Ger. *schellen*, 'to sound,' 'to tinkle'); the abbreviation *s.* is for L. *solidus*, 'a solid piece of money,' whence *soldier* 'a hired fighter.' *Pound* is the A.S. *pūnd*, from L. *pondo*, akin to *pondus*, 'weight' (cf. our *ponder*, 'to weigh a subject'); the abbreviation £ or *l.* is the Latin *libra*, 'a balance,' 'a weight' (whence *de-liber-ate*, and *level*, the latter coming, through the French, from the diminutive *libella*).

Dollar is from the Low Countries, — Low German *dahler*, whither it came from Ger. *Thaler*, short for *Joachims-thaler*, since dollars were first coined in the *Thal* ('valley,' cognate with English *dale*) of St. Joachim in Bohemia, in the sixteenth century. The word *dollar* was commonly applied to a Spanish silver coin at the time when our American monetary standards were devised. Spanish dollars were well known in this country. *Cent* was borrowed directly from L. *centum* at the same time, though the word already existed in English in *per cent;* and *mill* was similarly taken from L. *mille*, 'a thousand.' The clipped forms *cent* and *mill* are due to French influ-

---

[1] Or perhaps from Old Norse *skot*, really the same word.

ence,[1] but our American ancestors certainly had the Latin words in mind.

Florin is from *Florence*, where these coins were first struck. *Crown, louis, napoleon, sovereign, guinea* are specialized senses or nicknames. The last-mentioned comes from the fact that the first guineas were coined from Guinea gold. Such nicknames are originally slang, like *bob* or *tanner* for 'shilling,' *tenner* for 'ten-pound note,' *V* for 'five-dollar bill,' *cart-wheel* for 'silver dollar.' *Note* itself, in this sense, is short for *bank note*, like *bill* for *bank bill*. *Holy dollar* is an old punning Australian term for a Spanish or American dollar from which a circular piece had been cut; such coins passed in Australia when currency was scanty. Compare *slug*, for a stamped lump of gold in California; *dump*, for a similar thing in Australia. *Currency* itself is an abstract noun used collectively for *current money*.

A *necromancer* learns the future by calling up the spirits of the dead (Gr. νεκρός, *nekrós*, 'dead body,' and μαντεία, *manteía*, 'divination'). *Magic* is the art of the Persian *Magi*, a class of wizard-priests. *Wizard* is properly a 'wise man' (Milton calls the Three Magi 'the star-led wizards'); it is *wise* with the suffix *-ard* or *-art*[2] (as in *drunkard, coward, sluggard, braggart*). *Witch* (originally of common gender) seems also to mean 'a wise man,' and to be connected with the root seen in *wit*, 'knowledge.' *Sortilege* is divination by drawing lots, once regarded as a mysterious process controlled by the higher powers (Fr. *sortilège*, from L. *sors, sortis*, 'lot,' and *legere*, 'to

[1] French *cent, mille*.
[2] The suffix *-ard, -art*, came into English from the French, but is of Germanic origin, and once meant 'bold,' 'hardy.' It is the same as the English adjective *hard*, and appears in various proper names, as *Reginhard*.

choose'). *Soothsayer* is a 'truth-teller' (*sooth*, 'true,' 'truth'). *Juggler* is L. *joculator*, 'jester,' 'player of tricks.' *Exorcist* is a Greek word meaning 'one who lays a spell upon' evil spirits, and so bans them (from ἐξ, *ex*, and ὁρκίζειν, *horkízein*, 'to conjure or lay a spell upon,' from ὅρκος, *hórkos*, 'oath'). *Conjurer* is a similar word from the Latin *con*- (intensive) and *juro*, 'to swear'; to *conjure* is properly to pronounce the name of a god in such a way as to gain his assistance.

Prophet means 'spokesman,' that is, 'one who speaks for a divinity,' 'the interpreter of his will' (Gr. προφήτης, *prophḗtēs*, L. *prophēta*, from Gr. πρό, *pró*-, 'for,' and φάναι, *phánai*, 'to speak'); since *pró* also means 'before,' the usual modern sense is easily intelligible. A *seer* is 'one who sees.' *Druid* is a Celtic word for a kind of priest. The druids practised magic, and the Anglo-Saxons took the word in the form *drȳ*, in the sense of 'enchanter.' An *enchanter* is one who sings chants or charms (*incantations*), Fr. *enchanter*, from L. *in-cantare* (from *cantus*, 'song,' whence *chant*). To *augur* is to interpret the omens given by the flight of birds, as the Roman *augures* (perhaps from *avis*, 'bird') did.

Town is a very concrete word in its origin. It is native Germanic (A.S. *tūn*);[1] it means, literally, an 'enclosure,' or 'fenced place,' and points to the stockaded settlements of a time long before the Angles and Saxons saw Britain. The cognate Ger. *Zaun* has kept the older sense of 'hedge.' *City*, on the other hand, is abstract. It is the French *cité* from L. *civitas*. *Civitas* meant originally 'citizenship' (being the abstract from *civis*, 'citizen'), but was easily transferred to the citizens in their collective capacity; and so came, at last, to be a mere synonym of

---

[1] Cognate with the Celtic *dūn*, 'fortress,' seen in *Lugdūnum*, 'Lyons.'

urbs, 'city.' In its origin, then, *city* suggests the 'body politic,' whereas *town* suggests merely the actual place, the fenced stronghold; and some traces of this old distinction have persisted to modern times, though the words have received new conventional senses, different in different parts of the English-speaking world. *Village* is French, from L. *villaticus*, 'belonging to a country-house'[1] (cf. Milton's 'tame *villatic* fowl,' in Samson Agonistes), and suggests the manor-house with its adjoining cluster of cottages. *Hamlet* is a double diminutive. We derive it from O. Fr. *hamelet*, a diminutive of *hamel* (modern *hameau*), which is itself a diminutive of W. Ger. *haim* (A.S. *hām*, Eng. *home*, Ger. *Heim*). Thus *hamlet* is closely related to our *home*, though it has reached us through the French, and has not descended, like *home*, from Anglo-Saxon. *Home* (A.S. *hām*) is a general Indo-European word for 'abiding-place,' 'dwelling.' In the oldest English it was purely descriptive, and apparently as destitute of tender or sentimental associations as *town* or *city* with us. As early as the sixteenth century we meet with the proverb 'Home's homely,' that is, 'Home is homelike, or comfortable,' and since that time the growth of the modern connotations has been rapid. John Howard Payne's famous song, 'Sweet Home,' expressed in simple language the feelings that had become vaguely connected with the word. In itself, the song could not have produced the sentiments which we feel in the word *home*. Yet, since it fell in with the popular sentiment, and was easy to sing and pleasant to hear, it became almost immediately the common expression of

[1] The modern English word *villa* is a direct borrowing from the Italian, which had preserved the word from the Roman times without change of form. See pp. 321-2.

those sentiments for all English-speaking persons, and thus intensified a hundred fold the tender connotations which it aimed merely to express. In this way, *home*, at first a mere concrete term, has become an abstract expression for all that is best in family life. There is at present a tendency to overuse the word (at least in this country) as little more than a softer synonym for 'house' or 'place where one lives.' The result of this process would finally be to strip the word of all its associations, and reduce it once more to the position of a colorless descriptive term.[1] Conservatism, and the inevitable revolt against overdone sentimentality, may be strong enough to save the word.

County is properly the domain of a count or earl. *Count* is French (O. Fr. *counte*, modern *comte*), from L. *comes*, 'companion' (member of the imperial court). The influence of French on our language was sufficient to bring in *countess* and *county*, but *count* is still a foreign title. The English word is *earl*. The history of this word is almost the history of England. In A.S. *eorl* simply meant a 'nobleman,' a person of higher rank than an ordinary freeman. Among the Danes, the kindred word *jarl* was applied to a special class of noblemen of very high rank, who often exercised viceregal sway over particular districts, the same class that were called *aldermen* (*ealdormenn*) in Anglo-Saxon. When Cnut, the Dane, became king of England, *jarl* was of course used by the Danish nobles in England, and the corresponding English word *eorl* soon took on this special sense. The Normans found it in use, and it was recognized as equivalent to their term *count*.

---

[1] This is a natural tendency of all language, and must not be regarded as anything specially objectionable or noteworthy in itself. In the case of this particular word, it seems a pity: that is all. There is nothing abnormal or unusual about the process.

Thereafter, *count* was used by French-speaking Englishmen, and *earl* by those who spoke the vernacular; but though *count* entered our language, it never displaced *earl* as the legal and popular English term. *Countess*, however, for 'earl's wife,' came in almost immediately, and is one of the oldest French words in our language. It occurs in the Peterborough continuation of the Anglo-Saxon Chronicle under the year 1140, and was certainly in use considerably earlier. *Earl* continued to be the highest rank in the English peerage until the fourteenth century, when the French titles of *duke* and *marquess* were bestowed on certain members of the royal family. These titles were later extended beyond their royal limits, and thus grew up the present system. *Earl* has now no territorial significance, but is a mere title of rank, inferior to that of *duke* and *marquess*. The old name of *alderman* did not go out of use when *earl* was substituted for it. It ceased to be a title of nobility, but was applied to the head of a guild or trade-company. Towns were governed by the heads of guilds, and hence *alderman* easily passed into its present civic meanings with the development of municipal government in England and America. Thus the complete history of the single word *earl* involves the Anglo-Saxon, the Danish, and the Norman Conquest, the amalgamation of the different races into the present English nation, the growth of the social system of Great Britain, and the development of municipal government on both sides of the Atlantic.

But this is not all. The etymology of *earl* is uncertain (perhaps it meant in the first place merely 'man'). But *alderman* is derived from *aldor*, 'chief,' literally an 'elder,' and so conducts us back to very primitive times, when the community was a family, and the head of the clan was the father or patriarch. We have before us, then, not merely the history of England, but the history of government itself. The vicissitudes of a word like *alderman*, which once meant 'viceroy,' and now means a 'city official,' are curious enough; but the interest in them is far from that of mere curiosity.

CHAPTER XI

UNITY OF THE ENGLISH VOCABULARY

THE assimilating power of the English language is not less remarkable than the complexity of its sources. Our commonest words, as we have just seen, come from every corner of the world, and have been subjected to almost every conceivable process in form and meaning. Yet the language is consistent with itself, and has its distinctive character. *A priori*, one might expect that a tongue like our own would be like the learned jargon of Hudibras:—

> But, when he pleased to show't, his speech
> In loftiness of sound was rich;
> A Babylonish dialect,
> Which learnèd pedants much affect.
> It was a parti-colored dress
> Of patched and piebald languages;
> 'Twas English cut on Greek and Latin,
> Like fustian heretofore on satin;
> It had an odd, promiscuous tone
> As if h' had talked three parts in one;
> Which made some think, when he did gabble,
> Th' had heard three laborers of Babel;
> Or Cerberus himself pronounce
> A leash of languages at once.

In fact, however, English produces no such effect. Our *Sprachgefühl*, the 'genius of the language,' or whatever one may call the great conservative force which we have already considered, has not only kept English true to itself through long periods of time, but revolts instantly against any neologism that does not accord with our idiom. English is full of French words, but it is none the less English. Transfer a French sentence[1] into English words, *literally*, without regard to our idiom, and the vigor with which our language resents a Gallicism is evident at once; and the argument is clinched by the admitted impossibility of translating Macbeth or Hamlet into the language of Racine.

The diverse sources of English have been abundantly exemplified in the preceding chapter by the citation of groups of words for common things or familiar ideas. The harmony with which these diverse elements combine to make a consistent language may best be seen by examining the words that make up a particular passage of connected discourse.

Let us take, then, the following brief paragraph of recent narrative prose: —

The negro pilot was naturally of a gloomy and savage expression of countenance, and at these unwelcome tidings his forbidding features were so hideously distorted with anger and terror that he looked more like a demon than a man of this world. Springing to his feet, he tore his cap from his head with a spasmodic twitch that half detached the glazed visor, threw off his tattered pea-jacket, seized a harpoon, and rushed toward the companion-way. The captain, poor, peevish martinet, was at his wit's end. How should he exorcise the roaring devil that his own cantankerous folly had raised?

This is somewhat wordy, but not unusually so, and no one will challenge any of its words as 'un-English.' It

[1] This favorite trick of schoolboys and other humorists has, then, a real scientific value, though it does not prove that French is inferior to English as a medium of intellectual expression. The classic example of the joke is Mark Twain's Jumping Frog, which has amused two continents.

UNITY OF THE ENGLISH VOCABULARY 149

produces, on the whole, a consistent stylistic effect, though *peevish* and *cantankerous* might be objected to as affectedly simple or colloquial. At all events, it is by no means a Babylonish dialect; it does not suggest 'a leash of languages at once.' Yet a study of its components reveals a bewildering diversity of tongues, nations, dates, professions, and linguistic processes.

Negro is a Spanish (or Portuguese) form, from the Latin *niger*, 'black.'[1]

Pilot comes immediately from Fr. *pilote*, but this appears to be merely the Dutch *peillood*, — from *peil*, 'measure,' and *lood*, 'lead.'

Gloomy belongs to a puzzling group of words in which the ideas of light and darkness seem inextricably mingled. The Anglo-Saxon *glōm*, 'twilight,' is from the same root as *glow;* and there is a word *glome, gloom*, recorded from the sixteenth to the eighteenth century, which means 'heat.' From A.S. *glōm* comes *gloaming*, a Scottish and North of England word, recently introduced into English literature, like so many other dialect words.[2] Our ordinary noun *gloom*, however, is first recorded in the sense of a 'frown,' or 'scowl,' and the verb *to gloom*, for 'to frown,' seems to be older than this noun. It is hard to separate this from *glōm*, 'twilight,' but there are phonetic difficulties in the way.

Naturally is a Latin word with an English suffix.

Savage is French, from L. *silvaticus*, 'living in the woods' (*silva*, whence *sylvan* and the proper name *Sylvanus*). The form *salvages*, which occurs so often in the early history of America, looks like the Old French *salvage* (modern *sauvage*), but the *l* is more likely to be a learned insertion under Latin influence. Of course this has nothing to do

[1] See p. 356.   [2] *Croon*, for example (see p. 58).

with the maritime *salvage*, which comes (also through the French) from L. *salvo*, 'save.'

Expression is a Latin word meaning, literally, 'the act of pressing out,' or 'modelling.' 'Moulding' is extended to 'representation' in general, and hence come all our figurative meanings.

Countenance once meant 'one's bearing,' 'demeanor,' and the like, — literally, the way in which a person 'holds himself together' (L. *continentia*, from *con-* and *teneo*). So Chaucer is described by the Host of the Tabard Inn as 'seeming elvish by his countenance,' that is, 'shy (like an elf among men), to judge by his bearing' (since he does not chat with the other pilgrims).[1] From 'bearing,' in general, the word was specialized to the bearing or expression of the face, and in Modern English is used concretely for the face itself. So *gesture*, which once meant one's 'bearing' in general (from *gero*, 'carry'), has been limited to expressive motions with the hands, and so on. *Continence* is a direct borrowing from L. *continentia*, and has a special sense.

Unwelcome is a native word remade under foreign influences. Anglo-Saxon has *wil-cuma*, 'a pleasure-comer,' that is, one whose coming accords with one's *will* or wish. Later this was corrupted to *wel-come*, which has an obvious sense. The French *bien venu* is partly responsible for this change.

Tidings is apparently formed from the verb *to tide* (A.S. *tīdan*, 'to happen') under the influence of the Scandinavian *tīthinde*, 'happenings,' which was of kindred origin. The

---

[1] The passage is commonly misunderstood, as if *countenance* had the modern meaning. Thus one of Chaucer's editors describes him as having 'a weird expression of countenance,' which is amusing in itself and does not accord with his portrait.

connection between 'occurrences' and 'news' is obvious enough.

Forbid is a native verb. The prefix *for-* has a negative sense like the German *ver-*, to which it is related. The two senses of *bid*, 'order' and 'offer' (as in *bidding* at an auction) are due to confusion (which began in the Anglo-Saxon period) between *bēodan*, 'offer,' and *biddan*, 'pray' (Ger. *bieten* and *bitten*). Compare the more modern (and therefore 'vulgar') confusions between *lie* and *lay*, *sit* and *set*. 'To bid one's beads' preserves the old sense of *biddan*. *Bead* is properly 'prayer,' and has acquired its modern sense from the custom of counting one's prayers on the rosary.

Feature is literally one's 'make' (French, from L. *factura*). In Shakspere's time it often meant one's 'form' or 'figure'; but it is now specialized to the parts which make up the face. Compare the somewhat similar lot of *countenance*.

Hideous we get from the French. Its older history is very uncertain. It is usually referred to L. *hispidosus*, from *hispidus*, 'bristly.' An Old High German derivation has also been suggested: *egidī*, 'horror,' related to our word *awe*. The Germanic conquerors of the Gallic provinces contributed many words to French.

Distort is simply 'twist out of shape,'—L. *torqueo, tortus*, 'twist,' whence, in different ways, our *tortuous, torture*, and the law term *tort*.

Anger and *terror* are equally good English now, but the former is the Old Norse *angr* and the latter the Latin *terror*, both taken into our language bodily.

Look is a native verb. Its use in the sense of 'appear' illustrates the process of transference which will be discussed in Chapter XIX.

Demon is a Greek word for 'a divinity.' Its change in sense is due to Christianity. The fathers of the Church did not deny the existence of the heathen gods; they regarded them as evil spirits that had long deceived mankind. This view is familiar to all through Paradise Lost.

World is interesting as a compound that has become so reduced as to seem like a perfectly simple word. It was once *weorold*, from *wer*, 'man' (as in *were-wolf*), and an old noun meaning 'age' (related to our adjective *old*). Thus it meant 'the age of man,' and easily passed into the sense of 'mankind.' Similarly we use *the age* and *the times* for 'the people of the age' (cf. L. *saeculum*).

Cap is a very old (Anglo-Saxon) borrowing from the Low Latin *cappa, capa*. This *cappa* has been appropriated by our language over and over again. *Cappa* has given us *cap* (A.S. *cæppe*); the other form, *capa*, has given us *cope*. From *cappa* comes the French *chape*, which we have borrowed in the sense of 'the metal tip of a sheath,' and also (later) the French *cape* (through Spanish or Italian), which gives us *cape*. From the Latin diminutive *cappella* comes (through the French) our *chapel*. The change of meaning is curious, but has been traced. St. Martin's *cloak* (*cappella*) was preserved by the Frankish kings as a most sacred relic; and the name *chapel* came to be applied to other sanctuaries besides that in which this *cappella* was kept. From this to 'the singers in a choir' was an easy step (cf. *choir* itself), and hence we have *Kapelle* in German particularly applied to a 'military band.' The interest that one feels in this remarkable word *capa* is not a little enhanced by an additional circumstance. It first turns up in Spain, and, since it is certainly not of Latin origin, it has been thought to be really an

Iberian word, — one of the scanty remnants of the language of the native Spanish tribes whom the Romans subdued. Other English words that come from the same source are *chaplain; chaplet*, 'a garland'; *chapelet*, 'a pair of stirrups,' 'a kind of pump'; *chaperon*, literally 'a hood.'

Spasmodic and *twitch* repeat the same idea, for *spasm* is merely the Greek word for 'twitching' or 'convulsion.' It affords a good instance of a learned medical word that has become popular (see pp. 30-3). *Span* is thought to be from the same Indo-European root, and also *spin* and *space*.

Detach is French. The second syllable is the same as that seen in *attach, attack*, and *tack*, 'a small nail.' This *tack* is probably Celtic. If so, we have here a curious parallel to the relations in the case of *cap*. *Attach* is another good instance of the transfer of a technical word to general uses, — this time a legal word.

Glaze is from *glass* (A.S. *glœs*), perhaps connected (like *gloom*) with the root seen in *glow*.

Visor is Fr. *visière*, from *vis*, 'face.' It leads us back to the days of chivalry, when the word was applied to a movable part of the helmet. *Vis* is of course from L. *video, visus*. The termination *-or* for *-er* shows the Latinizing influence, as in the spelling *bettor* for *better* ('one who bets').

Throw has a remarkable history, which will be given in a later chapter (see pp. 242-4).

Tatter is Scandinavian, and is more or less remotely related to *tetter, dander, dandruff, tear, tar, tree, trough, tart*, and a number of other words. The general sense of the root is 'to split.'

Pea-jacket seems to be both a hybrid and a tautological compound, for the Dutch *pij* is a kind of coat. *Jacket* is

Fr. *jaquette*, and is a diminutive of *jack* (Fr. *jaque*), 'a leather coat.' This seems to be soldiers' slang, for there is little doubt that it is a jocose application of the proper name *Jacques* (cf. pp. 386-7).

Seize is a word which has increased in intensity of meaning. Its earliest meaning is to 'set' or 'put in possession of,' and this is still seen in the law-phrase *seized of* for 'possessed of' (cf. 'livery of *seisin*'). The word is of Germanic origin (related to *set*), but we took it from the French.

Harpoon (formerly *harpon*) is French (*harpon*) from *harpe*, 'dog's claw,' 'clamp,' which is derived, through the Latin from Gr. ἅρπη (*hárpē*), 'hook,' 'clutch.' The Greek *Harpies* are the 'Snatchers.' It is possible, however, that the Germanic *harp*, 'a musical instrument,' is the source of the French *harpe*, — the curve of the harp suggesting a hook.

Rush is Teutonic and has many relatives, all implying either haste or noise. *Toward* is an adjective in Anglo-Saxon (*tōweard*), meaning 'coming,' 'impending,' and this sense lasted till Shakspere's time (cf. *untoward* and *froward*). It is a compound of *to* and an old Germanic word akin to L. *verto*, 'turn.'

Companion-way is a hybrid compound, *way* being a native and *companion* a borrowed word. The latter has a diversified history. In its ordinary sense of 'associate,' it is the French *compagnon*, from a late Latin term signifying 'bread-sharer' (*com-*, and *panis*, 'bread'). As a nautical term, however, it is a corruption (under the influence of the ordinary word) of the French *chambre à la compagne* (or the Italian *camera della compagna*), which meant the 'pantry' or 'storeroom' on a ship's deck. Perhaps the English word passed through the Dutch language (*kompanje*), whence so many sailors' terms have come. This *compagna*, 'provisions,' is of the same origin as the word for 'associate.'

Captain is French, from Late L. *capitaneus* (from *caput*, 'head'). An older French form from the same is *chevetain*, which gives us *chieftain*.

Poor is Fr. *pauvre* (older *povre*), from L. *pauper*. The generalizing of the sense from 'indigent' to 'unfortunate' or 'contemptible' is interesting. Observe that we have also borrowed the word *pauper*, and have given it a technical sense, stronger than that which it bore in Latin.

Peevish is of unknown etymology. It is perhaps an imitative word, suggesting the fretful whining of an infant. At all events, it once meant 'childish,' and is still particularly applicable to fretful children or to those who resemble them. The inevitable union of both senses, 'childish' and 'fretful,' in such a passage as the following, goes far to establish the onomatopoetic character of the word: —

> As I remember, Henry the Sixth
> Did prophesy that Richmond should be king,
> When Richmond was a little peevish boy.
> Richard III, iv, 2, 98–100.

Martinet is an example of a proper name which has become a common noun (like 'a Solon,' 'a Solomon,' 'a Daniel come to judgment').[1] Martinet was a French officer in the time of Louis XIV, and introduced new regulations into the infantry service.

---

[1] See pp. 372 ff. This is the accepted etymology, but the history of the word needs investigation. It was slang in the latter part of the eighteenth century, but passed into the legitimate vocabulary in the first quarter of the nineteenth. *Martinet* has no such sense in French, but does mean, among other things, a 'cat-o'-nine-tails.'

Wit is preserved in this phrase in its old sense of 'wisdom' or 'knowledge.' The word belongs to an extremely productive Indo-European root meaning 'to see,' found in the Latin *video* (whence, in various ways, come *vision*, *revise*, *invidious*, *envy*, *vie*, *visage*, *visor*, etc.) and in the Greek ἰδεῖν (*ideîn*, whence *idea*, *idol*), as well as in our *wise*, *to wit* (*wot*, *wist*), *twit*, etc. The development of meaning in the English noun is worth notice. Compare 'a *knowing* fellow,' ' to live by one's *wits*,' and similar phrases.

Exorcise came into our language during the 'learned times' described in Chapter VIII. Its first occurrence is in the sixteenth century. We need have no hesitation, then, in refusing to derive it directly from the French verb *exorciser*. It was certainly adapted from the Greek ἐξορκίζω (*exorkízō*), 'to put under oath,' or 'to put under the ban,' with a side influence from the borrowed Latin verb *exorcizo*, which was a theological word for 'laying' evil spirits (see p. 142). It was, then, technical in its origin, but is now less so, though it has never become a popular word.

Roar and *raise* are native words, and require no special comment in this place.

Devil is the Greek διάβολος (*diábolos*), 'slanderer,' 'traducer.' This word was used as a Greek equivalent of the Hebrew *Sātān* ('the adversary'), who was the accuser or slanderer of the just, as in the first chapter of Job. Roman Christianity took the Greek word into Latin as *diabolus*, and it has also passed into the Germanic tongues. These must have borrowed it very early. The East Germanic Goths had the word in the fourth century, adopting it directly from the Greek. The Christianity of the West Germanic tribes was Roman, not Greek; yet the

UNITY OF THE ENGLISH VOCABULARY 157

behavior of this word in their dialects suggests that *devil* may have been passed along from the Christian Goths to the pagan High Germans, and so westward to the Angles and Saxons in their continental home. There is nothing improbable in this theory, in view of *church*, which had a similar history.[1] The name of a god or an evil spirit readily travels from tribe to tribe, even when religions are at variance. At all events, the Anglo-Saxons had the Greek (or Latin) word *devil* as well as the Greek word *church* before they went to Britain, and long before they were converted to Christianity.

We have found, in one short English passage, besides the native element, no less than a dozen languages represented,— Greek, Latin, French, Spanish (or Portuguese), Dutch, Old Norse, the Celtic of Gaul, the Iberian of the Spanish aborigines, and possibly Gothic and Old High German. The borrowings have taken place at all periods,— before the Anglo-Saxon Conquest, during the Anglo-Saxon period, between the Norman Conquest and Chaucer, in the learned times of the sixteenth century, in recent days. We have Latin words that have come through the French, others that have come from the Latin but have been affected by French fashions, and one that has entered the language bodily, without the change of a letter.

The technical dialects of law, medicine, and theology are all represented in words that have passed from their special vocabularies into the general stock. Slang, chivalry, and seamanship have contributed their quotas. The whole history of European Christianity is involved in the passage. Its conflict with classical paganism is suggested

---

[1] A.S. *cirice, circe,* from Gr. κυριακόν, 'the Lord's (house).'

by *demon*. The early conversion of the Goths, proceeding from the Eastern Church (in its heretical Arian offshoot), and the later conversion of the West Germanic tribes, proceeding from the Church of Rome, are mirrored in *devil*. Side by side with the name of the great Hebrew spirit of evil, we have the name of an obscure French infantry officer, both serving as 'common nouns' in English.

Many linguistic processes are also exemplified. We have seen native words modified by foreign influences, and foreign words subjected to native modifications. 'Popular etymology,' which changes a word so as to make it consistent with some fancied relation to another,[1] is also present. Hybrid and tautological compounds are illustrated. Metaphorical shifts of meaning abound. Generalization and specialization are manifest everywhere.

In short, our brief passage of simple narrative is a great panorama of linguistic history, and we discover, on surveying it, that the history of language is the history of mankind.

[1] See Chapter XXIII.

CHAPTER XII

COGNATES AND BORROWED WORDS

IN studying a language like our own, which has enriched its native stock by adopting thousands of words from foreign tongues, the difference between 'cognate' and 'borrowed' words is of great moment. Thus we say that *fraternal* is 'borrowed' from the Latin *fraternalis*. *Brother*, however, is not borrowed from the Latin *frater*, but 'cognate' with it or 'akin' to it. The distinction is particularly important in judging the relations between English and German. Every educated Englishman knows that a large part of his vocabulary is borrowed from Latin or French; but he is aware of a great residuum of words that he does not associate with those languages, such as *bread, fiend, friend, book, wife*. When he is first introduced to German, and meets with *Brod, Feind, Freund, Buch, Weib*, he is of course struck with their resemblance to these hitherto unexplained native words, and, since he knows that much of his native language is borrowed, he jumps at the conclusion that the same is true of *bread, friend*, and so on. Hence the popular error, which it seems almost impossible to eradicate in England, that words like this were borrowed by English from the German. The fact is, our actual borrowings from that language are almost *nil*. The resemblances that mislead the uninstructed reader are due to the fact that the English and the German words are cognate.

The meaning of 'cognate' in this etymological use may easily be seen in the Romance languages. We know that French, Italian, Spanish, and Portuguese are all descended from a single language, — the Latin. This is not a matter of inference, but of settled historical fact. When, therefore, we find the word for 'son' appearing as *fils* in French, *figlio* in Italian, *hijo* in Spanish, *filho* in Portuguese, and remember that the Latin word for son is *filius*, we have no difficulty in accounting for the similarity between the various forms without supposing that Italian has borrowed from French, or Portuguese from Italian. The French, Italian, Spanish, and Portuguese words resemble each other because they all come from the same mother-language, — Latin. Thus we explain the likeness of Fr. *mère*, Ital. *madre*, Sp. *madre*, Pg. *mãi*, as due to their common origin (L. *mater*, *matrem*), and so on with almost the whole vocabulary of the Romance languages. That is, the ancestors of the French, Italian, Spanish, and Portuguese peoples once had substantially the same words for the same things; but these words have gradually changed their forms, whether much or little, with changing conditions of government and society. Such languages, then, are *cognate*, or related languages, and the words which they possess in common, by virtue of their descent from a common mother-speech, are called *cognate words*.

In the case of the Germanic languages, as English, German, Danish, Dutch, we find a similar state of things. Thus we have *son* (A.S. *sunu*) in English, *Sohn* in German, *sön* in Danish, *zoon* in Dutch, and so on with a large part of our vocabulary. This leads us to infer that there was once a Germanic mother-language from which these words have descended independently in different tribes;

COGNATES AND BORROWED WORDS 161

and this is established by much historical evidence, though we have not (as in the case of the Romance tongue) the mother-language actually preserved (as Latin is) in ancient documents. The Gothic, a Germanic dialect which was reduced to writing in the fourth century, affords us much assistance in reconstructing the primitive Germanic forms.

Similar processes with other groups of related languages enable us to postulate a number of similar mother-languages, as Celtic (whence Irish and Welsh), Slavic (whence Russian and Bulgarian), Greek (whence various dialects like Attic and Ionic), and so on.

But we can carry our investigations still farther by this method of observing cognate words.

Thus the English *mother* (a Germanic word) is certainly not derived from the Latin *mater*, though it strongly resembles that word, and the same is true of Gr. μήτηρ (*mētēr*), Celt. *mathair*, Russ. *mate*, and Skt. *mātr̥*. No one of these words can be borrowed from any other; yet their similarities are too great to be accidental, and the words must be related in some way. The natural inference is that they are *cognates*, and that Germanic, Latin, Greek, Celtic, Slavic, and Sanskrit are all descended from a single mother-language (the so-called 'Indo-European'), as French, Italian, and Spanish are descended from Latin. Such an inference is established beyond cavil by the multitude of correspondences which these languages show.

Where this Indo-European mother-language was first spoken nobody knows. The 'home of the Aryans' was once thought to be somewhere in Asia, but this is extremely doubtful. Nor is the question important. We are only certain that the family which it has produced extended from Ireland in the West to India in the East, including almost all the languages of Europe, and several important Asiatic tongues. The nature of the movements which spread the Indo-European over so large an area is also obscure enough. We may be sure, however, that they were excessively complicated, including almost every possible means by which one tribe may influence another. Collectively, they are often styled the Indo-European Migration, but we must take care not to accept all that this term may seem to imply. Identity of language does not always mean identity of race. We know of many instances in which a whole people has given up its language : the Celts, for example, in Gaul ; the Iberians in Spain ; the Franks and the Normans in France ; the Normans in England ; the Danes in East Anglia. Sometimes the conqueror communicates his speech to the conquered ; at other times (as with the Normans), the victors adopt the language of those whom they have subdued. There are 'migrations of culture,' as well as migrations of tribes, and sometimes a very little leaven suffices to leaven a large lump. No schematic account of the Indo-European migration can be right in all its details, and however complicated the scheme which scholarly ingenuity may devise, the truth, if we could discover it, would be much more complicated. Still, we can tabulate the Indo-European Family of Languages as follows : —

I. Indian. (Sanskrit, Pali, etc.)
II. Iranian. (Avestan, Old Persian, etc.)
III. Armenian.
IV. Greek.
V. Italic. (Latin, with its descendants the Romance languages, — Italian, French, Spanish, etc.; Oscan, Umbrian, etc.)
VI. Celtic. (Irish and Highland Gaelic, Welsh and Armorican.)

VII. Slavonic. (Russian, Bulgarian, Polish, Bohemian, etc.)
VIII. Baltic. (Lithuanian, Lettish, Old Prussian.)
IX. Teutonic or Germanic.
    A. East Germanic   (Gothic.)
    B. Scandinavian.   (Icelandic, Dano-Norwegian, Swedish.)
    C. West Germanic.
        a. High Germanic.   (German.)
        b. Low Germanic. (Old Frisian, Anglo-Saxon, Old Saxon, Old Frankish; Frisian, English, Plattdeutsch, Dutch, Flemish.)

The position of our own language in this table should be carefully observed. It belongs to the Low or Coast division of the West Germanic dialects, as German belongs to the High or Inland division of these dialects. Thus it is more closely related to Frisian, Dutch, Flemish, and *Plattdeutsch*[1] than to German. Besides the West Germanic dialects, the Teutonic branch includes East Germanic (Gothic) and Scandinavian, to both of which English is allied, but less closely than to the West Germanic languages. Finally, the Germanic group as a whole is akin to every other branch of the Indo-European family. We must, therefore, expect to find in any Germanic language — English, for instance — a multitude of native words which show similarities to Latin and Greek, for example, not because they are taken from the classic tongues (as so many of our words are), but by virtue of the common descent of all these from the Indo-European parent speech. Thus our word *guest*, which once meant 'stranger,' and the Latin *hostis*, 'enemy,' are the same word, but neither is borrowed from the other; they are cognates. Similarly, *six* and *seven* are akin to *sex* and *septem*, *knee* to *genu*, *fish* to *piscis*, *father* to *pater*, *yoke* to

---

[1] 'Low German' in the special sense.

jugum, and so on with a large proportion of the native element in our speech. These correspondences are sometimes striking even to the casual observer, — as in *six* and *sex*, for example, — at other times it requires considerable knowledge of the subject to perceive them. Since Latin is in one sense an older language than our own (though from another point of view all Indo-European languages are equally old, as being independently descended from the parent stock), we expect to find the words less decayed in Latin than in English, especially modern English, which has undergone so many changes since the Anglo-Saxon time. But this is not always the case, for different Indo-European peoples have had different habits of linguistic conservatism. Thus our word *snow* shows an Indo-European initial *s* which the Latin *(s)nix, nivis,* and the Greek (σ)νίφα, *(s)nípha*, have lost, and so in many instances.

Comparison of cognates has shown that the changes in human speech, arbitrary as they seem to be, proceed in accordance with definite and ascertainable laws. For any united body of people form certain habits of utterance which affect their whole language in a remarkably uniform way, so that — when these are once discovered — one can predict with reasonable certainty what form the original word will take in a given dialect. Thus we find that it was the unconscious habit of the Spanish provincials to change Latin *f* to *h* at the beginning of a word, so that *fabulare*, 'to speak,' became *hablár*, *facere* became *hacér*, and so on. Hence we look for the Latin *falco*, 'falcon,' under *h* in the Spanish dictionary, and find it appearing as *halcón; formosus* appears as *hermóso*, and so on. Such habits, or 'laws of sound-change,' are equally noticeable in studying the development of the various Indo-European languages from the parent-speech. They may be followed

COGNATES AND BORROWED WORDS 165

out in minute detail, and their existence and regularity have made Comparative Grammar almost an exact science.

It is in great part our knowledge of such laws as this that enables us to distinguish with precision between cognates and borrowed words. For when a word is simply taken by one language from another, it suffers at first comparatively little change in its form. Thus we know that the Indo-European *p* was preserved in Latin but became *f* in Germanic, — and this makes it easy to recognize the Latin *pecus* and our *fee* as cognates, — that is, as the common descendants of an Indo-European word. Both originally meant 'cattle,' a sense which the Latin has kept, while in English *fee* has come to mean 'property' in general, and has then suffered further changes of meaning. Similarly we recognize *piscis* and *fish* as cognates. When, however, we find *piscatorial* in English, and *piscatorius* in Latin, we have no hesitation in recognizing the former as borrowed from the latter, and so in thousands of instances.

We have said that Comparative Grammar is *almost* an exact science. The qualification is necessary, for appearances are deceitful, in linguistics as in life, and phenomena have to be examined with the greatest care, even when all the facts are in our possession, which is rarely the case. As an example of the difficulties that beset the investigator, take the so-called 'New England ŏ.' It is well known that the long sound of *o* represented by *oa* in *road*, tends, in the natural speech of New England, to become a short open *o*, difficult for those who are unfamiliar with it to imitate, but equally hard for a born Yankee to avoid. Thus we have cŏat, tŏad, lŏad, bŏat, and so on. We should at once infer that a New Englander would say gŏat, but in fact, this word is never so pronounced, but is always *gōat*, without the shortening. The reason is clear enough in this case, for the phenomena are all recent, and the facts are known. The goat is not a familiar animal in this region, so that the name for it is rather a literary than a popular word; it is not properly *in* the dialect, and hence does not share in its peculiarities. The tendency in question had thus no opportunity to make itself felt as in *cŏat* and *tŏad*, which every child learns not from books, but from common talk. Suppose, however, we were dealing with a word that became obsolete two or three thousand years ago. We should be at a loss to account for the 'exception to the law,' and might even be tempted to provide *goat* with some strange etymology or ascribe a peculiar quality to its vowel in order to explain the facts.

Furthermore, there are many opportunities for analogy and for hybrids and cross-breedings in language. Thus our *nephew* is, in a manner, both a native and a borrowed word. In Anglo-Saxon it was *nefa* (*f* pronounced as *v*), and this is cognate with the Latin *nepos, nepotis*. The French *neveu*, however, which is the Latin word in a decayed form, influenced the English word, and the result is our *nephew*, which is neither Anglo-Saxon nor French, but an amalgam of both. Such processes as this may have been operative at any time in the history of the Indo-European family, and their action interferes a good deal with the certainty of prehistoric etymologizing.

Still, when all deductions have been made, there remains enough that is regular and undoubted to substantiate the claim of Comparative Grammar to be a true science. It has occupied some of the keenest intellects among scholars during the past century, and the results justify us in speaking with great confidence about the relations of the Indo-European tongues to each other and to the parent-speech which has been obsolete for so many thousand years. These results afford the only firm basis for investigating the history of words. In particular, they enable us to reason with assurance about certain very ancient processes in the growth of the inflectional languages, as we shall have to do in the next chapter.

CHAPTER XIII

THE DEVELOPMENT OF WORDS

I. ROOTS, STEMS, INFLECTION[1]

THE origin of language, as we have already seen, is an unsolved problem; yet the study of single words reveals many facts about the development of their form which make the question of their origin at least a simpler one. We find in our own words, on comparing them with other languages from which they have been borrowed or which have had a common origin with our own, certain obvious joints, as it were, which show clearly that the words have been built up of simpler elements by a process of aggrega-

[1] This chapter sets forth the main principles that have governed the development of words, *as to their form*, in our family of languages. For the sake of clearness, distinctions have been somewhat sharply made, and cautionary provisos have been omitted whenever there was danger that they would rather confuse than enlighten. Any orderly statement of these phenomena must be somewhat misleading; for, though the development of language is in general what is indicated, no single process ceased to act at the moment when another process began. The actual operations of speech-making in the Indo-European family must have been almost unimaginably complicated. The most minutely scientific investigation can arrive at only a part of the truth. A general outline must therefore be content to omit qualifications and parentheses. In particular, however, the reader should remember that the growth of stems did not immediately put an end to the root-period, and that the rise of inflection did not instantly put an end to the development of stems. Everything was gradual. The old processes survived alongside of the new, and only died out after long periods of time.

A further caution is necessary. The principles here set forth accord with the accepted results of philological science. In other words, they

THE DEVELOPMENT OF WORDS

tion or combination; that is, we find in the words certain sounds (letters or syllables) which appear elsewhere in other combinations, always with essentially the same significance. It seems justifiable to conclude that these parts were once independent, and were afterward put together, just as we might infer with reference to frame and strings, handle and blade, wheel and axle, or the parts of any other complex tool. To these component parts in their last analysis we give the name of *roots*. Of these roots we find two kinds: (1) roots which express actions, states, qualities, and other definite conceptions, and (2) roots which express less definite conceptions, such as place, direction, and the like. To the first class we give the name of *verbal roots*, because they seem to carry the idea expressed in verbs, though they are in fact no more

furnish the most probable explanation of linguistic phenomena, as the Copernican astronomy is the simplest hypothesis yet found to account for the phenomena of the heavens. Some details, however, are by no means settled. Thus the exact nature of stem-suffixes is far from certain. It is convenient to call them 'pronominal roots,' but we should remember that what seems to us a simple stem-suffix may be merely a fragment of a longer root, or even a remnant of another fully developed stem. Furthermore, the forms given to roots are simply such forms as we can infer from the fully developed words. We are by no means sure of the actual forms of these roots at the time when they alone constituted language; nor can we be sure that everything that seems to be a root actually goes back to this root-period in any form. Again, in selecting words to illustrate stem-formation, composition, and the like, we cannot always know that the example is old enough to belong to the period which we use it to illustrate. It may have been formed long afterward on the analogy of older formations of the stem-period which set the fashion for later derivation and composition. All these are questions of importance in a minutely scientific study of single roots and stems. But they do not affect the main theory of linguistic development, and hence they are of no immediate consequence in a brief outline of the subject.

One point, however, should never be lost sight of: in spite of the distinctions we have to make between stem-formation, word-composition, derivation, and inflection, these processes are all substantially identical. They are all *composition* in the larger sense of the word.

verbal than nominal in their significance. To the second class we give the name of *pronominal roots*, because a great number of them occur in pronouns, and because they seem to express ideas of a relative nature, such as are found in pronouns and indefinite adverbs. There are many apparent elements which we cannot surely assign to either class, and it is doubtful whether the distinction is fundamental. It is not certain whether at some period in the development of language either kind could not be used in place of the other. For instance, the first *i* in *itinerary* is called a verbal root because it means 'go' in many languages (as in L. *ire*, Gr. ἰέναι, *iénai*), while the first *i* in *iteration* is called pronominal, because it often appears in pronominal words, such as *it* and the like. Yet it seems probable that these two roots were once identical, and so with many others.

The process of aggregation indicated above seems not to have been promiscuous and at haphazard, but orderly and proceeding in a definite manner. In most instances we find the root of the first kind at the beginning of words, amplified by the addition of one or more roots of the second kind. Of course some words of the pronominal sort contain no verbal root, and in this case they consist of a similar aggregation of pronominal roots; but the more significant and definite words have a verbal root at the beginning. To take the two examples just cited: *itinerary* (L. *itinerarium*) is analyzable into $i + ti + no + er + \bar{a} + ri + (o)$, all except the first found elsewhere as pronominal roots; and *iteration* (L. *iteratio*) may be broken up into $i + ti + ro + \bar{a} + ti + \bar{o}n$, all found as pronominal. These examples illustrate the two forms of combination that are regular in our family of languages.

A *root*, then, is the simplest form that can be recognized

THE DEVELOPMENT OF WORDS 171

as having once had an independent existence and meaning in the development of words.

As these roots are common to many words of very different senses, it is sometimes difficult to distinguish what was the original conception that a root expressed. Accordingly we assign to each root that meaning from which it is possible to develop all the various ideas attached to the words in which it appears. This sense is often very vague, and it becomes a question how a primitive people, whose ideas are closely connected with the senses, could be satisfied with such representations of ideas as these. The answer is, that a conception that is very graphic to the senses may include a great variety of associated ideas which it may represent. For example, the root PET seems vague to us. It is defined as 'fall, fly, aim,' and clearly shows all these varied senses in its different forms and derivatives. Yet the root may have originally stood for a 'motion in a certain direction through the air'—a very graphic and sensible conception, from which the other meanings were specialized as time went on. The cause, or else the result, of such motion might be either 'falling,' 'flight,' or 'aim,' and so the same sound PET could express either of these ideas. So with DUC, 'lead,' AG, 'drive,' ED, 'eat,' PA, 'drink,' CAD, 'fall,' and many others. It is not necessary that we should consider such signs as representing nouns or verbs. It is probable that the distinction had not been developed in the root-period, and that a sign could be used for either or both, just as a child can employ any word that he knows for anything that he wants to say about the thing or its associated ideas.[1] From this con-

---

[1] Here the potency of significant tones and inflections of the voice may well be taken into account as a means of distinction. Gestures may also have helped to indicate the special sense in some instances.

sideration of roots and their meaning it is evident that roots are no mere abstractions, though they now have to be dug out, or abstracted, from words by comparison, and no longer exist independently in actual speech. They once did so exist, and expressed thought.

The next step in linguistic growth is the formation of *stems*, which takes place long before the development of what we call inflection. Stems came into existence by the union of verbal and pronominal roots. That is to say, the vague meaning and general application of the verbal root were limited or specialized by the addition of one or more pronominal roots, and thus was produced a new complex (the stem) capable of being used for the conveyance of ideas in the same manner as the root, but with a greater definiteness of meaning. Stems are not yet *words*, and hence we must not expect to find them existing *separately* in any language, for all these processes precede the formation of real words as we know them. Yet stems may still be clearly seen in the first part of compound words. Thus the stem *agro-* (root AG + *ro*), which meant (vaguely) 'field' is seen in the Greek compound word ἀγρο-νόμος (*agro-nómos*), 'inhabiting the country,' and, in the form *agri-*, in the Latin *agri-cola*, 'farmer' (literally 'field-cultivator'). This form *agro-* (*agri-*) nowhere exists by itself, but it must once have so existed, or it could not have been used in making compounds. The second part of the compound *agri-cola* is from the stem *colā-* (root COL + *ā*). Similarly *armi-ger* is made up of two stems *armo-* (from AR + *mo*), and *gero* (from GER + *o*).

Since stems are not words, and no such thing as syntax existed in the stem-period, we cannot designate stems as parts of speech, — nouns, verbs, and so on. Yet there was doubtless sufficient specialization to differentiate stems in

THE DEVELOPMENT OF WORDS 173

a vague way as nominal or verbal, — so that one stem vaguely suggested (like *agro-* or *armo-*) the name of a thing, another (like *colā-* or *gero-*) produced an idea more active in its nature, a partly verbal idea. Yet nouns and verbs as such could hardly exist before the inflectional period. In the stem-period, it was still possible to express a verbal idea by a stem which seems to us chiefly nominal, and *vice versa*. This state of things accounts for certain phenomena which seem anomalous to the young student of grammar. Thus in Latin a noun *tactio*, 'the act of touching,' may sometimes govern the accusative case : as, *hanc tactio*, 'the act of touching her,' where *hanc* is the object of the verbal idea contained in the noun *tactio*. In English a whole class of nouns (the so-called verbal nouns in *-ing*) have this power. Thus in such a sentence as 'Eating fruit is good for the health,' *eating* is a noun; yet it has sufficient verbal force to take *fruit* as its object.[1]

Sometimes a stem was formed by merely repeating the root, as the Italian uses *piano piano*, the French *beau beau*, or a child *goody goody*, to express a high degree of the idea intended. Examples are found in all reduplicated words like *murmur*, L. *turtur*, 'turtle dove,' and also (much modified) in such forms of reduplication as *momordi*, 'I have bitten,' used for inflectional purposes.[2]

A stem, then, is a complex of sounds expressing an idea,

---

[1] Our infinitive is also an old noun; yet we feel it as a verb even when its nominal nature is clearest : as in ' *To eat* fruit is good for the health.' Compare also the old idiom in ' What went ye out *for to see ?* '

[2] So Latin *sisto* shows a reduplication of the root STA seen in the simpler verb *sto*. Usually the first part of the reduplication is that which has been modified. Sometimes, however, it is the second, and we get what is called ' broken reduplication,' as in *gargle* (connected with L. *gurgulio*, ' gullet') ; cf. *gargoyle*.

and ready for composition and inflection, but *not yet subjected to either.*[1]

The endings which were added to roots to make stems such as we have been describing were very simple elements, such as *-o, -ā, -u, -vo, -ko, -no, -tu,* and the like. The stems themselves were later more or less specialized in sense; but originally they must have been, from the nature of the materials out of which they were formed, pretty indefinite in their signification. Many of them had a kind of adjective nature, expressing in a loose and indeterminate way almost any relation between the primitive idea of the root and some other conception or conceptions to which the stem might be applied.

The system must have attained an enormous development before words, as such, came into existence. Thus there were produced in this prehistoric period of language an immense number of such vague adjective stem-forms, many of which have survived in the languages of our family, with their senses somewhat specialized, but, in accordance with their origin, preserving (even after they have become definite parts of speech) much of their original vagueness, so that they easily acquire new special meanings as time goes on. There was also a tendency to add further stem-endings of a similar sort to stems already formed; and by this heaping up of stem-suffixes, new suffixes came into existence, and new and more complicated stems were constantly growing

---

[1] Though the stem-period of language is said to follow the root-period, it must be remembered that the development of stems did not immediately put an end to the independent existence of roots. In fact, the root-period in a manner extends throughout the stem-period, for roots were often used as stems without the addition of pronominal (stem) suffixes. Indeed, except for clearness, it would be better to regard the stem-period as merely a second stage of the root-period.

THE DEVELOPMENT OF WORDS 175

up.[1] Thus arose the system of derivative endings (such as *-er*, *-ness*, *-est*, and so on), which is still one of the most prolific sources of new words in our language.[2]

The original vagueness of all such stem-formations may be seen in the senses which the resultant words bear in even the most highly developed periods of cultivated languages. The adjective *fox-y*, for instance, may be applied to anything resembling a fox either in color, in actions, or in craft. A better example may be seen in a number of words derived from the root PAK, 'to feed.' First we have L. *pecu*, 'a flock.' From this comes *peculium*, (1) 'a little part of the flock reserved for the slave's private property,' or (2) 'a little garden-plot given to a child.' Then we have the adjective *peculiaris*, 'belonging or pertaining in any way to this little part of the flock,' and hence comes the idea of *peculiar*, in its variety of applications: as in 'my peculiar (*i.e.* personal) property,' 'the Lord's peculiar people,' 'a peculiar institution,' 'peculiar notions,' 'a peculiar fellow,' 'the story seems somewhat peculiar.' Then, by further growth, we get the abstract noun *peculiarity*. So *familiaris* means originally 'belonging to the *familia* or household,' and we easily get *familiar* in its different shades of meaning, and *familiarity* and *familiarly*. All this shows how vague the

---

[1] This multiplication of suffixes is especially seen in the languages that (like Greek and Latin) received literary cultivation at an early period. The more 'barbarous' tongues, not feeling the need of so many or so finely discriminated words, escaped this tendency. Thus in the Teutonic languages we usually have shorter words than in Latin. The English vocabulary consists of two large classes of words, — Teutonic (from Anglo-Saxon) and Latin (from Latin and French); hence we can see this difference in the component parts of our own speech.

[2] The details of this system will be studied later. Here it is only intended to suggest the general principles of development.

connection of meaning between the primitive form and its various derivative stems must have been. The processes are all easy and natural, but very little is actually expressed in each step of derivation. All that was needed was a loose connection with the primitive idea; the imagination and the conventions of speech have done the rest.[1]

All the processes which we have so far studied are processes of *composition*, that is, they consist in the combination of significant elements to make a new complex of a somewhat different meaning. But we have not yet considered composition in the ordinary sense, — that process which results in giving us compound words, like *butterfly*, *torchbearer*, *railroad*, and the like. The type for such formations goes back to the stem-period: that is, though we now make new compounds by putting together distinct *words*, we do so in accordance with a method which developed when there were no words, properly so called, but only stems.

Stems, as we have seen, early become somewhat differentiated, so that it is possible to speak of nominal and verbal stems, though the distinction was not by any means so sharp as that between our nouns and verbs. Many stems, as we have also seen, had a kind of vague adjective signification. An important step in linguistic development was taken when two stems, thus differentiated, were juxtaposed, and finally united into a single complex stem-form, or compound, having a sense far more definite than attached to either stem alone. This is *composition*, which has remained one of the commonest

---

[1] Compare what has been said of the poetic faculty as the most active influence in linguistic development (pp. 7 ff.).

means of manufacturing new words in our family of languages.

By this process of stem-composition a kind of rudimentary syntax arose. Thus, the stem *colā-* (the root COL + *ā*) meant vaguely a 'cultivator.' To this was prefixed the stem *agri-* (*agro-*), 'a field,' and the compound *agri-colā-* signified vaguely the kind of cultivator that stood in some relation to a field. Of course this could only mean what we should express syntactically in the form 'the cultivator of a field,' or 'one who cultivates the field,' or 'a man who tills the soil.' Thus this stem-compound *agri-colā-* served, before there was any such thing as syntax, to suggest by association of ideas the sense which syntax now definitely expresses. So L. *lucifer* (stem *luci-fero-*) means 'light-bearer,' 'one who brings light,' L. *auceps* (stem *avi-cap-*), 'he who catches birds,' and so on. Of course, we actually know such stem-compounds only in a later form, — as real words (*agricola* being the Latin word for 'farmer'). Hence we cannot be sure that any particular example is old enough to go back to the stem-period. But this makes no difference for our present purpose. Compounds made after the end of the stem-period simply followed the model of the older forms, and are equally good to illustrate the principles under discussion. That the suggestions conveyed by the complexes in question were originally far more vague than they seem to us, and that the meanings of the stems of which they are composed were therefore still more vague, may be seen by examining a number of compound words in English. It will at once appear that the relation of the two ideas to each other varies widely in different compounds. Thus we have *butterball*, a ball that consists of butter; *butterfly*, a fly that is yellow like butter; *buttermilk*, the milk that remains after the butter has been made; *buttertub*, a tub in which butter is kept; *butterwoman*, a woman who sells butter; *butterfingers*, a person whose fingers are slippery so that he cannot hold anything, a careless person. Compare also the variety shown in *hodman, ashman (dustman), motorman, milkman, fisherman, shipman, clergyman*.[1] The hodman *carries* the hod; the ashman or dustman *collects* and *takes away* ashes; the motorman *manages* the motor; the milkman *distributes* milk; the fisherman *is* a fisher; the shipman *sails in* a ship; the clergyman *belongs to* the clergy.

We see that language, even in the highly developed stage in which we know it, suggests much more than it expresses. We may learn the same lesson from any conversation. It is seldom necessary to hear the whole of a sentence in order to know what the speaker means. Such considerations make it easy to comprehend how language was intelligible enough before the dawn of syntax.

We have now traced the history of language through its earliest ascertainable periods. Beginning with roots, the simplest elements, we have traced the development of simple stems, and have seen some of the ways in which these became more complicated by the addition of further suffixes and by composition. All this, however, is intensely prehistoric. We have not yet arrived at *words* independently usable as such, and we have therefore no proper syntax. A further step is necessary, — namely *inflection*, and this we must now consider.

The phenomenon of inflection consists in the addition

[1] *Man* in these words has sunk almost to the rank of a mere suffix, so that the compounds illustrate the essential identity of the processes that we are studying.

to stems of certain suffixes which so limit the application of the stems in various ways, that they are capable of combining syntactically in sentences to express all those distinctions of time, place, action, existence, manner, description, and the like, which we include under the grammatical terms of *parts of speech*, *mood*, *tense*, *gender*, *active*, *passive*, and the rest. We have no actual knowledge of any language of our family at a period antedating inflection. In fact, at the earliest stage of the Indo-European parent-speech at which we can arrive with scientific certainty, the language was already highly inflected. Yet we may feel confident of the general nature of the process which advanced language from the stem-period to the period of inflection and syntax. Like all the processes which we have been studying, this, too, was essentially a process of *composition*.

In compound words, as we can observe in our own habits of speech, there is often a tendency to clip or sink the less important member. Thus *man* in *fisherman*, *workman*, *clergyman*, is less fully pronounced than when it stands alone. Yet the abrasion has not disassociated the *man* in *fisherman* from the ordinary word *man*; we still recognize the identity of the two. In *king-dom*, however, we no longer recognize the last syllable *-dom* as identical with our word *doom* (A.S. *dōm*), partly because of the abrasion, and partly because of a difference in sense. The *-dom* in *kingdom*, then, has sunk to the position of a mere *suffix*. We should never suspect that it had once been an independent word. This abrasion is still more marked in *-ly*, which is the Anglo-Saxon *-lĭcĕ*, our *like*, but which, though it keeps the sense which it had when it was a word, has become a pure suffix. We add *-ly* to an adjective to form an adverb, just as we add *-er* and *-est* to form the comparative and the superlative, or *-ing* to a verb to form a present participle or a verbal noun.

We may suppose that inflectional forms were gained in a similar manner during the stem-period, — that is, by processes of petrified and abraded composition, — though in these inflections we can no longer identify the component parts. Occasional phenomena in later periods of linguistic history tend to substantiate this view. Thus the English ending *-est*, in the second person of verbs (as in *bindest, runnest*) occurs in Anglo-Saxon both as *-est* and as *-es*. The form in *-es* is the older; that in *-est* came from the habit of suffixing the pronoun *thū*, 'thou.' Hence *bindes thū* became *bindestū*, and the *t*, which really belonged to the pronoun, was felt as a part of the verb, so that in time *bindest* replaced *bindes* as the regular form. The same thing has taken place in High German. A somewhat similar example occurs in recent 'vulgar English.' *Let's* for *let us* is often pronounced *less*, which has, in the mouths of ignorant speakers, become a petrified hortative form, — so that 'less us go' is frequently heard.

How easily inflection may grow out of composition may also be seen in such a form as *heavenward*. Here *-ward* is a suffix (cognate with L. *verto*) denoting 'to.' Nobody feels it as an independent word, yet it certainly was such at one time. It is used in making adverbs of direction from nouns; but we can easily imagine its having become so universal as to be attached at will to any noun to indicate 'direction toward,' — and if this had taken place, *-ward* would have become practically a case-suffix, expressing the 'limit of motion' (like the Latin accusative ending in *Romam*).

By these processes of composition and abrasion, then, there grew up in the Indo-European family a great number of inflectional forms, indicating the relations of words within the sentence, and other general modifications of word-meaning, such as time, place, manner, and the like. These inflections denoted three genders, eight or nine cases, three numbers, three voices, five moods, seven tenses with three numbers and three persons.

These inflections, so far as they were used in verbs, began early, it may be from the very outset, to be confused together, so that they do not all appear distinctly in any Indo-European tongue. Thus, as we might expect from the shifting and occasional nature of speech itself, some forms are wanting to a complete scheme, and many others might be imagined, or are found in other families, which would be convenient, but of which there is no trace among the Indo-Europeans. Indeed, the whole process seems to have gone on *pro re nata*, a new form being essayed only when a need was felt for it. It should be remembered that our grammatical paradigms are long subsequent to the forms of which they consist, and that the first makers of grammar did not know they had any grammar, any more than the makers of history are aware that they are making history. Still, we must not suppose that our inflections came into being at haphazard or without system. That pervasive influence which we call the *Sprachgefühl*[1] must always have exerted a controlling effect on the action of the early language-makers, just as it does upon us to-day.

It is a significant fact that there are many inflectional forms in the Indo-European family that never seem to have been gathered into a scheme at all, but were variants from the first, though of course these may also be remnants of a more complete scheme still. Such is the

[1] See p. 126.

Sanskrit *-tas*, used as an ablative, and we may compare adverbs like *thereby, therefrom*. In general, adverbs are survivals of lost forms of inflection; but often their original form cannot be recognized, and there will always be reason for uncertainty whether they were ever real cases, as is commonly supposed.

Few inflections survive in ordinary English: *-s* and *-es* in the genitive and the plural of nouns; *-en* in a few plurals; *-es* (*-s*), *-ed* (*-d, -t*) in verbs; *-ing, -ed*, and *-en* in participles, and a few remnants in pronouns, almost complete the list of our living inflectional suffixes. Yet the earlier history of our language, and comparison with other Germanic tongues, especially the Gothic, a Germanic dialect which was reduced to writing in the fourth century, reveal the fact that English belongs to a highly inflected family, other members of which are Sanskrit, Greek, Latin, and the Iranian, Slavic, and Celtic languages. Not only has there been a steady decay of inflections since the Anglo-Saxon period, but we find that the language of the Angles and Saxons themselves was already far gone in the same process. The relations may be conveniently seen by a comparative table of the preterite of *have*.

GOTHIC
Indicative

	SINGULAR	DUAL	PLURAL
1st Person.	habai-da	habai-dêdu	habai-dêdum
2d "	habai-dês	habai-dêduts	habai-dêduth
3d "	habai-da		habai-dêdun

Subjunctive (Optative)

	SINGULAR	DUAL	PLURAL
1st Person.	habai-dêdjau	habai-dêdeiva	habai-dêdeima
2d "	habai-dêdeis	habai-dêdeits	habai-dêdeith
3d "	habai-dêdi		habai-dêdeina

Anglo-Saxon	Chaucer	Modern English
	Indicative	
1. hæfde	hadde	had
2. hæfdes(t)	haddest	had
3. hæfde	hadde	had
Plural 1, 2, 3. hæfdon	hadde(n)	had
	Subjunctive	
1. hæfde	hadde	had
2. hæfde	haddest	had
later hæfdest		
3. hæfde	hadde	had
Plural 1, 2, 3. hæfden	hadde(n)	had

Observe that the Anglo-Saxon has lost the dual number altogether, and that the subjunctive forms differ very slightly from the indicative. In Chaucer the indicative and the subjunctive have become identical. In modern English the whole complicated system is reduced to a single form, *had*, which serves for all the persons and numbers of both the indicative and subjunctive. The contrast with the fully inflected Gothic is startling. *Our 'had,' in the preterite, takes the place of fifteen distinct forms in the fourth-century Gothic.* Decay of inflections could hardly go farther.

The development of our family of languages, then, proceeds from simple elements of vague meanings to an elaborate system of inflections, nicely differentiated to express a great variety of ideas and relations. No sooner is this great system built up, however, than it begins to go to pieces, until, in our own speech, there are scarcely any inflections remaining. This decay, as we have seen, may coincide with an enormous advance in civilization. Our ancient relatives, the Goths of the fourth century, were as much our inferiors in complexity of civilization as our language is inferior to theirs in complexity of inflectional forms. At first this seems paradoxical,— but only at first. The decay is merely formal; it has in no way impaired the expressive power of our language. The Goths used fifteen distinct forms of *have* in the preterite, some of them extending to twelve letters; we have a single form *had*, three letters in length, to perform the functions of the whole fifteen. Yet this one short form proves to be entirely competent for the task imposed upon it. There has been no loss, but an incalculable gain,— the gain involved in accomplishing a given result with an enormous economy of effort. The apparent demolition is only the destruction of a scaffolding that is useless after the building is finished, or— to change the figure — a short cut adopted instead of a roundabout road when the landmarks are so well known that there is no fear of losing one's way.

CHAPTER XIV

THE DEVELOPMENT OF WORDS

II. DERIVATION AND COMPOSITION

WE have already considered the beginnings of composition and derivation, and have observed that these processes are essentially identical, and that inflection is but a special result of their operations. The importance of the two processes, however, makes it necessary to study them further, even at the risk of a certain amount of repetition.

The enormous system of derivational endings (like *-ness*, *-ship*, *-dom*, *-ty*, *-ly*, *-ish*, *-ic*, etc.) which characterizes our family of languages is the result of the slow operation of the forces already described, extending over thousands of years, and acting in every period of our linguistic history, from the remote 'Indo-European' times to the present day. New stems were made, as we have seen, by the addition of modifying forms, either verbal or pronominal (chiefly the latter), all in themselves once significant.

The development of the endings is easily traced by means of modern analogies. *Home-like* is a recent formation, both parts of which are recognizable as independent elements preserving their full significance. There is no difference between the word *home-like* and the phrase *like home*. An older *homelike*, however, which has, by decay of the second element, become *homely*, is no longer recognized as a compound, and has acquired new meanings quite different from those which the full form *home-like* conveys to our minds. The second syllable is no longer felt as an independent word. It has become an effete adjective suffix of wide application,—as in *ruffianly*, *ghastly*, *ghostly*, *fleshly*, *goodly*, *comely*. Another form of *-like* has in a similar way become a universal termination for the manufacture of adverbs from adjectives,—as *truly*, *beautifully*, *elegantly*, *terribly*, *willingly*, and so on *ad infinitum*. All the suffixes in our language have a similar history. The beginnings of the process, however, lie so far back that we cannot be sure of the original forms of many suffixes; and we are certain that the oldest of them lie within the root and stem period, and hence were not words, but roots, verbal and pronominal (chiefly the latter). But that makes no difference in the principle. The essence of the matter is that a significant element, originally independent, is added to another element, and that, as time goes on, the second loses its identity and comes to be a mere derivational ending, widely applicable in the formation of new units of expression. After the advent of inflection, these units are no longer stems, but words, though stem-forms long continue to be usable as the material for composition and derivation. Finally, as in English, all feeling for stems disappears, and full-fledged words are freely compounded. The tendency of the second member to lose its identity still continues, and the production of derivational suffixes goes on.

Our language has a huge number of derivational suffixes, native and borrowed. Some of these are still alive, —that is, they may be used at will to make new words. Such are *-ly*, *-ness*, *-ish*, *-y*. Others are dead,— that is, though still felt as suffixes, and existing in a considerable number of words, they can no longer be used as formative elements. Thus, *-ant* (a French descendant of the Latin participial ending *-ans, -antis*) is visible in *militant, recalcitrant, reluctant, rampant, blatant*, and so on, but we have no power to make a new word in *-ant*. Contrast with this the native suffix *-ing*, which is fully alive. If a new verb like *to railroad* is manufactured (see p. 191), we are able, at will, to form a noun from it, and to speak of 'the *railroading* of a bill through the House of Representatives.'

Some of our derivational suffixes may be traced back to their independent existence as words. Such are *-dom* (the same as *doom*), *-hood* (A.S. *hād*, 'station,' 'condition'), *-ly* ('like'). Most of them, however, are known only as suffixes. Such are *-ish, -ness, -y, -ty, -ing, -ling, -ic, -ical*, and many others.

New suffixes sometimes arise from a mistake in the application of old ones, the termination being cut off behind its ears, as it were. Thus, having borrowed the word *habitable* which is properly *habita+ble* (L. *-bilis*), we conceive the ending as *-able* and make *saleable, eatable* (cf. *edible*), and *bearable*. (See pp. 293-4.)

The development of prefixes is parallel to that of suffixes; but the number of genuine prefixes is much smaller. Most of the prefixes now in use were really independent words associated syntactically with verbs after the beginning of the inflectional period (see p. 188). Of living prefixes *un-, re-, out-, semi-*, and *half-*, may be specially noted.

Besides the old stem-compounds and the word-compounds that are their descendants or collateral relatives, there are also many compounds which belong to a later stage of linguistic development, being formed by the growing together of phrases or syntactic complexes. Of this kind are all verbs compounded with prepositions or similar particles. These prefixes were originally adverbs, which, from being habitually used with verbs, have become necessary to the sense, and have accordingly united with the verb to make a single unit. Thus we have the native verbs *undergo*, *outdo*, *forego*, *withstand*, etc., besides a very large number of similar formations borrowed from Latin or French : as,—*transcend, admit, deter, depose, adjoin.* The Greek has furnished us with a good many words of similar character,—*hypo-crite, hyper-phosphite, meta-thesis,* and so, in a less degree, of other languages.

Native phrase-compounds are *beside* (for *by-side*), *betimes* (for *by-times*), *undershot, overlord, outlaw, outdoor,* and so on. We may compare *meanwhile, meantime, henceforth, forthright, towards, offhand, throughout, wherewith, therein, himself, oftentimes, somewhere,*[1] *somewhat, everybody, nobody,* and many others, originally phrases, and still easily taken apart. Longer examples are *rough-and-ready, well-to-do, matter-of-fact, tooth and nail, devil-may-care, through and through, by-and-by, inside out,* and so on,—some of which are still felt as phrases rather than as single compound words. So we use the old greeting 'Hail, fellow, well-met!' (*i.e.* 'Health to you, companion! Glad to meet you!') as an adjective to describe one who is familiar with everybody he falls in with. We may even attach derivative suffixes to long phrase compounds, as in *lackadaisical* (from *lack-a-daisy,* an elaborated form of *lack-a-day,* i.e. *alack-a-day*),[2] *alamodeness* (William Penn), and

[1] The provincial *some-place* for *somewhere* (as in 'I have seen him *some-place*') shows how strongly *somewhere* is felt as a phrase rather than as a single word.

[2] *Alack* is doubtless *ah! lack!* the second word being used in the obsolete sense of 'misfortune.'

the colloquial monstrosities *get-at-able* and *go-ahead-itiveness*.

If the phrase is very old, its component parts may be no longer recognizable, and we have a simple word, not a compound at all. Thus *wassail* is the Anglo-Saxon *wes hāl!* 'be well!' a sentence used in drinking healths. The same result is often produced when a foreign phrase is adopted into English. *Aid-de-camp*, *bas-relief*, *belles lettres*, *embonpoint*, *extempore*, *locum tenens* (whence *lieutenant*), are still felt as phrases or phrase-compounds; but *alarm*, *carouse*, *jeopardy*, *kickshaws*, and *hoax* are not so recognized except by the etymologist. *Alarm* (Fr. *alarme*) is the Italian call 'to arms!' (*all' arme!*). *Carouse* is the German *gar aus!* 'quite out!' *i.e.* 'empty your glass.'[1] *Jeopardy* (in Chaucer, *jupartie*) is Fr. *jeu parti*, 'even (*literally*, divided) game,' *i.e.* a game in which the chances are equal. From the noun we have formed a verb, *to jeopardize*. *Kickshaws* is a corruption of Fr. *quelque chose*, 'something'; it was at first singular (plural, *kickshawses*). *Hoax*, which was formerly slang, and is still undignified, though accepted into the legitimate vocabulary, is a shortening of *hocus pocus*. So is *to hocus*, for 'to drug.' *Hocus pocus* seems to be a bit of juggler's mock Latin,—a fragment of a longer formula used by a particular magician in the seventeenth century.

A peculiar form of phrase-composition is found in numerous words consisting of a verb and its object used as names, more commonly of an abusive character. Some of these look like imperative phrases used in ironical address. At any rate, the category must have originated in quotation. This is seen from the peculiar relation of the two

[1] *Carouse* came to us through the French *carous* (later *carrousse*), whence the form of the English word.

parts. Thus, *a spendthrift* is a person who spends what others have saved; so *telltale, do-nothing, ne'er-do-well, dreadnaught, daredevil, singsong, killjoy, makeshift, turncoat, catchpoll, holdback, holdfast, Johnny-jump-up* (the name of a flower), *forget-me-not*. We may compare the subjunctive phrase-compounds *hit or miss, live or die, willy nilly*, used adverbially. Here again, as usual, slang is very fertile: as, *kiss me quick, hug me tight, follow me lads*, names for articles of female attire. The distinctive mark of these is that they have a verb and an object, so that they must not be confounded with a few others which are like them, but can hardly be quotations, such as *catchbasin, turnstile, ramrod*. These seem to arise from a confusion between noun and verb in the first member. Words like *go-between* and *hangdog* are somewhat doubtful.

A curious tendency of our language is that of making virtual new compounds of verbs and prepositions without actual union, not unlike the separative compounds in Homer. This shows itself in neuter (intransitive) verbs, which become capable of having a passive by taking up the preposition which properly governs the following case. Thus one might *speak to a woman*, in which case we should say that *to* governed *woman*, but it would not be surprising if the woman should complain of being *spoken to* in the street. So an adversary may be *reckoned with*, a book *quoted from*, a house *lived in*, a divinity *sworn by*, a man *run through*, or *run over*, or *stared at*, or *despaired of*, or *talked about*, or *looked after*. A doctrine may be *fought against*. An argument may be *insisted on*, or *lost sight of*, and in newspaper English, an opportunity may be *availed of*. Not all sorts of such combinations can be made, for nothing is so freaky as language in new formations by analogy, but many have become good English, and the number is increasing. Perhaps the future antiquarian will revive the figure 'tmesis' to account for the separation of the verb from its preposition in these cases!

The almost entire loss of inflections in English has brought about a curious result in the possibilities of our language, namely, the free interchangeableness of verb and noun. The tendency in this direction is visible very early in our family of languages; but, so long as inflections exist, a verb must be distinguished from a noun by some termination. Hence, though the change of noun to verb has been a universal want, yet it had to be accomplished by means of a system of derivative suffixes gradually adapted to the purpose, and so in like manner of the change from verb to noun. Indeed, so common have these changes and parallelisms been, that in some cases one of the members has been supplied by a false analogy. Thus in French almost all verbs in *-er* have (or once had) a corresponding noun in *-e*: as *voyager*, *voyage*; *ménager*, *ménage*, and the like. Hence, *coucher* (L. *col-locare*) not having a noun to match inasmuch as the noun (*locus*) was never compounded with *con-*, one was made, out of hand, to correspond with the others. Thus the French have the noun *couche*, whence our *couch* is borrowed. As it happens, this proceeding gives a curious combination. The Latin *locus* became *lieu* in French (a word which we have borrowed), so that *couch* and *lieu* are cognates, though they have only a single letter in common.

When inflections are lost, as in English, there is nothing to distinguish the form of verb and noun. Hence any noun or adjective can at once become a verb if employed as such, and conversely almost any verb may be used to express the idea of its action or result.

Thus we have *to cudgel, to powder, to oil, to pipe* (for gas), *to wall in, to brick up, to bell* (the cat), *to metal, to provision, to wood and water, to color, to yellow, to black, to serenade, to paper, to match, to fire, to fringe, to cover* (a book), *to letter, to carpet, to coach, to tutor, to gum, to ground, to varnish, to hedge about, to man, to chaperon, to people, to tar, to plane, to counterfeit.* Indeed, a whole phrase may be used as a verb : *to blackball, to copperbottom, mastheaded.* Conversely are found the nouns : *a sell, a pull up, a setback, a walk-over, an upper cut, a knock-down, a run-over, a spin, a hit;* and many such terms are used even in literary English. In general, however, we are not so free in using verbs as nouns, as in using nouns as verbs. Our inclination is rather to have recourse to derivation by means of nominal suffixes (as in *starvation* from *starve*, and the countless noun-formations in *-ing*), or to employ a readymade synonym from our enormous stock of borrowed words (as *to climb, ascent; to break, fracture*). Thus every part of our complicated vocabulary works together in perfect harmony in the expression of thought in all its varieties.

CHAPTER XV

FOSSILS

A LANGUAGE which is not given to borrowing foreign elements, but develops its vocabulary out of its native resources, makes an immediate impression of consistency. In such a language the same inflectional and derivative endings are almost universally applicable, and composition goes on in accordance with fixed linguistic habits. The formative processes are therefore almost sure to yield words of like character and sound. And, though phonetic decay works incessantly to alter the form of a language, yet the habits of speech are so regular and the associative forces so strong, that words when they change are likely to go in groups or classes, so that they retain the same similarity of sound to each other, though the sound itself may be altered beyond recognition.

In an omnivorous language like English the same forces work, though with slightly less energy. Words are borrowed in blocks, as it were, or — what amounts to the same thing — one after another in the same line merely because a similar word has been borrowed before. We have many long-tailed Latin words in *-osity* and *-ation*, not because they are peculiarly adapted to our tongue, but because, having found a use for a number of them, the language is impelled to borrow more to match those it has already. Notice also the huge quantity of verbs in *-ate* (adapted from Latin past participles in *-atus*). The tendency is helped by the subtle association between sound and meaning which manifests itself in rhyme, alliteration, assonance, and so on, ever attempting to assimilate to each other words which have a similar sense, or to give a similar sense to words that resemble each other in sound. Two examples will make this clear: —

Citizen and *denizen* are old synonyms which have influenced each other's form. *Citizen* is O. Fr. *citeain*[1] (from L. *civitas*); the unoriginal *z* makes its first appearance in Anglo-French and is borrowed from *denizen*, which is O. Fr. *denzein* or *deinzein* (from *denz,* 'within,' modern *dans*). *Denizen*, in its turn, has taken its *i* from *citizen*.

Restive and *restless* are etymologically unrelated. Their similarity of form is quite accidental. *Restive* is from L. *restare*, 'to stand back,' 'to hang back,' and means properly 'unwilling to go forward.' *Restless* is from A.S. *rest*, and means 'refusing to stand still.' Yet the similarity of sound has so brought the words together in our consciousness that *restive* has, in common speech, become a synonym for *restless*, which is properly almost its express opposite.[2]

The tendencies which we have considered operate to keep the parts of a language together, so that words and forms do not stand each by itself, but make larger or smaller groups pretty firmly bound together in our consciousness.

But there is at the same time a strong counter-influence. Thought is constantly tending to individualize this or that expression by ascribing to it an idea or a function which is not shared by the other members of its group. Thus it

[1] Modern *citoyen*. The ending *-ain* is L. *-anus*.
[2] The error is assisted, no doubt, by the fact that a balky or 'restive' horse is in fact also 'restless,' *i.e.* nervous and uneasy.

often happens that a word which was one of a thousand, or a form which was universal, becomes isolated. Dissociated from its fellows, it ceases to share their future destiny. If they perish, it does not perish with them. Nor is its preservation assisted by their survival. It may become the centre of a new group. Or it may remain isolated, — embedded, as it were, in amber, and lost or preserved to future ages, not as one of the swarm but with the individuality of a fossil.

English abounds in such fossils, and they are of every conceivable kind. Sometimes a word or a meaning has become obsolete except in an idiom or two, which, however, are still in common use. Again, an old construction, once widespread, has died out in general, but still lingers in a few phrases. So also an old grammatical form may occasionally survive, because it has become petrified, as it were, in a single expression or a small group of words.

A considerable number of survivals will now be studied. We may begin with certain old forms or constructions that often excite unnecessary scruples in the minds of speakers who are nervous about their grammar.

Whilom, 'in former days,' 'quondam,' is familiar to every one as an archaic adverb. It happens to be the only word in the language that preserves the universal Anglo-Saxon *-um* of the dative plural. In the gradual simplification of language, *-um* went out of use, so that to-day there is no special form for the case which it represented. Meantime, the form *hwīlum* (from *hwīl*, 'while,' 'time'), which meant 'at times,' had become petrified in the sense of 'formerly,' and consequently the decay of inflections did not affect it. It was not conceived as the dative case of a noun, but simply as an adverb. Our conjunctive *while* is the accusative singular of the same word;

and *whiles* (of which *whilst* is a corruption) is an adverbial genitive. Most adverbs, in all the languages of our family, have originated in case-forms.[1]

The adverb *needs*, 'necessarily,' is another interesting survival. There were a number of Anglo-Saxon adverbs formed by means of the genitive ending *-es*, and these multiplied in the Middle English period. The proper genitive of A.S. *nēd* was *nēdë*, and this, as well as *nēdes*, was used adverbially. In Middle English *nedë* and *nedes* were used indifferently. In Modern English, *nede* is quite dead, and many of the old adverbs in *-es* have also perished. *Needs*, however, still remains as an apparently anomalous formation, commonly attached to *must*, as in the well-known proverb. Other examples of the same construction are *nights* and *days* in such expressions as 'Do you sit up late *nights*?' 'What do you do *days*?' Here *nights* and *days* are old adverbial genitives meaning 'by night,' 'by day'; but they are felt as plurals by most speakers, even by those who know better, and hence a tendency to regard them as incorrect has grown up.[2] In England, the idiom 'early *days*' is still used, as 'It is *early days* to tell what will come of this'; in America, however, it is seldom heard, though 'early in the day' is common.

Once, *twice*, and *thrice* are likewise adverbial genitives, though their formation is disguised by the spelling. In Chaucer they are spelt *ones*, *twyes*, *thryes*, which at once makes their origin clear. The vulgar *lives* for *lief*, as in 'I had just as *lives* do it' shows the same formation. So *whilst* for *whiles* (see p. 195), which has the excrescent *t* seen in *amidst* (for *amiddes*), *amongst* (for *amonges*),

[1] See p. 182.
[2] Compare also such expressions as 'He always comes *Tuesdays*' (for which 'of a Tuesday' is often heard); 'Where do you go *winters*?'

against (for *ageynes*), the obsolete *alongst* (for *alonges*), and the vulgar *onst* and *twicet* (for *once* and *twice*).[1]

Since is a curious instance of the same adverbial *-es*. The Anglo-Saxon had *sith-than* (cf. Ger. *seitdem*), compounded of *sīth*, 'afterwards,' literally 'later' (akin to Ger. *seit*), and *thon*, an instrumental case of *that*. *Siththan* became *sithen-es* in Middle English, and this was shortened to *sithence* and *since*. The spelling in *ce* was intended (as in *once*, *twice*, *thrice*) to prevent the pronunciation *sinz* (as in the plural of *sin*). *Hence* and *thence* are also for *hennes* and *thennes*.

Nonce is a curious fossil word, occurring only in the single phrase *for the nonce*, 'for the occasion,' 'for the time being.' The *n* of *nonce* really belongs to the preceding word, so that the phrase was formerly *for then once*. *Then* is a corruption of an old dative form (no longer used) of the demonstrative *that*,[2] so that *for the nonce* means literally 'for that one time.' The transference of *n* from the end of *then* to the beginning of *once* is parallel to what we often see in the case of the article *an*, when followed by a noun beginning with a vowel. Thus children say *a napple* instead of *an apple*, and then sometimes, regarding *napple* as the name of the fruit, *the napple*. So *the nagent* is sometimes heard for *the agent*. These two forms, *napple* and *nagent*, have not established themselves in the language, but many other forms originally quite as incorrect have come in from the same tendency. Thus *newt* owes its *n* to a preceding article *an*. The Anglo-Saxon

---

[1] The adverbial *-es* occurs also in *-wards* (*towards, upwards*, etc.), *always, algates* (perhaps originally a plural), *besides, betimes, thereabouts, hereabouts*. *Somewheres* and *nowheres*, though not in good use, illustrate the strength of the tendency.

[2] The adverb *then* (really the same word as *than*) is another formation from the same pronominal stem.

efete is also preserved as *eft* and *evet*. Conversely, in a number of words, an *n* which properly belongs to the noun, has parted company with it and joined the preceding article, thus depriving the noun of its first letter. *Adder*, for example, was originally *nadder*; *apron* was *napron* (Fr. *napperon*); *umpire* was originally *nomper* (O. Fr., from L. *non par*, 'not equal,' that is, 'odd,' the umpire being the 'odd man' who decides a dispute).[1]

Our *yore* is descended from an Anglo-Saxon adverb in -*a*, *gēara*, really the genitive plural of *gēar*, 'year.' *Soon* was *sōna* in Anglo-Saxon, and was felt as belonging to the same class as *gēara*. In fact, however, the -*a* in *sōna* is not a termination, but a decayed remnant of a noun meaning 'time.' Both *a*'s became weakened to -*e*, and in Chaucer we have *yorë* and *soonë*. In Modern English the adverbs appear to have no ending, since the final *e* has disappeared.[2]

There are many adverbs in modern English which have no ending, but are identical in form with the corresponding adjectives. Such are *fast*, *slow*, *quick*, *cheap*, *sound* (in 'to sleep sound'), *high*, *low*, *still*, and the like. These give the young grammarian much trouble, and he is seldom assisted by his school-books, which usually inform him (erroneously) that such words are 'adjectives used as adverbs.' There is even a tendency to banish them from the language, just as *had better* is stigmatized by many as

[1] A very learned and equally interesting study of 'English Words which have gained or lost an Initial Consonant by Attraction,' by Dr. Charles P. G. Scott, may be found in the Transactions of the American Philological Association for 1892, XXIII, 179–305.

[2] Disappeared, that is, in speech. The fact that we *write* an *e* at the end of *yore* is neither here nor there. This -*e* is simply a graphic sign to indicate the length of the preceding vowel. It is no more an ending than a long mark over the *o* would be. In Chaucer's time, on the contrary, the final *ĕ* was a *sound*.

an impropriety. In fact, however, these words are merely the survivors of a large class of adverbs in *-ĕ*; and it is the disappearance of this adverbial termination (in common with all weak final *e*'s in our language) that makes them coincide in form with the adjectives from which they are derived. Not all of our 'flat adverbs' actually go back to such *-ĕ* forms, since analogy has brought new ones into existence, and a few (like *right* and *full*) are really old adjectives used in an adverbial construction. However derived, the 'flat adverbs' are an ancient and dignified part of our language, and the pedantry which discountenances them is not to be encouraged. Still, one must admit that such pedantry itself obeys a natural linguistic law, — the tendency to associate particular endings with particular syntactic functions. Most English adverbs of manner do end in *-ly* (a decayed form of *-līce*, 'like'), and the feeling that such a termination is indispensable is easy to understand. But until the language has actually shown some disposition to reject the 'flat adverbs,' it is pedantic to attempt to put them under a ban.

Fro, an Old Norse form, once common as a preposition (as in *fro the fire*, *fro the land*), has gone out of use, except in a single adverbial phrase, *to and fro*.

The adverb *ago* is really the same as *agone*, the past participle of *ago(n)*, 'to go on,' 'depart.' Thus 'six years ago' is literally 'six years having elapsed.'

Elder and *eldest* are the regular ancient comparative and superlative of *old* (which, like Ger. *alt*, shows the umlaut, or change of vowel, in the comparative and superlative). *Elder* and *eldest* have been almost universally replaced by *older* and *oldest*, — new formations made directly from *old*, and keeping the same vowel as the positive. Other ancient forms showing the same vowel-change are *strenger* and *strengest* from *strong*, and *lenger* and *lengest* from *long;* but these have disappeared from the language. *Elder* and *eldest* survive because they were so often employed in special family phrases, *elder brother*, *eldest son*, and the like, and they are almost entirely confined to this use. *Elder* has also survived as a noun in a special sense.

Near and *next* show a similar umlaut. They are really the comparative and superlative of the adjective *nigh* (A.S. *nēah*), but they are no longer associated with *nigh* in our consciousness. They survive as independent words. *Near* has become a positive, and a new comparative has been formed from it, — *nearer*, which really shows a double comparative ending. *Far*, which we also feel as a positive, was originally in the comparative degree. There has always been a tendency to use comparatives as positives, and so to accumulate endings of comparison. Thus *farther* shows two such endings, and the children's word *fartherer* shows three. (The *th* in these words results from a confusion with *further*, which is really a comparative of *forth*.) The accumulation of comparative endings in successive periods of our family of languages is well illustrated in *nethermost*. The Indo-European had a particle *ni*, meaning 'down.' This is seen in L. *ni-dus* and in the first two letters of *nest*, the last two (*st*) being a clipped form of *sedó-z, 'sitting place' (connected with *sit*, *set*, and akin to L. *sedeo*). This *ni* appears in Anglo-Saxon in the comparative *nith-er* and the superlative *nithemest*, where the *-th* is an old comparative ending. *Nithemest* has the superlative ending *-mest*, itself a union of a superlative ending *-mo* (seen in L. *pri-mus*, 'foremost') and the familiar *-st* (*-est*) ending (seen in *first*, *latest*). This *-mest* ending was subsequently confused with the

English *most*, which itself has the same *-st* but is from the root found in L. *magis* and *major*. Thus *nethermost* has at least four endings denoting comparison, — *-th*, *-er*, *-mo*, and *-st*. Many other ancient forms are similarly accumulative, for tautology is an ineradicable tendency of language. The so-called double comparison, now vulgar, but formerly in good use, illustrates the point. Everybody remembers instances enough in Shakspere: 'his *more braver* daughter,' 'the *most unkindest* cut of all.'

Alive is a singular example of a fossil form. It is descended from the Anglo-Saxon *on līfe* (pronounced *on leevë*), 'in life.' *Līfe* was the dative form, *līf* the nominative. At the end of a word, *f* was pronounced as we pronounce it. Between two vowels it was pronounced like *v*. The final *e* was the dative ending. This dative ending disappeared from the language long ago, but before its disappearance *on-livë* or *alivë* (for the *a* is merely a clipped form of *on*) had become established as an independent word; hence the *v*-sound, which owed its existence only to the dative ending *e*, remained. When we say *alive*, then, we are in a manner preserving the Anglo-Saxon dative; otherwise, we should say *alife*. In *abed*, which is also descended from a dative (*on bedde*), the modern word shows no remnant of inflection; for the ending *e* had no effect on the preceding *d*, and when the *e* disappeared, it left no trace behind it.

Down to very recent times the use of *year* as a plural was extremely common, and it is still heard in careless or colloquial language. It is not a corruption, but a survival. Indeed, from the historical point of view, it is a better form than *years*. *Year*, in Anglo-Saxon, belonged to a class of nouns which took no ending in the nominative and accusative plural. In Middle English, the differences between the old declensions broke down, so that nearly all plurals came to be formed by means of the ending *-es* (A.S. *-as*). Thus, *yeeres* was soon substituted for *yeer*, but the older *yeer* was still used. In Chaucer, for example, both forms are common. Compare *ten pound*, *six mile*, *three foot*, and other expressions of measure, formerly correct, but now regarded as colloquial or vulgar. *Stone*, however, as a weight, has never been superseded by *stones*.

The, in such sentences as ' *The* harder he tries, *the* less successful he is,' is not the definite article, but the instrumental case of the demonstrative pronoun *that*, like the Latin 'ablative of degree of difference.' In the sentence just quoted, the first *the* is a relative, the second a demonstrative, for *that* had both functions in Anglo-Saxon, as it has to-day. Thus, 'the more . . . the less' is exactly equivalent to the Latin *quo magis . . . eo minus*. The instrumental case of *that* survives in Modern English in this idiom only. Another petrified instrumental is *why*, which is really a form of the interrogative pronoun *who*, *what*.

The pronominal *'em*, *'m*, *um* of rapid speech is usually felt as a fragment of *them*, but is, in fact, quite a different word. It is the Anglo-Saxon *heom* (or *him*), Chaucer's *hem*, the regular dative plural of *he*. *Them* (Anglo-Saxon *thæm*), on the contrary, was not the personal pronoun. It was the dative plural of the demonstrative *that*. The Scandinavians used their form of this demonstrative (*theim*) as a personal pronoun, and it was partly under this influence that a similar usage of *them* sprang up in English, but did not extend to Chaucer's dialect. *Their* is the Old Norse genitive plural *theira;* the Anglo-Saxons used *hira* (Chaucer's *hire*, *here*), also from *he*. The variation between Chaucer and Modern English in the matter of *their* and *them* is one sign that our literary language is of a somewhat more northern character than his dialect.[1]

The pronoun *thee* has gone out of use entirely, except dialectically, or in the poetical or solemn style. It still survives in the colloquial *thank'ee*. Compare the vulgar *don't-ee* often heard in England, but probably never in the United States. *Prithee* is now poetical, but was once extremely popular.

An old ending *-en* (akin to L. *-īnus*[2] in *serpentinus*, 'snaky') produced a number of 'adjectives of material': as, *golden, leaden, brazen, wooden, earthen*. These have decreased in number, and some of those which survive are poetical or figurative. The modern habit in such cases is to use the noun itself as an adjective. Thus, we say 'a *gold* watch,' but '*golden* hair.' *Wooden* and *earthen*, however, are still common in the literal prosaic use. In the case of the participial ending *-en*, once universal in strong verbs, there is great diversity. Most of the old participles have lost the termination: as, *sung, hung, spun, found, bound*. But others have kept it: as, *stolen, born, ridden*. There is a tendency to retain the forms in *-en* as adjectives, even when the participles are commonly shortened. Thus, *drunken, sodden, swollen*, 'ill-*gotten* gains,' '*cloven* foot,' 'a *riven* oak,' 'that labor and are heavy-*laden*,' 'all *shaven* and *shorn*,' '*shrunken* cheeks.' Hence the anomalous *boughten*, as opposed to *home-made*. The old adjectives of material in *-en* may possibly have assisted here.

---

[1] See p. 92.

[2] The Latin termination became familiar in English in a great number of borrowed words. It is a living suffix in our language, being much used in scientific coinages (*quinine*, etc.), and (by imitation) in such terms as *vaseline, pearline*, etc., made up to name commercial products.

Still another ending *-en* was once common as a feminine termination, and is identical with the German *-in*, as in *Königin*, 'queen' (cf. *König*, 'king'). It is preserved in the single word *vixen* (from *fox*), 'a she-fox,' and hence 'a snarling woman,' 'a scold.' Observe also that *vixen* shows the umlaut of *o* to *i* (cf. Ger. *Fuchs*, *Füchsin*).

Verbs show many curious survivals, only a few of which can be mentioned here.

Wol, an old form of *will*, is never used except in the colloquial negative *won't* (for *wol not*, the *l* having disappeared as in *shan't* for *shall not*). *Woo't*, as in Hamlet's 'Woo't drink up esil, eat a crocodile?' is simply *wolt* without its *l*. *Nil* (that is, *ne will*) survives in the fossilized subjunctive phrase *willy nilly* (for 'will I, nil I,' that is, 'will I, will I not'), meaning 'whether I will or no.' A similar phrase (in the indicative) is *shilly shally*, for 'Shall I, shall I?' — the natural hesitating question of an undecided person. From this we have formed the extraordinary verb *to shilly-shally*, which is made up of two nouns and two pronouns, but which may be inflected like any other verb, as, 'He *shilly-shallied* a good while.'

'If you *please*' is an old subjunctive phrase, and *you* is in the dative case — 'if it be pleasing to you.' 'If you *like*' is the same thing, since the old meaning of *like* is 'be agreeable' to one. After the old dative, *you*, began to be used as a nominative also, the dative *you* in these phrases, however, was erroneously taken as the subject of the verb, and, as the result of the misapprehension, we now say, 'if I like' or 'if I please' instead of the older 'if *me* like.' Observe that the idiom is none the less accepted because it sprang from a blunder, and, further, that no one thinks of challenging 'if I please' because it is impossible to 'parse' the *I* without giving an unheard-of sense to the verb.

The subjunctive mood is rapidly going out of use. In particular, it is no longer generally employed, as it formerly was, to express wishes. In a few phrases, however, which originally had a religious significance, the old construction survives. Thus we can say 'God bless me!' 'Heaven help me!' 'The saints preserve us!' But we can hardly *say*, 'Fortune favor us!' though we might venture it in poetry. Curses survive as well as prayers, and the subjunctive 'God curse him!' is quite as idiomatic as 'God bless him!'

A few other idiomatic uses of the subjunctive also survive in particular phrases: as, '*Come* what will, I will make the attempt,' '*Act* as he may, he cannot alienate his friends,' '*Try* as hard as he can, he will never climb the tree.'

A peculiar idiom with the preterite subjunctive *had* survives in a few phrases. Thus, 'I *had as lief* go as stay,' 'You *had better* not do this,' 'We *had rather* ride than walk.' In this particular use *had* is really the preterite subjunctive of *have* in the sense of 'regard.' The meaning may be clearly seen in the first example. *I had as lief* means literally 'I should regard it as *as pleasant* to go as to stay.' The extension of the same construction to *had rather* is due to analogy. Naturally *I had*, *we had*, etc., were contracted to *I'd*, *we'd*, etc., in these phrases (as elsewhere), and many persons suppose that *I had* in the expressions just quoted is a mistaken expansion of *I'd* (the contraction of *I would*). Such a notion is not strange, since this use of *had* is confined to so small a number of phrases. The result has been a determined attempt to stigmatize the idiom as an error, and to substitute *I would rather*, *I would better*, etc., for it. The idiom, however, is perfectly established, has been in use for centuries, and is habitually employed by the best writers.[1] In some cases the substitution of *I would* results in downright error. Thus, 'I would better go' is positively ungrammatical.

In older English the indicative *have* and *hath* are common in such phrases, as well as the subjunctive *had*. Thus, —

> 'Yet *have I levere* maken him good chere
> In honour than myn emes [*i.e.* uncle's] lyf to lese.'
>
> Chaucer, Troilus, ii, 471–2.

The meaning 'hold,' 'regard' (cf. L. *habere*), is also seen in such phrases as 'I pray thee have me excused,' *i.e.* not '*procure* an excuse for me,' but '*hold* me excused (in your own mind),' 'pardon me.'

In the case of idioms like 'I had better,' one frequently hears the objection that *had* 'will not parse.' As a matter of fact, it *will* parse, easily enough, if one knows how to parse it. But the objection would have no validity even if the phrases were grammatically inexplicable. The grammarian has no business to object to an established idiom, for idioms are superior to paradigms and analytical diagrams. Grammar was made (pretty imperfectly) from language, not language from grammar.

As particular grammatical forms or old constructions often remain in only a few phrases or in single words, so obsolete words occasionally survive in a few expressions, or even a single one.

Fine, an old noun meaning 'end' (Fr. *fin*, L. *finis*),

[1] See Fitzedward Hall, in the American Journal of Philology, II, 281 ff.

survives only in the adverbial phrase *in fine*. The noun *hallow*, 'a saint,' survives only in *All Hallows*, and in *Hallowe'en*, that is, the 'eve or vigil of All Saints' Day.' The Anglo-Saxon *rīce*, 'kingdom,' 'domain' (Ger. *Reich*), survives only in *bishopric;* the Anglo-Saxon *lāc*, 'offering,' only in *wedlock;* the Anglo-Saxon *rǣden* (a word connected with *rǣdan*, 'to counsel,' but used as an abstract termination) in *hatred* and *kindred* only.

To 'revoke' at cards is to *renege* (often pronounced *renig* and shortened to *nig*). This is L. *renegare*, and is seen in its general sense of 'deny' in Shakspere's 'Renege, affirm, and turn their halcyon beaks with every gale and vary of their masters.' The Spanish *renegado*, which came into our language bodily, and was also adapted as *renegade*, is L. *renegatus*, 'one who has denied his faith,' 'an apostate.' *Runagate* is the same thing, but comes from the French *rénegat*, and has been corrupted by 'popular etymology'[1] as if it meant 'runaway' and were from *run* and *gate*, 'a way.' This *gate* comes from O.N. *gata*, whence also *gait*. *Gate*, 'a door,' is another word, but may be related.

Weasand, an old word for 'windpipe,' is practically obsolete, except in the half-jocose phrase 'slit his weasand.'

Stead is our regular native word for *place* (which is French, see p. 244). The borrowed word, however, has narrowed the use of the native term to compounds (like *homestead, farmstead, roadstead*) and special phrases *instead of, in his stead, to stand me in good stead* (cf. *to stead me* or *bestead me*). Even in so idiomatic an expression as *instead of* the French *lieu* (L. *locus*) has made a bid for favor, but is felt by most speakers as somewhat bookish.

[1] See Chapter XXIII.

Welkin is an old word for the 'clouds' (cf. Ger. *Wolken*). It is kept only in the phrase 'to make the welkin ring.'

Umbrage, 'offence,' survives in 'to take umbrage' (less commonly, 'to give umbrage'). It is a special sense of *umbrage*, 'shade' (from Fr. *ombrage*, which also has both meanings). The figure is rather striking. One originally 'took umbrage' when one was 'thrown into the shade' by another. *Dudgeon* is almost as limited as *umbrage* in its use. It is practically confined to the phrase *in dudgeon* ('in great dudgeon,' 'to take a thing in dudgeon'). The etymology is quite unknown, and the same is true of *dudgeon*, 'a dagger,'—formerly *dudgeon dagger*, *i.e.* one with a hilt of dudgeon or boxwood. The progress of meaning in this word is curious: (1) a kind of wood, (2) a dagger-hilt of this wood, (3) any dagger-hilt, (4) a dudgeon-hilted dagger, (5) any dagger. It is not impossible that *dudgeon*, 'resentment,' is the same word. We speak of 'looking daggers,' and a bitter speech is 'a dagger in one's heart.' The sense in question is not found till the Elizabethan age, when, for a time, the continental fashion of *stabbing* in resentment of an insult was rather ostentatiously followed by the English. Possibly 'to take a thing in dudgeon' was to resent it by planting your dagger in the speaker's breast; but this is not so likely.

Suborn is a good example of a word that is kept only in a very limited application. It means to 'procure or fit out secretly' (L. *sub-orno*), and was used in English for the act of inducing another person to commit a crime. Thus Macduff speaks of the attendants 'suborned' to murder Duncan, and Hotspur talks of 'murtherous subornation.' Nowadays both the verb and the noun are confined to perjury and treason. 'Subornation of perjury' is a well-known offence; subornation of *murder* is never heard of.

Sometimes an obsolete word is retained in an idiom in which it is associated with another word of similar meaning. We understand the whole phrase as a kind of compound and get the sense out of the word which has survived in ordinary use. A good example is 'without *let* or hindrance.' *Let* means 'hindrance,' but is obsolete except in this idiom. In Anglo-Saxon there were two verbs, *lettan*, 'to hinder,'[1] and *lǣtan*, 'to permit,' 'to let go,' 'to let.' The forms of these verbs were originally quite distinct. Gradually, however, they fell together, so that in the time of Shakspere there appeared to be a single verb, *to let*, which sometimes meant 'to hinder' and sometimes 'to permit.' The ambiguity of such a verb led to the abandonment of one set of meanings, and with this abandonment went the noun *let* in the sense of 'hindrance,' except in the single phrase just noted.

Mete, an old word for 'boundary,' is similarly preserved in the legal phrase *metes and bounds*.

Hue and cry (A.N. *hu e cri*, connected with *huer*, 'to shout') is a good example of the same thing.

Obsolete or unusual words are often preserved as family names. So *Fletcher*, 'arrow maker' (Fr. *flèche*, 'arrow'); *Bowyer*, 'bow maker'; *Spicer*, 'dealer in spices,' 'grocer' (cf. O. Fr. *espicier*, Fr. *épicier*); *Webster*, 'weaver' (with *-ster*, the old feminine ending); *Baxter* (for *backster*), 'baker'; *Sumner*, 'summoner,' 'somnour' (officer of the ecclesiastical courts); *Day*, 'dairyman' (O.N. *deigja*); *Chapman*, 'merchant'; *Lorimer*, 'maker of bits, etc.'; *Latimer* (*i.e.* 'Latiner'), 'interpreter.'

---

[1] It is etymologically related to the adjective *late*, and properly meant 'to retard,' 'to make slow' (*late* having the meaning of 'slow').

Fain was once freely used in the sense of 'glad'; and it was possible to say, 'I am fain,' exactly as we now say, 'I am happy.' We now have the word only in the phrase, 'to be fain to do so and so,' where it apparently means 'forced' or 'obliged.' This curious shift in meaning is easily understood. Falstaff, according to his own account (Merry Wives of Windsor, act ii, scene 2), 'leaving the fear of God on the left hand and hiding his honor in his *necessity*, was *fain* to shuffle, to hedge, and to lurch.'

A great many obsolete words remain embedded in the language as parts of compounds.

Gār, an old word for 'spear,' found also among the Celts (whence Cæsar's *gaesum*), survives in *garlic*[1] and *gar-pike*, and in the noun *gore*, for a 'triangular piece.' It is also, in all probability, the source of the verb *gore*, 'to pierce.' *Gore*, 'blood,' is not connected; it is the Anglo-Saxon *gor*, 'filth,' and had no poetical associations in the eighth century.

Many native compounds have ceased to be felt as other than simple words, and in such cases the meaning of their component parts has been utterly forgotten. *Lord* is A.S. *hlāford*, from *hlāf*, 'bread' (our *loaf*), and *weard*, *ward*, 'guardian.' *Lady* is A.S. *hlāfdige*, of which the first part is also *hlāf*, but the *-dige* is uncertain. The connection with *dough*, which has been suggested, as if *lady* were 'kneader of bread,' is attractive, but not quite easy. At all events, both *lord* and *lady* had lost their literal meaning before the end of the Anglo-Saxon period.

Stirrup is *sty-rope*, that is, 'mounting rope,' from A.S. *stīgan*, 'to mount' (cf. Ger. *steigen*), and *rāp*, 'rope.'

---

[1] A.S. *gārlēac*, literally 'spear-leek' or 'spear-plant,' from the shape of the leaves.

The literal meaning of the word, and the fact that it was a compound, must have remained in people's minds until the verb *to sty* (*stīgan, stien*) became obsolete. We have a trace of this verb in our *sty* (in the eye), which means, literally, a 'rising' or 'swelling.'

Handiwork is not a compound of *handy* and *work*, but of *hand* and A.S. *ge-weorc*, where *ge-* is a collective prefix, which later wore down to *i-*. *Handicraft* has no hereditary right to its *i*, which it has appropriated from *handiwork*.

The *step-* in *stepson* and the like is the adjective *stēop*, 'destitute,' 'bereaved,' so that *stepson* or *stepchild* is the same as *orphan*, which comes from the Greek for 'bereaved.' *Stepfather* and *stepmother* are therefore terms which could only have arisen after the *step-* had lost its proper sense. A *stepmother* is not a 'bereaved mother,' but one who takes the place of a mother to the bereaved children. This illustrates the tendency of language to form groups, and to make new words to fill out any gaps that may be observed in any group.

The *nightmare* is not a she-horse, but a nymph or demonic creature. The Anglo-Saxon *mara*, 'incubus,' is quite distinct from *mearh*, 'mare'; but the words were later confused, so that one even hears *night-horse* as a jocose variation. The origin of *mara*, 'incubus,' is uncertain, though the word is found in several languages of our family. The suggestion that it means 'crusher,' and is connected with *mar*, is not free from difficulties.

Mermaid preserves the Anglo-Saxon noun *mere*, 'lake,' 'sea' (akin to L. *mare*), which is obsolete except in poetry or dialect. The word is thought to have the same root as L. *morior*, 'die,' so that the sea was so called as being a 'dead waste,' a 'wilderness of waters.' *Marsh* is a derivative of A.S. *mere*; *morass* (Fr. *marais*), seems to be from

L. *mare*. *Moor* doubtless belongs to the same group. It is A.S. *mōr*, which meant both 'moor' and 'morass' as well as 'mountain.'

Just as many old forms remain fossilized in the language, and an obsolete word may survive in a single idiom or a compound, so now and then a peculiar phrase or group of phrases preserves some ancient meaning of a term that is otherwise common in a different sense. Thus *ghostly* originally meant 'spiritual' in any sense; but it is now specialized to disembodied spirits, except in *Holy Ghost* and *ghostly father* or *counsellor*, and the like. In this case, the survival is due to the sacred associations, which always act as conservative forces. *Confound*, in the sense of 'destroy,' is quite obsolete, except in the colloquial *confound you!* that is literally 'God destroy you!' which is used, however, like most oaths and curses, with slight feeling for its tremendous significance. *Damn* has been specialized in the theological sense of 'condemn to eternal punishment.' Its old meaning of 'condemn' in general (as in *damned to death*) is still alive in 'the play was damned.' *Condition*, in the sense of 'character' or 'nature,' is extremely common in Elizabethan English. Thus when Gloster in King Lear says that 'the stars above us govern our conditions,' he means that we owe our characters to the influence of the heavenly bodies, — we do not derive them from our parents. 'An *ill-conditioned* fellow' still shows a trace of the Elizabethan sense.

Comfort (from L. *com-* and *fortis*, 'strong,' through the French) originally meant 'to strengthen,' 'support.' It now means 'to console'; but the literal sense is preserved in one phrase, 'giving aid and comfort to the enemy,' a legal formula which has become 'popular.' Observe that *aid* and *comfort* mean much the same thing; and that **in** our modern use we take them together as if they were a single word, getting our understanding of the phrase from *aid*, and not attaching any definite sense to *comfort*. Compare *let or hindrance* (p. 209).

Abuse is literally 'to misuse,' and this is the regular modern sense. The secondary meaning, 'deceive,' was once very common, but is now quite obsolete. *Disabuse*, however, still signifies 'to undeceive.'

Nerve once meant 'sinew' (L. *nervus*),[1] as in Shakspere's 'hardy as the Nemean lion's *nerve*.' *Nervous* was therefore 'vigorous,'—a sense which remains in 'a nervous style' or 'writer.' With the advance of physiology, however, the name *nerve* received a different sense, with the result that, in ordinary use, *nervous* suggests almost the opposite of sinewy strength. It is worth notice that we have transferred to *nerves* in the modern sense a number of expressive words which are literally applicable to the muscles and sinews. Thus we speak of 'nervous tension,' and say 'every nerve was tense with excitement,' or in the vernacular, 'his nerves were on the stretch.' Compare 'nervous strain.' 'To lose one's nerve' is really 'to lose one's sinewy fibre,' to become weak and 'flabby.' In modern usage, a man 'loses his nerve' in proportion as he becomes conscious that he *has nerves*,—a curious contradiction, but natural enough when we know the history of the word.

Thorough and *through* are merely different ways of pronouncing the same word. As often happens, we have utilized the variation to make two words of one.[2] We no longer employ *thorough* as a preposition ('thorough bush, thorough brier') or *throughly* as an adverb. Yet we still

[1] *Nervus* is for an earlier *snervus*, perhaps cognate with *snare*.
[2] See p. 355.

speak of a *thoroughfare*, a '*thorough-lighted* room,' the '*thorough-shot* of a boom'; [1] and conversely, 'through and through' is a synonym for 'thoroughly.'

'Prosper,' curiously enough, seems to be the older sense of *speed* rather than 'swiftness.' We have it still in 'God speed!' 'Speed the plough!' 'good speed,' and the much misunderstood proverb, 'The more haste, the worse speed.'

Just, in the sense of 'exact,' is still found in the adverbial use, and also in the printer's term *justify*, for 'straighten' (type); cf. *adjust*.

An old sense of *favor*, 'features,' 'looks,' survives only in *hard-favored*, *ill-* (or *well-*) *favored*, and two or three phrases like 'He *favors* his father,' that is, 'looks like him.' So 'Kissing goes by favor,' a proverb that is generally misunderstood.

All that Chaucer's Clerk of Oxenford spoke was '*souning in* moral vertu,' that is, it 'had a tendency' in that direction, 'was colored' by morality or consonant with it. The idiom is obsolete in common talk, but the lawyers have it still: 'to *sound in* damages,' 'to *sound in* tort.'

Lust formerly signified 'pleasure' in general (as Ger. *Lust* still does). A by-form of the noun was *list*, which is now obsolete except in *listless*, ' taking no pleasure in anything,' hence 'apathetic.'

Read in the old sense of 'interpret' or 'guess' (whence the ordinary meaning) is poetically alive in one phrase,— 'to *read* a riddle.' *Riddle* itself is from this same verb.[2]

To *wink* was once extremely common in the sense of

[1] A lumberman's term for the opening where the logs are allowed to 'shoot through.'

[2] It is A.S. *rǣdels*, the ending *-els* being the same that is seen in Ger. *Räthsel*. This *-els* also survives in our *burial*, — A.S. *byrgels*, with the *s* lost (because it looked like a plural) and the *-el* respelled as if it were from the Latin termination *-alis*.

'*shut* the eyes,' which survives only in the figurative phrase 'to *wink* at,' *i.e.* 'to connive' (from L. *conniveo*, 'to shut the eyes to').

Liberal retains something of its old sense of 'gentlemanly' (L. *liberalis*, 'free-born') in 'liberal arts' and 'liberal education.' The contest that is still raging over the nature of a 'liberal education' affords very pretty examples of the tyranny of words when the 'term is allowed to govern the meaning,' especially when the term is interpreted awry at the outset. Here, as in so many other wordy combats, the etymon of the Stoics[1] 'umpire sits, and by decision more embroils the fray.'

As yet is a relic of an ancient idiom. In former times it was possible to prefix *as* to almost any expression of time or place without appreciably changing the sense. Thus we find *as now* in the sense of 'now,' *as in this place*, *as then*, *as at this time*, and so on. Of all these phrases only *as yet* has survived in Modern English.

On was once common in the sense of 'because of,' a meaning which has survived in only two or three phrases, like *on purpose* and *on compulsion*. The preposition *with*[1] originally signified 'against,' 'in opposition to,' but it has lost this meaning except in a few compounds,—such as *withstand* and *withhold*. The latter word means 'to hold in opposition to somebody else,' and hence 'to retain.' *Withsay* has been replaced by *gainsay* (*gain* = *against*), and that by the Latin synonym *contradict*. This is an interesting example of the substitution of a learned for a popular word. *Withsay* is pure Anglo-Saxon, and *contradict* is a 'learned' borrowing. Yet few words are now more truly 'popular' than *contradict*. The reason is

---
[1] See p. 230.
[2] Cf. the *withers* of a horse, *against* which the harness draws.

obvious. It is a familiar term in the nursery. 'You must not *contradict*' is one of the earliest lessons in courtesy that children have to learn. Thus they become acquainted with this cumbrous and seemingly erudite term long before they see it in print.[1] There is no other test of complete popularity.

Other phrases containing words or senses seldom found in other contexts are: *in durance* (especially 'in durance vile,' from Shakspere); 'a *foregone* conclusion'; 'at this *juncture*'; 'in a *trice*'; 'the *livelong* day'; 'to *mew* up'; 'a good *riddance*'; 'much *exercised*'; 'soft *impeachment*'; '*sneaking* fondness'; '*madding* crowd'; '*damn* with faint praise'; 'special *dispensation*'; 'might and *main*'; 'aid and *abet*'; 'watch and *ward*'; '*meat* and drink'; '*doubling* capes'; 'in this *connection*'; '*hugging* the shore'; '*skirting* the bushes'; 'the *wherewithal*'; 'on his own *recognizance*.'

Some of the phrases just quoted will be recognized as bits of proverbial lore or as fragments from the poets. In such cases, the peculiar word or the ancient sense accounts for itself immediately, on the principal of quotation. So with the survival of archaic language in legal formulas like 'hue and cry,' and, indeed, in many other expressions.

The fate of a quotation that cuts loose from the exclusive society of its context and joins the mixed company of idiomatic phrases, is always instructive, and often extremely curious. 'A foregone conclusion' now means 'a result (or action) that may be predicted with absolute certainty.' Quite different is the sense which the words bear in their original context. When Othello says 'This denoted a foregone conclusion,' he means that this dream

[1] See p. 29.

of Cassio's *pointed back* to an actual deed in the past.[1] It will be seen that, in adopting Shakspere's phrase as an idiom, we have gradually inverted its application.[2]

An almost equally striking example is the famous line, 'One touch of nature makes the whole world kin,' from Shakspere's Troilus and Cressida. It has become an assertion of universal brotherhood. In its context, however, the verse means simply, — 'All men are alike in one natural trait,' — the love of novelty.

> One touch of nature makes the whole world kin, —
> That all, with one consent, praise new-born gauds,
> Though they are made and moulded of things past,
> And give to dust that is a little gilt
> More laud than gilt o'er-dusted. (Act iii, sc. 3, ll. 174–8.)

Thus we have gradually and unconsciously modified the sense of two Shaksperean passages until the contrast between the meaning which we attach to them and that which they bear in the original context is nothing less than startling. The same process goes on incessantly throughout the vocabulary of any living language. The old terms shift their senses continually as they adapt themselves to changed circumstances and novel ideas, — that is, to new necessities in expressing thought. Language develops by the felicitous misapplication of words.

Stray relics of ancient usage are often challenged by critics who observe their isolation, and infer that they are either erroneous or at best 'contrary to the spirit of the language.' Such views are quite wrong, as the briefest study will show. The correctness of a form or a con-

---

[1] Othello, act iii, sc. 3, l. 428.
[2] Cf. L. *cui bono ?* 'for *whose* advantage ?' usually taken as meaning 'for *what* advantage ?'

struction is not impaired by the fact that there is nothing exactly like it in English, any more than the correctness of a word is to be called in question merely because our language has no other that is identical with it in sound and spelling.

CHAPTER XVI

THE CONVENTIONAL CHARACTER OF LANGUAGE

We have now studied a number of the most significant processes in the development of our language. We have seen how words grow up and how they change their forms. We have examined the machinery which makes new terms by derivation and composition. We have considered the way in which a vocabulary accumulates by borrowing from other languages. We have also discriminated between the learned and the popular words in our vocabulary, and have traced the slow growth of a literary language from a mere tribal dialect. Incidentally, we have had occasion to notice a great many shifts in sense, great and small, natural and paradoxical. It is now time to study more systematically the general and particular processes by which such changes in signification take place. In other words, we must ask the question: How do words behave in the development of their various *meanings?*

The changes which the meanings of words undergo in the development of a language seem, at first sight, purely fortuitous in some instances. In fact, however, the appearance of chance is due merely to our ignorance of the causes that have operated in each case. Such causes may be simple and easily understood, or so complex as never to be discoverable in their entirety. But so long as thought proceeds in obedience to definite laws, language, which is the expression of thought by means of conventional signs, must also obey rules which, if we could discover them, would account for every variation.

We often speak of the 'proper or essential meaning' of a word. The term is convenient, and one could not well dispense with it in etymological study. Yet it may easily become misleading, if certain cautionary limitations are not borne in mind. In the absolute sense of the term a word has no 'essential' meaning. Words are conventional signs.[1] They mean what they are intended to mean by the speaker and understood to mean by the hearer. There is no other sense in which language can be properly said to signify anything. Thus when a boy in the street declares that he 'hain't seen no dog,' it is not true that his 'two negatives make one affirmative,' for he intends simply an emphatic negation, and we inevitably understand him in that way, however nice we may be about our own *not*'s. In other words, two negatives may make an affirmative in logic, but they seldom do in English speech.[2] The rule in Anglo-Saxon and Middle English was like that in Greek: 'Use as many negatives as you can.' Thus in King Alfred's description of the effects of the harping of Orpheus: 'No hart shunned-not no lion, nor no hare no hound, nor no beast knew-not no hatred nor no fear from another, for the pleasure they took in the sound.'

Many current social phrases show in a moment how conventional are the meanings of words. Thus, 'Beg your pardon!' with a questioning inflection of the voice, has come to mean simply 'What?'—an inquiry when one has failed to catch another's remark. The only dif-

---

[1] See p. 312.
[2] The somewhat artificial 'not unnecessary,' 'not impossible,' and the like (imitated from the Latin) are almost the only exceptions in English.

ference between 'Beg pardon' and 'What?' is a difference in courtesy, — the former involving an apology for inattention. 'Dear Sir' at the beginning of a letter, and 'Your humble servant' (or 'yours' anyway) at the end, may mean very much, but commonly mean very little; they are no more than a notification to your correspondent that a letter is beginning and ending (like *salutem* and *vale* in Latin). 'Please' or 'if you please,' annexed to a command, carries no suggestion that the person who receives the order is to obey it or not, as he chooses. 'An early remittance will greatly oblige' does not necessarily indicate that your tailor feels himself under an obligation when you pay your old bill. 'Your favor of the 30th' is a common commercial phrase for any letter, though we all know that letters are hardly favors to busy men. 'Be so good as to go home!' 'Kindly let me see no more of you!' 'Not at home!' 'So glad to see you!' 'Give my love to ——,' 'Sorry to be out when you called!'—are all phrases which mean just as much and just as little as they are understood to mean by the speaker and the person spoken to.

Perhaps the final test of the fact that language is a convention,—that words have no natural and essential meaning which belongs to them more than any other,—is seen in irony. Here we use a word in a sense which is the direct opposite of that which it usually bears,—and we are understood without difficulty. Thus, 'He is a very courageous person' may mean, if it is so intended and so taken, 'He is an arrant coward!' Nor is it absolutely necessary that the remark should be uttered in any special tone of voice in order to convey this ironical meaning. The intention of the speaker and the understanding of the hearer are all that is required. There is a whole class of expressions (more or less colloquial) which have become idiomatic in an ironical sense: as, 'A precious rascal!' 'That's a pretty thing to say!' 'Fine work, this!' 'Here's a pretty how-d'ye-do!' 'A nice mess!' 'You're too kind!' 'How *very* good of you!' 'Here's richness!' 'This is pleasant!' 'Much good may it do him!' 'I wish you joy of it!' So *merci!* and *danke!* may mean 'No, thank you!' and the Romans used *benigne* (like the Greek καλῶς) in a similar sense.

The truth of these considerations may be tested in another way. Many words have so changed their meanings in the course of time that their present sense has no necessary logical connection with that which they formerly bore.

Thus the Latin *rivalis* is an adjective that meant 'pertaining to a brook' (L. *rivus;* cf. *river, rivulet*); but a *rival* is a 'competitor.' There is no necessary connection of thought between the two senses. Philologists know the history of this curious change, and see that it is easy and natural. *Rivales* in Latin came to mean 'neighbors who got water from the same stream,' — and it is thus used in the Roman Digest, which discusses the contests that often rose between such persons respecting their riparian rights. But this connection between the senses is a mere matter of history. It does not effect us to-day. We do not think of brooks when we talk of rivals in politics, or business, or love.

Chamberlain once meant a servant who attended to the chambers of a house or inn. The *Chamberlain* of London is the city treasurer.

Phaethon was a Greek participle that meant 'shining,' and was appropriately applied to the son of Phœbus. Phaethon once drove a chariot with disastrous results, and his name now designates a kind of vehicle. But we do not call such vehicles *phaetons* because they *shine*.

Explodo meant, in Latin, 'to drive off an actor by clapping the hands,' then 'to hoot off' by any noisy sign of disapproval. Thus Cicero speaks of a player as being 'exploded not merely by hissing, but by abusive words.' The modern intransitive use of *explode* is very modern indeed, but it suggests neither actors nor catcalls. The bridge between the senses is the idea of 'driving out' in such phrases as 'the ball was exploded from the gun.' So powerful, however, are the modern associations of the word that even the bookish phrase 'an exploded fallacy,' which preserves the old sense, is commonly understood as an error that has been 'blown up' or 'blown to pieces' by the arguments of an adversary.

Ingenium originally meant 'that which is born in a man' (cf. *generate*, *genus*). Now, in the form *engine* (taken into English through the French), it means a machine for the application of 'power,'—a locomotive, for instance. The intermediate steps are well known ('mother-wit,' 'contrivance,' 'device'); but it would be manifestly absurd to interpret our English word by appealing to *in* and the root GEN, 'to be born.'

These are merely a few examples out of thousands, but they suffice to enforce what has been said of the conventional nature of words.

To be sure, the course by which these same words have strayed so far from their former selves may usually be traced; and the clew which has guided their wanderings may then become evident. But this does not alter the case; for the present signification of each of them *is* its meaning, and something very different *was* its meaning a hundred or a thousand years ago, and between the two is a great gap, which the memory and the linguistic consciousness of the modern speaker does not span, and could not if it would. It is as if the word had been annihilated and created anew. The modern user knows nothing of the former meaning.

Words, then, have no character in themselves. They are merely conventional signs, and consequently they can be good or bad, dignified or vulgar, only in accordance with the ideas which they conventionally denote or suggest in the mind of the speaker and his hearers. Yet under this head of *suggestions* comes in an important consideration, which accounts for a great deal that would otherwise be inexplicable. Most words, from their use, acquire special connotations or associations, which almost seem to give them a character of their own.

Thus the word *fist* means simply 'the hand with the fingers doubled up against the palm.' In the idiomatic comparison 'as big as your fist,' it is purely descriptive, and has no particular character, good or bad. The use of the fist in fighting, however, has given a peculiar connotation to the term. We may say 'He hit his opponent with his clenched fist,' for here again *fist* is purely descriptive and occurs in an appropriate environment. Similarly, we may say 'The boy cried dismally, wiping his eyes with his dingy fist,' for here there is a certain grotesqueness in the scene which justifies the use of undignified language. But we can no longer say, as was formerly possible, 'The lady held a lily in her delicate fist.' In other words, the associations of *fist* are either pugnacious, vulgar, or jocose.

These suggestive associations are partly general and partly individual. If certain phrases are habitually associated in our minds with low or disagreeable persons or things, they will inevitably be relegated to the category of

CONVENTIONAL CHARACTER OF LANGUAGE 225

unseemly terms; and, on the other hand, phrases that are associated with dignified and reputable persons or circumstances, will acquire a kind of respectability independent of the exact meaning which they convey.

The associations in question may be purely personal. Everybody remembers certain words which he dislikes intensely, though they are in common use, convey no bad or disagreeable meaning, and are quite euphonious. We may even remember our reason for such dislikes. Perhaps the word is associated with an unpleasant experience; more likely, however, our antipathy is due to its habitual use by some one whom we do not fancy.[1] Or we may have been bored by hearing the word over-used, so that every new repetition gives us a feeling of satiety.

We have already averted to this doctrine of association in discussing slang.[2] One of the chief objections to the excessive use of this pariah dialect is not that there is anything objectionable about the words themselves, but that their associations are low, or at least undignified, and perhaps disgusting. If they secure a position in the vocabulary, their origin is likely to be forgotten, and they cease to be offensive.

The associations of words are always shifting, even when the meaning remains unchanged. Hence we continually meet with expressions in our older poets which have lost their dignity, and appear to us out of harmony with the context, though they were quite irreproachable when the author used them. Examples are *brag, candy, pate, slubber, mope, fry, portly, smug, pother, liver, wink, blab, feed,* and many others. The effect referred to may be felt in such a passage as the following: —

[1] So we often feel an aversion to the very names of people whom we do not like.   [2] See p. 72.

> I have dispatch'd in post
> To sacred Delphos, to Apollo's temple,
> Cleomenes and Dion, whom you know
> Of *stuff'd* sufficiency.
>
> SHAKSPERE, The Winter's Tale, act ii, sc. 1, ll. 182-5.

It is largely these indefinable connotations of words that make it so difficult to speak a foreign tongue. We may be well trained in grammar and command a large vocabulary, and yet use words which, though they express our meaning accurately enough, suggest ridiculous or inopportune associations to a native. 'Baboo English' is proverbial. The awkward and equivocal remarks into which one frequently blunders in speaking one's own language, 'the things one would rather have left unsaid,' depend on a momentary forgetfulness of some more or less obscure connotation which the words that we are using may bear.

Clearly, then, we are dealing with a very real phenomenon in the operations of language. When a word has been long used in a particular sense, there cluster about it a great variety of traditional associations, — religious, historical, literary, or sentimental, which, though not a part of its meaning, properly so called, are still a considerable factor in its significant power. A rose by any other name would smell as sweet, no doubt; yet no other name would so vividly suggest to us its fragrance. The noun *lily* is no whiter, nor is it more graceful, than, for example, *nilly*. Yet if it were possible to substitute *nilly* for *lily*, it would be long before the new term would call up in our minds either the whiteness or the grace of the lily as the accustomed word presents them, — not by virtue of any inherent quality, but merely because of its traditional and poetic associations.

The power of such connotations becomes very great when the word is an old one, which has been much used, and is in some manner, therefore, bound up with the most intense experiences of great numbers of men. Words like *father*, *mother*, *home*, or the name of one's country, may have a tremendous effect in a great crisis. A mob may be roused to fury by the utterance of a single word; yet in all such cases it is of course not the word at all that produces the effect, but its associations. Cæsar's mutinous army was reduced to tearful submission by the one word *Quirites!* 'fellow-citizens,' which reminded them that they were no longer *commilitones*, the 'fellow-soldiers' of their beloved leader.

Indeed, language is sometimes translated into conduct. A figure of speech may even suggest a course of action. To '*bridle* one's tongue' is an old and very natural metaphor. Is it too much to believe that it suggested the particular form of gag used in the seventeenth and eighteenth centuries to confine the tongue of a convicted shrew? At all events, the figure of speech is centuries older than the actual 'scold's bridle.' A mistaken etymology may react in a similar manner. A *forlorn hope* is a body of soldiers who undertake some service of extraordinary peril. The phrase is an adaptation of the Dutch *verloren hoop*, 'lost band' (in Fr., *enfants perdus*). *Hoop* is cognate with our *heap*, which formerly signified a multitude of persons as well as of things. Who can doubt that the happy confusion of tongues which illuminated with a ray of *hope* the desperate valor of the old phrase, has had its effect on the fortune of war?

As we have already remarked, we seem to ourselves to speak by nature, for we cannot remember learning to talk. This fact, taken in connection with the powerful influence which words often produce upon our minds through the association of ideas, enables us readily to understand how it is often thought that words have some natural power or meaning independently of usage or convention.[1] This idea is widespread, and manifests itself alike in the savage and in the philosopher.

Thus we find amongst men of all degrees of civilization a deep-seated belief in the magic potency of words. This belief underlies all kinds of charms and incantations. It is not the magician who forces the demon to appear or produces the convulsion of nature, but the words themselves which the magician speaks. His power consists only in knowing the words. There are stories of ignorant persons, and even children, who have accidentally read a passage, to them unintelligible, from a book of magic, with precisely the same effect which the spell would have had if recited by the enchanter. Similarly, it is often thought that the name of a person, an animal, or an object, has a mysterious connection with its bearer. A werewolf may be restored to his human form by calling him by name. If a berserk champion was addressed by his right name in the midst of a battle, he instantly lost his demonic strength. In invoking a god, or other supernatural being, it was

---

[1] So complex a phenomenon is language that even this possibility cannot be utterly denied. Any such essential meaning, however, lies so very far back that it is useless to attempt to discover it in the case of any particular term. In other words, if there ever was such an essential element of meaning involved in a particular combination of sounds, so many changes have occurred in the thousands of years during which the term has passed current among men that it must have lost this original significance. Indeed, the sounds themselves must be something quite different from what they were at the outset. Hence we are obliged in the present discussion to regard the essential element of meaning in any particular word as either non-existent in the beginning, or as now undiscoverable, and therefore, for our purposes, *nil*.

CONVENTIONAL CHARACTER OF LANGUAGE 229

customary to use many different names.[1] Often, in later times, the object of this variety was thought to be the winning of the deity's favor by employing that title which he might prefer. Originally, however, the purpose was to make sure of uttering the one true and essential name of the divinity, — that name which would control him instantly and force him to grant your request. It is well known that the real name of the city of Rome was supposed to be kept secret, lest, if it became known to the enemy, they might use it in incantations which would deprive the city of its protecting gods.[2] So, among some savages, it is a deadly insult to call a man by his right name, — an idea which has left its traces in the apologetic Latin formula 'quem honoris causa nomino,' and in the parliamentary phrase 'the gentleman from Ohio.'

All these superstitions, primitive as they seem to us, have had considerable effect on men's opinions about language, and, consequently, on language itself. They have even found philosophic expression in the Stoic doctrine of etymology, which has exerted a profound influence on modern thought, and still sways us in our judgment of words.

When, in the fourth or fifth century before Christ, the Greek philosophers began to connect the study of words with that of things, one of the questions which confronted them was, whether words and their meanings came 'by nature' ($\phi\acute{u}\sigma\epsilon\iota$), or artificially and 'by convention' ($\theta\acute{\epsilon}\sigma\epsilon\iota$). The Stoics, in accordance with their general theory of the

---

[1] The custom passed into a literary convention in invoking the higher powers to aid the poet. See the opening passage in Book iii of Paradise Lost.

[2] See the formula of *evocatio* (or calling out the gods of a beleaguered city) in Macrobius, Saturnalia, iii, 9, 7–8.

universe,[1] decided in favor of a 'natural' origin, and held that if the 'true' (ἔτυμος, *étumos*), or original meaning of a word could only be discovered, we should at once gain an insight into the divinely constituted nature of the thing which the word denotes. The search for this 'true meaning' (ἔτυμον, *étumon*) was therefore called *etymology*, or 'the science of true meanings.'

The doctrine of the Stoics has long been exploded, and the term *etymology* has entirely changed its sense. Yet the old notion dies hard. In the popular mind there still lingers a haunting suspicion that it is true, and accordingly one often hears, from the pulpit or the platform, and even from the professor's chair, serious arguments based on the supposed original or essential meaning of this or that word. The fallacy of such reasoning may be illustrated by an anecdote. The writer recently asked a friend, in jest, whether a particular service came within the functions of an *amanuensis*. 'Oh! yes,' was the reply, 'she does it *with her hands!*' Now, it is true that *amanuensis* comes from *manus*, 'the hand'; yet the jocose remark just quoted was none the less an absurdity, as, indeed, it was meant to be. The Romans, who were accustomed to dictating their compositions, designated the slaves who wrote for them as *servi a manu*, *i.e.* 'writing-servants,' for *manus* was often used for 'handwriting' (like our *hand*). Later they made, somewhat irregularly, a noun, *amanuensis* (like *Atheniensis*), and this we have borrowed in the same sense, and in that sense only. Hence the absurdity of drawing from the general meaning of *manus*, 'hand,' any inferences as to the proper duties of an amanuensis.

Yet similar 'etymological' arguments are extremely

[1] See p. 38.

common in serious discourse. One can hardly take up a periodical without reading that *education* is derived from L. *e-dūco*, 'draw out,' and that *therefore* all education must be a 'drawing out' of the child's faculties. Nothing could be more erroneous. In the first place, *education* is not derived from *e-dūco;* and if it were, it is absurd to suppose that the first Roman who used the noun *edŭcatio* had any such sublimated and refined idea of education. The whole argument depends on the antiquated doctrine of the Stoic etymon.

Now, the fact is, that the Romans compounded the verb *dūco*, 'to lead,' with *ex*, meaning 'out' or 'up.' This compound *edūco* they used for all kinds of 'leading' (in distinction from *agere*, 'to drive'), and particularly for 'bringing up' from the egg to the chicken, or from infancy to mature years; always, however, with personal objects, that is, always with reference to the creature that was 'brought up.' As *edūco* also came to be employed in many other senses, a special verb, *edŭco*,[1] was made for this special meaning, and later, this *edŭco*, with its derivative noun, *edŭcatio*, was applied especially to the 'training' of children. We may believe that the proper method of education is to draw out the latent faculties of the pupil, but we can find no suggestion of that method in the etymology of the word itself.

It is equally misleading to seek for light as to the nature of the religious principle in men from the etymology of the word *religion*. Yet we are often told that the very name of this principle reveals its true quality as the *bond* that unites the human and the divine. There is,

[1] *Edŭco* is only possible as a denominative verb from a real or supposed noun, *edux*, 'one who brings up or rears,' formed from the same root, DŬC, to which *dūco* belongs.

to be sure, a bare possibility of deriving *religio* (irregularly) from *religo*, 'to bind'; but even if that were its origin, the sense in which the first heathen users of the word conceived the figure could not throw any light on the central principles of spiritual life. It is far more likely, however, that the word is an abstract from *relego*. This is Cicero's own derivation, and the use of the cognate words undoubtedly confirms it. The verb *relego*, 'to pick up,' and so 'to notice,' 'take cognizance of,'[1] is compounded of *lego*, 'to pick,' and *red-*, 'again' (the prefix being used somewhat in the sense of *re-* in *regard*, as we also have it in *respicio*, *respecto*). It undoubtedly meant 'to notice carefully,' 'to observe closely' (cf. *diligens*), especially of noticing omens, portents, and other divine intimations. Hence we have *religiosus*, 'inclined to' this action, often in a bad sense, 'excessively so inclined,' and hence 'superstitious': compare the dictum quoted by Aulus Gellius (iv, 9, 1), — 'religentem esse oportet, religiosum nefas,' 'One ought to be scrupulous, — it is wrong to be superstitious.' At a time when man's connection with the gods was entirely through omens and the like, it would be natural that a 'painful regard' (for divine intimations) should be 'superstition' or 'religion,' either of which ideas *religio* expresses. The word *neglegere* is used of the opposite idea (though not, like *relegere*, without an object). It is only by taking into account the customs and beliefs that prevailed when a word was made, that we can have any just conception of its origin.

Such false linguistic doctrine as this of *education* and *religion* must not be confused with a proper study of 'root-meanings.' The history of every word begins with

[1] Cf. *relegere scripta*, 'to reread writings'; *relegere litora*, 'to revisit the shores.'

its root, if the root can be ascertained, as is not always the case. Yet we must not expect the root to contain, as in the germ, all the significance that successive civilizations have attached to the words that have grown out of it. We should never forget that words are conventional symbols, and that any word — whatever its origin — bears, at any moment, that meaning which the speakers of the language have tacitly agreed to assign to it. And this meaning may, or may not, have a direct logical connection with the original sense of the root.

This principle does not do away with the distinctions of right and wrong in speaking a language. The purpose of speech is to express one's thoughts so that they may be understood by others. Hence, the consensus of usage determines the meaning which a word bears, and this consensus is governed at all times by the *Sprachgefühl*, so that a language always remains true to itself, as we have had occasion to remark before.[1] Within the limits of this feeling, however, hardly any influence is too slight to produce a variation in sense.

[1] See pp. 126–7.

CHAPTER XVII

GENERALIZATION AND SPECIALIZATION OF MEANING

WHETHER in literature or in common talk, a word is never the exact sign of an unchangeable idea. Words are not mathematical formulæ. The character π always represents the same thing,—namely, the ratio of the circumference of a circle to its diameter, or $3.14159+$. There cannot be two correct opinions about the meaning of the symbol. Take, on the other hand, such a word as *boy* or *man* or *hatred* or *virtue*. There may be a dozen opinions about the applicability of these terms to a particular person or quality. Science, it is true, aspires to absolutely definite nomenclature, but the technical denotements of science are not so much words as formulæ or hieroglyphics. At any rate, they stand outside of the domain of ordinary speech.

We need only consider what different ideas are attached by different persons to *father*, *God*, *ruler*, *infidel*, *wealth*, *honesty*, *morals*, *patriotism*, *government*, to see the inexactness of separate words as expressions of thought. It is only when words are put together and 'modified,' when they are expounded (by the circumstances or the context, or by stress and modulation of the voice), that we can interpret their meaning with much accuracy. The Clown's 'O Lord, sir!' in Shakspere was a good answer to all the remarks of the Countess.[1] We may try the same

---

[1] All's Well that Ends Well, act ii, scene 2.

experiment by uttering the interjection *oh!* in various ways. It will readily express surprise, indignation, pain, terror, joy, compassion, or we may use it simply to attract the attention of some one whom we wish to address.

So every language has its special stock of words that mean little or nothing, but may stand for almost anything. They are the counters and markers of the game of speech. Such words are, in Modern English, *thing, affair, business, concern, regard, account, article, circumstance, fact, state, condition, position, situation, way, means, respect, matter.* Each of these may, it is true, be used in a pretty definite sense, but they are also extremely common in the function indicated. We infer that they once meant something rather definite, but have gradually faded into their present vague and shadowy condition. And such is, in fact, their history.

Thus, *state* is L. *status*, 'the act or manner of standing,' 'attitude,' 'position.' The Latin word had taken almost all the senses in which we use *state*, general and particular, except that of a concrete 'body politic.' *Estate*, the same word in an Old French form, was formerly an absolute English synonym for *state*, but is no longer used in either the political or the vague sense, being more or less appropriated to 'property' (abstractly or concretely), and to 'condition in life.' *Status* we have borrowed again, intact, but in a comparatively limited sense. *Position* and *situation* are similar to *state* in their literal meaning, but have not faded quite so much. *Posture* is vague in 'the *posture* of affairs,' but preserves its literal sense in most contexts. *Condition*, which has become quite as vague as *state*, is, literally, 'stipulation,' 'agreement,' or 'terms' (from L. *con-* and *dico*). *Thing* must have had a somewhat similar history. Its special modern sense of 'inanimate object' (usually regarded as its 'real meaning') is certainly due to generalization. The Anglo-Saxon noun *thing* often meant 'terms,' and also 'a council or court,' and the verb *thingian*, 'to make conditions,' 'to arrange.' So *be-dingen* in German. *Thing* was the Old Norse word for a legislative and judicial assembly, as it still is in the Scandinavian languages. Thus, the *Storthing* (or Great Thing) is the Norwegian parliament. The word is thought to be cognate with L. *tempus*, 'the (fitting) time,' 'the right moment.' If so, we may feel confident that the oldest sense at which we can arrive in English is 'that which is agreed upon as fitting.' From the 'terms' of a bargain to a concrete 'object of value' is a short step, — and from this to 'anything' (actual or ideal) is no long stride.

Circumstances, literally, 'things that stand round one,' has become so vague that we say, without hesitation, 'under the following circumstances.' The phrase, it will be observed, includes three inconsistent expressions of direction or position: *under*, *after*, and *around*. Yet we do not feel the inconsistency, and even those stylists who prefer '*in* these circumstances' to *under*, rest undisturbed by the contradiction involved in *following*.

Such vague counters of the game change from generation to generation. Thus, in the Elizabethan time, *gear* was used almost as we use *thing* or *matter:* as, 'This is fine gear' for 'a fine state of things.' Similarly, *effect* was often used in the sense of *fact* or *act*, *passage* for 'act or action,' as in Fluellen's 'gallant and most prave passages at the pridge,' or in 'passages of proof' for 'facts of experience.' *Part* was common for 'deed' (from the *part* or *rôle* one plays[1]) and so on. On the other hand, *fact*

[1] Cf. the Latin *primas (secundas) partes agere*.

GENERALIZATION OF MEANING

itself was less vague then than now. It often signified a 'deed' or 'act,'—especially 'wicked deed' or 'crime.'

The different words which have so faded as to be mere synonyms for *become* are interesting. The old verb *to worth* (A.S. *weorthan*), cognate with Ger. *werden*, has disappeared, except in the poetical phrase, 'Woe worth the day!' (*i.e.* 'May woe happen to the day!'), a curse used as an exclamation of sorrow. *Become*, once meaning 'arrive,' has taken its place, but is now so colorless that other more vivid words have been summoned to its aid. Thus we say: 'The weather *grew* cold,' 'He *turned* green with envy,' and in older English *wax*, 'to grow,' was similarly used, as in the biblical 'Jeshurun *waxed* fat and kicked.'[1] *Go*, which has long been common in such phrases as 'go lame,' said of a horse, is somewhat overused by recent writers in expressions like 'she went white,' 'he went stale,' 'Old Adrian, penned in the landing corner, went gray of face,' and the like. *Get* is another synonym, as in 'to get tired,' and Coleridge's 'His chariot wheels *get* hot by driving fast.' It is peculiarly idiomatic in certain phrases, as *to get rid of*, *to get angry*.[2] Martinets frequently object to these *get*'s, because they think that the verb must always mean 'to acquire,' but such an objection ignores all linguistic principles, as well as the facts of good usage.

A striking example of 'fading' is seen in the terms for 'existence.' This fading is demonstrable in all the words for 'being' in our family of languages, except, apparently

[1] *Wax* is one of those curious words which nobody uses, but everybody knows. Literature (particularly the Bible and Shakspere) still keeps it alive in its general sense, and it is specially applied to the increase of the moon.

[2] On these uses see C. A. Smith, in Publications of the Modern Language Association of America, XV, 108–10.

in *is* and its cognates, that is, in the group of Indo-European terms that come from the root ES. In fact, it is doubtful whether the primitive languages had any such category as 'being.'

Important as a 'copula' seems to us for predication, it is certain that such a tool is really unnecessary, and that predication can be and is constantly performed without its aid. The mere naming of an object is a true predication, and the first person who called men 'mortals' asserted the mortality of man quite as effectively as the logician with his 'All men *are* mortal.'

Further, as a 'substantive verb,' the ancestor of our *am* and *is* (and the Latin *sum*, *est*) must have meant something far less abstract than 'pure existence' when it was first ventured on by the primitive language-maker of the Indo-European family. What was the sensuous idea behind these words we cannot now divine, whether it was 'breathe' or 'sit' or one of a thousand others. But that there was some sensuous image is proved by the analogy of all other words for 'being,' by the freedom with which adverbs of manner have been used from the earliest times with these ES-verbs,[1] and finally by the constant effort of the poets to revivify such images by using words which actually mean something (as in Sophocles' πέλει, Virgil's 'incedo regina,' Scott's 'Breathes there a man?'). There was, then, a time when the primitive language-maker did not feel the need of an *ergo sum*, or a 'solvitur ambulando,' or of Dr. Johnson's vigorous action. Some sensuously observable idea was implied in the words which have now faded by abstraction into mere words for 'existence.'

---

[1] As in '*How* is he?' 'He's not very *well*.' Compare the colloquial 'I am nicely, thank you!' So in Shakspere's 'That's verily!' and the Latin *bene est*.

GENERALIZATION OF MEANING

However difficult the problems of ontology may be, it is as idle to discuss them on the ground of words as it would be to seek the Stoic etymon of *religion* or *education* or *amanuensis*.[1]

Such fading is demonstrable, as we have said, in all words for existence except those from ES. Thus *be* and the Latin *fui* are from a root that meant 'to grow,' a sense preserved in the Greek φύω, *phúo* (whence *physical*, *physiology*, etc.), which also was sometimes used in the faded sense of 'be.' *Was* and *were* are parts of an Anglo-Saxon *wesan*, from a root meaning 'dwell,' seen in that sense in Sanskrit and in the Latin *verna*, 'a slave born in his owner's house,' whence *vernaculus*, 'native,' and our loan-word *vernacular*.

The fading is obvious (because not so prehistoric) in our *stand* in 'it stands (=is) approved,' and the Italian *sta* in 'come sta ella?' (from *stare*); in Gr. γίγνομαι (*gignomai*), 'be born,' then 'become' or 'be' (cf. L. *gigno*); in our many synonyms for 'How are you?': 'Comment vous portez-vous?' 'Wie geht's?' 'How goes it?' 'How fare ye?' 'How do you do?' 'How do you prosper?' Compare the rustic 'How do you git along?' made popular by Artemas Ward. *Exist* itself means literally 'to stand out' and so 'to come into view.'

Sometimes words lose almost all their definiteness in particular phrases: as, 'on the one *hand*,' 'on the other *hand*,' from which all idea of *hand* in the literal sense has disappeared. It is doubtful, indeed, if we think even of the right *side* or the left *side* in using these phrases. So also 'in the first *place*' in such a sentence as, 'In the first place, I do not like this street; in the second place, I find the house disagreeable,' where the phrases mean no more

[1] See pp. 230 ff.

than 'first' and 'secondly.' So *stands* is often almost equivalent to *is:* as, 'It *stands* recorded on page 253.' This use of *stands* was much commoner in the Elizabethan time than at present. It is well preserved in 'stands approved' (p. 239) and in the antiquated phrase 'stands affected': as, 'I do not know how he stands affected toward me,' that is, how he *is* affected or feels. Compare also the following three phrases, which are entirely synonymous as we use them, though a moment's consideration will show that they differ widely in their literal sense: *at any rate* (a figure from reckoning); *at all events* (however the matter may *come out* or 'eventuate'); *in any case* (in any happening, that is, however things may befall or happen). In these idioms, *rate*, *events*, and *case* have pretty nearly lost their meaning. The phrases are all synonymous with *anyhow*.

The last result of this fading process may be seen in such meaningless ejaculations as *well, you know, you see, don't you know? of course*, without which conversation cannot get on at all. Every such phrase is capable of resuming its original meaning at any moment, but in ordinary discourse they seldom stand for anything. They merely fill pauses. Indeed, they may be called the punctuation marks of spoken language. With persons addicted to profane swearing, oaths and curses have become similarly colorless to the speaker, who inserts them without regard to their appropriateness and merely to emphasize what he wishes to say, or to round out his period.

In discussing the vague and even meaningless way in which some words are used, we have really been considering extreme cases of one of the two universal tendencies of all language, — *specialization* and *generalization*. The operations that we have noticed are simply generalization carried to its last results. The word becomes so very general that it ceases to distinguish anything in particular from everything else. That is, a term that can be applied to everything means nothing, as a man who is equally intimate with everybody has no real friends.

Generalization and specialization of words are so closely associated that they can hardly be treated separately, for there is scarcely a word in the language which does not show the results of both processes. As we have seen, words are not exact signs for definite and unchanging conceptions (as are the formulæ of mathematics). Every word is capable of covering a great variety of conceptions, and the area which it covers may be vastly enlarged by the adoption of senses belonging to foreign synonyms which it is used to translate into the vernacular. Circumstances and the trend of a people's thought alone determine whether, in its commonest use, it shall include all of these conceptions, or a few of them, or shall be confined to a single one. And since circumstances vary infinitely, and nothing is more susceptible than language to every eddy and chance whirl of popular feeling, we shall expect to discover in many words a complicated history of generalization and specialization which, if we could analyze it completely, would depict the intellectual life of the race in no uncertain colors.

We may illustrate these processes in two common words belonging to very different classes, — the abstract noun *virtue* and the verb *throw*.

The starting-point of the noun *virtue* is the Latin word *virtus*, from *vir*, 'man.' *Virtus* meant literally 'manliness' in general. But 'manliness' is not a simple quality, but rather a collection of qualities; and one of these, 'courage' or 'prowess in war,' was so important in the eyes of the early Romans that the word was unconsciously specialized by them in that sense. The changed circumstances of an advancing civilization suggested that other good qualities are always associated with 'manliness,' and a need was felt for a more comprehensive term. Thus, doubtless under the influence of Greek culture, *virtus* was so generalized as to include all good qualities, as in our *virtue*. With reference to individual objects this general sense was easily limited to the special excellence of the object, and thus *virtus* was used, for example, of the 'potency' of drugs. A particular application to artistic merit gave the Italian *virtù* (which we use in the phrase 'articles of *virtù*').

The word entered English from the French, bringing with it the general ethical sense as well as the meaning of 'any excellent quality,' moral, mental, or physical. Hence, in the Elizabethan time, it was a *virtue* to dance gracefully as well as to speak the truth. The tendency, however, has been more or less to limit the application of the term to moral excellence, and this leads to frequent misconceptions in reading our older authors. There is nothing in English to remind us of the original connection of the word with '*man*liness,' and, in fact, we have given it a newly specialized sense with regard to women, — 'chastity.'[1] A somewhat similar history may be seen in *vice*, from L. *vitium*, 'a flaw' or 'defect,' and in *moral* and *immoral* (from L. *mores*, 'customs,' 'manners,' then 'character').

The history of the different English verbs that have successively expressed the general idea of 'throwing' is equally curious. The earliest of our verbs to be used in

[1] Literally, 'purity,' especially 'ceremonial or religious purity,' 'cleanness of hands.'

this sense was *warp* (A.S. *weorpan*), which is cognate with
the German *werfen*. The German verb has retained its
general sense of 'throw' down to the present time. The
English *warp*, however, was ousted by *cast* (a borrowing
from the Scandinavian). *Warp* did not go out of existence, but was limited or specialized to a particular kind
of throwing. A piece of wood, which, in drying, throws
itself out of the plane, is said to *warp*, and we speak, figuratively, of the *warping* of a man's judgment by prejudice.
Thus a word of completely general signification has become extremely special. *Cast* maintained itself for a good
while; but it acquired numerous special senses, such as
'to compute' (to *cast* accounts), 'to lay plans,' 'to mould,'
etc. The effect of this swarm of particular meanings was
to drive out *cast* as the general term for 'throwing,' and
there was substituted for it *throw*, — the verb which we
now use. This substitution of *throw* was an extraordinary case of generalization in sense; for *throw* (A.S.
thráwan) originally meant 'to turn,' 'to twist,' and was
especially applied to torture ('to rack'; cf. *torqueo*).
On being generalized, however, it lost its special sense
altogether, so that we are no longer conscious that it
has any connection with twisting or racking. By the
time that *throw* became the common word for the general
action, our language was so fixed by literature and the
schools that no further substitutions seem imminent. Still,
we may observe in the untrammelled language of boys a
strong tendency to replace *throw* by some word that is less
vague, and therefore more picturesque. Thus *fire* (from
gunnery) is popular with American boys, who constantly
speak of 'firing a stone,' and *sling* is not uncommon in
the same general sense. The reason is not far to seek.
'Throwing' is specially connected in the boy's mind with

the projection of a missile, like a stone or a ball. The boy's ideal missile used to be a stone from a sling, but is now a bullet from a rifle.

A few striking examples of generalization may now be considered. *Place* came originally (through L. *platea*) from the Greek word for 'broad,' and signified a 'wide street' or 'square' in a city. It is now our regular term for any kind of locality, or for 'locality' or 'situation' in the abstract; that is, it has become about as general as a word can possibly be and still retain a meaning. *Piazza*, the Italian descendant of *platea*, still means 'a square' in that language; but in English it is an architectural term for 'a roofed arcade,' and in the United States it is often used for the 'veranda' of a house. The origin of both meanings has been traced.[1] Covent Garden was laid out as a square, Italian fashion, between 1631 and 1634, with an arcade running along two sides. The square was named 'Covent Garden Piazza'; but the term *piazza* was soon applied to the arcades themselves, and this gave rise to the architectural sense which it still has in England, and which was adopted in this country some two hundred years ago. In America, however, it was rapidly extended to its present meaning, which alone survives, though the East Indian word *veranda* is increasing in favor.

Picture meant first a 'painting,' but is now applied to any flat representation of an object or scene, except a mere plan or diagram. Thus photographs, pencil sketches, and drawings with pen or crayon, are all included with paintings under the general term *pictures*.

Religion seems to have originally signified a 'scrupulous regard for omens,' that is, for the signs by which the

[1] See a note by Albert Matthews in The Nation, New York, June 1, 1899, vol. LXVIII, p. 416.

GENERALIZATION OF MEANING

gods communicated their purposes to mortals.[1] Christianity has broadened and deepened its meaning in a very striking way. Again, the adjective *religious*, in the Middle Ages, was applied solely to persons who had taken some special vow as members of a holy order. Thus monks, friars, nuns, hermits, and palmers were 'religious persons.' A layman could not be so called, however pious he might be. In modern usage the word is applied to any devout person. *Miscreant* originally meant a 'misbeliever,' that is, a person who did not accept the Christian faith, — a Saracen, for example, or a heathen. It is now used as a general term for a person of bad character, without regard to the orthodoxy of his opinions.

Injury once meant 'injustice.'[2] It is now applied to any kind of harm or damage. Indeed, it is perhaps commonest in its application to physical hurts. The Latin *poena* meant first a 'fine,' or money compensation for an offence, but was generalized to comprehend all sorts of punishment (cf. '*pains* and penalties,' '*peine* forte et dure'); and our *pain*, its descendant, has come to include all acute bodily or mental suffering, whether inflicted by way of punishment or not.

A few other examples of generalization may be briefly indicated: *layman* (originally 'one not in holy orders,' now often applied to any non-professional man or 'outsider'); *conduct* (originally the 'act of guiding' a person; now 'the way in which a man conducts *himself* or behaves'); *paper* (originally a substitute for parchment manufactured from the papyrus plant, now any similar flexible substance used for the same purpose, whether made of rags, rice, or wood-pulp; or any 'document');

---
[1] See pp. 231–2.
[2] Cf. the legal formula *damnum absque injuria*.

wall (originally 'a rampart,' L. *vallum;* now used of any similar structure, whether of earth, stone, or brick; applied also to the sides of a house, even if they are made of wood); *sail* (literally, to 'travel in a vessel propelled by sails,' now applied to steam navigation as well); *street* (literally, 'a paved way,' *strata* [*via*], borrowed from Latin by the Germanic languages to distinguish the great Roman military roads, the only paved ways with which our ancestors were acquainted; now applied to a definitely laid out road in a city or town, quite irrespective of the question of pavement); *apathy* (a Stoic term for ideal freedom from domination by the passions;[1] now vaguely applied to any sluggish condition of mind or body); *assassin* (originally a member of a fanatical sect in the East, who intoxicated themselves with *hashish*, and committed murders for the glory of their divinity; cf. *thug*); *scene* (originally 'a tent'; then the booth in front of which the actors played; then a permanent structure in the Greek theatre, forming the background of the stage or orchestra; cf. our 'behind the scenes': now used in the most general way for anything that lies open to the view or may be taken in by one glance of the eyes).[2]

The generalization of a word may be due in the first instance to some special figure of speech. Take, for example, our use of *body* as applied to a collection of persons — as 'a body of men.' In former times, philosophy liked to regard the individual as a miniature analogue of

[1] See p. 39.

[2] Doubtless the accidental resemblance of this Greek word in its English pronunciation to our native participle *seen* has assisted in this enormous extension of meaning, though a somewhat similar extension has taken place in French, where of course no such cause is operative. Words are constantly influenced by each other even when they have no etymological connection. See Chapter XXIII.

the great universe. The universe (*cosmos*) was an orderly system on a large scale. A man, body and soul, was a similar orderly system on a small scale. Hence, man was often called a *microcosm* ('little universe') as opposed to the *macrocosm* ('great universe'). Closely connected with this idea, which, though merely an analogy, was constantly used as if it enshrined a physical truth, was the conception of the state as a kind of body—'the body politic'—of which the citizens were the 'members.' So taking was this figure that statesmen often argued from the behavior of the human body in health and disease to the larger operations of government and society. Thus Lord Bacon observed that inactivity and neglect of exercise make a man's system sluggish and generate disease. From this he chose to infer that long-continued peace might induce a diseased condition in a commonwealth, and that the strenuous exercise of war was then needed to restore the state to health. From this use of *body* as a figure for the state, it was easy to pass to its employment for any collection of individuals, whether persons or things. Another figure, however, assisted in the development of the extremely general way in which we now use this word for *any kind* of collection: 'a body of men,' 'a body of facts,' 'a formidable body of arguments.' A particular codification of the common law was known as the *corpus juris*, because it collected and arranged the isolated facts and principles in a systematic order, as the human body is an assemblage of different parts working harmoniously together. From 'body of law' it was easy to pass to 'body of divinity' for a systematic treatise on theology, and this learned figure has contributed to generalize the meaning of *anybody*.

The phenomena of *specialization* are no less important

than those of generalization, and they are perhaps even more striking in their effects.

When a word is equally applicable to a number of different objects which resemble each other in some respects, or to a vague or general category of ideas, it may at any moment become specialized by being used to name *one* of those objects or to express *one* of those ideas. And if this particular application gains currency in the language, a new and specialized sense is the result. Thus, the Latin *liquor* means simply 'liquid,' but in English it often designates 'ardent spirits,' and in the French form *liqueur* it is still further specialized to an 'aromatic cordial.'[1] *Ballad* means any 'dance song,'[2] but it is frequently used for a particular kind of simple narrative poem. Here the tendency to generalization has also been operative, for the ballad is no longer confined to the uses of the dance. The French *ballade* (also adopted in English) is further limited to a very special lyrical form.

Disease was formerly used for any kind of 'discomfort.' *Wedlock* is literally a 'pledge' of any kind (A.S. *wedlāc*, a compound of *wedd*, 'pledge,' and *lāc*, 'offering'). *Ghost* once meant 'spirit' in general, — not specifically a disembodied spirit appearing to mortal eyes. *Poet* is literally 'maker' (L. *poeta*, from Gr. ποιητής, *poiētḗs*), but it was borrowed by us in the special sense, so that we cannot use the literal meaning to interpret the English word. *Charm* is *carmen*, 'song,' in a French form (cf. *in-cantation en-chant*). *Minister* in Latin means 'attendant,' 'servant.' *Affection* meant 'feeling' in Elizabethan English. *Auction* is literally 'the act of increasing' in any way. *Tyrant*

---

[1] Cf. *humor* (p. 30).
[2] It is from Prov. *ballada* (*ballare*, 'to dance'), through the French *ballade*.

meant simply 'king' or 'absolute ruler' in Greek; but it was specially applied to one who usurped the rule over a democratic state, and hence it has gradually come to mean 'a cruel or irresponsible monarch.' *Goods* is literally 'good things.' *Myth* is merely the Greek for 'story.' *Focus* meant 'hearth' or 'brazier' in Latin. *Crime* is L. *crimen*, 'an issue' at law, then any 'charge' or 'accusation' which one must answer.

Doctrine is 'instruction,' — now specially used in a theological sense, whence, however, it has been transferred to scientific and philosophical theories. *Mansion* is 'residence' (L. *maneo, mansus*, 'remain,' especially 'to stay over night'); cf. the German *Residenz* for a city where the sovereign resides. *Pocket* meant a 'little bag' (cf. *poke*). *Meat* was once 'food' of any kind, — a sense preserved in *sweetmeat*. *Spill* is literally 'destroy'; the most effectual way to destroy a liquid is to tip over the vessel that contains it. *Stick* was 'piece' (as in Ger. *Stück*). *Doom* was formerly any 'judgment' (cf. *deemster* 'judge,' the family name *Dempster, doomsman*, and *to deem*). *Adventure* is 'that which comes' or 'happens' to one; in Chaucer the word often meant simply 'chance,' being less suggestive than *fortune* of a personal power.

Coast was 'side' or 'border,' — not always 'seacoast' (it is French, from L. *costa*, 'rib,' 'side'). *Fable* meant any 'tale.' *Fate* is L. *fatum* (participle of *fari*, 'speak'), 'that which is said,' — then, 'the utterance of the divinity.' *Chaos* is the Greek word for 'yawning' (from χαίνω, *chaínō*, 'yawn'), and is closely related to *chasm*. *Deer* was formerly any 'animal' (cognate with Ger. *Thier*). *Lesson* (French, from L. *lectionem*) is a 'reading' (a meaning which survives in religious services). *Epos* (whence *epic*) is the Greek for 'word,' then 'story' or 'song.'

Fond is *fonned*, the past participle of *fonnen*, 'to be foolish,' and once meant 'foolish' in general; it was then specialized to foolish or doting affection, and that sense has in turn become more general by the gradual evaporation of the idea of 'foolish.' *Dote* has a somewhat similar history. It is from an old verb for 'doze,' 'be stupid.'

Sometimes the specialization is very slight but extremely significant, and in such cases the change in sense is baffling to the modern reader of our older authors. An amusing instance is *hint*, which in Shakspere's time meant 'an occasion' or 'opportunity' (from *hent*, 'to take'), but which now carries the special implication of 'the intentional suggestion' of such an opportunity. Thus, when Othello says to the Senators, in describing the course of his wooing, 'Upon this *hint* I spake,' he means merely that he *seized the occasion* unintentionally afforded by Desdemona's *naïve* remark. Yet modern readers almost inevitably understand him in the modern sense, as if Desdemona had been 'hinting' that an offer of marriage would not be unwelcome.

The manner in which a word may carry numerous specialized senses along with its more general meaning, and yet no confusion arise among them all, appears almost miraculous when one takes the word by itself, as an isolated phenomenon. But words are not used by themselves. It is their different combination in different contexts or circumstances that enables the same term to symbolize so many different things.

The noun *play* (A.S. *plega*) seems to have meant originally 'motion' (rapid motion) of almost any kind, — a sense preserved in technical language, as 'The piston-rod does not *play* freely,' 'the *play* of the valve.' The specialization to 'sport' or 'game' is natural, and took place very early,—and this is the regular sense among children, who require a context of some kind if they are to understand the word in any other way. The gambler has a still narrower limitation of *play* as his regular understanding of the word,—a specialization of the already specialized sense of 'game.' So has the musician, the base-ball or cricket player, the actor. This last-mentioned specialization to the drama is perhaps the commonest of all. 'Are you going to the *play?*' without any further context, would first suggest this meaning to almost anybody. Probably *play* in this sense is, at least in part, a translation of the Latin *ludus*. It affords a good example of the influence of foreign languages in giving special senses to native words, even when the corresponding foreign terms are not actually borrowed.

We can easily study these processes in our own experience, by noticing what we first think of when we hear the word *engine*, or *machine*, or *range*, or *register*. For 'every man is his own specializer.' Such special senses are dependent, mainly, on our business, profession, or chief interest in life, but in some cases they come from accidental associations of ideas or from obscure habits of thought. *Machine* is a term of general application to all kinds of mechanical contrivances. To the bicycle-rider, however, it suggests at first the particular kind of mechanical contrivance on which he is in the habit of riding. To the seamstress, on the contrary, it is likely to suggest at first the sewing-machine by means of which she gets her living. The use of the still more general term *wheel* as a familiar synonym for *bicycle* is an even more striking example of specialization. *Pump* calls up one picture in the mind of the country boy, another in that of an engineer in charge of a great system of waterworks. *Stone* suggests to the lithographer the lithographic stone; to the dealer in jewels, the mason, the maker of tombstones, the workman on a macadamized road, the epigraphist, it suggests other and quite different ideas, though the fundamental basis of meaning is the same in all cases. *Cataract* means one thing to the physical geographer, another to the oculist. *Devil* conveys one meaning to the preacher, another to the printer. The laborer engaged in laying a water-main and in smoking his 'T. D.' at the same time may be thought to have both meanings of the word *pipe* equally present to his mind; yet he will seldom hesitate as to what is meant if the 'boss' tells him that 'the pipe is broken.' *Boss*, by the way, means one thing to a workman, another to a politician. *Gas* to most people means illuminating gas. To the chemist it has no such special sense; for this is but one of a thousand gases in the midst of which he lives. As to abstract ideas, we need only mention the specially limited senses which the fanatic assigns to *religion*, the ward politician to *honesty*, the pedant to *scholarship*, and Mrs. Grundy to *propriety*. If men enough happen to agree in any such specialization, the general meaning may go out of use, either locally or universally, and we have a complete specialization of the word itself. *Medium* (Latin, 'middle') means 'anything through which an influence is transmitted.' To the Spiritualist, however, this general sense is practically obsolete, and the word exists only in a rigidly limited application to the persons through whom the spirits manifest themselves to mortals.

Specialization frequently results from the omission of some adjective or other modifier. Thus *undertaker* once meant simply 'one who undertakes' to do a particular job, a 'contractor' or the like (cf. Fr. *entrepreneur* and Ger.

Unternehmer).[1] The phrase 'funeral undertaker' means, of course, a 'contractor for funerals.' Usually, however, the limiting adjective is omitted, so that *undertaker* has acquired a very special sense. Other examples are: *duties* for *port duties*; *fall* for *fall of the leaf* ('autumn'); 'in a predicament' for *bad predicament*; *plight* for *bad plight*; *success* for *good success*; *paper* for *newspaper*.

It is often impossible to discover that any definite limiting words have actually been omitted, but equally clear that specialization has been accomplished by a similar omission or ellipsis in thought. The omitted idea need never have been expressed in plain terms; it is enough that it should have been vaguely present to the mind in a general way. Thus, *suggestion* in Elizabethan English frequently meant 'evil suggestion' or 'temptation'; *broker*, 'a go-between'; *practice*, 'a plot'; *fact*, 'a crime.' So *officious*, properly 'dutiful' or 'serviceable' (cf. L. *officia*, 'good offices'), has come to mean 'too forward in offering one's services.' *Wanton*, 'sportive' (in an innocent sense), illustrates by its change of meaning

> How mirth can into folly glide,
> And folly into sin.

Revel carries riotous suggestions which it had not in Chaucer's day.[2]

Per contra, specialization frequently results from the omission of the noun and the retention of the adjective

[1] This meaning survives in formal language. The special sense of a 'projector' or 'adventurer' (one who risks his capital) seems to have developed in connection with the colonization of America.

[2] It has a good right to them, however, being really the same word as *rebel*, from L. *rebellare*, 'to renew hostilities.' *Rebel* is the 'learned' and *revel* the 'popular' word in French.

word in the sense which the whole phrase was intended to express. *Main* means 'strong' or 'great,' then 'principal.' Its special use for 'the sea' comes from the omission of the noun in the phrase 'the *main* ocean.' Similarly, *main* was formerly used for *mainland*, but the ambiguity drove out this sense, leaving the clipped phrase *main* for 'ocean,' and the full phrase *mainland* (made into a compound word) to designate the correlative idea. Thus many adjectives (or nouns used adjectively) have become pure substantives. A *natural* was once common for 'a natural (born) fool,' 'an idiot.' A *private* is 'a private *soldier*'; a *general*, 'a general *officer*.' The same tendency has given us *editorial* for 'editorial *article*' or 'leader,' despite all protests against the neologism. A *lyric* is 'a lyric poem' (literally, one composed for the *lyre*). The *Mediterranean* is the 'Mediterranean' or 'midland' sea. A *meridian* in astronomy is 'a meridian line,'—one crossed by the sun at noon (L. *meridianus*, from *meri-dies*, older *medi-dies*, 'mid-day'). Its use in geography is due to a transference from the celestial to the terrestrial sphere. *Terrier* is for *chien terrier* (L.L. *terrarium*, 'hillock' or 'burrow,' a burrow always implying a mound), from the fondness of these dogs for hunting animals that burrow. *Planet* means 'wandering'; the full phrase was Gr. ἀστὴρ πλανήτης (*astèr planétēs*), 'wandering star' (as opposed to the fixed stars). *Cordovan* or *cordwain* was 'leather from Cordova.'

In this way, the material of which a thing is composed may become the special name of the article itself. Thus, *meerschaum* (Ger., 'sea-foam')[1] for 'meerschaum pipe,' *irons* for 'fetters,' *glasses* for either 'spectacles' or 'drink-

[1] *Meerschaum* has been thought to be a corruption (by 'popular etymology,' see pp. 330 ff.) for *myrsen*, the Tartar name for the substance.

ing glasses,' *the glass* for 'the barometer,' *brasses* for 'brass tablets,' *corduroys* (Fr. *corde du roi,* 'king's cord').[1]

India rubber (gum) overshoes are colloquially known as *rubbers* in some parts of America, as *gums* in others. The history of this word, *rubber*, by the way, is very curious. When caoutchouc was first introduced, it came in thick, heavy pieces, and was used chiefly to rub out pencil marks. It came from Brazil, which was confounded with the West Indies,[2] and thus originated the name *India rubber*, often shortened into *rubber*. The simple word is now freely used as an adjective or as the first part of a compound. Recent slang has coined the word *rubber-neck* for a gaping fellow in the street, who turns his head this way and that; and still more recently, this term, once more cut down to *rubber*, has become a general word of reproach, used especially to express incredulity. All this slang has arisen and become obsolescent in so short a time that it affords us peculiar opportunities for studying linguistic processes.

The omission of the noun is one of the chief means by which names of places or persons become names of things.[3] The object may be called after the place whence it comes or where it originates, or after its inventor, or a 'fancy name' may be applied to it. When the noun that actually names the object vanishes, the descriptive term becomes the name of the object itself. Thus we have *mocha, java, oolong, madras, calico* (from Calicut), *japan, china, Wellingtons* and *Bluchers* (kinds of *boots*), a *mackintosh*, a *basque* (*waist*), a *jersey*, a *polonaise*, a *brougham*, a

---

[1] See p. 15.
[2] Observe that *West Indies* itself is a misnomer, due in the first place to geographical confusion.
[3] See Chapter XXVI, pp. 382–3.

victoria, a *surrey*, and so on. Often the noun is kept, as in *Concord wagon*, *Wellington boots*, *China oranges*, *Jamestown* (corrupted to *jimson*) *weed*, etc., and this enables us to trace the history of those terms in which it is omitted.

We need not suppose that all such designations are clipped forms of actual phrases. The type once established by means of this process of omission, other such names would inevitably be formed without the intervention of the phrase. Thus, the *sandwich* was named directly after the Earl of Sandwich, and the *spencer* after the third Earl Spencer. No one ever said a 'Sandwich lunch' or a 'Spencer coat.'

One of the commonest transformations in language is from an abstract meaning to a concrete. Every language has machinery to make words signifying qualities or actions in the abstract; but no sooner are these formed than thought tends to consider each case of the occurrence of the quality or action in the abstract as a separate entity, and to use its name as a concrete noun. Thus, *heat*, *cold*, *magnitude*, *terror*, *mercy*, *kindness*, *opportunity*, *propriety*, and the like, would seem to be only abstract names of qualities or actions, and, consequently, not limitable to a given case or admitting a plural; but in many languages we hear of 'the heats of summer,' 'the colds of winter,' 'greater and lesser magnitudes,' 'the terrors of the law,' 'the mercies of the Lord,' 'many kindnesses,' 'great opportunities,' 'the proprieties.' So, also, as every action may result in a concrete entity, the name of the action is used, by an easy metonymy, for the resultant concrete idea. Thus, a *congregation* signifies 'a body of worshippers'; a *legion* ('levying of troops'), 'a body of men'; *provisions* ('a foreseeing'), the 'edibles' prepared.

One striking use of the abstract for the concrete is the

application of the name of a quality to a person or thing. This may be regarded as the reverse of personification. In personification a quality is spoken of as a person ('Vice is a monster'); in the use which we are now discussing, a person is designated as if he were the quality incarnate: as, — 'My father was goodness itself,' 'She is perfection.' The Elizabethan poets went very far in applying abstract nouns to persons. Thus Shakspere uses *admiration* for 'wonderful creature' ('Bring in the admiration'); Polyxenes addresses Perdita as *enchantment*, meaning that she has bewitched his son by her beauty. Juliet goes so far in her excitement as to call her old nurse 'ancient damnation.' Though none of these phrases would be possible in Modern English, we can still see many cases of the application of abstract nouns to persons. So colloquially, a man may be described as a 'failure,' a 'fraud,' a 'terror,' a 'success,' an 'awful warning,' an 'inspiration,' one's 'despair,' or 'hope,' or 'dependence,' or 'aversion,' one's 'ruin,' or 'destruction,' or 'salvation'; a child is 'his mother's joy and his father's hope'; Hamlet was 'the expectancy and rose of the fair state.'

There is one form of expression which, though not strictly the use of abstract words for concrete, is yet a peculiar use of the abstract idea by which it is substituted for a concrete notion, so that ultimately the same effect is produced.

The Greek had an idiom by which, when a person was to be mentioned with special reference to one of his qualities, an abstract noun was used to express the quality, and the name of the person was put in the form of an adjective or a genitive. Thus 'the might of Hercules,' or 'the Herculean might,' was practically equivalent to 'the mighty Hercules,' but was felt as a more forcible and picturesque expression. This is really not unlike what one might write to a friend, 'I hope *your experience* will suggest a solution of the problem,' which would be natural in English.

The Greek idiom was imitated in Latin, but the delicate elusiveness of the Greek was lost in the coarser Roman mind. Horace says more crudely, 'virtus Scipiadae et mitis sapientia Laeli,' 'the valor of the son of the Scipios and the kindly wisdom of Laelius,' when he really means no more than 'the valorous Scipio and the wise and kindly Laelius.'

Later the same 'figure' got into prose, as courtesy or servility increased, was seized upon for flattery, and took the form of address: as in 'tua majestas,' 'tua serenitas,' which finally became actual titles. Such titles multiplied, and were also transferred to the third person, so that we have 'his Majesty,' 'your Highness,' 'your Excellency,' 'his Reverence,' 'his Holiness,' 'his Imperial Majesty,' 'his Lordship,' and so on.

English poetry also utilized the figure, — often with superb effect, as when Milton speaks of the 'scaly horror' of the Old Serpent's tail, meaning his 'horrible scaly tail,' and in Shakspere's 'deep damnation of his taking off.'

The English Bible has an extraordinary example of the same kind, 'spiritual wickedness in high places.'[1] What is meant, as appears instantly from the original, is 'wicked demons of the upper air.' But the translators have substituted the abstract *wickedness* for *wicked*, and used *spiritual* for 'of spirits,' thus obscuring or completely changing the sense to the mind of the ordinary reader.

Hardly anything illustrates better the continuity of our civilization than such survivals in common speech of what is regarded as a forcible figure in Greek poetry.

[1] Ephesians vi. 12.

CHAPTER XVIII

SPECIAL PROCESSES IN THE DEVELOPMENT OF MEANING: RADIATION, ETC.

EVERYBODY has envied the magician's talent of being in two places at once. Words, in the development of their several meanings, seem to have mastered the trick. *Power*, for example, is almost ubiquitous in its special senses. Thus it may signify (1) control over one's subordinates, sway ('the power of the king'); (2) delegated authority ('the envoy exceeded his powers'); (3) physical strength ('all the power of his muscles'); (4) mechanical energy ('water-power,' 'steam-power,' 'the power is shut off'); (5) one of the so-called 'mechanical powers' (as a lever); (6) moral or intellectual force; (7) a person of influence ('a power in the community'); (8) one of the great nations of the world ('the concert of the powers'); (9) a mathematical conception ('the fourth power of 6'); (10) an 'army' or 'troop' of soldiers (now obsolete; but cf. *force* and *forces*); (11) an effective quality of style in writing or oratory ('a writer of great power'). Yet in all these vagarious specializations, the 'primary meaning' of *power*, 'the state of being able' to do something (O. Fr. *pouer*, modern *pouvoir*, 'to be able,' from L.L. *potere*[1]), is still present, so that we may almost say that the word accomplishes the feat of being in eleven

---

[1] Which supplanted the classical *posse* in Low Latin.

more or less widely separated places at the same time without ceasing to hold its original position.

The phenomenon is familiar enough. One finds it illustrated on every page of a large dictionary. Yet its significance is disguised by the necessary limitations of printing. The lexicographer must put the primary meaning at the head, and arrange the others below it in an unbroken series. Yet his fifteenth special sense may bear as close a relation to the primary meaning as the fifth. It would be more logical to arrange the whole article in the form of a sunburst or a starfish. *Radiation* is the true history of this process. The simplest meaning stands at the centre, and the secondary meanings proceed out of it in every direction like rays. Each of them is independent of all the rest, and may be traced back to the central signification as if there were no other derivative meaning in existence.[1]

Thus in the case of *power*, the various senses may be arranged in a kind of diagram. (See p. 261.)

Each of the derived senses, it will be seen, might easily have developed from the central meaning 'to be able' without regard to any of the others. Consequently, any one of them might go out of use without affecting the others in the slightest degree.

If we study these radiating senses of *power*, we immediately perceive that they do not all come from the central idea by the same process. Thus 'sway' (of a ruler) is mere specialization. The sense of 'effectiveness' (in style) is both specialized and figurative. The writer's diction is, as it were, personified, and has attributed to it the ability to move the thoughts or feelings of his readers. It is actually the writer who has *power*, but the idea is

[1] See A. Darmesteter, La Vie des Mots, 2d ed., pp. 73–6.

SPECIAL PROCESSES 261

easily ascribed (by transference)[1] to the implement by means of which he exerts it. Again, when a man is called 'a power in the community,' we have the very common use of the abstract for the concrete. The same is true when a nation is called a *power*, or when the term is applied to a lever or a pulley. Some of our special meanings might be derived from one or another of their fellows rather than from the central idea of 'be able.' Thus 'mental or moral power' (No. 6) may be a figurative use

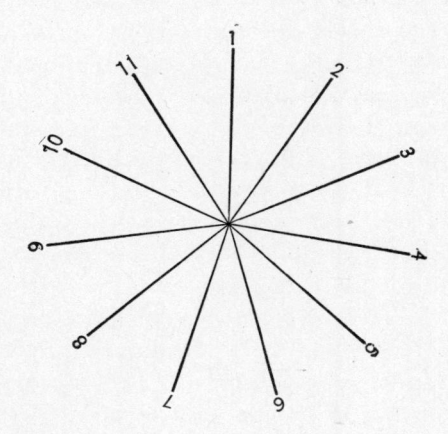

of 'muscular power' (No. 3), and, more probably, the concrete sense of 'lever' or 'wheel-and-axle' (No. 5) may come from the abstract 'mechanical power' (No. 4) ; but we will ignore these minor considerations for the moment.

The word *head* affords a good example of radiation. We may regard as the central meaning that with which we are most familiar, — a part of the body. From this we get **(1)** the 'top' of anything, literally or figuratively,

[1] See Chapter XIX.

whether it resembles a head in shape (as the head of a cane, a pin, or a nail), or merely in position or preëminence (as the head of a page, the head of the table, the head of the hall); (2) figuratively, 'leadership,' or concretely, 'a leader' (the head of the army, the head of the school); (3) the 'head' of a coin (the side on which the ruler's head is stamped); (4) the 'source' of a stream, 'spring,' 'well-head,' 'fountain-head'; (5) the hydraulic sense ('head of water'); (6) a 'promontory,' as *Flamborough Head, Beechy Head;* (7) 'an armed force,' 'a troop' (now obsolete); (8) a single person or individual, as in 'five head of cattle'; (9) the 'main points,' as in 'the heads of a discourse' (also 'notes' of such points); (10) mental power, 'intellectual force.'

Here again there is no reason for deriving any of our ten special senses from any other. They are mutually independent, each proceeding in a direct line from the central or primary meaning of *head*.

The main process of radiation is so simple that it is useless to multiply examples. We may proceed, therefore, to scrutinize its operations in certain matters of detail.

In the first place, we observe that any derived meaning may itself become the source of one or more further derivatives. It may even act as a centre whence such derivatives radiate in considerable numbers, precisely as if it were the primary sense of the word.

Thus, in the case of *head*, the sense of the 'top' of anything immediately divides into that which resembles a human head in (1) shape, or (2) position merely. And each of these senses may radiate in several directions. Thus from (1) we have the head of a pin, of a nail, of a barrel, of an ulcer, 'a bud' (in Shakspere); from (2) the head of a table, of a hall, of a printed page, of a subscription-list. And some of these meanings may also be further developed. 'The head of the table,' for instance, may indicate position, or may be transferred to the person who sits in that position. From the head of an ulcer, we have the disagreeable figure (so common that its literal meaning is quite forgotten), 'to come to a head' for 'to mature' — as in 'his plan came to a head,' and Prospero's 'Now does my project gather to a head' in The Tempest.

Sense No. 2, the 'forefront' of a body of persons, the 'leader,' cannot be altogether separated from No. 1. But it may come perfectly well from the central meaning. In every animal but man the head actually precedes the rest of the body as the creature moves. At all events, the sense of 'leadership' or 'leader' (it is impossible to keep them apart) has given rise to an infinity of particular applications and idiomatic phrases. The head of a procession, of an army, of a class, of a revolt, of a 'reform movement,' of a new school of philosophy — these phrases all suggest personal leadership, but in different degrees and very various relations to the persons who are led, so that they may all be regarded as radiating from a common centre.

By a succession of radiations the development of meanings may become almost infinitely complex. No dictionary can ever register a tithe of them, for, so long as a language is alive, every speaker is constantly making new specialized applications of its words. Each particular definition in the fullest lexicon represents, after all, not so much a single meaning as a little group of connected ideas, unconsciously agreed upon in a vague way by the consensus of those who use the language. The limits of the definition must always be vague, and even within these limits there is large scope for variety.

If the speaker does not much transgress these limits in a given instance, we understand his meaning. Yet we do not and cannot see all the connotations which the word has in the speaker's mind. He has given us a conventional sign or symbol for his idea. Our interpretation of the sign will depend partly on the context or the circumstances, partly on what we know of the speaker, and partly on the associations which we ourselves attach to the word in question. These considerations conduct us, once more, to the principle on which we have so often insisted. Once more we are forced to admit that language, after all, is essentially poetry. For it is the function of poetry, as Sainte Beuve says, not to tell us everything, but to set our imaginations at work: 'La poésie ne consiste pas à tout dire, mais à tout faire rêver.'

Besides the complexity that comes from successive radiation, there is a perpetual exchange of influences among the meanings themselves. Thus when we speak of a man as the 'intellectual head of a movement,' *head* means 'leader' (No. 3), but has also a suggestion of the tenth sense, 'mind.' If two very different senses of a word are present to the mind at the same moment, the result is a pun, intentional or unintentional. If the senses are subtly related, so that they enforce or complement each other, our phrase becomes imaginatively forcible, or, in other words, recognizable poetry as distinguished from the unconscious poetry of language.

So, too, the sudden re-association of a derived sense with the central meaning of the word may produce a considerable change in the effect. *Head* for 'leader' is no longer felt as metaphorical, and so of several other of the radiating senses of this word. Yet it may, at any moment, flash back to the literal meaning, and be revivified as a conscious metaphor for the nonce. 'He is not the *head* of his party, but their mask'; 'The leader fell, and the crowd was a body without a *head*.'

Radiation is a very simple process, though its results may become beyond measure complicated. It consists merely in divergent specialization from a general centre. It is always easy to follow the spokes back to the hub.

Quite different is the next process that we have to study, in which a word moves gradually away from its first meaning by successive steps of alternate specialization and generalization until, in many cases, there is not a shadow of connection between the sense that is finally developed and that which the term bore at the outset. The history of many such words is well ascertained. If the evidence is fragmentary, however, the etymologist is often baffled in his attempts to reconstruct it.[1]

We have already observed that a word may get a new meaning by the addition of a modifying idea (expressed or implied) to the old one.[2] Thus *congregation* means simply an 'assembly' of any kind, but it has developed the special sense of an 'assembly gathered for worship.' Here we may represent the first meaning ('assembly') by A, and the modifying limitation ('religious') by B; the new meaning will be $A + B$, the sum of the two elements.

So far the process is simple enough; but the process may not stop with $A + B$. Thus L. *candidatus* (whence our *candidate*) meant 'a person dressed in white' (A); then, 'a white-robed seeker for office' ($A + B$), from the Roman custom of wearing one's freshest robes when ask-

[1] Cf. A. Darmesteter, La Vie des Mots, 2d ed., pp. 76 ff.
[2] See p. 253.

ing the suffrages of the people; in our *candidate*, all idea of 'white attire' (*A*) has disappeared, leaving only the sense of 'an applicant for office' (*B*), which has no obvious connection with the first meaning of the word.

Again *cheater* meant first 'an officer who attended to escheats,' 'an escheator' (*A*); then 'an escheator who was dishonest' (*A* + *B*); and finally (by loss of *A*), a 'dishonest person' (*B*). *Squire* is (*A*) 'shieldman' (*scutarius*); then (*A* + *B*) 'shield-bearer' who attends on a knight; then (*B*) 'attendant on a knight' (without reference to the carrying of a shield). *Tally* is (*A*) 'cutting'; then (*A* + *B*) a cutting of notches to keep an account; then (*B*) 'an account,' whether kept by notched sticks or otherwise. *Score* is (*A*) 'a notch' or 'cut'; (*A* + *B*) a notch or mark to indicate a charge or computation; then (*B*) 'a bill or account' (without reference to cuts or notches).

None of the examples cited has wandered far from its first sense. The development is still very simple, and the chain of meanings is easy to follow. But the process may continue until all logical connection disappears and we find ourselves wondering how a single word has come to stand for such disconnected and even inconsistent ideas. *Treacle* is undoubtedly derived from the Greek θηριακόν (*thēriakón*), 'pertaining to a wild beast.' It now means 'sugar syrup' or 'molasses.' If we were ignorant of the history of the word, we should be at a loss to account for this peculiar state of things; but the process which we are studying explains the apparent anomaly as a natural development. The Greek word *thēriakón*, 'pertaining to a wild beast,' may be called *A*. From this there arises the modified sense, 'a *remedy* for the bite of a wild animal (*A* + *B*). The next step is to reject *A* altogether, so that *treacle* comes to mean any 'antidote' or 'sovereign remedy' (*B*). Now ancient remedies were frequently put up in the form of electuaries or thick syrups. Thus *B*, 'a remedy,' developed into $B + C$, 'a remedy in the form of a *syrup*.' This meaning is treated precisely as $A + B$ was treated. *B* is rejected and only *C*, 'a syrup,' remains. By this time there is no connection at all between *C*, 'a syrup,' and *A*, 'pertaining to a wild beast,' since the middle term *B*, 'a remedy,' has vanished altogether, and it was only this middle term that connected *C* with *A*.

The process may be graphically represented. Thus:—

1.	A	pertaining to a wild beast.
2.	$A + B$	remedy for a wild beast's bite.
3.	B	antidote or remedy in general.
4.	$B + C$	remedy in the form of a syrup.
5.	C	syrup in general.

At any stage of the process, a meaning is capable of being treated as if it were the original sense of the word. Thus when *treacle* had come to mean 'a remedy' in general (*B*), and people had forgotten that it had anything to do with the bite of an animal, it was used (1) literally, for the 'antidote' to any poison, and (2) figuratively, of that which relieves one's sorrow, a 'comfort' or 'consolation'; and finally (3) of a personal comforter. So Chaucer speaks of Christ as 'treacle of every harm,' *i.e.* a sovereign remedy for every grief. Again, the general simplified meaning 'syrup' (*C*) has been affected by radiation, so that, in modern usage, *treacle* is applied indifferently to the 'spume of sugar,' to 'maple syrup,' and to 'molasses.'

The paradoxical effects of the $A + B$ process, as well as the complications that result from its working in combination with other linguistic forces, may be studied in the extremely interesting words *parson* and *person*, which are simply variants of the same word, like *clark* and *clerk*.[1]

The Latin *persona* means properly 'a mask,' such as the ancient actors wore.[2] This meaning we may call A. Such masks were typical of various parts or *rôles*, and thus arises $A + B$, 'a dramatic character as indicated by the appropriate mask.' Then A disappears and B remains, so that *persona* means 'a character or *rôle* in a play.' To B is then added a further modifier (C), 'one who represents,' and we have $B + C$, 'one who represents a dramatic character,' 'one who takes a *rôle*.' Next B disappears, so that *persona* means merely 'a representative.' C is then modified by the addition of 'the church' (D), and we get $C + D$, 'the representative of the church (*persona ecclesiae*) in a parish.' Finally the main idea of C ('representative') disappears, and *parson* in the sense of 'parish priest' results. The relation between a mask and a *curé* would be unintelligible (except on grounds of satirical humor) if we could not trace the word step by step.

1. A mask.
2. $A + B$ character indicated by mask.
3. B character or *rôle* (in play).
4. $B + C$ one who represents a character.
5. C representative in general.
6. $C + D$ representative of church in parish.
7. D parson.

---

[1] *Clark* is preserved only as a proper name. *Clerk* is pronounced *clark* in England, but *clerk* (*e* as in *fern*) in America, though the other pronunciation is well known, and may still be heard occasionally from old people. For the etymology, see p. 44.

[2] *Per-*, 'through,' and *sonare*, 'to sound,' since the actor 'talked through' the large mouth of his mask.

This whole development took place in Latin, whence the word was borrowed (under French influence) as *persoun*, the form which Chaucer uses.

Meantime *persona* had taken another course. From *B*, 'dramatic part' or 'rôle,' had come (in classic Latin) the figurative meaning of the 'part' or 'character' which one sustains in the world, and then, by transference and fading out of the metaphor, a 'personage' or 'person' in the modern sense.

In English the old *persoun* has split into two words,[1] which are not felt by most speakers as having any connection in sense or etymology. *Parson* is reserved for the ecclesiastical sense, and *person* is used for 'bodily form' or for 'human being' in general. It has lately acquired a somewhat slighting connotation, which, however, is not always felt. The form *person* is habitually associated with *persona* by everybody who has any acquaintance with Latin, which in part accounts for its pronunciation. *Parson* is a phonetic spelling of the Middle English word. For 'characters in a play' we have borrowed the Latin phrase *dramatis personae*, which is to all intents and purposes an English term.

Strange transformations of meaning may come by the simple and natural process of applying the name of an object to something else which resembles it or is used for the same purpose. The progress of invention makes this process very common in the names of utensils and the like. *Pen* (L. *penna*) is originally a 'feather.' The name was appropriately applied to pens so long as quills were used for writing. It is kept, however, for various modern implements (steel pens, gold pens, stylographic pens) which have replaced feathers in this

[1] Cf. pp. 355-7.

function.[1] The change is comparatively slight in this instance, since steel pens actually resemble quills. *Pencil* is more noteworthy. The word was borrowed from L. *penicillus*, and meant a fine painter's brush, made of fur, hair, or bristles, like a 'camel's-hair pencil.' *Penicillus* is a diminutive of *peniculus*, 'a little tail,' such as was used by the Romans for purposes of cleaning, as we use brushes or brooms. From 'a painter's brush,' the name *pencil* was passed along to a marking instrument made of lead; hence the term *lead-pencil*, which we now apply to a stick of graphite enclosed in wood, where there is really neither *lead* nor *pencil*.

Chimney comes (through the French) from L. *camīnus*, a 'forge' or 'smelting-furnace.' It came to be used for any 'fireplace' (the earliest sense in English), then, in particular, for the 'smoke flue.' *Lamp-chimney* shows a further narrowing in sense.

Chandelier (from L. *candelabrum*), 'a receptacle for candles,' has been so extended as to include gas-jets and electric lights. *Scales* (from L. *scala*, 'a ladder') now means 'a weighing instrument,' from the graduated marks on the beam of the balance, which suggest the equidistant rounds of a ladder. It has also been extended to musical *scales*.

A capital example of the shifting process is seen in *handkerchief*. A small piece of cloth to cover the head was naturally enough called a *coverchef* (O. Fr. *couvre-chef*; *chef* from L. *caput*) or *kerchief* (cf. *curfew*). When fashion decreed that a somewhat similar piece should be carried in the hand, *handkerchief* was coined, with no thought of the literal sense of *kerchief*. The next step was *pocket-handkerchief*, which is literally, it will be observed, a thing to

---

[1] The same thing has happened to the German *Feder*.

cover the head, to be carried in the hand, to be put in the pocket.

The history of railroading illustrates the point in question remarkably well. English and American railroads developed independently, and long after the separation of the colonies from the mother-country. The special vocabulary, therefore, differs widely in the two countries. In Great Britain, coaching terms were utilized. Hence we find *coaches*, *drivers*, *guards*, and *booking-offices* in England, but *cars*, *engineers*, *conductors*, and *ticket-offices* in the United States. *Booking-office* is a particularly interesting transference. It was originally the bureau at which one entered or 'booked' one's name in advance, in order to secure a place in the coach. Many of the differences between the language of England and that of America depend, in like manner, on the independent development of industries or occupations in the two countries. Compare *lift* with *elevator*, *tram* with *horse-car* (or *electric car*), *parish council* with *selectmen*, and so on. The investigation of such divergences is a matter of much interest, but has usually been pursued in a somewhat perfunctory way, with little regard to linguistic principles. The conservative tendency to retain familiar terms in a new application is probably stronger in England than in America.

CHAPTER XIX

TRANSFERENCE OF MEANING

THE Romans had a proverb, 'Everything has two handles'; and nowhere is this more true than in mental conceptions and the words that express them. Almost every conception has two aspects; (1) that of the person or thing that possesses or exercises it; (2) that of the person or thing that is affected by it. This difference between the active agent and the effect produced, between the cause and that which it causes, between the subjective and the objective, is very great indeed. But, obvious as it seems, it has been slow to arise in the consciousness of the race. In the Latin vocabulary, to which we are so deeply indebted, little account is made of this fundamental distinction, so that the same word is often used indifferently for either side of the conception. Thus the Latin *opinio* means both *opinion* (from the point of view of him who *has* it) and *reputation* (from the point of view of him concerning whom it is held); and the same is true of the English word *opinion* in Shakspere. Nothing could be more natural, for 'my opinion of Richard Roe' is of course identical with 'Roe's *reputation* with me.' The difference is simply in the person from whose point of view the conception is regarded. As time goes on, however, we feel more and more that, although *opinion* and *reputation* are the same thing, yet they differ widely in their relations to other ideas which we may wish to express. The distinction between them seems so important that we feel the need of making it clear in the vocabulary. Accordingly, we have limited or specialized *opinion* to its modern meaning, and have adopted *reputation* (from *re-puto*, 'to think over') to signify the other side of the same idea. It is to be observed, however, that there is no inherent difference between these two words, since both mean properly 'the act or process of considering,' 'consideration.' Their distinction in our vocabulary is due merely to the fact that *opinion* has been specialized in one direction, *reputation* in the other, with the result that we have two carefully discriminated words, which cannot possibly be confused, even if they have no context to fix their bearings.

A few examples will make clearer this important point. In '*shame* kept him silent,' the subjective feeling of the person who is ashamed is meant; in '*shameful* treatment,' the character of the act is objectively described. *Honor* may be the sentiment which a man cherishes in his own heart and which keeps him true to his better nature, or it may be the tribute of respect which others pay to such a man. Compare 'an *honorable* gentleman,' with 'an *honorable* invitation.' Our *odium* is the Latin word for 'hatred,' but it never means 'hatred' in English. It signifies the objective result of the hatred of others, — something like 'unpopularity' (but in a stronger sense).[1] In *odium theologicum*, however, we have borrowed the same word again, this time in the sense of 'hatred' pure and simple.

The same confusion between subjective and objective may be seen in the uses of cases and propositions, and in

---

[1] This was also a Latin meaning, in accordance with the habit of that language, in which almost any abstract noun may express both sides of an idea.

other linguistic machinery for expressing the relations of ideas. The Latin *amor Dei*, and our 'the love of God,' may mean either God's love for us or ours for him. So *caedes Clodiana* may mean a murder committed by Clodius or a murder of which Clodius was the victim; and such phrases as 'the Fontenoy forgery case,' 'the Williamson assault' are equally ambiguous. There is a like uncertainty in compound words: compare *walking stick* with *pruning hook*, *headsman* with *head man*, *ink stain* with *ink eraser*, *lovesick* with *lovelock*, *heart-wished* with *heart-whole*. The Elizabethans were very venturesome in the matter of compounds. Thus (in Shakspere), *death-marked* might be 'marked *by* death' or 'marked *for* death,' but in 'the fearful passage of their *death-marked* love '[1] it is probably the latter. The 'death-practised duke'[2] is Albany, whose *death* is *plotted* (to practise = to plot). 'Be *simple-answered*'[3] means 'Be provided with a simple answer,' *i.e.* 'Answer simply.' But *full-acorned*[4] is 'stuffed full of acorns.' *Foolish-compounded*[5] is 'composed of folly,' not 'foolishly put together.' *Folly-fallen*[6] is 'fallen into folly.' '*Neighbor-stained* steel'[7] is 'stained by neighbors' blood.' *Hell-hated*[8] is not 'hated by hell' but 'hateful as hell.' And so on. The exact relations of the ideas expressed by the parts of the compound have to be interpreted by the context in each case.

The English infinitive illustrates the point incomparably. *To wear*, for instance, is active in 'I am *to wear* my black coat,' but it seems to be passive in 'My coat isn't fit to wear!' In fact, however, *wear* has no 'voice' in these

[1] Prologue to Romeo and Juliet.
[2] King Lear, act iv, sc. 6, l. 284.
[3] King Lear, act iii, sc. 7, l. 43.
[4] Cymbeline, act ii, sc. 5, l. 16.
[5] Henry IV, Part I, act i, sc. 2, l. 8.
[6] Twelfth Night, act iii, sc. 1, l. 75.
[7] Romeo and Juliet, act i, sc. 1, l. 89.
[8] King Lear, act v, sc. 3, l. 147.

sentences. It is really a noun of action. *To wear* is thus equivalent to 'for wearing'; it includes both the idea of somebody who *wears* and of something that *is worn*, and the application is left to the acumen of the hearer. Compare 'a journey to go,' 'a sight to behold,' 'dreadful to see,' 'a sad tale to hear,' 'fish to sell (or *for sale*),' 'nothing to eat.' The placard 'To Be Let,' sometimes seen instead of the usual 'To Let,' is a comical specimen of grammatical prudishness. It shows, however, the anxiety that we feel to avoid, if possible, all concession to the 'facing-both-ways' element in our language.

Now it is precisely in this debatable land between two aspects of the same conception that some of the most curious freaks of language take place. *Transference*, or a sudden shift in the 'point of view' (from subject to object), is likely to happen at any moment. It may pass unnoticed; it may serve only to give point to an epigram or felicity to a poetical figure, but in countless instances it has had a permanent effect on our vocabulary.

Adjectives are much affected by transference. Many adjectives have since been limited to one side or the other of a conception, as the need for specialization has made itself felt, that were once equally applicable to both. There was extreme confusion between active and passive adjectives.[1] Thus '*feeling* sorrows' in Shakspere means 'sorrows that are deeply *felt*'; 'the *unexpressive* she' is the 'inexpressible' or 'ineffable' lady; *uncomprehensive* is 'incomprehensible.' *Per contra*, *tuneable* meant 'tuneful,' 'harmonious'; *separable*, 'causing separation'; *imaginary*, 'imaginative'; an '*intenible* sieve' was one

[1] This comes of course from the fact that most adjectives are in origin neither active nor passive, but only indicate likeness or relationship in a vague way. Cf. p. 174.

that *could hold* nothing; *deceivable* was 'deceptive'; *reverent* and *reverend* were practically interchangeable.

There was a similar uncertainty with regard to adjectives in *-ful*. *Awful* meant 'awe-inspiring' or 'filled with terror'; '*distressful* bread' in Henry IV's soliloquy on sleep is not 'bread that distresses the eater,' but 'hard-earned bread' won by distressful toil; *dreadful* shared the ambiguity of *awful*; *hateful* meant 'full of hate' as well as 'odious'; *painful* was common in the sense of 'painstaking,' 'laborious,' — a 'painful preacher' was a complimentary phrase in the seventeenth century. Some of these *-ful* adjectives are still unsettled. One may be *doubtful* about a *doubtful* question. But in most cases the die has been cast. Thus *pitiful* is now seldom used in the sense of 'compassionate'; it signifies either 'proper to excite one's pity,' or, with a scornful connotation, 'contemptible.' In Shakspere's time the three meanings were about equally common. We no longer say 'a fretful corrosive' (Henry IV). Our *fretful* carries only the neuter or reflexive meaning of the verb, — 'to fret *one's self*,' 'to let one's self be fretted,' and we have almost forgotten that *fret* is literally 'to eat away,' or 'devour,' like the German *fressen* with which it is cognate.[1]

The transference of an adjective from the *person* who has the quality denoted to some *object* (person or thing) with reference to which he manifests that quality, is one of the commonest of all linguistic phenomena. Poetry is full of such instances. The thane of Cawdor resigned his life 'as 'twere a *careless* trifle.' Lear's fool 'labored

---

[1] A.S. *fretan* is for *for-etan*, like Ger. *fressen* for *ver-essen*. The old sense is seen in 'a moth *fretting* a garment.' '*Fret-work* and *fret-saw* are not related to this verb, but come from *frætwan*, 'to adorn.' So 'yon gray lines that *fret* the clouds' in Julius Cæsar.

to outjest' the 'heart-struck injuries' of his master. Of course, in plain prose, it was *Lear* who was struck to the heart by the wrongs that his daughters had done him. A 'sleepy language,' in The Tempest, is such a language as one might speak in one's sleep. 'Trusty business' in All's Well is the kind of business that we commit to trusty agents. 'Drunken prophecies' is a happy phrase in Richard III.

But the shift in question is not confined to the poets. It is characteristic of language itself; for language, as we saw at the outset, is the unrecognized and instinctive poetry of the mass of men. 'Glad tidings,' 'joyful news,' 'hopeless efforts,' 'a malignant speech,' 'a jealous look,' 'a friendly glance,' 'a flattering offer,' 'wise counsel,' 'treacherous plots' are examples of precisely similar transference. The colloquial dialect shows the same tendency. *Elegant, nice, superb,* denote a subjective personal quality, but are transferred in ordinary language to objects with reference to which the quality is manifested. Thus a '*nice* person' is no longer (except in books) a 'fastidious' person, but one who might satisfy a fastidious person. *Superb* is the Latin *superbus,* 'proud,' but it has lost that meaning by transference and is always applied objectively.

A few additional examples will bring out the importance of these processes in the development of the English vocabulary. *Curious* is the Latin *curiosus,* 'careful,' 'care-taking.' It retains its personal meaning in the sense of 'inquisitive.' Transferred to things, it came to mean 'requiring care,' as in '*curious* business,' or 'elaborately wrought,' as in 'a *curious* tale' (both from Shakspere). From this to the everyday sense of 'odd,' 'peculiar' was but a step. *Quaint* has a similar history. It is the Old French *cointe,* 'cultivated,' 'agreeable' (from L. *cognitus,* 'known'). Its development in English is from 'wise' or 'skilful' to 'elaborate,' 'well-wrought,' and thence to 'fanciful,' 'odd,' or 'peculiar.' Its special modern connotation seems to be 'old-fashioned,' — for the studied elegance of one generation becomes singularity in the age that follows.

Secure, with its doublet *sure*, and their numerous derivatives show a like transference of epithets. *Secure* is originally the Latin *securus*, 'without anxiety' (from *se-*, 'without,' and *cura*), an epithet of course applicable to persons only; and in that sense it is constantly used in Latin and even in early English. But in modern use it has been transferred (in the main) to the thing about which one feels *secure*, and in this sense we have also *assurance*, *insurance*, and other derivatives. *Sure*, which is *securus* in a French form (O. Fr. *seür*, modern *sûr*) is still usable in the old meaning: as, — 'I am *sure* of my ground.' Compare also the derivative *surety*.

The transference from things to persons, from the objective to the subjective, is less common, but is found often enough. Thus *pompous* is a derivative from L. *pompa*,[1] 'a procession,' and denotes properly the splendor and 'pomp' that characterize a festal march. So the poet Sidonius has *pomposus incessus* for a stately or 'processional' gait. Transferred to persons, *pompous* suggests the same stateliness, with a ridiculous connotation. *Solemn* is an excellent parallel. The Latin is *solemnis*, *sollennis*, from *sollus*, 'whole,' and *annus*, 'year,' and signifies 'annual,' with special reference to religious celebrations; hence *solemnize*, and a *solemnity*. 'A *solemn* person' shows a transference of the epithet.

---

[1] The Latin *pompa* is borrowed from Gr. πομπή in the same sense (from πέμπω, 'to send').

Other instances are *downright, straightforward*. 'Downright speech' and 'straightforward language' are easy figures; but it is only by transference that we can speak of a downright or straightforward *person*. The 'superfluous and lust-dieted man' in King Lear is one who has more than he needs, a pampered epicure. Other examples are 'a very *literal* person,' 'a *prolix* talker,' 'a *navigable* merchant,' 'a *logical* thinker,' 'a *profound* investigator,' '*mellifluous* songsters.'

Transference operates also in verbs, producing many curious shifts of meaning. To *sprinkle* is literally to 'scatter.' But in sprinkling we not only act directly on the liquid but indirectly on some other object: we '*sprinkle the water* on the plants,' for example. Hence, by transference, we speak of 'sprinkling the plants' themselves. In like manner, *spatter* (connected with *spit*) has suffered transference, — so that one may 'spatter blood upon the floor' or 'spatter the floor with blood.' To *empty* is literally to 'make empty,' — 'I emptied the bag of its contents'; but we do not hesitate to 'empty the silver out of the bag,' or to 'empty the water out of the glass.' By a still further transference a river may be said 'to empty into the sea,' in which the action of emptying is said to be done by the river itself. So, with *spatter*, one might say, 'I cut an artery and the *blood spattered* all over the floor.'

This last-mentioned kind of transference has had far-reaching results in our syntax and vocabulary. It enables us to use a great many verbs not only transitively ('he poured oil on the flame') but intransitively ('the rain poured dismally'). Thus we have, without change of form or fear of ambiguity, a satisfactory substitute for the Greek middle and the reflexive verbs of German and

French. 'He turned round' is simpler than 'he turned himself round,' and equally clear. In Greek 'I turn' (a thing), transitively, is one form, τρέπω, *trépō* (in the active voice); 'I turn (myself),' intransitively, is another form, τρέπομαι, *trépomai* (in the so-called 'middle voice,' *i.e.* neither active nor passive). The beginner is struck by the grammatical distinction (which has probably never attracted his attention in English), as well as by the elegance with which the Greek inflection indicates it. He may easily infer that the absence of the middle voice is a defect in our language. A moment's thought, however, convinces one that no inflectional distinction is necessary, and that the abandonment of a third 'voice' (for the Germanic languages once had a 'middle' too) is not deterioration, but advance. We accomplish the same end with simpler means and less trouble. In this respect, as in certain others, we have gone farther than most languages of our family. In German, for instance, to 'turn (anything)' is *wenden;* to 'turn (one's self)' is '*sich* wenden.' In English, the reflexive is not used, and our experience proves that it is not requisite.[1]

Engage is a good example of the process that we are studying. It means literally 'to put (a person or thing) in or under a pledge (*en gage*),'[2] 'to impledge' in any manner, literal or figurative: as, — 'I *engage* my word,' 'He suffered his kinsman to be *engaged*' (that is, held as prisoner or hostage), 'He *engaged* himself to carry out the plan,' 'He *engaged* the servant.' But it is now especially common in an intransitive use: as, — 'He *engaged* in the practice of law.' So *prove*, 'to test' (L. *probare*), may

[1] Cf. pp. 183-4.
[2] A *gage* is a 'pledge'; cf. *wage, wages, wager*, 'throw down the *gage.*'

mean 'to turn out' (so and so, under the test of time): as,—
'His efforts *proved* unsuccessful.' Even such verbs as
strengthen, *weaken*, *tighten*, *loosen*, and *sharpen*, though
they are specially formed with the suffix -*en*, 'to make or
cause,' are not infrequently heard in the sense of '*become*
strong,' etc. Similar instances are innumerable.[1] Such
colloquialisms as 'He *takes* a good photograph' for 'He
always succeeds in getting a good photograph of himself,'
and the butcher's encouraging 'This beef will *eat* well'
may sound grotesque. In fact, however, they illustrate,
as such things usually do, a governing principle of our
language.

English shows similar freedom in making intransitive
verbs transitive by giving them a causative force. 'To
fly a kite' is 'to cause it to fly.' So one may *grow*
wheat, *run* an engine, *gallop* a horse, *float* a corporation,
or *stand* a man on his head. Like other languages,
English once had its machinery for making verbs of
causation. Thus, to *fell* is the causative of *fall*, to *drench*
of *drink*, to *singe* (older *sengen*) of *sing*, to *quench* of
A.S. *cwincan* ('disappear'), to *blench*[2] of *blink*. But this
machinery ceased to operate long ago, though some of its
products are still in stock. Transference has proved a
simpler means of accomplishing the end desired.

In view of all these facts it is not surprising that the
distinction between *sit* and *set*, *lie* and *lay*, has broken
down in vulgar English, and has not always maintained
itself in literature. In the first half of the last century
lay was pretty common for *lie*, even in respectable authors.
The sun still *sets*, and it is excessively difficult (hardly

---

[1] Compare the transitive and the intransitive use of *twist, draw, drag, settle, stay, putrefy, submit, oppose, pretend, warp.*

[2] *Blench* has lost its causative sense.

desirable) for a poultry farmer to speak of 'a *sitting* hen.'

In conclusion, a few miscellaneous examples of transference are given to illustrate the variety of its operations. An *omen*[1] is a sign that foreshadows calamity, but in Elizabethan English it is sometimes transferred to the calamity that is foreshadowed by the sign,— as in Shakspere's 'prologue to the *omen* coming on.' This is a close parallel to *disaster*, which has passed from 'ill-boding appearance of the stars' to 'ruin and misfortune.' To *challenge* is literally to ' bring a charge against' a *person*, being derived (through the French) from L. *calumniari*, 'to calumniate'; hence, by an easy shift, it gets the sense of 'laying claim to ' a *thing* or a privilege,— as in 'challenge attention.' *Polite* is 'polished' (L. *politus*, p.p. of *polio*, 'to polish'); its application to *persons*, at first metaphorical, has ceased to be figurative so far as English is concerned, and the word is freely transferred to manners or bearing; compare *courteous* and *courtly*.[2] *Game* is 'sport' of any kind; with reference to hunting, it means the material result of the sport, — the 'quarry.' *Venison* is L. *venatio*, 'hunting,' and has developed its meaning in a precisely similar fashion. A 'hollow sound' is one that sounds as if it were reëchoed from a pit or hollow; so 'a hollow roaring,' 'a hollow groan.' There is transference of the epithet in 'a terrible night,' where the terror has nothing to do with the night except for the relation of time, and in 'an anxious week,' since only a person can be anxious.

[1] Of course there are good omens as well as bad, but the word has been more or less specialized in its disastrous sense.

[2] *Court* is an old borrowing from Norman French. It is L. *cohors, cohortis*, 'cohort.'

One can *blow* a *blast* on a horn in actual pneumatical fact. To *blow* the *horn* requires an imaginative transference, which, however, was made so long ago that we forget that it is imaginative. More recently, a famous lyric poet could, without fear of criticism (indeed, with much force and elegance), exhort a bugle to blow itself. Here, as always, the individual poet is merely following out, with the certainty of genius, the path in which the language guides him.

No poet proceeds more daringly than Milton in this path: 'Let the bass of Heaven's deep organ blow,' 'happier union,' 'dolorous mansions,' 'speckled vanity,' 'like glories wearing,' 'the scaly horror of his folded tail,' are well-known examples from his Hymn on the Nativity. But they are, in fact, no bolder than many a phrase which we habitually employ without a thought of its logical history.

Thus English is full of happy misapplications of words. They should serve as warnings to the puristic pedant, and may, perhaps, encourage aspiring neologists. One caution, however, must in conscience be added. The only safe course is to be sure that the misapplication is so happy that the rest of the world will adopt it. Then, despite the purists, you have enriched the English language. Otherwise,—well, you have not!

CHAPTER XX

DEGENERATION OF MEANING

DESCENT is easy, and words, like people, show a propensity to fall away from their better selves. The degeneration is sometimes due to special causes. Usually, however, the word takes its first step in the downward path when it is used in slight, perhaps in jocose, disparagement. As time goes on, it gets into worse and worse odor, until at last it may become a term of extreme contempt or reprobation.

A good example is our word *villain* (from the French *vilain*). *Villain* originally signified 'a farm-laborer.' It is derived from the Latin *villa*, 'farmhouse,' through *villanus*, 'a slave attached to one's country-place.' In English it was at first merely a descriptive term for a particular station in life, replacing the native word *churl* (A.S. *ceorl*), which had the same sense. Soon, however, it became a term of contempt for one who did not belong to the gentry. Gradually there was built up a set of ideas associating with *villain* and *villany* all the qualities opposed to the comprehensive word *courtesy*,[1] which signified in the Middle Ages 'the continent of what part a gentleman would see.' Thus *villain* was applied to a 'low fellow' in general, and *villany* was used for low conduct, or low

[1] The injustice which Tennyson has done to the character of the matchless Gawain, 'with his olde curteisye,' comes in part from too limited and modern an understanding of this fine old word.

language, or low thoughts. From this to the present meaning is a short step; the implied moral reprobation has simply been intensified. In this process *villain* and *villany* have quite lost their association with any particular rank in life. A king, as well as a peasant, may be described as a villain, if he is morally wicked.[1] Several other words which properly mean 'farm-hand,' or the like, have become more or less debased. Thus *churl* no longer means 'serf,' or 'bumpkin,' but is applied to any one who is rude in his manners or a curmudgeon in disposition. But the word is little used; *boor*, literally 'farmer,' has taken its place.[2] In this country, *farmer* itself is sometimes jocosely applied to a 'greenhorn,' or to a person who has made himself ridiculous, particularly by awkwardness or stupidity. If our language were not so fixed by the conservative forces of literature and education, it is not impossible that *farmer* would go the way of its predecessors. *Clown* was perhaps contemptuous in its very origin. It seems to have meant literally 'a clod.'[3] It appears in English in the senses of 'rustic' and 'jester' at about the same date (late sixteenth century), but there is evidence that the latter is a derived meaning. At all events, the comic 'clowns' of the drama frequently represented countrymen who amused the audience by their mingled simplicity and mother-wit.

Knave has had a history similar to that of *villain*. It

---

[1] When *villain* was borrowed from the French, it had both the first and the second meanings here given to it, so that the development indicated did not take place in English. Both the more primitive and the more developed sense were borrowed at the same time.

[2] See p. 347.

[3] Cf. *clod* for a gross or stupid fellow. A *clodpoll* or *clotpoll* is a man who had a sod or a clod of earth for a head (cf. *blockhead*). Cf. Emilia's 'as ignorant as dirt,' in Othello. *Clodhopper* tells its own story.

meant originally (like Ger. *Knabe*) 'boy'; then *servant*, from the habit of calling servants 'boys' (as in Greek and Latin, and the South before the war). Thus it came to be used as a general term of disparagement for a person of inferior station, and finally it developed the sense of moral worthlessness. *Valet* and *varlet* are Old French diminutives of *vassal*. They literally meant 'boy' or 'youth,' just as *vassal* meant 'man.' Specialized in the sense of 'servant,' however, they tended to deteriorate, and *varlet* became, in English, a synonym for 'saucy fellow.' All such words, as soon as they acquire a reproachful or contemptuous connotation, tend to go out of use in their literal descriptive meaning, for the *knave* or *villain* in the old sense refuses to answer to the discredited name. *Vassalage* is an interesting example of a word which has been specialized in two directions. Since the *vassal* was his lord's inferior, *vassalage* sank to the sense of 'servitude.' On the other hand, it rose by an equally obvious chain of thought to the meaning of 'valorous deeds,' 'splendid service in war,' such as a vassal performs for his suzerain, and this is its meaning in Chaucer.

Several words for 'woman' or 'girl' have lost caste in one way or another. *Wench* was once perfectly respectable; it meant nothing but 'daughter,' 'orphan,' or 'pupil' (A.S. *wencel*, *wencle*, from *wencel*, 'weak' and so needing protection). *Quean* (A.S. *cwene*) is cognate with Gr. γυνή (*gunḗ*), and meant 'woman.' A related word (A.S. *cwēn*) has given us *queen*, and the Sanskrit *gnā*, another related term, is even more dignified, since it stands for 'goddess.' *Hussy* is from *housewife*. The German *Dirne*, 'loose woman,' once meant 'virgin,' and in Old High German is even applied to the Virgin Mary. It would be hard to find a more extraordinary instance of verbal degradation. *Woman* and Ger. *Weib* have also gone down in the world (see p. 326).

Fellow, now either contemptuous or else used lightly for 'man' in general, once meant 'partner.' It was A.S. *fēolaga*,[1] — one who *laid* down his property (*fee*) along with yours. Hence came the meaning of 'companion,' then 'idle companion,' and thus we arrive at the slighting modern sense. The literal meaning has also been preserved, by virtue of certain combinations into which *fellow* had entered before it began to lose caste, such as *fellowship*, *fellow-feeling*, *yokefellow*, and compound words like *fellow-Christian*. '*Fellow* of a college' is a translation of *socius;* its academic isolation has preserved its dignity.

Companion and *mate* were also used contemptuously at one time, probably because they were synonymous with *fellow*. *Chapman*, the native English word for 'merchant,' is obsolete, except as a proper name. The clipped form *chap*, however, is still used disparagingly, and in older English both *chapman* and *merchant* were common terms of contempt for a saucy or otherwise objectionable person. Observe that *companion*, *merchant*, and *mate* have succeeded in rehabilitating themselves — always a difficult feat for either a word or a person to accomplish.

Caitiff is an old French word for 'captive' (modern *chétif*, L. *captivus*). It often meant 'poor creature,' since the condition of captives was peculiarly miserable, and it was quite as often applied in pity as in contempt. Borrowed by us in both the literal and the developed meaning, it was later specialized in the peculiarly odious sense of 'coward.' It is now obsolete in common language, though

[1] From O.N. *fēlage*, in the same sense.

it is one of those curious words which everybody knows but nobody uses. Compare the history of *wretch*, the Anglo-Saxon word for 'exile.'[1]

Almost any term of reproach or word that suggests inferiority may come to imply moral badness: as, — *low*, *base*, *degraded* (literally 'put down a step, or grade'), *debased*, *sunk very low*. *Rascal* means first 'the rabble,' and probably comes ultimately from L. *rado*, *rasus*, 'scrape': cf. 'the offscourings of society.' So Chaucer speaks of Jove, Apollo, Mars, and the other heathen gods, as 'rascaille.'[2] In hunting-language a *rascal* was a lean deer, out of condition and not fit for venison.

The degradation of a descriptive term may tell a sad story of human frailty. Tax-gatherers are never welcome guests, but the mere word suggests no moral turpitude. It was otherwise with the Roman *publicans*, whose business became a synonym for extortion.[3] The English *escheators* (or *cheaters*) had a similar fate. They were officers who looked out for lands that might revert to the king in default of heirs (French, from *ex-* and *cadere*, 'fall away'). But their actual or supposed dishonesty gave their name an evil sense.

Simple, *guileless*, and *innocent* are good words, but they have not remained so 'in the corrupted currents of this world.' Even *silly*[4] once meant 'blessed' or 'good,' being

[1] *Wrecca*, from *wrecan*, 'to drive out or punish,' whence *wreck* and *wreak*.

[2] O. Fr. *rascaille* (modern *racaille*).

[3] The modern sense of 'keeper of a *public* house' originated in an obvious pun, and has never become serious.

[4] A.S. *sǣlig*, M.E. *sely*. Another adjective, *sellic*, 'strange,' is thought by some to have become confused with *sely*, and thus to have helped it down, but no such contamination is necessary to account for its fall from grace. The Greek εὐήθης, 'good-hearted,' came to mean 'foolish,' and our *good-natured* often has a slighting connotation.

DEGENERATION OF MEANING

akin to the German *selig*. *Unsophisticated* is literally 'unadulterated,' 'unspoiled,' but is almost always a term of contempt. We have here a long history of degradation; for *sophist* is properly 'a wise teacher,' and owes its evil sense to the dialogues of Plato, in which the reasoning of these professors was attacked by Socrates.

Cunning,[1] *sly*, and *crafty* were also commendatory adjectives at first. *Cunning* is 'knowing,' hence 'skilful,' as in 'a *cunning* workman.' *Crafty* was 'skilful,' especially in a handicraft (cf. *craftsman*). *Sly* (borrowed from the Scandinavian) was 'wise' or 'skilful' in any way, but with no evil meaning. All such words deteriorate easily. Even *knowing* has come to have a suspicious sound. Compare *keen*, *sharp*, *smart* (in the American sense), *clever*, *cute* (for *acute*), and 'to live by one's *wits*.' The line between *craft* and *diplomacy* is as hard to draw as that between *piracy* and *privateering*. Sir Henry Wotton wrote, punningly, that an 'ambassador was a man sent to *lie* abroad for his country.' Subtlety is a recognized virtue among primitive peoples, and no civilized nation has yet climbed high enough to look down on Themistocles.

To *counterfeit* had at first no evil suggestion. It meant simply to 'imitate' or 'copy,'[2] — hence, a counterfeit was, among other things, a 'portrait,' — as in 'fair Portia's counterfeit' (*i.e.* portrait), and 'the counterfeit presentment of two brothers.' To copy another man's hand and seal, or to imitate the coin of the realm, however, was

[1] The innocent sense is preserved in the American nursery: 'a *cunning* child' is commendatory.

[2] *Counter* is *contra* and *feit* is *factum*. *Counter* may imply opposition or merely comparison. Thus *counterpart*, which properly means that which completes or complements anything by supplying contrasted qualities (as the 'stub' or counterfoil, and the *check*), has acquired, also, the sense of 'exact copy.'

felony, and the word soon acquired the sinister associations which always attend it to-day. Compare *coiner* and *coining* for 'counterfeiter' and 'counterfeiting.'

Sanctimonious once meant 'devout,' 'holy,' or 'sacred.' To modern ears it always carries an implication of hypocrisy. The case is perfectly typical. Persevering innuendo will ruin the reputation of any word, and religious observances are immemorial targets for sneering suspicion. Compare *pious, saint, sanctified, priestcraft, forms and ceremonies, zealot, devotee*. *Religious* itself once meant 'superstitious' (see p. 232). *Enthusiasm* is a Greek word for 'inspiration,' or possession by a divine spirit (from ἐν, *en*, 'in,' and θεός, *theós*, 'god'), — yet in the eighteenth century it was the regular English term for *fanaticism*. Madness and prophetic inspiration, we remember, are identical in the opinion of savages, among whom all lunatics are sacred, and the ancient religions had not outgrown this idea.[1] *Fanatic* is a Latin synonym for *enthusiastic*. It is literally 'belonging to the fane'; then, 'inspired by the divinity.' The Romans applied it especially to the frantic priests of Mars and Cybele, and found no difficulty in extending it to madness in general. It entered our language in the seventeenth century, and is always taken *in malam partem*.

Other examples of words that have deteriorated are *lust*, which originally meant simply 'pleasure,' as it still does in German; *lewd*, 'belonging to the laity,' then 'ignorant' (since only the clergy were learned), then, 'low' in any sense, as in 'lewd fellows of the baser sort,'

---

[1] *Vates*, the Latin for 'prophet' (also 'bard,' 'poet'), is properly the 'raging seer.' Genius and madness are thought to be near allied. At all events, the Anglo-Saxon *wōd*, 'insane,' is cognate with *vates* (cf. Ger. *Wuth*). Cf. *vaticination* (borrowed from Latin).

and, finally, 'lascivious'; *vile*, literally 'cheap'; *vice*, literally 'flaw,' 'defect'; *illicit*, formerly 'unallowed'; *revel*, formerly simply 'joy,' 'festivity'; *reckless*, once simply 'careless,' now always 'extremely careless,' often used as a synonym for 'desperate'; *erring*, formerly 'wandering' (cf. *knight errant*), now always in a moral sense; *plausible*, literally 'praiseworthy' (from L. *plaudo*, 'to clap the hands'), then 'pleasing'; *rash*, literally 'quick,' 'active.'

If we go back to the original sense of a borrowed word, we frequently find that it was innocent enough but had become unpleasant or evil before the word entered our language. In such cases, we have, of course, no right to cite the original meaning in interpreting the English use. Thus, *pirate* has always meant 'sea-robber' in English. We borrowed it from the Latin in that sense. Nor had *pirata* any other signification in Latin, which borrowed it from the Greek with the same meaning. In Greek, however, we can easily see that the word originally meant 'one who tries' or 'makes an attempt,' and that it acquired its special denotation through the comparatively harmless meaning of 'one who goes on an enterprise,' 'an adventurer.' This points to an age when piracy was a respectable occupation among the sea-going Greeks, as it was among the Angles and Saxons before they conquered Britain, and among the Norsemen at a still later period. The *vikings* were pirates when robbery was an honorable profession. They got their name from O.N. *vīk*, 'bay,' for piracy loves 'nook-shotten' coasts, as Pompey found when he conquered the Cilician marauders. We of New England should not forget the proverb that 'piracy and privateering both begin with a *p*.' The celebrated Captain Kidd began as a privateer.

So far we have considered pretty serious cases of

degradation. The words that we have studied, though innocent in their origin, have come to express moral reprobation, or, at the very least, a high degree of contempt. Often, however, the same tendencies have operated to produce less striking changes, affecting rather the dignity of the term than its actual signification. Thus, *worthy* (from *worth*) once meant distinctly 'honorable,' but has acquired a condescending connotation. *Worship* (also from *worth*) meant 'honor,' but has been heightened in sense (except in 'your Worship'); *worshipful*, however, has kept its meaning more exactly, but it is an old-fashioned word, hardly used except with a half-humorous suggestion.

Respectable has fared in the same way. Once a term of positive honor, it has imperceptibly slid down to its present apologetic position. It is still dignified, however, to be a 'respectable author,'— since that fine old-fashioned phrase is seldom used except by those who feel its full force, — a writer whose language commands respect, one who may be cited as an 'authority.'

An amusing instance of verbal degradation is afforded by a little group of words which should mean 'instantly,' but to which the procrastinating habit of mankind has attached an implication of delay. *Soon* is the Anglo-Saxon word for 'immediately.' *By and by* once meant the same thing,[1] and so did *presently* and *directly*. All four have fallen off in promptitude. 'I will attend to your business *soon*' is cold comfort to the waiting petitioner. *Presently* and *directly* are better, especially the

[1] *By and by* was originally an adverb of place, meaning 'side by side.' Thus, Palamon and Arcite were found on the battlefield lying 'by and by,' severely wounded. From adjacent place it was transferred to time immediately future. Compare *on the spot* in 'Tell me *on the spot*,' 'in the *nick* of time,' *sur le champ*, *main-tenant*.

latter, for they are newer words and have not had time to break down utterly. But *by and by* has become the proverbial motto of the determined procrastinator. Even *immediately* is backsliding a little. *Instantly* stands firm, but will doubtless go the way of all the rest.

Sometimes a word shows deterioration in some of its uses, but maintains itself in others. This may be seen in the case of *execute*, which has long been used for putting to death by legal process, but which is still perfectly familiar in its general meaning of 'carry out,' 'follow out,' or 'fulfil.' The peculiar sense of *execute* appears to come from a kind of ellipsis. The judgment of the court is *executed*, that is, 'carried out,' when a murderer is hanged. Hence, the hanging is called an *execution*, that is to say, a carrying out of the judgment pronounced; and, by transference, the *man* is said to be *executed* as well as the sentence. This special development has had no effect whatever on the other meanings of the word, perhaps because it relates to a class of ideas that are pretty thoroughly isolated. The *executive* is still one of the three coördinate high powers of the government. Observe that *executor*, the appropriate term for 'one who executes' in any sense, but particularly applied, in legal language, to one who carries out the terms of a will or testament, was formerly used for the hangman or headsman; but, for the sake of distinction, a new term for this officer has grown up, formed by attaching to *execution* the suffix *-er*, which designates one's trade or occupation (as in *grocer*, *moneyer*, etc.). When the electric chair was substituted for the scaffold in New York, the need of a special verb was felt, and the monstrosity *electrocute* was cobbled together from the first part of *electric* and the last part of *execute*, — the syllable *-cute* being felt as in some sort a suffix indicating 'to put to death by judicial process.' This uncouth term was much laughed at for a time, but, although it cannot be said to have taken its place for good and all in our vocabulary, *electrocute* (as well as *electrocution*) has stood its ground with unexpected courage. Good or bad, *electrocute* is a highly instructive phenomenon in half a dozen ways. *Electro-* is the stem of the Greek ἤλεκτρον (*élektron*), 'amber,' and *-cute* (the supposed suffix) is the Latin participle *secutus*, 'following' (from *sequor*). Yet the compound signifies 'to put to death judicially by means of an electric shock.' Every step of this wonderful change is easily followed and may be paralleled in other cases. The last syllable we have already traced. As to *electro-*, we have but to remember that the phenomena of electricity were first observed in amber, and were believed to be peculiar to that substance, — so that *electric*, 'pertaining to amber,' and *electricity*, 'amberness,' as it were, were coined to express the new 'force.' As science advanced, the need of a shorter form was felt for the purposes of composition, and the Greek stem *electro-* was extended to the full sense of the longer word, *electricity*, and utilized in numerous formations, like *electro-physics, electrolysis*, etc. Thus, when an amalgam of *electricity* and *execution* was attempted, *electrocution* was the result.[1]

Even slight changes in connotation may render a word

[1] We may compare the equally barbarous, but more natural, *electrolier* for an 'electric chande*lier*.' Here *-lier* was taken as a termination, though the *l* is really a part of L. *candela*, 'candle,' from which *candelabrum* (the original of *chandelier*) is derived. *Motoneer*, from *motor* and *-neer* (a part of *engin-eer*), shows a similiar confusion as to the boundary between word and suffix. These two words are not likely to get a place in the language, but they illustrate the confusion of suffixes which is constantly manifesting itself in legitimate speech and has produced many new endings (see p. 187).

too prosaic or undignified for poetical use, though its real meaning has not changed at all. This is the subtlest kind of degradation, and is of peculiar interest to the student of literature. Again and again have passages in our older authors been stigmatized as vulgar or out of taste, when the fault was with the critics, who had not the grounds of opinion. And not seldom has intentional incongruity for the sake of humor been suspected where, in fact, there was actually no incongruity at all, except that which lapse of time had made. Chaucer says the *friar* was 'a noble *post* unto his order,' — we should have to say *pillar*, or, abandoning the vividness of the figure, *support*, for *post* has sunk in dignity. The *liver* is essentially as poetical an organ as the heart, and it was formerly much mentioned in poetry, being regarded as the seat of courage and of passion. Physiology has changed its opinions, and nobody would venture to mention 'liver, brain, and heart' in a line of verse, as Shakspere did. *White-livered*, for 'cowardly,' preserves a trace of the old physiology. Other words which have lost their place in the poetical vocabulary are *blubber*, 'to cry hard,' *fry* (which Spenser applies to the torments of the damned), *brine* for 'tears,' *crack* for 'loud noise' (as in 'the *crack* of doom'), *spout* ('her eyes became two spouts').[1]

Occasionally a word has risen in dignity or agreeableness. The ascent, however, is not in obedience to any general tendency, but occurs in response to some peculiar cause. *Marshal* meant 'horse-boy'; *seneschal*, 'old servant'; *constable*, 'stall-attendant,' *comes stabuli; chamberlain*, 'the servant in charge of the chambers.' But when the king was the master, menial service was dignified, and, as royalty grew more splendid and the life of

[1] Shakspere, Winter's Tale, act iii, scene 3, l. 25.

palaces more ceremonious, the old plain terms became titles of honor. This process was, in some cases, assisted by forgetfulness of their original meaning. *Marshal* and *seneschal* are Teutonic words adopted into French from Old High German. As the Frankish invaders gradually gave up their Germanic tongue, no one remembered that *-shal* was *scalc* (modern Ger. *Schalk*), 'servant,' or that *mar* was 'horse' (akin to Eng. *mare*), or that *sene-* meant 'old' (cognate with L. *senex*). *Constable* has sunk again in some of its uses. It was once the highest military title under the kings of France. Compare the difference in rank between the *steward* on a steamboat and the Lord High Steward of England, and observe that the royal family of the *Stuarts* got their name from being the hereditary stewards of the Scottish kings. Other names of offices or occupations have risen in rank with changing circumstances or under peculiar influences: as, — *broker, minister, engineer, ambassador*.

A happy figure of speech may dignify a word forever. *Pioneers* (earlier *pioners*)[1] were soldiers who cleared the way for an army by felling trees, building roads, and doing all manner of hard and disagreeable work. They were regarded as the lowest portion of the army: 'the general camp,' says Othello, 'pioners and all.' It occurred to somebody, not so very long ago, that the settlers in a new country or on the borders of the wilderness are the *pioneers* of the great march of civilization. For a time this *pioneer* was a metaphor, but it has lost its figurative character, is usually conceived as the literal sense of the term, and is employed to make new metaphors, as in '*pioneers* of scientific discovery.'

More than once a derisive nickname has been accepted

[1] Fr. *pionnier*, from *pion*, the same word as the *pawn* in chess.

by those to whom it is applied, and has thus risen to the rank of an ordinary descriptive term. *Yankee*, *Hoosier*, and *Whig* are familiar examples. If some investigators are to be trusted, many of the early Germanic tribal names were of this character. There are abundant examples in religious history: as, *Puritan*, *Quaker*, *Shaker*, etc. It is possible enough that when the 'disciples were called *Christians* first in Antioch,' it was by their enemies, or, at best, by those who despised them as the dupes of a false prophet.

The adjective *nice* is a peculiar example of linguistic processes. It originally meant 'foolish,' being derived (through the French) from the Latin *nescius*. This is the regular sense in Chaucer. It was gradually specialized in the sense of 'foolishly particular about trifles,' or, as we say, 'more *nice* than wise.' By transference, it meant 'trivial' as applied to the objects themselves, — 'The letter was not *nice*, but full of charge.' Then the idea of folly was lost, and 'particular about small things,' 'accurate,' a distinctly commendatory sense, came into existence. In this sense *nice* was naturally applied to persons, as 'a nice observer,' or (by transference) to actions or qualities, as 'nice discrimination,' 'a nice distinction.' Thence the passage was easy to the colloquial sense of 'excellent,' 'good of its kind,' etc., in which it is applied to everything in the universe. 'A nice apple,' for example, is such an apple as a nice (or discriminating) judge of apples would pick out for his own eating. In this use *nice* has never risen to the dignity of being a literary word, yet it has made good its position in respectable colloquial language in America, in spite of the vehement opposition of purists. Nor is it merely an Americanism, as many have supposed. Indeed, it is far from certain that the use originated on this side of the water. However that may be, the passage from 'foolish' (applied to persons) to 'excellent' (applied to either persons or things) seems inexplicable until the history of the word is known, and gives us one more example of the folly of appealing to the Stoic etymon.[1]

Naughty is a curious example of the ups and downs to which words are subject,— particularly words of approval or reproach. It is from *naught*, and meant originally either 'destitute,' or 'good-for-nothing.' In the latter sense it became a general synonym for 'bad.' King Lear's fool says 'This is a *naughty* night to swim in'; the records of Plymouth Colony speak of 'small and *naughty* canoes' (1661). In its application to morals, *naughty* was perhaps a euphemism at first, but it soon came to be a term of extreme reprobation. 'A naughty world' and 'naughty lady' in Shakspere are exactly equivalent to 'wicked' in Modern English.[2] Since his time the word has lost all dignity on account of its application to the peccadillos of children. When used of older persons, it is purely sportive, and has far less force than it possessed at the very beginning of its career.

The whimsicality of affection takes delight in transforming abusive words into caresses. 'Lie still, ye *thief*,' says Lady Percy to her husband. Desdemona is Othello's 'excellent *wretch*' before Iago springs his snares. The dead Cordelia is 'my poor *fool*' to King Lear. *Rogue, rascal, toad, tyke* ('cur'), and even *snake*, are pet names for little children. All this is akin to the employment of grotesque pet names like *chuck* (in Macbeth), *honey, baw-*

---

[1] See p. 230.
[2] We may compare the Latin *nequam* and our *good-for-nothing*, 'a *nobody*,' and the colloquial 'no *sort* (or *kind*) of a man.'

cock (from *beau*, 'fine,' or *baud*, 'bold'), and queer diminutives. Intimacy or familiarity explains these phenomena, and supplies the common term between abusive language and the dialect of tender fondness. On the one hand we have the familiarity of affection; on the other, the familiarity of contempt.[1]

Whenever a word comes to have a disagreeable sense, some synonym begins to take its place in ordinary language. The synonym may be a new word borrowed for the express purpose, but it is more commonly a word already established, which may suffer a slight change of meaning, perhaps by being more generalized. Thus, when *knave* began to acquire a disagreeable signification, *servant*, from the French, took its place. *Servant* was already in the language, but was a somewhat more dignified and special word than *knave*. In modern usage, with the spread of democratic feeling, there has been, particularly in America, a tendency to abandon this word *servant* in favor of *help*, or *domestic*, or some other less plain-spoken term.[2] This conducts us directly to *euphemism*, which will be treated in the following chapter.

[1] Compare *fellow* (p. 287), in which the influences here described have made themselves felt.

[2] The history of *help* in this sense is fully discussed by Albert Matthews in the Transactions of the Colonial Society of Massachusetts, V, 225 ff.

CHAPTER XXI

EUPHEMISM

DECENCY and propriety are powerful forces in changing the meanings of words, or in driving them out of use. They are also very ancient forces. Indeed, it is hard to imagine a state of society so low as to be exempt from their operations. Prudery may be ridiculous, but it is not unnatural. It is merely the self-conscious expression of tendencies that have affected language from the remotest times, and that have their roots in the most primitive philosophy of the human race. The propriety of the Hottentot may differ from the white man's propriety, but, such as it is, he feels under bonds to observe it, and the bonds are quite as stringent as those which regulate our own society. In particular, he is very loath to 'call a spade a spade.'

The origins of euphemism, then, are to be sought not in our complex civilization, but in those conceptions of language which are common to men in every stage of culture. We instinctively avoid the mention of death, and take refuge in such vague or softened phrases as 'he has passed away,' 'he is gone,' 'the deceased,' 'the departed,' 'the *late* Mr. Smith.' The savage feels still greater reluctance. Sometimes he even refuses to utter the name of a person who is no longer living, or to give it to a child, so that the name actually becomes obsolete among the tribe. This

EUPHEMISM

agreement between the civilized man and the savage points to the solution of the whole problem. It is unlucky to speak of death or misfortune, for, in all men's minds, there is a mysterious but indissoluble connection between the thing and the word. To pronounce the *word* may bring the *thing* to pass. Here we are on familiar ground. The 'power of the word,' as we have already seen,[1] is a conception that appeals with equal force to the Stoic philosopher (with his etymon) and the medicine-man with his rigmarole of senseless charms.

Thus euphemism becomes immediately intelligible. Nothing that the savage does or says is free from ceremonial restrictions. The most innocent acts or speeches may be fraught with tremendous consequences if they violate a taboo or run counter to a religious requirement. Such and such words are allowable under one set of circumstances, but forbidden under another. The habit of linguistic caution is thus formed, and what we call decency of language is the last result.

The Australian aborigines are very near the bottom of the social scale. Yet they have many rigid rules of decency and propriety in speech. They feel no hesitation, to be sure, in speaking of all sorts of things which we never mention in polite society. Yet they have two words for almost every such idea, and they shudder at the thought of employing the wrong synonym in a mixed company. In short, the language of these naked savages is provided with all the apparatus of an elaborated euphemism.

The Greek word *euphemism* itself has ceremonial connections. It comes from εὖ (*eû*), 'well,' and φημί (*phēmí*), 'to speak.' Εὐφημεῖτε (*euphēmeîte*), 'speak fair,' the im-

[1] See pp. 228 ff.

perative of the corresponding verb, was the solemn warning to the worshipper not to disturb the sacrifice by speaking, lest he might utter some ill-omened word. The Romans had a similar formula, — *favete linguis*, 'favor with your tongues.' 'Utter nothing ominous' would have been itself an ominous utterance. Even 'keep silence' was too suggestive of evil speech.

The superstitious notion involved in these formulæ manifests itself in all languages. *Absit omen*, said the Romans, when they found it necessary to mention an unlucky or disastrous thing. 'God save the mark!'[1] is the nurse's interjection when she describes the wound in Tybalt's breast and touches her own body in significant gesture. Our 'Don't speak of it!' gives vague expression to the same feeling.

Death and disaster, then, afford a starting-point for our study of euphemism. We have already mentioned a number of euphemistic synonyms, like *depart, decease*, and *pass away*. Compare *the end, dissolution, expire, go to a better world, last sickness* (or *illness*), *breathe one's last, lifeless, the silent majority, gone before, fall asleep, among the missing, he lost fifty men, he is no more, he cannot recover, he fell in battle, he was lost at sea*.[2] The French *feu* (as in *feu roi*, 'the late king') is for *fatutus*, from *fatum* (cf. 'to meet one's fate'). There are like synonyms for *kill:* as, 'to make way with'[3]

---

[1] Nobody knows the origin of this phrase, but its use is clear enough. The many explanations suggested for its origin are all more or less clever guesses.

[2] The habit of using trivial or slang phrases for *death* is a coarser expression of the same feeling.

[3] Compare L. *tollo*, as in the punning epigram on Nero's murdering his mother (Suetonius, Nero, 39) : —

> Quis negat Aeneae magna de stirpe Neronem?
> Sustulit hic matrem, sustulit ille patrem.

(or 'make away'), 'to put away,' 'to finish,' 'settle,' 'do for,' or 'remove,' 'he must *disappear*' (for 'be slain'), and so on. The use of a borrowed word may serve the purpose of veiling the truth, — as *mortal* or *fatal* for 'deadly'; *post mortem*, *obituary*. The last-mentioned word refers us back to a well-known Latin euphemism, *obiit*, for *obiit diem supremam*, 'he has met his last day.' Compare *post obit* (for *post obitum*), an agreement to pay money after some one's death. *Suicide* (from L. *sui*, 'of one's self,' and *-cidium*, 'killing,' as in *homicidium; caedo*, 'slay') is a milder term than Hamlet's *self-slaughter*. And *felo de se* is also felt as less plain-spoken, though in fact it embodies the savage legal doctrine that a suicide is a 'felon against himself' (or 'in his own case').

Misfortune, mischance, accident (literally 'happening'; *accidere*, 'to befall'), *casualty* (L. *casus*, 'falling,' 'chance'), *disaster* ('bad aspect of the planets'), *injury* (literally 'injustice,' 'wrong'), *ruin* (L. *ruo*, 'to fall'), are all euphemistic in origin, though some of them have ceased to be so felt. *Ill*, as applied to sickness, means literally 'uncomfortable' (cf. *disease*), but has come to have a much more serious sense.[1] *Serious* itself is often euphemistic when applied to illness.

So far the superstitious sources of euphemism have revealed themselves unmistakably. We are justified, therefore, in assuming a similar origin when, as in some of the examples that we must now examine, no obvious fear of ill luck attends the practice. The habit of employing softened or veiled expressions, once established, spreads to all the relations of life, and may at any moment be intensified by

---

[1] Our ancestors used *sick* for all kinds of disease, grave or trivial, and *ill* for the discomfort or distress attending them. 'Sick and ill' was a common phrase.

special causes, whether of reverence or courtesy or passing fashion.

Profane language has long been regarded as not only irreverent, but vulgar; yet the propensity to curse and swear is deep-seated. The result is a singular compromise which has produced a large body of euphemistic expressions. Some of these are ordinary words substituted for oaths or curses; but others are grotesque distortions, resembling the originals in sound, but having a different meaning or none at all. Thus arise *darn* and *dum; all-fired* (for *hell fire*); *geewhillikens, Jerusalem, Jerusalem crickets, geewhiz,* and other suggestions of *Jesus; Godfrey, goodness, goodness gracious,* suggesting *God*. The divine name has been strangely treated in such expressions. *Gosh, golly, gorry,* and so on are mere vulgar distortions. *Cox my passion, by Cock, Cock's bones,* and the like, are attempts to avoid profanity by substituting a trivial word. *Odd's*, as in *Odd's bodkins* ('little body'), *Odd's pitikins* ('pity'), and *Odd's my life*, are clipped forms. *'Sdeath, 'slife, zounds* ('God's wounds'), and so on, preserve only the final letter of the genitive *God's*. *Gad* differs from *God* only in an affected pronunciation of the short *o*; yet even this slight change is enough to satisfy most consciences.[1]

As refinement progresses, great reluctance manifests itself to mention various parts of the body in plain terms, and this avoidance is extended (by association) to different articles of attire. The extreme of vulgar prudery is thought to have been reached in *limbs* for *legs*, but the substitution is not different in kind from many others that have established themselves in the language. *Shift* was originally a euphemism for *smock* (cf. Italian *mutande*, 'drawers'), but it became obsolete because it was in time

[1] Cf. p. 34, note.

associated with the body itself, and the French *chemise* replaced it. *Drawers*, also a euphemism, is avoided for the same reason. Even *underclothes* is out of favor (though *underwear* is the trade term). *Flannels* or *linen* have become the general name for such garments, and the French *lingerie* (literally 'linen' collectively) has lately been introduced in a somewhat special sense. *Breeches* gave way to *smallclothes* and *knickerbockers*. *Waist* (literally 'growth,' cf. *to wax*) is a very old euphemism. *Corsage* is later. *Neck* and Fr. *gorge* are extended beyond their original sense. *Petticoat* (literally 'little coat'), in itself a sufficiently inoffensive term, has shown a tendency to give way to *skirt*. By the irony of fate, this substitution is made in ignorance of the original meaning of *skirt*, which is, in fact, merely the Old Norse word for *shirt*, and less 'delicate,' therefore, than *petticoat*.

Moral delinquency is the constant object of courteous euphemism. *Misconduct*, *misguided*, *misdemeanor*, *offence* (from *offendo*, 'to run into one'), *fault* ('lack,' 'failure,' from *fallo*, 'deceive'), a *slip*, a *lapse* (L. *lapsus*, 'slip'), *transgression*, *excesses*, *immorality* (*mores*, 'manners,' then 'character') are examples. In Australia a transported convict used to be called an 'old hand'; one who had served his time and been discharged was an *expiree*, or more politely, an *emancipist*. 'He is short in his accounts' is often said of an embezzler in this country. Any right-minded man had rather be called a *defaulter* than a *thief*. 'In trouble' may be used of a person who is accused of a crime. One for whom the police are searching is said to be 'wanted.' 'Sent up' means 'put in prison'; 'executed' is a politer term than 'hanged.' 'You lie' is an insult, and there are various less offensive ways of accusing a man of falsehood, from suggesting that he is 'somewhat distorting the facts,' or 'not making an accurate statement,' to the courteous Elizabethan 'I fear you have done yourself some wrong.' So *to romance*, 'to draw the *long bow*,' 'to give a free rein to one's *imagination*.' *Falsehood, misrepresentation, misstatement*, and the colloquial or slangy *fib, big story, whopper, taradiddle, fish story*,[1] *fairy tale*, are all common euphemisms.

Wanton is an interesting word both as to structure and meaning. It is a shortened form of *wan-towen; wan-* being a negative prefix meaning *un-*, and *towen* (A.S. *togen*) being the past participle of an old verb (A.S. *tēon*), 'to draw' (related with *tug*, Ger. *ziehen*, and L. *duco*). Hence *wanton* meant literally 'not (well) brought up,' 'untrained,' and was applied (as noun or adjective) to a 'spoiled child.' It is easy to understand the rise of the meaning 'playful,' 'sportive' (in an innocent way), as in '*wanton* lambs,' and from this the modern evil sense developed readily. From the 'spoiled child' meaning came also the sense of 'perverse,' 'without motive,' as in '*wanton* mischief,' '*wanton* malice.' The old literal sense of 'untrained' led also to the meaning 'rank,' 'luxuriant' (of vegetation); and the sense of 'self-indulgent,' 'luxurious,' came from the 'spoiled child,' who is pampered.

Sometimes a learned or scientific term is used as a euphemism, and thus becomes popular. We have *effluvium* for *stench; perspiration* for *sweat; intestines* for *inwards* or *insides; indigestion* for *surfeit* or *over-eating; intoxication* for *drunkenness; dipsomaniac* for *sot; idiot* for *fool; maniac* for *madman*, and so on.

Euphemism often consists in substituting for a positive word a denial of the opposite idea. Thus, for *dirty* we

[1] From the tendency to exaggerate the weight of the fish one has caught.

may say *untidy* or *unclean;* for *lying*, *untruthful;* for *drunken*, *intemperate;* for *foolish*, *unwise;* for *perfidious*, *unfaithful;* for *deceitful*, *insincere;* for *abandoned* or *depraved*, *worthless;* for *mad*, *insane* (literally *not healthy* or *sound*); for *dangerous*, *unsafe;* for *anxious*, *uneasy;* for *rude* or *boorish*, *impolite* or *uncivil;* for *blundering*, *inaccurate*, and so on. In most of these cases the euphemistic word has become quite as severe a reprobation as the more outspoken term.

Crazy (literally 'cracked') and *insane* ('unsound') were at first milder terms for *mad*, but they now carry the full force of the idea in question. *Disease* (properly 'discomfort') is no longer felt as a euphemism. *Vile* (literally 'cheap,' of 'small value'), *vice* ('a flaw or fault'), *base* (literally 'low'), *caitiff* ('a captive,' 'a poor fellow'), *mercenary* ('serving for hire'), *indiscretion* ('lack of judgment'), *transgression* (a 'stepping across' the borders), are similar examples of the effect of euphemism in degrading the sense of comparatively innocent words.

Observe that the degeneration of words (Chapter XX) is often due to euphemism. The mild or decent word, when applied to the disagreeable or indecent idea, begins to be shunned by speakers on account of its dubious meaning, and soon comes actually to express the meaning which it was intended at first merely to suggest, or even to conceal. Thus, for *dissolute* (itself a euphemism) we have almost every possible word that means 'lively' or 'sportive,' and hence these words acquire a doubtful character. Such is *wanton*, just discussed, which has come to have a distinctly bad sense, and such are *gay*, *lively*, *fast*, *reckless*, *a sport*. This use may be merely slang at the outset. This was the case with *fast*, which has a curious history. Originally, the adjective signified 'fixed,' 'firm.' The corresponding adverb *fastë* (later *fast*) became very common in the sense of 'vigorously,' 'extremely,' and (vaguely) 'very much,' and, when attached to verbs of motion, soon acquired the special sense of 'rapidly': 'to run *vigorously*' and 'to run *rapidly*' mean the same thing. From the adverb the sense of 'rapid' was early attached to the adjective. The special meaning of 'dissipated' developed first in the expressive phrase 'to live *fast*,' — which got into literature about 1700, but must have been colloquial or society slang some years earlier. Thence came the adjective use in such phrases as 'a *fast* life,' '*fast* living,' and then, by transference to persons, 'a *fast* man.' Recent slang (partly from euphemism, partly from the tendency of all slang to achieve variety by means of synonyms[1]) has substituted *rapid* and *swift* for *fast*, in this sense, but neither of these words has yet secured admission to respectable society.

[1] See p. 69.

CHAPTER XXII

HYPERBOLE OR EXAGGERATION

EXAGGERATION is often regarded as an abuse of language, and so, indeed, it may become if it is recklessly indulged in. But it is a natural and ineradicable tendency of human speech, and has played its part in the development of our vocabulary. The psychology of exaggeration is simple enough. Strong feeling demands strong words. If, as often happens, we feel more strongly than the occasion warrants, we use terms which, though not too strong for our feeling, are disproportionate to the facts of the case. If others do the like, and employ the same words, the vocabulary of the language is affected. Our strong word becomes the sign of a less emphatic idea. It loses vigor and relaxes its hold on its original meaning.

Examples will crowd upon the reader's mind. A single one may therefore suffice in this place. *Astonish* is literally 'to thunderstrike' (L. *ex-* and *tonare*, 'to thunder'), and was once common in the physical sense of 'stun,' as when Fluellen 'astonished' Pistol by hitting him on the head with a cudgel. It was also used metaphorically for the extreme effect of terror or wonder in paralyzing the faculties for the moment, — a man who was 'astonished' was in a kind of trance. But the word has gradually lost its force, till nowadays it is hardly more than an emphatic synonym for 'surprise' or 'excite wonder.' *Amaze* has behaved in a similar way. In its earliest uses it conveyed the idea of utter physical stupefaction, or loss of one's wits. It is still somewhat more emphatic than *astonish*, but is far from maintaining its pristine vigor. *Surprise*, which meant literally 'to seize upon,' 'to capture' (compare the military sense), has become purely descriptive, and is as dispassionate as a quadratic equation. When we wish to express the idea in its full force, we resort to emphatic adverbs (*'utterly* amazed,' *'profoundly* surprised,' *'unutterably* astonished'), or we employ new terms of similar meaning, like *thunderstruck*, or *stupefied*, or *'petrified* with wonder,' or the colloquial *dumbfounded*, *flabbergasted*, *paralyzed*. All of these show a tendency to lose force as time goes on.

Words and phrases of affirmation and negation have been particularly affected by the tendency to hyperbole, and sometimes in very curious ways. *Yea* is the regular old particle for a simple unemphatic affirmative. It is related to the pronominal root seen in our *yon* (properly 'that') and the German *jen-er*, and must originally have meant 'in that way,' *i.e.* in the same way in which the previous speaker has said the thing happened. Compare the biblical 'thou sayest it' as a polite expression of assent. In Anglo-Saxon, however, *yea* (A.S. *gēa*) had become a mere affirmative particle. *Yes* is also found in Anglo-Saxon in the form *gese* or *gise*, which seems to be a compound of *yea* (*gēa*) and *so* (*swā*). It was a stronger affirmative than *yea*, being equivalent to our 'just so!' or 'exactly so!' or 'yes, indeed.' In time, however, it lost its emphasis and is now the regular particle of affirmation. We may compare the modern 'quite so,' originally emphatic (since *quite* meant 'entirely'), but now a mere substitute for 'yes.'[1] *Yea* has gone out of use, except in

[1] This use of *quite so!* has grown up in England since the settlement of America and has never been adopted in this country, though it is sometimes heard in conscious or unconscious imitation.

dialectic, poetical, or solemn language. Its unfamiliarity and archaic quality make it seem more emphatic than *yes*, though, as we have seen, the latter was formerly the stronger term. All sorts of hyperbolical substitutes for *yes* have grown up: such as, — *by all means, certainly, of course, to be sure, surely* (and in recent slang, *sure*). Here courtesy has been active. It is good manners to make one's assent as cordial as possible. In time, however, as we have seen, all such expressions grow weaker till at last they are hardly distinguishable from a simple 'yes.'

No has a somewhat similar history. It is an old word for *never*, being the adverb *ā*, 'ever,' with the negative *ne* prefixed. *Nay* is the related Old Norse *nei*, of similar meaning. Originally, then, *no* and *nay* were as strong a negative as 'never!' is to-day. Substitutes have grown up in plenty, — like *not at all, by no means,* and so on. Courtesy, however, which demands an emphatic *yes*, suggests, on the other hand, the propriety of softening a negative answer. Hence we have *hardly, scarcely, I think not*, and a score of similar phrases, all of which have come to have the full negative force.

The tendency to emphasize the negative may also be seen in a number of figurative expressions with *not*. *Not* itself is merely a clipped pronunciation of *naught*, 'nothing,' and meant originally 'not a bit,' 'not a whit.' Its origin was soon forgotten, and such phrases as *not a mite* and the like came into use. Our older language has a multitude of these, some of them very grotesque: as, *not worth an oyster, a hen, a leek. Not a jot* is scriptural: 'One jot or one tittle shall in no wise pass from the law' (Matthew iv. 18). *Jot* is *iota*, the Greek letter *ι* (our *i*): cf. 'not an *iota*.' *Tittle* means a 'little bit'; its etymology is doubtful. If such a phrase becomes idiomatic, the *not* sometimes disappears, leaving behind it, however, its full force attached to a word which has in itself absolutely no negative sense. We may compare the contemptuous *much* in Elizabethan English in the sense of '*not much!*' as when Falstaff speaks of men as their fathers' shadows, adding 'but *much* of the father's substance!'[1] This process explains the French *point*, 'point'; *rien*, 'thing'; and *pas*, 'step' (L. *passus*), in their negative use, and illustrates in a striking way the truth of the statement on which we have already insisted, that language is conventional, and that words mean what the speaker intends and the hearer understands.

Emphasis is also responsible for the double negative, which, however much it may make an affirmative in logic, has rarely any such effect in language.[2]

The examples which we have studied suffice to illustrate the effect of hyperbole or exaggeration on legitimate speech. The same tendencies come out with even greater clearness in the colloquial dialect and in slang, since here, as we have already remarked,[3] the changes are so rapid that we can actually see them taking place. For this reason, the very absurdities of slang and (since the word must have a feminine) polite inelegance, may throw a strong light on the processes of legitimate speech, as monstrosities guide the naturalist in investigating the normal development of species. We may select the special category of adjectives and adverbs of degree, which will be found particularly instructive.

Such words are somewhat inexact in themselves, since the feelings that prompt them are seldom well defined.

[1] This use of *Much*, however, is more likely to be irony. Cf. '*Much* he knows!' '*Much* you care!'
[2] See p. 220. [3] See p. 56.

HYPERBOLE OR EXAGGERATION

They are, therefore, peculiarly exposed to the inroads of slang and fantastic colloquialism. The general tendency to exaggeration is strikingly exemplified. Take, for instance, the descriptive terms or ejaculations of pleasure evoked by a view or spectacle. *Beautiful* and *fine* are natural and simple expressions; but they soon become too weak to satisfy the enthusiastic tourist or spectator, and stronger words are substituted, — such as *lovely, delightful, splendid, glorious, superb, grand, wonderful, gorgeous, heavenly, sublime, magnificent, perfect, divine, tremendous, entrancing, stupendous, enchanting*. Of the same sort are the genuine slang words *bang-up, rattling good, tip-top, first-rate, immense* (cf. Ger. *kolossal*), *stunning, corking*. It is to be feared that some of these occasionally force their way into the less vulgar list. *Charming* has been omitted from the enumeration because, though originally referring to superstitious ideas from which the minds of men have only lately been liberated, yet the decay of the word has been so rapid that it is now, in its ordinary use, a pretty tame epithet.[1]

In accordance with the general habit of language, all the epithets just mentioned are applied not merely to beautiful scenes but to other objects of sense, and also to things that do not appeal to the senses at all. In fact, they are employed with so little discrimination that they

[1] *Enchanting* and *bewitching* have retained more of their force. *Take* was once synonymous with 'bewitch,' both in the literal and the figurative sense, as in Shakspere: 'No fairy *takes* nor witch hath power to charm, So hallow'd and so gracious is the time' (Hamlet); 'Daffodils that . . . *take* the winds of March with beauty' (Winter's Tale). 'A *taking* person,' however, or 'a *taking* manner' carries but little of this old sense. *Fetching* has been recently substituted for *taking* in polite slang, — 'a very *fetching* costume.' Thus language, legitimate and illegitimate, insists on novelty. 'Men loven of propre kinde newefangelnesse,' as Chaucer says.

are almost as destitute of thought or definite emotion as the contented purr of a cat on the hearth-rug. A few similar terms, however, as *nice, dear, sweet, powerful, thrilling,* are sufficiently discriminated to exclude them from the list, but even these are made to cover a considerable range of objects.

The terms of disapproval in this dialect are also very numerous, and quite as undiscriminating as those which express satisfaction. Thus we have *nasty, beastly, rotten, loathsome, shameful, miserable, outrageous, atrocious, distressing, horrid, horrible, awful, dreadful, frightful, hateful, disgusting.* The fondness for coarsish words is noteworthy; but since the dialect that we are considering is particularly affected by students, society buds, and other callow persons, the attractions of the *fruit défendu* no doubt have much to do with the matter. Such words, however, frequently find their way into graver dialects, and one must infer that the bend of the twig occasionally reappears in the inclination of pretty well-grown trees. At any rate, this vulgar tendency may often be observed in adults not otherwise ticketed as vulgar.

When such adjectives seem too tame (as, from inordinate repetition, they constantly do), an adverb of the same kind is attached to them, with the like amount of discrimination. Thus we get 'superlatively fine,' 'ravishingly beautiful,' 'awfully fine,' or, on the other hand, 'awfully horrid,' 'horridly rotten.'

There is nothing 'modern' about these tendencies. Our ancestors succumbed to the same temptation in their 'monstrous fine,' 'vastly pretty,' and the like, which appeal to the modern reader with the factitious charm of a bygone age.

This hyperbole is occasionally seen in other connections,

as 'extravagantly fond,' 'passionately fond,' and the like. Sometimes it crosses itself with courteous tendencies, stealing the livery of the devil to serve heaven in. Thus one may hear, in sober utterance, monstrosities like 'Thanks! awfully!' and 'Awfully good of you!' In the same dialect the hyperbolic *infinite* and *infinitely* have been replaced by 'no end,' thus giving the somewhat ludicrous 'Thanks! no end!' and other exaggerated expressions which embody this jocular substitutionary form.

One method of superlative-making is peculiarly subtle. It is a general tendency of language to employ absolute words (like *perfect* or *true*) as if they were relative, as when we 'compare' absolute adjectives: — 'more perfect,' 'most perfect,' 'very true,' 'more true.' *Per contra*, an adjective that is ordinarily relative (like *horrid* or *nauseous*) is unconsciously assumed to have an absolute sense, and thus to be capable of expressing a consummate degree of the quality in question. Hence arise such phrases as '*perfectly* horrid,' 'absolutely nauseous,' 'disgusting in the extreme,' 'extremely objectionable.' The emphatic use of *superlatively*, *extremely*, *utterly*, originated in this manner; but these, like many overdrawn words, have lost their force, and become mere synonyms for *very*. An extreme case is that of *simply*, in 'simply loathsome,' 'simply ridiculous.'

We may compare such expressions as 'fine and wet,' 'good and ready,' 'nice and warm,' where the first adjective does not logically belong to the subject, but defines the degree of perfection in which the quality expressed by the second adjective exists. Thus, 'fine and wet' is 'finely wet,' 'nice and warm' is 'nicely warm,' 'good and ready' is 'well ready.' So, in '*finely* cheated,' the adverb refers to the degree of perfection with which the cheating is done;

but in '*badly* cheated' the case is different. The distinction may be clearly seen in Latin. Take, for example, any adverb with a 'bad' signification, like *male* or *misere*. If it is used with an adjective or participle of a similarly 'bad' meaning, it enhances the degree of the second member: as, — *male mulcatus*, 'badly punished'; *misere deceptus*, 'miserably deceived.' But if it is used with an adjective expressing a 'good' quality, it contradicts or neutralizes the second member, and hence is equivalent to a negative: as, — *male sanus*, '*un*sound.' Contrast, in English, *badly beaten* (which is practically equivalent to *well beaten*) with *badly fed* (which is the opposite of *well fed*).

One hyperbolical phrase of degree, *ever so*, now firmly rooted in our language, has a curious elliptical form and an equally curious history. In the Prayer-book version of the Psalms occurs the passage, 'Which refuseth to hear the voice of the charmer, *charm* he *never so* wisely.' Modern English would lead us to expect 'ever so wisely,' though the negative form is still occasionally used. In fact, both are equally logical. 'Charm he' is of course the old subjunctive, equivalent to 'let him charm,' which might be followed by '*ever so* wisely,' *i.e.* 'however wisely he may charm,' or by '*never so* wisely,' *i.e.* 'as wisely as no one ever charmed before.' The latter is easily abbreviated to *never so*, which sometimes crops up as an isolated phrase; the former is abbreviated to *ever so*, and in this form becomes an idiomatic intensive, as in, 'I liked it *ever so* much,' 'He can run *ever so* fast.' Considered by itself, the abstracted fragment seems ludicrous and irrational; but it is, in fact, equivalent to 'however *much* (or *fast*) you can imagine' or 'as *much* (or *fast*) as possible,' — a perfectly logical form of expression.

HYPERBOLE OR EXAGGERATION

The examples which we have drawn from 'words of degree' show conclusively how impossible it is to separate the operations of slang from those that go on in legitimate speech. Exaggeration permeates this category of words, and has been active alike in the slow processes of gradual modification by which our vocabulary is affected in the lapse of centuries, and in the 'lightning changes' to which the dialect of the streets and the jargon of society are subject. We may now turn to certain special fields in which the tendency to hyperbole has manifested itself in a peculiarly interesting fashion. We shall find, as we have so often found before, that the study of words is in reality the study of civilization. The investigator of language has his finger on the pulse of human society.

There is one tendency of speech which, though founded on a firm basis of psychology, is constantly spoken of by those who know nothing of the ways of linguistics, as 'new' and vulgar in the extreme. This is the inclination to use words more grandiloquent or more honorable than the occasion calls for or admits. Such a tendency has characterized the languages of all cultivated nations, and seems to be inherent in the human mind. Vanity and social ambition, on the one hand, combine with courtesy and servility on the other, to support and enforce this natural bent, and the disposition to 'magnify one's office' contributes its share in producing the final result. Contrast the 'Men of Athens' of St. Paul (Acts xvii. 22) with the 'Ladies and Gentlemen' of a modern orator. Think, too, how many ages of active and passive snobbery are involved in giving the title of *princeps*, the official designation of the Roman emperor, the master of the world, to a petty fortune-hunting princelet, without power, money, brains, or morals, the laughing-stock of his own order and the dupe of those who pay court to his station. One might as well call an acolyte an archangel! But the tendency is slow in operation, though persistent and unceasing, and we may well be surprised at its effect in a long lapse of time. We recognize its operations in such queer phrases as *saleslady* and '*professor* of bootblacking,' but we fail to see its potency in *patriarch* and *patron*.

Abundant examples of this tendency are found in the names of places where people live. If a new quarter or village is to be laid out, every motive of magniloquence comes into play. In America, the attraction and dignity of urban life seem greater than those of the country, and therefore our new 'residential district' will be 'in the vicinity' of a city, but never 'on the outskirts.' It will be furnished with some name that has 'smart' associations, — like, 'Hyde Park' or the 'Charles River Embankment.' Perhaps a 'boulevard' will be laid out, without consideration of the original meaning of that term or its later derived sense. 'Avenues' will be numerous, and in this country 'streets.' But in England 'street' smacks of commerce, which, as Cicero says of Rome, is in disrepute except on a large scale, and 'road' will be preferred as more suggestive of the country-loving gentry. Thus, at Oxford, 'Banbury Road' is really the old road to Banbury Cross of famous memory, but 'Bardwell Road' is a brand-new side street, leading nowhere in particular, certainly not to Bardwell, which is miles away in Suffolk.

This matter of *road* and *street* is a great curiosity. In America, where trade is still highly respectable, the tendency to magniloquence has changed many genuine 'roads' to 'streets,' for the sake of the urban suggestion. But lately, in blind imitation of the English fashion, little 'roads' have begun to be laid out over newly improved land, in defiance of every topographical principle. 'Squares,' 'places,' and 'circles' are sure to abound; but 'lanes' and 'alleys' disappear from the map. A 'park' will certainly be found, if there is a foot of ground dedicated to the uses of the public. When a man puts up a house, we hear that the 'residence' of the Honorable Mr. Jones is 'in process of erection.' 'Villa' has hardly domesticated itself in America, but is extremely common in England and on the continent. If houses must be closely built, 'block' is avoided in favor of 'terrace.'

All this is obviously magniloquence; but 'cottage' is a different matter. The history of *cottage* in America is not a little curious. In the strict sense of 'a laborer's dwelling,' the word has never been adopted into popular American use. In fact, we have never really had the *thing* in America. The conditions of our rustic life have, from colonial times to the present day, differed essentially from those in England, and few contrasts are greater than that between a rural village here and in the mother-country. *Cottage*, then, has always had literary and sentimental connotations with us, — like *rill* and *rivulet* and 'woodland glade.' Of late years, however, the habit of spending a part of the summer in the country or at the sea has become almost universal. Small houses for the accommodation of 'summer people' called for a special name, and *cottage* seemed to meet the demand. It had precisely the rural and sentimental associations required, and it served to distinguish these temporary shelters from the larger and more substantial 'houses' in the neighborhood. Hence, *cottage* came to mean a 'summer residence,' however splendid, like the cottages at Newport, which are really villas on a very grand scale. *Cottager*, which in England signifies a person of humble condition, has thus become in America a term of social distinction in contrast to those who take up their summer quarters at boarding-houses or hotels. A somewhat similar development of meaning has taken place in England since the middle of the eighteenth century, so that *cottage* is freely applied to a 'small residence' or 'detached suburban villa.' It is not likely, however, that this has had much effect on the American sense, which has a history easily traceable on this side of the water. Every one will remember that Coleridge's devil grinned at the 'cottage of gentility' with the double coach-house which he saw in his walk.

> For his darling sin
> Is pride that apes humility.

There is none of this false humility, at all events, in the American word, which has got its meaning by legitimate inheritance. Its rise in dignity is not deliberate or self-conscious, but due to changed circumstances, like the rise of *marshal* and *seneschal*.[1]

The derivation and original sense of some of the words which we have just examined will show how far they have wandered in obedience to the magniloquent tendency.

Boulevard is a French corruption of the German *Bollwerk*, 'bulwark.' It means, therefore, a street laid out on the site of an ancient fortification. As this is never done until a city has far outgrown its walls, a boulevard is generally in a thickly settled quarter and has no suburban associations. On the contrary, an *avenue* (from Fr. *avenir*, 'arrive') is properly an 'approach' to a city or to some conspicuous part of it. A *road* is properly a way by which one *rides* or travels, a 'highway,' and is naturally

---

[1] See p. 295.

HYPERBOLE OR EXAGGERATION

named from the place to which it leads (as 'the London Road') or its direction ('the Northern Road').

Street is a very old word for a 'paved way,' — L. *strata* (*via*). It was first applied to the great military roads of the Romans. It is now, however, associated with towns, since cross-country roads are seldom paved.

Way is the most general term for any kind of road or street or passage. It is connected with the Latin *via*, and means literally, 'that over which one moves.'

A *lane* is a narrow country way, not a highroad. The term is crowded with poetical associations, which are lost in the dismal reality of city surroundings. A narrow way is seldom pleasant in a city. Hence the term is not in favor in urban nomenclature.

An *alley* (Fr. *allée*) has long been a rather disparaging name for a means of transit. Surviving or revived associations, however, may preserve its respectability.

Villa is the Latin name for a 'farmhouse' with its accompaniments, and from the nature of Roman landholding might be used of a very splendid estate. Many of the houses in our suburbs would be properly 'villas.' As we have said, the word has never made itself at home in America. When this country was settled it was not used in English except in speaking of the villas of the Italian nobility, — that is, it was still a foreign word confined to its proper application. Thus Evelyn in his Diary (Nov. 12, 1644) speaks of walking 'to Villa Borghesi,' which he describes as 'a house and ample garden' appearing 'at a distance like a little town,' and again (Nov. 10): 'We went to see Prince Ludovisio's villa. . . . The house is very magnificent, and the extent of the ground is exceeding large considering that it is in a city.' The extensive use of *villa* in England, and its magniloquent application to cheap suburban houses, have had no effect on American English. We did not inherit this application and have not imported it.

From the magniloquence of vulgar display we may pass to a subtle influence of the same general kind, though different in its motives, — the exaggeration that comes from courtesy. The extension of *lady* and *gentleman* to all human beings is often unthinkingly ascribed to pushing self-assertion. In fact, however, it comes rather from politeness than from bumptious democracy. A woman in humble circumstances compliments her neighbor by calling her a 'lady'; the attention is reciprocated, and, the usage once established, the kindly feeling of social superiors prompts them to employ the same term in their intercourse with those below them. It is the courtesy of democracy, not its assertiveness, that brings about the results which amuse us in *saleslady* or *washerlady* or the *gentleman* who sweeps the crossing.

We can study these tendencies in our ordinary terms of courteous address. These depend first on the institution of slavery,[1] second, on respect for age, and third, on apprenticeship and education. From the first relation come all the words that represent *dominus* and *domina*, such as *don*, *dame*, etc.; from the second, all that represent *senior*, such as *signor*, *sieur*, and *sir;* from the third, all that represent *magister*, such as *Mister* and *Miss*. The word *lady* is of the same kind, but is of native origin, and has had an independent development, as we shall see hereafter.

The progress of the magniloquent tendency in two

[1] White, of course, because generally the social effects which we are considering can only be produced where there is no permanent physical distinction between master and slave.

HYPERBOLE OR EXAGGERATION

thousand years is well illustrated by a French speaker's address to his audience, 'Messieurs et Dames,' literally 'My Elders, and Mistresses,' which has become a mere courteous equivalent for 'Men and Women.' It is unnecessary to follow all the steps which this example implies. We must rest content with mentioning enough of them to establish the general tendency and to indicate the result as we see it to-day.

In the society of the Roman Republic, a man who owned slaves was addressed by them as *dominus*. This term implied rather 'ownership' than mastership. For the latter idea there was an old word (*h*)*erus*, which was gradually displaced by *dominus*, no doubt for the reasons that we are now considering. The wife of the *dominus* was called *domina*, — a mere courtesy title (like *Frau Professorin* in German), since no woman could be properly *domina* unless she held slaves in her own right. At all events, it had become customary for a household to address its female head as *domina*, — a title which marks the social superiority of the Roman lady over her Greek sister. Of course a slave could never be addressed as *dominus* by anybody except a slave of his own; but many slaves were manumitted and grew rich, and when this was the case, a freedman might be *dominus* to a large circle of dependents. When the establishment of the Empire made all Romans virtual slaves of the court, the terms *dominus* and *domina* were regularly used by the whole population as titles of the highest respect, and became more and more common, until finally we get the Spanish *don* and *doña*, the Italian *donna*, the French *dame* and *madame*, and (from the French) the English *dame* (once common as a title, as in 'Dame Quickly,' 'Dame Trot') and *madam*. It will be observed that the application of the feminine forms is more general than that of the corresponding masculines, as might be expected from the greater courtesy that is habitually shown to women. All women are *dames* in France and *donne* in Italy, while the masculine is still slightly restricted. This is precisely what is now happening with the English *lady*, but no one ascribes the change to democratic self-assertion among the Italian peasantry.

Magister is in classical Latin more nearly equivalent to 'boss' than to any other word, and has to do with joint-stock companies, or other associations for trade, commerce, and the arts. Probably its first ennobling use comes from *ludi magister*, 'schoolmaster,' which appears in early classical times, and still survives in its English form; but we have *master workman* and *past master* as well, which suggest the sense which was mentioned at the outset. The Anglo-Saxons borrowed *magister* without real change (as *mægister*), but this was afterward replaced by the French form *maistre* (our *master*, modern Fr. *maître*), which became to all intents and purposes a native word, and was therefore employed to translate *domine*. Hence we have *Master* as a term of respectful address, later corrupted to *Mister*, always written *Mr.* except in imitation of vulgar English. The fully pronounced *master*, however, is still kept as a title for boys, as well as in the various uses of the word as an ordinary noun. This splitting of one word into two is a familiar phenomenon.[1]

The feminine *magistra* was early used in the school sense. Low Latin developed a new form *magistrissa*, whence O. Fr. *maistresse* (modern *maîtresse*) and our *mistress*. The latter was later corrupted to *Mrs.* (pronounced *missis*, but never written at length), which was long used as the title of both married and unmarried

[1] See pp. 355–7.

women. Finally, however, the abbreviated *Miss* was applied to the latter. Both *Mr.* and *Mrs.* have ceased to be specific titles of honor. They are applied to all men and women of whatever rank. But they are still titles merely. They have never become ordinary synonyms for 'men' and 'women.' The reason is, in part, that we have other courteous designations for this purpose, namely, *gentlemen* and *ladies*, which we shall examine in a moment.

In the development of titles of courtesy from the sentiment of respect for age, magniloquence is not so obvious, but it appears on a moment's consideration. *Senior*, 'elder' (the comparative of *senex*), does not regularly appear as a form of address in classic Latin, but we find it now and then as a respectful designation for an individual (as in Virgil's *senior Acestes*), and the use of similar words in other languages is common enough. The Greek πρεσβύς (*presbús*), 'old,' and its derivatives are familiar examples. St. Isidore informs us that '*presbyter* in Greek and *senior* in Latin indicate not mere age or the decrepitude of years, but are used for honor and dignity.' At all events, *senior* had established itself in the sense of 'lord' or 'master' as early as the sixth century, and it has given us the Italian *signore*, *signora*, and *signorina*, the Spanish *señor*, the Portuguese *senhor*, the French *sieur*, *sire*, and *seigneur*, and the English *sir* and *sire* (both borrowed from the French). It is certain, then, that this word had become a title of distinction (opposed to *vassal*), and that courtesy extended it beyond its proper boundaries, with the result that we have already observed in *dominus* and *magister*. We may compare the slang use of *old man* for 'boss' or 'employer.'

Lord and *lady* have developed their meanings somewhat differently. *Lord* was originally 'bread-conserver' or 'guardian of bread' (from *hlāf*, 'bread,' and *weard*, 'guardian'), and *lady* is thought to mean 'bread-kneader' (though the last part of the word is doubtful). From their etymology, then, *lord* and *lady* seem to have signified 'husband' and 'wife,' or, perhaps, to have been distinguishing terms for a husband and wife of some rank. At all events, *lord* occurs early as a translation of *Dominus* and the Greek Κύριος (*Kúrios*), as applied to the Supreme Being, and *lady* is also found in respectful address and appellation: observe especially 'Our Lady' for the Virgin. But, unlike the other terms which we have examined, *lord* has never been generalized.[1] It remains a kind of title to the present day. With *lady*, however, the case is different. This has resolutely gone through the generalizing or vulgarizing process, in spite of every attempt to confine its application.[2] The effect of this on the word *woman* is well known. Of late, however, a reaction has set in, and *woman* seems likely to be restored to its full rights as a self-respecting word. Meantime *person* has suffered an amusing deterioration. It has been more or less employed as a substitute for *woman* by those who did not wish to countenance the vulgar abuse of *lady* and yet shrank from giving offence. The result has been to give a comically slighting connotation to one of the most innocent words imaginable.[3]

The adjective *gentle* (whence *gentleman*) is from the

[1] The French *milord* for 'gentleman' and the modern Greek *lórdos* (for κύριος), 'Mr.,' illustrate what might well have taken place in English.

[2] The substitution of *Frau* for *Weib* in German affords a precise parallel. 'Washerlady' for 'washerwoman' is not different from *Waschfrau* for *Waschweib*, except that in German the change has been accepted in legitimate speech. *Frau* is a highly honorable word in its origin, being cognate with A.S. *frēa*, 'lord,' 'prince,' and the Old Norse *Freyr* and *Freyja*, the names of a god and a goddess respectively.

[3] For the etymology of *person* see p. 268.

Latin *gens*, and means properly 'belonging to one of the great families or *gentes* of Rome.' It implied, therefore, in its first use in English, high station and what we may call 'gentle breeding,' and came, in England, to be applied to a definite rank in society, corresponding to that of the 'lower' or untitled nobility of the Continent ('ye *gentles* all'). The adjective *gentle*, however, had acquired a secondary meaning in French before it was taken into our language. It had been applied, by association of ideas, to the characteristics supposed to accompany high birth (exactly as in the case of *noble, generous, courteous*, and the like), and this sense, still further limited, has prevailed in English. *Gentleman*, however, has not gone quite so far. In England it has retained its literal meaning of 'a man of good family.' Still, even there, the extension of the word has been so great that the phrase 'gentleman by birth' has often to be employed to prevent ambiguity. Indeed, the moral or ethical sense of *gentleman* was insisted on long ago by Chaucer, who defined the true gentleman as one who always tries to 'do the gentil dedes that he can.'[1] Pope's famous line 'Worth makes the man and want of it the fellow,' points the same distinction between *fellow* and *man* which many now make between *man* and *gentleman*, and Pope's verse correctly represents the usage in this country fifty years ago.

Courtesy, however, has affected *gentleman* exactly as it has affected *lady* and many other terms of respect. It has become, in vulgar use, a mere synonym for *man*, without regard to birth or breeding. A young woman once spoke

[1] The definition did not originate with Chaucer. Discussion of the true nature of gentility and courtesy, as opposed to the accident of birth, considerably antedates his time. There is a fine passage of the kind in the Roman de la Rose, which inspired the well-known homily of the lady in the Tale of the Wife of Bath.

of a room in an art museum as 'the room where all those *gentlemen* are,' referring to the casts of antique statuary. The incident is significant enough. It illustrates the tendency to call all men (even in plaster) 'gentlemen.' But it does more. It shows how free such language is from self-assertion. The same lesson may be learned from the respectful formula 'Gentlemen,' which is freely employed in addressing one's audience, even by speakers who would never be guilty of the vulgarism of making *gentleman* a mere synonym for 'male human being.' Courtesy, not democratic push, is the explanation of the kind of magniloquence which we have been studying. There is nothing 'new' or essentially vulgar in the process as demonstrated by the facts that we have presented. The history of the commonest forms of address in our family of languages is precisely parallel to the latest and most amusing extensions of *lady* and *gentleman*.

Thus we have examined the tendency to exaggeration in several of its most striking manifestations. We have seen its effect in weakening strong words like *astonish* and *amaze;* and we have followed its operations in words of degree, in self-assertive magniloquence, and in terms of courteous address. It has certainly made good its claim to be regarded as a considerable motive power in the development of our vocabulary.

Hyperbole is a favorite object for the animadversions of critical rhetoricians. It is undoubtedly necessary to control this tendency in 'forming a style.' But the same is true of metaphor, or simile, or antithesis, or alliteration — indeed, of every linguistic tendency that can be mentioned. *Ne quid nimis* is the most elementary of stylistic rules. To point the moral, however, by calling attention to the weakening effect which continuous hyperbole has had on this or that English word in the course of centuries, is ill-considered. For this effect is no more deplorable than any other linguistic change. Language can never stand still so long as it is alive, and hyperbole is merely one of the many causes which operate to alter it from age to age. Any loss is at once made good by the employment of less used synonyms, by fresh figures of speech, or by the coinage or borrowing of new words. Extravagant hyperbole is ridiculous because it is **extravagant**, not because it is hyperbole.

CHAPTER XXIII

FOLK-ETYMOLOGY

SYSTEMATIC etymology is a high mystery, requiring of its initiates long and painful preparation, and cultivated by its adepts at the price of eternal vigilance. But scholars are not the only etymologists. Curiosity about the make-up of words and about their sources is universal. We are continually proposing to ourselves problems in derivations, and solving them to our own satisfaction without regard to the dictionaries. Many words, to be sure, are passively accepted without inquiry. It seldom occurs to us to ask why a stone is called a *stone*, or why bread goes by the name of *bread*, — and so of most of the very familiar words in our vocabulary. In such cases we accept the name as belonging to the thing by nature. But we are not always so easily satisfied. We are aware that a vast number of words are actually derived from something else. *Kindness* and *kindly* are manifestly formed from *kind*, *friendship* from *friend*, *blackish* from *black*. Many compounds also tell their own story : as, *knifeblade* and *dogwhip* and *schoolboy* and *breakfast* and *fisherman*. Further, we see that words are gregarious, that they live and move in groups, larger or smaller, and many such groups are always present to our minds: as, — *true, truth, untrue, untruth, truthful,* etc.; *strong, strongly, strength, strengthen; fill, full, fulness, fulsome, fulfil.*[1] Hence we

[1] Cf. p. 193.

unconsciously attempt to associate every strange word with its group, or at all events with some other word whose company shall preserve it from utter loneliness. Thus every speaker of any language is to some extent his own etymologist. Children, even, have their theories of etymological relations. A little girl who had heard many stories about the mischievous doings of an imaginary 'Wilhelmina,' asked whether this personage was not so called because she was so *mean*. The question was typical of a process which is always active in linguistic history, and which goes by the name of *folk-etymology*.[1]

In its simplest operations, folk-etymology merely associates together words which resemble each other in sound and show a real or fancied similarity of meaning, but which are not at all related in their origin: as,—*hag* and *haggle; hawk* (the bird) and *hawker; raven* (the bird) and *ravening; horse* and *hostler*. Often, however, the erroneous association has a perceptible effect on the form or the sense of a word, so that folk-etymology becomes a transmuting power in language.

The change may be very slight, affecting only the orthography. Thus *surloin* (from *sur-*, 'above') is usually spelled *sirloin*, as if from *sir*. A ludicrous anecdote tells how an English king once knighted a loin of beef in enthusiastic appreciation of the national dish. So 'Welsh *rabbit*' is often spelled *rarebit* (and even so pronounced), from a whimsical notion that it is compounded of *rare* and *bit*. In fact, however, 'Welsh rabbit' is merely a joke, like 'Cape Cod *turkey*' for *codfish*, the Australian 'colonial

[1] An adaptation of the German *Volksetymologie*. 'Popular etymology' is an attempt to translate the same word. In fact, our language is somewhat at a loss for a graceful and convenient term under which to classify the phenomena.

goose' for a leg of mutton with savory herbs, and the old
'French of Norfolk' for the Norfolk dialect of English.[1]
Slowworm is not from *slow*. The Anglo-Saxon form is
slā-wyrm, probably related to *slēan*, 'strike,' 'slay' (akin
to Ger. *schlagen*). Though quite harmless, the creature
has always been regarded with terror by the people.
Slāworm would regularly give *slō-worm* in Modern English.
Hiccough is variously spelled in older English (*hickup*,
hicock, *hicket*) and is doubtless an imitative word; it is
certainly not derived from *cough*.

A recent French novelist renders *teetotaller* by *totaliseur
du thé*, as if it were *tea-totaller*,[2] though in fact it is from
teetotal, which is merely a reduplicated form of *total* (cf.
mishmash, *tittle-tattle*, *bibble-babble*, the German *Wirrwarr*,
and the like). Recent slang gives the name *teetotum* to a
tea or coffee-house conducted by the charitable as an offset
to the dramshop. This is merely a poor pun, and nobody
ever thought that *teetotum* and *teetotaller* were etymologically connected, but its coinage differs from folk-etymology
merely in being jocose and intentional. *Teetotum*, by the
way, is *T' totum*. When used for gambling, the *teetotum*
had a T on one of its four sides, standing for 'take all the
stakes.'

But changes in spelling come oftener from scholars than
from the people, and the learned have done their part in
disguising English words. *Rhyme*, for instance, is the
Anglo-Saxon *rīm*, 'measure,' and would naturally be *rime*
in Modern English. But scholars attempted to derive it

[1] Cf. 'peddlers' French' for the *argot* of vagabonds (thieves' slang).
[2] This derivation has often been seriously entertained. The opposite
phenomenon is seen in *tea-tree*, the name of various Australian shrubs
whose foliage has been used as a substitute for *tea*. This is sometimes
written *ti-tree* and even *ti-tri*, under the mistaken impression that it is an
aboriginal word.

from the Greek *rhythmos* (whence *rhythm* comes), and the absurd spelling *rhyme* is the result of their efforts. *Rime* is now preferred by many writers, and is steadily gaining ground; but printers are stubborn, and it is hard to resign the hard-won spoils of our youthful campaigns in the spelling-book. The adoption of the 'learned' spelling *rhyme* had of course had no effect on the pronunciation.[1] In many instances, however, a new spelling has changed a word considerably. Thus *perfect* was *parfit* or *parfet*, being derived not directly from the Latin *perfectus* but from the Old French *parfit*, *parfet* (modern *parfait*). Scholars, however, substituted the form *perfect* in the sixteenth century, and for some decades the word was thus spelled, though still pronounced *parfit* or *perfet*.[2] In time, however, the spelling carried the pronunciation with it, and we have the modern word.

But we must return to popular etymology, from which the parallel phenomenon of learned error has diverted us for a moment.

Folk-etymology ordinarily affects more than the associations of a word or its spelling. It transforms the word, in whole or in part, so to bring it nearer to the word or words with which it is ignorantly thought to be connected. The process is not confined to any single constituent part of our vocabulary, but its effects are most

[1] Other examples of spelling influenced by erroneous etymology may be seen in *scissors*, which is not from L. *scissor*, 'cutter,' but from O. Fr. *cisoires* (modern *ciseaux*), from L. *caedo*; *style*, which is L. *stilus*, not Gr. στῦλος; *searcloth* for *cerecloth*, 'waxed cloth' (L. *cerum* 'wax'); and the obsolete *satyr(e)* for *satire*, adopted under the impression that the word came from *satyr*, whereas it is really the Latin [*lanx*] *satura*, 'full plate,' a name given by the Romans to an 'olio' or 'mixed dish,' and transferred in Latin to a 'poetical medley' and (somewhat later) to 'satire' in the usual sense.

[2] See Campion, 1602, Works, ed. Bullen, p. 259.

commonly felt in foreign derivations. The reason is clear, and may be seen in a familiar example: — the corruption of *asparagus* to *sparrow grass*, which is now regarded as vulgar but which was in good use in the eighteenth and early nineteenth centuries. Such a word as *asparagus* stands alone in our vocabulary. The learned knew that it was the Latin *asparagus*,[1] borrowed intact, like so many other terms from that language, and the fact that it had no relatives in English made no difference to them, for they associated it with the Latin. To the people, however, who knew nothing of its origin, it was an English word like any other; and their minds unconsciously attempted to associate it with some other word or words with which they were familiar. It was long enough to be a compound. Its last syllable sounded like a slovenly pronunciation of *grass*. There were already many plant names in which *grass* was the last syllable. *A-* is easily lost, and *sparrow* is vulgarly *sparra*. The result was inevitably *sparrowgrass*, — a form which immediately satisfied the popular conscience. True, the plant had nothing to do with sparrows, but one cannot have everything in this world. What has *dog-grass* to do with dogs? In general, the etymologizing tendency which we are studying is easily satisfied. Half a loaf is better than no bread.

Take *cutlass*, for instance. It is the French *coutelas* (from L. *cultellus*, 'knife'), but owes its present form to a fancied connection with *cut*.[2] *Lass* seemed to be English enough already, and suffered no change at first, though lasses have nothing to do with swords. Half of

[1] The Latin took the word from the Greek ἀσπάραγος (perhaps connected with σπαργᾶν, 'to swell with sap').

[2] The *l* of *cultellus* would regularly disappear in French. *Cut* has nothing to do with either French or Latin, but is thought to be of Celtic origin.

the word had an appropriate meaning, at all events, and for a time the popular feeling was content. And it has remained content except among sailors, who did not like to call their favorite weapon by a name that was not completely intelligible. *Cutlass* seemed wrong, somehow, and accordingly they made it into *cutlash*, both parts of which were eminently satisfactory, just as they made the old man-o'-war *Bellerophon* into *Bully Ruffian*.

Often there is only the slenderest connection in sense, or none at all, between two words that are thus associated by popular etymology. In such cases we think it enough to give the strange term a familiar sound. Sense may take care of itself, as it does in so large a part of our vocabulary. Thus *lanyard* is the French *lanière*, 'thong' (L. *lacinia*), transformed by association with *yard*. The first syllable is left undisturbed. *Lutestring*, a kind of silk, is for *lustring*, itself a corruption of Fr. *lustrine* (from the gloss or *lustre* of the material). Nowadays the name is practically confined to ribbon, perhaps because this resembles string.

But popular etymology is not confined to foreign borrowings. It affects native words as well. *Sand-blind*, for instance, is for *samblind*, in which *sam-* is an Anglo-Saxon prefix, meaning 'half' (akin to L. *semi-*). So long as this prefix remained intelligible, there was no temptation to change it. But *sam-* became obsolete, and was therefore as tantalizing to the etymological consciousness of the folk as if it had been exotic. *Sand* in the eyes would cause temporary blindness: cf. 'throw *dust* in one's eyes' for 'deceive.' A very pretty song describes with much particularity the function of 'the *Sand*-man' who puts babies to sleep.

Shamefaced was formerly *shamefast*. The second syllable was the adjective *fast*, literally 'confirmed,' which was used in Anglo-Saxon to make adjectives. *Shame* meant 'modesty' and *shamefast* was merely 'modest' in a good sense. When the old termination went out of use, popular etymology got hold of the word, and, in its eagerness to make things intelligible, transformed it into *shamefaced*. In this instance (as in many others) the new associations of the word, consequent on its new etymology, have somewhat modified its sense. *Shamefaced* now means not so much 'modest' as 'bashful' or 'disconcerted,'— showing shame in one's *face*.

A number of examples of native and foreign words that have been distorted by folk-etymology will now be given without any attempt at classification. The reader will see that in some instances the change has been slight; in others, thoroughgoing. The whole word may be affected, or only a part of it. When two syllables are equally unintelligible to the popular mind, one may be changed and the other remain as inscrutable as before. Sometimes there is an obvious appropriateness in the new form; at other times, there is not the remotest connection in sense between the word and its supposed etymon. Indeed, the result of the etymologizing instinct may be a conglomerate of incongruous words, each meaning something by itself, but having no possible relation to its fellows or to the idea which the term expresses as a whole. Everywhere, however, the principle is the same. The effort is to make the word sound familiar, and, if possible, to give a meaning to that which was meaningless before. If both ends are achieved, so much the better. If but one is accomplished, we make the best of a bad matter.

Crawfish or *crayfish* is not from *fish*, but is a distorted form of an older English *crevis* from O. Fr. *crevice* (modern *écrevisse*), itself derived from the Old High German *krebiz* (modern *Krebs*), which is cognate with the English *crab*.

Penthouse, 'lean-to,' has nothing to do with either *pent* or *house*. It was once pronounced *pentus* (Ben Jonson rhymes it with the Latin *juventus*) and *pentis*, and comes from the French *appentis* (L. *appendicium*).

Rake, 'a debauchee,' is a shortened form of the old word *rakel*, 'reckless,' perhaps from O.N. *reikall*, 'vagrant,' which is from *reika*, 'to rove,' whence the old verb *rake*, 'wander.' Popular etymology made *rakel* into *rakehell* and slang shortened it to *rake*. To *rake* in the sense of 'live dissolutely' is from the noun.

Belfrey is not connected with *bell*. It is O. Fr. *berfray*, from M. H. Ger. *ber(c)vrit* (modern *Bergfriede*), 'place of safety,' from *bergen*, 'conceal,' and *vride* (modern *Friede*), 'peace,' 'protection.' Its original sense was 'a kind of tower.' The bells came later and are unessential.

Primrose is M.E. and O. Fr. *primerole*, L.L. *primula*, a diminutive of *primus*, 'first.' It comes in the *prime* or spring of the year. Compare 'a violet in the youth of primy nature' (Hamlet). We may observe that the '*prime* of life' once meant the 'springtime of life,' that is, 'youth,' and not, as it now does, the fulness of manly strength.

Clove and its longer form, *clove gillyflower*, have a strange history. The starting-point for English is the Old French *clou de girofle* or *girofre*, that is a 'nail of girofle,' applied to the dried bud of the clove-plant, which resembles a nail in shape and is used as a spice. *Clou* is the Latin *clavus*, 'nail.' *Girofle* is worn down from the Greek καρυόφυλλον (*karuóphullon*), 'nut-leaf,' the name of the plant, — from κάρυον (*káruon*), 'nut,' and φύλλον (*phúllon*), 'leaf,' cognate with the Latin *folium*, whence our *foliage* and *folio*. By popular etymology, *girofre* became *gillyflower*, a name still applied to the 'pink.'

Cassimere is the French *casimir*, which, like our *cashmere*, is simply the name of the Indian state *Kashmír*, though the fabrics in question are different. *Kersey* is still another kind of woollen cloth, named from the town of Kersey in Suffolk; but folk-etymology has transformed *cassimere* into *Kerseymere*.

A *sackbut* was lengthened or shortened in playing, like the modern trombone. Hence its name (Fr. *saquebute*) from *sachier* or *saquier*, 'to pull,' and *bouter*, 'to push.' Curiously enough the popular etymology would here be in the right place. For to *butt* (with the horns) is from *bouter*, and *sachier* was perhaps originally 'to pull out of a *sack*.'

Touchy is not from *touch*. It is a corruption of *techy*, 'peevish,' literally 'faulty, vicious' (cf. 'a vicious horse' for one of bad temper). *Teche* (now obsolete) is O. Fr. *tache*, *teche*, 'spot,' 'blemish,' and so 'fault.' The change from *techy* to *touchy* is instructive. *Touch* is often vulgarly pronounced *tetch*, and it was therefore easy to infer that *techy* was a mispronunciation of *touchy*. Folk-etymology is often a corrector of errors that are not erroneous.

Curmudgeon is of unknown derivation, but *cur* suggests popular etymology. The word recalls one of the most famous of etymological blunders. Dr. Johnson recorded it as from the French *cœur méchant*, adding 'unknown correspondent' to indicate that this (truly preposterous) conjecture had been sent to him by some person to him unknown. Ash copied the etymology in the form '*cœur*, "unknown," *méchant*, "a correspondent."'

Many have doubtless wondered why a *tuberose* is so called, since it resembles not a rose, but a lily. In fact, the name is merely *tuberosa*, 'tuberous,' from the tuberous root of the plant. (*Tuber* is the Latin word for 'knob' or 'swelling,' adopted as a botanical term.) *Rosemary* was formerly *rosmarine*, from L. *ros marinus*, 'sea-dew,' 'sea-foam.' The Australians have corrupted *tarantula* into *triantelope*, which they employ as the name of a large native spider.

Warlock is A.S. *wǣrloga*, literally 'one who proves false to his pledge (or faith),' from *wǣr*, 'pledge,' and *loga*, 'liar.'

Purlieu has been assimilated to Fr. *lieu*, 'place' (L. *locus*). It is O. Fr. *puralée*, *poralée*, L.L. *perambulatio*, so called because of the 'perambulation' or 'survey' by means of which the land adjoining a royal forest and improperly included therein was disafforested and restored to its owners. The usual modern sense is 'outskirts' or 'suburbs,' commonly with a suggestion of disrepute, since the suburbs of a town were, in old times, the haunt of debauched and desperate persons.

Battledoor can hardly be from *battle* and the last syllable is certainly not the noun *door*. The earliest sense is 'a bat employed by washerwomen.' The derivation is extremely uncertain. Spanish *batallador*, 'hero of many battles,' has been suggested, and also Provençal *batedor*, 'little bat.'

Panther has been subjected to folk-etymology more than once. The Latin *panthēra*, which gave *panthère* in French (whence our word), was adapted from the Greek πάνθηρ (*pánthēr*). In Greek, παν- (*pan-*) means 'all' (as in '*Pan-Presbyterian* Council,' *Pan-American*, etc.), and θήρ (*thḗr*), 'wild beast'; but there is little doubt that the word is the Sanskrit *puṇdrīka*, 'tiger,' borrowed by the

Greeks and transformed so as to make sense in their language. The hunter's name for the American panther is *painter*. This also looks like popular etymology, but perhaps it also preserves a suggestion of the older English form *pantere*.

Pennyroyal is a compound of translation and folk-etymology. The Latin is *puleium* (or *pulegium*) *regium*, from *pulex*, 'flea,' the plant being thought to be efficacious as a flea-bane. The Latin name, partly adapted and partly translated, gave Eng. *puliall royal*, which was not like anything else in the language, and was promptly rationalized to *pennyroyal*.

Artichoke comes directly from the Italian (*articiocco*, probably from Arabic); the last syllable was formerly pronounced *chock*, but has been respelled and repronounced under the influence of the verb *choke*. A still better example of popular etymology is seen in *Jerusalem artichoke*, which has nothing to do with Jerusalem, but is corrupted from It. *girasole* ('turning with the sun'), the name of a plant with an edible root resembling the artichoke.

Walnut is not related to *wall*, but to *Welsh*. The first syllable is the Anglo-Saxon *wealh*, 'foreign,' which, however, is not a native word, but comes from the name of the Celtic tribe of *Volcae*, whence also *Welsh*. The Teutonic race regarded the Celts as 'foreigners' *par excellence*. In some parts of America the name *walnut* is given to the 'shagbark,' a kind of hickory nut, and the true walnut is known as the 'English walnut,' — a term which involves a curious etymological contradiction.

Mandrake is a corruption of *mandragoras*, the Greek (and Latin) name of the plant. The Anglo-Saxon *mandragora*, a direct borrowing, has also survived. *Drake* is an Old English word for *dragon* (A.S. *draca* from L. *draco*). There is no connection between the plant and dragons, but folk-etymology is careless about trifles. At all events, the *mandrake* was a mysterious thing, popularly supposed to be endowed with life, and to shriek so terribly when it was torn from the earth 'that living mortals, hearing it, run mad.' Perhaps the mere fact that dragons were also uncanny was enough to satisfy the popular mind. Doubtless the first syllable was identified with our *man* (with which it has no connection). The mandrake has a forked root, which often startlingly resembles the human figure. In this word one may see the action and reaction of popular superstition and popular etymology in a remarkable degree. The idea that the mandrake was alive did not spring from the accidental identity between the first syllable of its name and the name of a human being; but we cannot doubt that it was strengthened by this identity.

Standard is O. Fr. *estendart* (modern *étendard*), 'that which is spread out' (L. *extendo*). As soon as the word entered our language, however, it was associated with *stand*, so that the form *standard* appears in the twelfth century.[1] The supposed connection with *stand* has not only changed its form, but has given it the meaning of 'that which stands firm,' or 'is fixed.' Thus we have the '*standard* of weights and measures,' 'the *standard* bushel,' the *standard* of morals,' 'not up to the *standard*.' The notion of 'extension' or 'spreading' has quite vanished.

Purblind is *pure blind*, i.e. 'absolutely sightless.' Its commoner meaning of 'near-sighted' seems due, in part, to the erroneous idea that the first syllable is a cor-

[1] In the Peterborough Chronicle (cited by Skeat), and also in Henry of Huntingdon (v, 7): 'fixo *Standard*, id est regio insigni.'

ruption of *pore*. The form *pore-blind* actually arose under the influence of this idea.

Abominable (formerly spelled *abhominable*) seems to owe its special implication of 'unnatural' or 'inhuman' conduct to the mistaken derivation from *ab homine*, 'away from or contrary to a man.' The word is really from *ab* and *omen*. The Latin *abominari* is literally 'to deprecate anything as an evil omen,' and then 'to abhor.' The connection with *homo*, 'man,' is a very old error and antedates the adoption of the word into English.

Pantry and *buttery* are associated with *pan* and *butter* by most speakers. In fact, *pantry* comes (through the French) from L. *panis*, 'bread'; and *buttery* was originally the place where the *butts* and *bottles* were kept (L.L. *botaria*, from *bota*, *butta*, 'cask').

Reindeer does not mean a deer that is guided by *reins*. It is the Old Norse name of the animal, *hreinn*, with a superfluous English *deer* added. The German name for the creature, *Rennthier*, is also from the Norse, but is connected in the popular mind with *rennen*, 'to run.' The Scandinavian word was no doubt borrowed from the Lapps or the Finns.

Tweezers is vaguely associated in our minds with *squeeze* and with *pinchers* or *pincers*. But the name means simply 'implements carried in a *tweeze* or case' (Fr. *étuis*).

In *headlong*, *flatlong*, and *sidelong* the old suffix *-ling* (preserved in *darkling*) has been confused with *long*. *Endlong* (in Chaucer *endëlong*) is the A.S. *andlang* (cf. Ger. *entlang*) in which *and-* is an adverbial prefix akin to Gr. ἀντί (*antí*). Our noun *end* is the A.S. *ende*, which is cognate with *antí*.

In *foremost*, *nethermost*, etc., an old superlative suffix

FOLK-ETYMOLOGY 343

mest has been supplanted by the adverb *most*, so often used with adjectives (as in *most beautiful*).[1]

In all these examples of folk-etymology we have simply been observing strong cases of the operation of analogy, — a force which pervades all speech, as it pervades all thought, and which has caused far-reaching changes in the structure of our language. Confusion of grammatical constructions and inflectional and derivative forms is largely due to this force, which has operated with peculiar energy in English.[2] Countless instances might be given, but two or three will sufficiently illustrate the point.

Burial is for an older *buriels*, 'tomb,' in which the *s* was not the plural ending, any more than it is in *corps* and *corpse* (which are the same word pronounced in two ways). The form looked like a plural, however, and so *burial* was formed (like the vulgar *corp*).[3] The spelling *-al* is after the analogy of *manual*, *casual*, and other Latin derivatives in *-al(is)*.

Syllable is O. Fr. *sillabe* (L. *syllaba*).[4] It owes its *l* to association with the numerous English words in *-able*.

In Anglo-Saxon there were several declensions of nouns, differing greatly in their inflection. Modern English reduces these to the simple scheme with which we are familiar, partly through decay, but largely through the influence of analogy. The nouns which made their genitive singular in *-es*, for instance, have attracted to themselves those that had other genitive endings. The old differences between the singular and the plural in the preterite of strong verbs have disappeared; sometimes the singular form has carried the day, and

---
[1] See pp. 200–1.   [2] See pp. 181 ff.   [3] See p. 139.
[4] Gr. συλλαβή, 'something taken together,' from συν-, 'together,' and λαμβάνω, λαβεῖν, 'take.' The Modern French *syllabe* is a learned spelling.

sometimes the plural. The confusions of analogy are baffling to the philologist, but its effect has been, in the main, in the direction of simplicity, — and increased simplicity, as we have already remarked, is an advance in the usefulness of language.[1]

[1] See pp. 183-4.

CHAPTER XXIV

DOUBLETS AND HOMONYMS

THE borrowing habits of the English language have filled our vocabulary with 'doublets,' as they are called, — that is, with different words which go back, by diverse courses, to the same original form. For example, *dainty* and *dignity* are both derived from the Latin *dignitas*, but the former entered our language through the French (O. Fr. *deintié*), the latter was adapted directly from the Latin (or perhaps from the French *dignité*, a learned derivative from *dignitas*). Thus *dainty* and *dignity* are doublets. They were taken into English at different times, have distinct senses, and are not felt as related words except by the etymologist.

Again, *guest* is a native word, cognate with L. *hostis*, — that is, a word meaning 'stranger' in the Indo-European parent-speech has survived in Latin as *hostis*, in English as *guest*. Neither of the two is derived from the other. Possessing *guest* by right of inheritance, we have borrowed *hostile* (a derivative of *hostis*) from the Latin. The native *guest* and the borrowed *hostile* are therefore doublets in English, — both going back to an Indo-European word, but by different paths.

Shirt and *skirt* are also doublets. They are both descended from the same Germanic word, but *shirt* is native English, whereas *skirt* is Scandinavian, and its presence in our language is due to borrowing. Sometimes the doublets are both of native origin. Thus, *whit* and *wight* are both descended from the Anglo-Saxon *wiht*, though they have become differentiated in the period that intervenes between the Anglo-Saxon times and the present day.

The development of doublets is one cause of the richness of our vocabulary. Sometimes they are synonymous. More often, however, they have received special meanings, which, as well as their diversity of form, tend to conceal their original identity. Though we have studied a number of these words incidentally in previous chapters, their importance will justify us in examining several typical specimens by themselves.

Verdigris is the French *vert-de-gris*, 'green of gray.' The latter, however, is corrupted from L.L. *viride aeris*, 'green of brass.' *Ambergris*, on the other hand, really means 'gray amber' (Fr. *ambre gris*); cf. Milton's *grisamber*. The last syllable of the English word has been sometimes confused with *grease* or with *Greece*, whence the obsolete forms *ambergrease* and *amber-de-grece*.

Turtle (*dove*) is A.S. *turtle*, which was, however, not of native origin, but a very early borrowing from L. *turtur*, a reduplicated form (like *murmur*) that seems to go back to first principles, being an imitation of the bird's note. *Dove* was added to distinguish the bird after the name *turtle* had been applied to the tortoise. The latter application is comparatively late. English sailors of the sixteenth or seventeenth century, becoming acquainted with the sea tortoise under its Spanish name *tortuga* (cf. the islands called *Tortugas*) or its Portuguese name *tartaruga*, corrupted the strange term into one with which they were familiar, though there was no resemblance between the tortoise and the dove. These foreign names were derived from L. *tortus*, 'crooked' (in allusion to the creature's queer feet), whence came O. Fr. *tortis* and our *tortoise*.

Booth is probably from the Old Norse *būth* (or connected with it), which is from *būa*, 'to inhabit' (A.S. *būan*, Ger. *bauen*). Thus *booth* is connected with *bower* (A.S. *būr*), 'sleeping-place' (preserved in poetry), and with *boor*, 'peasant.' *Boor* is the Dutch *boer*, 'farmer'; recently introduced afresh in the pure Dutch form as a proper name for the Dutch in South Africa. *Busk*, 'to prepare,' is from the same Old Norse verb (*-sk* being an old suffixed reflexive pronoun), and *boun*, 'ready,' is the Anglo-Saxon participle (*ge*)*būn*, 'prepared,' from the corresponding Anglo-Saxon verb *būan*. *Bound* (on a journey) is the same *boun*, with *d* added under the influence of the participle of *bind*. *Bower*, for the 'knave' at cards, is the German *Bauer*, 'peasant,' from the corresponding High German verb *bauen*. Thus, in this group of words, our language has laid under contribution not only its native stock but the related words in three Teutonic tongues, — Old Norse, Dutch, and High German.

Lien is the French form of L. *ligamen*, 'bond' (*ligare*, 'bind'). *Ligament* is a direct borrowing from the same Latin word, influenced by the numerous French and English words in *-nt*. *League*, 'alliance,' is the French *ligue* (from L.L. *liga*), also from *ligare*.

Our ordinary *utterance* is from the verb *utter*, which comes in its turn from *out*. But the old phrase 'to the *utterance*' for 'to the death,' said especially of duels or other combats, is the French *à outrance* (from L. *ultra*, 'beyond'). The change from *outrance* to *utterance* was no doubt due, in part, to the emphatic sense which the adjective *utter* (really a comparative of *out ;* cf. *outer*) had acquired, — as in 'utter misery,' etc. It is one of the countless freaks of linguistic fortune that *outrance*, borrowed from the French, and *utterance*, of native origin, should resemble each other so closely both in form and sense, and yet should have no etymological relationship. The former goes back to L. *ultra*, the latter to Eng. *out*, and these two adverbs are in no way akin.

From the Latin *dominus*, 'lord, master,' we have borrowed almost every conceivable formation.[1] The vocative, applied as a title, we have taken in bodily as *domine* (or *dominie*), for a schoolmaster or a parson. *Dan*, as in Spenser's '*Dan* Chaucer,' is an Old French shortening of *dominus*, and corresponds to Sp. *don* and Port. *dom*. *Don* is jocosely used of a university dignitary in England, but never (except by imitation) in America. *Dame* is *domina*, — also French. *Domain* and *demesne* are really one and the same French word, from L. *dominicum*, *demesne* being Anglo-French (the *s* was simply a bad Law French spelling).

Donjon or *dungeon* means properly the 'master-tower' or 'keep' of a castle, — from L.L. *domnio*, for *dominio* (the source of Fr. *dominion*, which we have also borrowed). *Donjon-keep* is a tautological compound. The shift of meaning in *dungeon* is easy to understand.

The Latin verb *dominari* (from *dominus*) became *dominer* in French, and this was taken into Dutch as *domineren* (with infinitive ending *-en*). In the fifteenth century, apparently, the Dutch word furnished us with our *domineer*. *Dominate*, *dominant*, and *domination* we borrowed directly from the Latin.

Dominican is from St. Dominic, who founded the order. His name is the Latin *dominicus*, 'belonging to the Lord.' *Domino* is a modern word in English. It is found in

[1] Cf. pp. 323–4.

DOUBLETS AND HOMONYMS 349

French, Spanish, and Italian in this same form, and was applied originally to a canon's hood, and then to a masking habit. How the word was formed is matter for conjecture. The suggestion that it was a jocose application of a fragment of the Latin 'benedicamus *Domino*' is not improbable. At all events, it must have been in the first instance a bit of slang. The game of *dominos* is said to be named from the garment, because the pieces with which it is played have black backs — again a bit of humorous slang, which has established itself in the language. But all this is guesswork, as is so often true in the case of slang and cant.

Danger means originally 'mastership,' and comes from L.L. *dominarium* (through the French). So when Portia says to Antonio, 'You stand *within his danger*, do you not?' she means not 'in his debt,' as some have thought, but 'in his power,' 'absolutely under his control.' So, too, *dangerous* often meant 'offish,' 'distant,' 'defiant,' which are closely connected with the idea of 'lordliness' of demeanor. In the mediæval love allegory, *Danger*, one of the lover's fiercest opponents, typifies the lady's coldness.

Cross, in all senses, as noun, verb, adjective, and adverb (*across*, cf. *athwart*), comes ultimately from the Latin *crux*, *crucis*. Its introduction into our language depends on the crucifixion of Christ; hence, there is attached to it the whole history of the conversion of Western Europe. But that is not all. The noun *cross* did not reach England in any simple way. It is the Norse *cros*, borrowed from the Irish, which in turn borrowed it from Latin. Its proper English home is the North, where Scandinavian settlements greatly affected our language; but it spread into other dialects, and has finally become the universal form. Our texts of Chaucer have both *cros* and *crois*, the latter being from the French modification of L. *crucem* (O. Fr. *crois*, modern *croix*). Thus, in this single word, we have a trace of the early Christianity of Ireland ('the Isle of Saints') and of the conversion of Northumbria by Celtic missionaries. The pure Latin form appears in *cruci-al*, *cruci-fix*, *cruci-form*, and other borrowed words of a learned character, and we have taken in *crux* intact for 'a difficult question or passage in an author.' We have also *crusade* (from Sp. *cruzada*), *crusado*, 'a coin' (Port. *cruzado*), and *cruise* (from D. *kruisen*, a verb made from the noun *kruis*), all of which go back to the Latin *crux*.

An instructive case of successive borrowing of the same word is that of *reason*, *ration*, and *ratio*. The Latin *ratio*, 'reckoning,' became *resoun* in Old French (modern *raison*), and this gives us *reason*. Later, *ration* was borrowed by French directly from Latin, and by English from French, in the special military sense; and, finally, we have also the Latin word, unchanged, as a technical term in mathematics. Compare *gentile*, *gentle*, and *genteel*, all from L. *gentilis*, — the first directly, the second and third, by successive borrowing, through the French *gentil*.

The Latin *camera*, 'vault,' 'arch,' later 'chamber,' became *chambre* in French. We have borrowed both words, as well as another derivative *camber* (O. Fr. *cambre*), used as a technical term in shipbuilding and architecture.

Rose was adopted from L. *rosa* by the Anglo-Saxons. *Rosa* is doubtless related to the Greek ῥόδον (*rhódon*), which we have in *rhodo-dendron*, a Greek word meaning 'rose-tree,' taken into English bodily. Green vitriol was called by the alchemists 'rose of copper,' *cupri rosa*, which became *couperose* in French, and this latter word was gradually corrupted into *copperas* in English. The successive corruptions point to the fact that *copperas* has been much used in the arts. Words wear out like coins.

Tavern and *tabernacle* have very different associations; yet they are the same word at bottom. L. *taberna*, 'a booth,' 'shop,' 'tavern,' became *taverne* in French. English borrowed this word from French; and also, directly from Latin, the diminutive *tabernaculum*, 'tent.' The biblical use of *tabernacle* has given sacred associations to the term, so that it is often used in special senses, — *e.g.* for a canopied seat in the choir of a church.

Bench, *bank* (in all senses), *banco*, and *bunco*, are, to all intents and purposes, the same Germanic word. *Bench* is the native English form (A.S. *benc*). French borrowed the word from Old German in the form *banc*, and this gives us 'a *bank* of oars' (from the rowers' 'bench') and the legal phrase *in bank* (of the terms of a court). The Scandinavians had the Germanic word in a slightly different form, and from them we borrowed, at an early date, *bank*, in 'sandbank' or the 'bank of a river.' The Italians had also adopted the Germanic word, and used *banca* or *banco* for the bench or table of a money-changer. From *banca* the French made *banque*, which gives us *bank* in the financial sense; while we have also taken in the other Italian form *banco* intact. The Spaniards had corresponding forms *banca* for '(money) bank' and *banco* for a certain game at cards. The latter term has recently passed into American English, giving us *bunco* (or *bunko*) for a swindling card-game or mock-lottery, — whence the slang verb *to bunco*, for 'to cheat,' 'chouse,' or 'defraud' in almost any manner: as, — 'He was *buncoed* out of his seat in the House of Representatives.' It would be hard to find a better example of the omnium-gatherum character of the English vocabulary. We had this word *bench* by right of inheritance, yet we have, at different times, taken in the same word, in different senses, four times, — once from Old Norse, once from Spanish, and twice from French. Besides this, we have *mountebank* and *bankrupt*. The former is the Italian *montimbanco*, 'a quack' (who gets upon a *bench* to proclaim his nostrums). *Bankrupt* has been twice borrowed, — from It. *banca rotta*, 'broken bench,' and from Fr. *banqueroute* (which is also from Italian). Hence the older English *banke rota* and *bankrout*. *Rotta* is the Italian form of the Latin participle *rupta*, and hence, in the 'learned times' of the sixteenth century, the English word was brought nearer to the classic languages, and took the form *bankrupt*, which we now have. Observe that all the financial senses of *bank* go back to Italy, the cradle of modern banking.

Arch and *arc* are both from L. *arcus*, 'bow,' — the latter directly, the former through the French.

Hyena and *sow* are really the same word. The Anglo-Saxon had *sū*, 'pig,' and *sugu*, 'sow,' and these are cognate with L. *sûs*, Gr. σῦς (*sûs*) or ὗς (*hûs*). From ὗς comes *hyaena* (which is merely the Latin spelling of Gr. ὕαινα, *húaina*, 'sow'). *Swine* is A.S. *sū* with a diminutive ending, though its diminutive force vanished utterly long ago.

Star is a general Indo-European word. The English form (A.S. *steorra*) is cognate with L. *stella* (short for *sterula*) and Gr. ἀστήρ (*astér*), ἄστρον (*ástron*). Besides having the native word, we have borrowed freely from Greek and Latin: *stellar, stellate, stellify, constellation; aster*, 'the star-flower,' *disaster*, 'a bad star'; *astrology, astronomy, asteroid*.

The Romans had a word *cancer*, 'a crab,' perhaps old enough to be cognate with the Greek καρκίνος (*karkínos*),

but, from its appearance, more likely to be corrupted from
it. *Cancer* has continued to be the name of a constellation
for more than two thousand years. It was also applied
in Greek to a disease, from a fancied resemblance of the
swollen veins to a crab's claws, and, in its Latin form, has
been borrowed by later civilizations, giving rise to the
two English words *cancer* and *canker*, now very different
in sense. Modern science has distinguished various forms
of cancer, and, feeling the need of exacter terms than those
which satisfied the old physicians, has accordingly borrowed the Greek name *carcinoma* in a special sense.
Cancer had a Latin diminutive *cancelli*, 'a grating' (once
more from the resemblance to a crab's claws), especially
a structure separating a part of a large hall from the rest
when used as a court or audience-room. Hence, through
the French, we get the *chancel* of a church. A derivative
of it in Latin gives *chancellor*, and later developments
give *chancery*. Directly from the Latin comes the verb
cancel, literally to 'cross out' writing by means of lines
like the bars of a grating. *In chancery* came to have
a sinister sense from the delays and expenses incident to
suits in the chancellor's court. It was picked up by pugi-
listic slang, and has reëntered the colloquial vocabulary
with the associations of the prize-ring.

Legal, loyal, and *leal* are all from L. *legalis*, 'according
to law.' *Legal* is directly from the Latin. *Loyal* and
leal are from O. Fr. *loial* (modern *loyal*) and *leial* respectively, the former being Central and the latter Norman
French. The general currency of 'Land of the Leal'(*i.e.*
of those who have 'kept the faith') for 'heaven' is due
to the Scottish poem of that name.

Sire and *sir* are variant forms of Fr. *sire* which is
from L. *senior*, 'older.' For their use as terms of respect,

see p. 325. *Sirrah* seems to be the dissyllabic result of an angry or scornful pronunciation of *sir-r-r*, with a prolonged *r* (cf. Irish *sor-r-r!*). The derivation from O.N. *sīra*, 'sir' (later used scornfully), itself a borrowing from French, must be rejected. 'No, sir-reé!' common a few years ago in jocose or vulgar speech, is doubtless a variant of *sirrah*, or at all events a parallel phenomenon.

Clench and *clinch* are dialectic variations of the same word, and were formerly interchangeable. In present usage, however, there is a strong inclination to distinguish them. We '*clench* our fists,' but '*clinch* a bargain.'

Chaw is a dialectic variety of *chew*, and does not appear in literature before the sixteenth century. For a time it was interchangeable with *chew* in dignified speech. Witness Spenser's Phaon, who describes himself as 'chawing (*i.e.* ruminating) vengeaunce.'[1] At this moment, *chaw* is contemptuously used for violent or vulgar chewing (cf. *chawbacon*), and is therefore regarded as itself a word of dubious character.[2] The distinction between *chew* and *chaw*, however, is very much like that between *essen* and *fressen* in German, which, however, has established itself in the literary language. *Chew* itself is sometimes euphemistically avoided in favor of *masticate*, — a curious Latin word which seems to come from Gr. $\mu\alpha\sigma\tau i\chi\eta$ (*mastichē*), 'mastic,' a resinous gum used for chewing. No essential dignity attaches to *masticate*; its elegance consists in its being a Latin word used in technical language. In the figurative sense, again, *chew* is out of favor. A modern Brutus would not advise Cassius (as in Shakspere) to 'chew upon this.' He would say *ruminate*, which is sono-

[1] Faerie Queene, ii, 4, 29.
[2] It is common, however, in various dialects, as the ordinary verb for 'masticate.'

rous enough, but is after all only the Latin for 'chew the cud' (from *rumen*, 'throat,' 'gullet').

The two pronunciations of *gallant* (as *gállant* and as *gallánt*) are really doublets of a peculiar kind. The Old French adjective *galant* passed into English in the fourteenth century, and is now accented on the first syllable. Some three hundred years later, the same word was borrowed again in the sense of 'polite or attentive to ladies,' and this gives us *gallánt*. The French adjective is a present participle of the old verb *galer*, 'to make merry,' which is of Germanic origin. The Italian *gala* (which we have also borrowed) is from the same source. It corresponds to O. Fr. *gale*, 'merriment,' with which it is almost impossible not to connect the phrases 'a *gale* of laughter,' 'a *gale* of merriment,' 'to be in a perfect *gale*' (*i.e.* 'a state of great hilarity'). This use of *gale* is old in New England, and is not confined to this side of the Atlantic.

Our language often shows considerable diversity of usage in the pronunciation of the same word, especially with regard to accent. This is likely to be the case with borrowed words, which, as they become established in our vocabulary, conform more and more closely to our habits of speech. Thus, Tom Moore knew only *balcóny* (from It. *balcóne*), and there are still persons who would say 'you was' as soon as *bálcony*, though this has come to be the usual pronunciation. Occasionally, the language has taken advantage of such diversity to make two words out of one by attaching different meanings to the different pronunciations, as in the following examples.

In the Elizabethan time, *mettle* was simply a phonetic spelling of *metal*. There was no difference in sense, — both forms being freely used both in the literal sense and in the figurative meaning of 'one's composition,' 'the stuff out of which one is made,' 'one's nature.' In Modern English, we no longer even associate *mettle* with *metal*, — the two forms have become perfectly distinct words with widely different meanings.

Conjúre and *cónjure* are not distinguished in Shakspere. Either accentuation is used for either sense. To-day they are different words: to *cónjure* is 'to use charms or incantations'; to *conjúre* is 'to call upon one solemnly,' as it were with an oath.

Many dissyllabic adjectives like *profound*, *supreme*, *complete*, and the like, which are derived from Latin adjectives accented on the penult (*profúndus*, *suprémus*, *complétus*) had in the Elizabethan age a variable accent, *prófound* or *profóund*, etc., according to their position with respect to other stresses in the verse or sentence. As time went on, the accent became settled. In some instances, however, both pronunciations were retained, each with a special set of meanings, and thus the single term split into two distinct words. *Húman* carries the literal sense of the Latin *humanus;* *humáne*, the other pronunciation, is specialized to the ethical meaning. *Antíque* is literal; *ántic*, simply another accentuation of the same word, means first 'fantastic' (as *old* things seem to the moderns), and then 'a fantastic caper.'

Negro and *nigger* are interesting examples of the tendency to utilize variant pronunciations for the increase of our vocabulary. *Negro*, 'black,' was borrowed from the Spanish (or Portuguese) as a descriptive term for the black race proper. It is pronounced *negṛ* by many, in accordance with the tendency to develop a vowel *r* from *r* + vowel (cf. *chambre* from *camera*). Then *negṛ* becomes *nigger*, much as *chambre* becomes *chamber*. *Negro* is retained as the true racial designation, while *nigger* is utilized as a term of contempt or abuse not only for an 'Ethiopian' but, especially in England, for a member of any dark-skinned race.[1]

Sometimes the tendency to differentiate asserts itself in different inflectional forms of the same word. So especially in the so-called irregular verbs. We say 'the pirate was *hanged*,' but 'the crane *hung* in the fireplace'; 'he *hove* the lead,' but '*heaved* a sigh.'

It is a familiar fact that our vocabulary includes many pairs of words which, though entirely distinct in origin and meaning, are pronounced alike, and sometimes spelled in the same way. Such words are called 'homonyms.' Their presence in our language is often wondered at, but comes about in a perfectly natural way. It may be ascribed, in the main, to mere coincidence. Two different words may happen to sound alike, just as two persons who are not related may show a striking 'family resemblance.' The chances of coincidence are greatly increased by our habit of borrowing from every possible quarter. Sometimes, however, both homonyms are derived from the same language or belong to the native stock. Pure accident is not the sole cause of the existence of homonyms. Folk-etymology has often assisted in bringing into accord two words which have nothing in common except a slight resemblance of sound.

The study of homonyms is not altogether a matter of linguistic sport. It illustrates what we have so often remarked,—the varied history of our language and the complex civilization which it mirrors so accurately. A few

[1] The derivation of *nigger* from Fr. *nègre* is far less likely. The scholars who uphold it are unacquainted with the form *negr*, which is often heard in the South. *Neger* and *niger* are found (as serious designations) in the sixteenth century.

examples of these verbal curiosities will therefore be of interest.

Weed, 'a wild plant,' has nothing to do with the *weed* in a man's hat or a widow's *weeds*. The latter word is the A.S. *wǣde*, 'garment,' which we have specialized to 'mourning garments,' while *weed*, 'plant,' is A.S. *wēod*, from quite a different root.

Yearn, 'to desire,' is A.S. *geornian*, akin to Ger. *gerne*, 'gladly.' *Yearn*, 'to mourn,' as in Pistol's

> Falstaff he is dead,
> And we must *yearn* therefore, —

is corrupted (under the influence of the former word) from an older *erm*, from A.S. *yrman*, which is akin to Ger. *arm* (A.S. *earm*), 'poor,' 'miserable.'

Vice, 'fault,' is Fr. *vice* (L. *vitium*); *vice*, 'a clutching instrument,' is Fr. *vis*, 'screw' (L. *vitis*, 'vine'). *Vice-* in *vice-president* is the Latin ablative *vice*, 'in the place of' (from *vicis*, 'turn'), and so is different from either.

The *Tartars* are more properly *Tatars*, but their name was connected by the Europeans with *Tartarus*, because of their supposed fiendish nature. This points to the terror roused by the Tartar conquests of the thirteenth century.[1] *Cream of tartar* comes from the *tartar* that forms on the inside of wine-casks. It is Fr. *tartre*, and is thought to be of Arabic origin. At all events, it has no connection either with Tartarus or with Tartary. For *argol*, another name for this tartar, no plausible etymology has been suggested.

Temple, a part of the head, might easily be regarded as a figurative use of *temple*, a place of worship. But, in

---

[1] See Wiener, The Tartar Myth, in the Modern Language Quarterly, III, 25.

fact, the former is from L. *tempus*, which means both 'time' (properly 'the fit time'), and 'temple' (perhaps, 'the fitting place' *i.e.* for a fatal blow). From *tempus*, the French took *temps*, 'time' (our *tense* in grammar), while from the plural *tempora* they formed *tempe*, 'temple of the head.' A by-form in Old French, *temple*, determined the English word. The term for a place of worship is from L. *templum*, which was borrowed as *tempel* in the Anglo-Saxon period. *Templum* is from a root meaning 'to cut,' and signified originally the 'sacred precinct' rather than the building.

A *sorrel* horse gets his name from Fr. *saure* (older *sore*), probably a Germanic word (akin to *sere*) indicating the color of withered leaves. The plant *sorrel* is Fr. *surelle*, from *sur*, 'sour,' also of Germanic origin and identical with our English *sour*.

When we speak of a hog as *rooting*, we doubtless think we are using a verb from the noun *root*, as if the animal were seeking for roots to eat. In fact, however, though the words may be remotely connected, the verb is properly *to wroot*, being the A.S. *wrōtan*, and is connected with *wrōt*, 'snout'; whereas the noun *root* is the Scandinavian *rōt*, akin to *wort*, 'a plant' (as in *thoroughwort*).

Angle, 'fishhook,' is a native word (A.S. *angel*); but *angle*, 'corner,' is from L. *angulus* (through Fr. *angle*). Yet the two words are near akin, since both the Latin and the Anglo-Saxon word come (independently) from the same Indo-European root ANK, 'to bend.'

Ancient (earlier *auncien*), in its ordinary sense, is Fr. *ancien* from L.L. *antianus* (from *ante*). But Iago was Othello's *ancient*, and Falstaff's soldiers were 'more dishonorable-ragged than an old faced *ancient*.' Here we have a corruption of *ensign* (Fr. *enseigne*, from L. *insignia*).

Tattoo, 'drum-beat,' was formerly *tapto*. It is the Dutch *tap-toe,* 'tap to!' *i.e.* 'drinking-house shut!'[1] The *tattoo* is the signal for the soldiers to go to their quarters. The *tattooing* of the flesh is another matter. This *tattoo* is a South Sea Island word, imported, with the custom, by sailors. The chances that a Dutch military term and a Polynesian custom should independently give to the English vocabulary two words identical in form would seem unlikely enough, were not language full of such coincidences. A similar instance is *squash* (see p. 139).

Haggard, 'a wild hawk,' is French from Old German, and means literally 'of the *hedge.*' The ending is like that in *drunkard, coward,* etc. (see p. 141). *Hagged,* 'haunted by a *hag* or witch,' was confused in form with this word, and hence we have our common adjective *haggard. Hag* itself seems to be related to *hedge,* and thus to mean originally 'a wild creature.'

Periwinkle, the plant, and *periwinkle,* the shell, have exchanged influences. The plant is L. *pervinca,* adopted by the Anglo-Saxons as *pervince.* This provides the *per-* of both words. The shell is A.S. *pine-wincla,* from L. *pina* (*pinna*), 'mussel,' and *wincle,* 'winkle' (a shellfish). This has furnished the second part of both names.

[1] Compare our 'Shut the door *to*' and the German *zu* in *Thüre zu!*

CHAPTER XXV

WORDS FROM THE NAMES OF ANIMALS

OUR language has a great quantity of words and phrases in which the names of animals are figuratively used to describe human qualities. Several linguistic processes which we have been studying are well illustrated in this category, and there are, besides, interesting historical considerations attaching to the group.

In the first place, expressions of this type are of absolutely popular origin. They point to a time when everybody was familiar with out-of-door life, and when comparisons with animals lay, therefore, close at hand. The type once formed, literature would inevitably extend it by including the names of exotic or even fabulous animals;[1] but, in their beginning, the phenomena in question are intensely popular. More than this, they go back to a very primitive psychology. We now make a sharp distinction between man and the 'lower animals,' as we call them. To primitive man, however, it did not occur to classify the world in this fashion. He never doubted that beasts could talk and that it was possible for us to learn their language. He believed that men were frequently transformed into animals and animals into men. Indeed, it is still a tradition among many tribes that their ancestors had the forms of beasts or birds. Further, instead of denying reason to the lower animals, primitive man often

[1] See p. 117.

ascribed to them intellectual faculties superior to his own. All these beliefs survive among savages, and may be observed as well in young children. Nursery tales and classic mythology alike embody them, and what we call 'fables' spring from the same root. Long after such naïve conceptions had ceased to be seriously entertained by civilized races, they were still utilized in literature and art; and hence they form, in one way or another, a component part of every grade of language, from slang to the most elevated poetry.

English has a considerable stock of popular comparisons which illustrate these points in a very simple way. A man may be 'blind as a bat' (physically, morally, or intellectually), 'sly as a fox,' 'cross as a bear,'[1] 'bold as a lion,' 'stubborn as a mule,' 'gay as a lark,' 'dumb as an oyster,' 'busy as a bee,' 'hungry as a wolf,' 'gray as a badger.' He may 'work like a beaver,' 'puff like a grampus,' or 'drink like a fish.' Nowadays a talkative person 'chatters like a magpie.' In the fourteenth century he 'jangled as a jay.' 'Gentle (*i.e.* well-bred) as a falcon' is a pretty comparison of this kind, often applied to ladies in the days when hawking was a fashionable sport.

Still more primitive is the practice of designating a person, metaphorically, by the name of some animal whose qualities he is thought to exemplify. Thus a crafty fellow may be called a *fox;* a glutton, a *pig;* a surly person, a *bear*. A shrewish woman is a *vixen*, that is, a 'she-fox.'[2] Hamlet speaks of Osric, the fantastic, feather-

[1] Slang, which delights in elaborating simpler expressions, carried out the figure : 'as cross as a bear with a sore head.' Hence, apparently, the American word *sorehead*, for 'a disappointed politician.'
[2] See p. 204.

brained courtier, as a *waterfly*. *Caterpillar* (or 'caterpillar of the commonwealth') was an expressive old term for one who devours what other men earn, — that is, for what we sometimes call, in the language of political economy, an 'unproductive consumer.' Other similar terms which need no explanation are *sheep, monkey, duck, goose, viper, cat* (for a spiteful woman), *parrot, mole, skunk, snake, serpent, wolf, drone*. Few of us have ever seen the little grub which bores through the leaves and bindings of books, yet *bookworm*, in a figurative sense, is familiar to everybody and has literary associations. *Dog, hound, cur, tyke*, and *puppy*, are terms of contempt, and *worm* or *insect* is sometimes used in the same way. Such surnames or sobriquets as *Cœur de Lion* and 'the *Wild Boar* of Ardennes' may also be mentioned, and the *bulls*, *bears*, and *lambs* of the stock exchange must not be forgotten.

The names of various stupid birds have been used at different periods for 'fool' or 'dupe': — *gull* (properly a 'young bird' of any kind),[1] *pigeon, daw, dodo, dotterel*, and *rook*. *Rook* affords a curious instance of transference. From the noun *rook*, 'a dupe,' comes the verb *rook*, 'to cheat,' and from this verb the noun *rook* was rederived in the sense of 'swindler.' Thus we have the same word in two opposite senses: the blackleg and his victim. 'To pluck a *pigeon*' (or simply to *pluck*) is an obvious figure. A *stool pigeon*, used figuratively for a 'confederate in some swindling operation,' is a 'decoy pigeon,' so called from its being tied to a stool. *Dotterel* itself means 'silly thing' (from *dote*); and *dodo* is the Portuguese *doudo*, 'simpleton.' These three words have turned a complete somersault, returning, in their figurative application to stupid mortals, to the posture which they held before they

[1] See p. 365.

were applied to the birds. If the Portuguese *doudo* is really a corruption of the provincial English *dold* (our *dolt*), the whirligig of etymology is dizzy enough.

Loon for 'fool' is not the name of the bird. It is the Scotch *loun*, and is apparently identical with English *lown*, 'a worthless fellow,' which is perhaps akin to *lame*. Any physical defect may give rise to an abusive epithet: as, — *absurd* ('very deaf,' L. *surdus*), *blind*, *purblind*, '*scald knave*.'[1] Yet the popular feeling associates *loon* with *loony*, — which is *lunatic*, 'moonstruck,' from the supposed effect of the moon on insanity. *Woodcock* was once a synonym for 'silly creature,' for this bird was thought to have no brains and to walk into the snare with its eyes open. Indeed, old books on fowling assert that it catches itself, as it were, by examining the snare in idiotic curiosity. Compare the words of Laertes, who has been wounded with the poisoned rapier which he prepared for Hamlet: —

> Why, as a woodcock to mine own springe, Osric,
> I am justly kill'd with my own treachery.

Bull, for 'an absurd blunder,' particularly in speech, might well come from the bull's habit of charging with his head down so that he appears not to see where he is going; but the etymology is not known, and the word may have nothing to do with the animal.[2]

Horse is used as a kind of prefix to indicate size or coarseness: as in *horse-radish*, *horse-purslain*, *horse-mussel*, *horse sense*. Compare *sow-thistle*, *dog-rose*, and the Greek use of βοῦς (*boûs*), as in βού-συκον (*boú-sukon*), 'a large

---

[1] 'He that repreveth his neighebor, outher he repreveth him by some harm of peyne that he hath on his body, as *mesel, croked harlot*, or by som sinne that he doth.' Chaucer, Persones Tale, § 42.

[2] Compare *bull luck* for good fortune which a man blunders into.

WORDS FROM THE NAMES OF ANIMALS

kind of fig.' *Horse chestnuts*, however, are so called from being fed to horses.

Many adjectives (of the nature of similes, and closely comparable to the phrases cited on p. 362) exist in the language. Such are *lionlike, dogged, wolfish, cattish, currish, sheepish, elephantine* (for 'clumsy,' often used of literary style), *hoggish, piggish, bearish, mulish, apish*. We speak of 'mulish obstinacy' and 'owlish commentators.' Shakspere has *cowish* for 'cowardly,' probably because the cow is not valiant; but also, no doubt, under the influence of *coward*, which has really nothing to do with *cow* (being O. Fr. *couard*, from *coue*, L. *coda, cauda*, 'tail,' with the ending *-ard*[1]). Observe that many of these adjectives end in *-ish*, a termination meaning simply 'like' or 'resembling,' but frequently implying contempt (*boyish, childish, mannish, womanish*). *Foxy* is a colloquial term for 'shrewd'; compare the 'learned' *vulpine* (L. *vulpinus*).

A few verbs belong to this class of animal names. They come easily from our ability to use almost any noun as a verb.[2] To *ape* is to 'imitate' (especially in a ridiculous or ineffective way). To *gull* is to 'cheat.' *Gull* formerly meant 'a young bird' of any kind. In Elizabethan English it was applied to an unsophisticated youngster who wished to be thought knowing. To *monkey with* is slang for to 'meddle with,' monkeys being proverbially unable to let anything alone. A vulgar but expressive American warning is 'Don't monkey with the buzz-saw.' We may '*dog* one's steps,' or '*hound* a man,' or '*worm* our way into his confidence' (cf. *insinuate*, 'to wind in,' from L. *sinuo*). To *rat* is an expression for deserting one's party or associates, as rats are said to forsake a ship that is unseaworthy.

---

[1] See p. 141. [2] See p. 192.

It is common in England, but only imitative in this country. To *gawk* is to 'stare about' like an awkward greenhorn. A *gawk* is properly a *cuckoo* and comes from the Old Norse. *Cuckoo* itself was once used for 'simpleton,' as by Falstaff in addressing Prince Hal. To *badger* is to 'abuse with words' (as a badger is baited with dogs). To *crawfish* is an expressive American slang term for to 'back out' of an agreement or 'back down' in a contention. Two verbs of this class are illustrated by the omen in Macbeth: —

> A falcon, towering in her pride of place,
> Was by a *mousing* owl *hawk'd* at and kill'd.

The 'tame villatic fowl' has supplied our language with the verb *henpeck* (now commonest as an adjective, *henpecked*), for which Leontes, in The Winter's Tale, uses the ferocious synonym *woman-tired*, that is, 'torn' as a falcon tears its prey. '*Cock* of the walk,' '*cock* of the school,' to *crow over* (Shakspere's *overcrow*, as in Hamlet's 'the potent poison quite o'ercrows my spirit') are not from the barnyard, but from cock-fighting.[1]

Caprice comes (through the French) from the Italian *capriccio*, which seems originally to have meant the skipping movement of a goat (L. *caper*). *Capriola* (from L. *capra*, 'she-goat') means 'fawn' in Italian, and this has given us *capriole* (perhaps also through the French), shortened to *caper*. *Caper* (for sauce) comes from L. *capparis* (Gr. κάππαρις), the name of the plant, and is probably of Oriental origin.

Tools, utensils, or pieces of machinery are frequently named after animals. *Battering ram* (or simply *ram*) explains itself. The Romans called such an implement

[1] Cf. p. 57.

aries, 'ram,' and sometimes made the end of it into the shape of a ram's head. A warship provided with a beak for ramming is also called a *ram.* A *crowbar* (or *crow*) gets its name from the fancied resemblance of its bent and flattened point to the bill of a crow. A frying-pan is called a *spider* in some parts of New England. The *cock* of a gun and *cock*, 'a spigot,' are probably from some fancied resemblance to the comb of a cock. It is curious that the German *Hahn* (though not related to our word *cock*) has both of these senses. *Sawhorse* and *horse* are pieces of wooden framework used for carrying or supporting logs and the like. *Cheveaux-de-frise,* 'Frisian horses,' are pieces of timber set with long iron spikes and used as a defence, especially against cavalry. The name (now a technical military term) was, like many such words, originally slang, and came from the use of this device by the Frisians in the seventeenth century. The Roman *eculeus*, 'little horse,' was an instrument of torture. An English religious poet of the fourteenth century describes Christ on the cross under a similar figure: 'on stokky stede [steed] he rode.' Other implements which bear names of animals are *dogs, canting dogs, fire-dogs,* a *mule* (in spinning), a *summer beam* (also called a *summertree* ; that is, the beam which bears a burden on each side of it, as a *sumpter* mule or horse), *culverin* (from L. *coluber*, 'snake,' because the figure of a serpent was frequently engraved on ordnance of this kind; cf. *basilisk*[1] for a kind of cannon), *fly* (for a light carriage), *worm* (for the spiral part of a still), 'a *rat-tail* file.' Similar figures are the medical *lupus,* 'wolf,' and *cancer,* 'crab,' as names of diseases.[2]

There are many proverbial or idiomatic phrases containing the names of animals, and sometimes embodying

[1] See p. 368.   [2] See p. 353.

a bit of popular wisdom or rude satire. Such are *bee-line*, 'as the crow flies,' 'bird's-eye view,' 'wild-goose chase,' 'calf love,' 'wildcat financiering,' 'to send him away with a flea in his ear,' 'nine lives like a cat,' 'as wise as a Waltham calf,' 'as honest as Cooper's cow.' Most of these are perspicuous, but others allude to jests or anecdotic narratives that have suffered the iniquity of oblivion.

Blind bayard, literally 'bay horse,'[1] is an old term for a heedless man. Its use and meaning are well explained by a passage in Chaucer's Canon's Yeoman's Tale (ll. 860–1):—

> Ye ben as bold as is Bayard the blinde,
> That blundreth forth and peril casteth [imagines] noon.

A 'spread-eagle speech' comes from the old style of Fourth of July oratory in this country, in which the orator seemed to spread his wings like the national bird.

The Middle Ages possessed a great stock of fantastic natural history, derived in great part from Pliny the Elder, from the works of Aristotle and Ælian, and from a Greek treatise of the second century A.D. known as Physiologus, or 'The Naturalist.' Such lore was highly valued, and has been much utilized by literary men of all periods. A great deal of it became popular and traditional. Hence come several linguistic curiosities. The *basilisk*, 'royal serpent' or 'king snake' (Gr. βασιλίσκος, *basilískos*, from βασιλεύς, *basileús*, 'king'; cf. *basilica*, *Basil*) caused death by a subtle poison that emanated from its eyeballs. Hence 'to glare like a basilisk' means to stare at one with a petrifying or annihilating glance, like Tennyson's *gorgonize*. A person who can en-

---

[1] The termination *-ard* is that seen in *drunkard*, *braggart*, etc., and is cognate with the adjective *hard*. *Liard*, 'gray horse,' shows the same ending. (See p. 141.)

dure much heat is called a *salamander*, since this animal was supposed to live in the element of fire. *Phœnix* may denote a person of unique excellence, a 'nonpareil,' since there was never more than one phœnix in the world at a time. More commonly, however, we use the word in allusion to the legend that the phœnix rose from its own ashes to a new life. In former times, *pelican* was a symbol both of parental self-sacrifice and of filial ingratitude. The mother pelican was thought to feed her young with her own blood, which the nestlings were so eager to taste that they sometimes wounded the old bird with their beaks. The *dove* was supposed to have no gall, and hence to be incapable of resentment. *Scorpion* for 'flatterer' comes from the action of this reptile in curving its tail over its body in the act of stinging. Hence the scorpion (which was represented with a human countenance) was said to flatter with its face while it stung with its tail.[1] In addition to these conceptions, most of which were common property, countless other bits of unnatural history are scattered through the pages of our older writers. The Elizabethan Euphuists were fond of such figures and developed them with wearisome formality.[2] 'Deaf as an *adder*' is biblical and alludes to the old idea that the adder either could not or would not hear the music of the charmer. It was even asserted that in order to avoid the sound of the charmer's voice and pipe, the adder pressed one ear to the ground and inserted its tail in the other. *Crocodile tears*, for 'hypocritical weeping' alludes to the story that the crocodile shed tears over the prey which it devoured. Compare 'He plays with his victim as a cat plays with a mouse.' The *chimera* and the *cha-*

[1] See Chaucer, Man of Law's Tale, vv. 404–6.
[2] See p. 117.

meleon may also be mentioned. 'An unlicked *cub*' alludes to the belief that young bears are born as formless lumps, and have to be 'licked into shape' by their dam. The phrase is popularly associated with *lick*, 'to beat,' on the principle that to spare the rod will spoil the child.

We have already mentioned fables. These have a complicated history, into which it is impossible to enter. Their origin, however, goes far back in the history of our race, suggesting a stage of civilization in which the psychological differences which we feel between man and the lower animals were not recognized. The stories of 'Uncle Remus' illustrate a developed form of this type. As civilization advanced, naïve beast-stories, founded on such primitive conceptions of animated nature, grew slowly into the literary apologue which we know as the Æsopic fable. These fables have given us a number of proverbial phrases, of which 'to cry *wolf*,' 'to nurse an *adder* in one's bosom,' and 'the *lion's* share' are perhaps the most familiar and picturesque. 'A *wolf* in sheep's clothing' is biblical (Matthew vii. 15). In addition to this, the Middle Ages had a well-developed beast-epic or beast-romance, partly based on the literary Æsopic fable and partly on traditional stories about animals. In this epic, the leading characters had various names, two of which have maintained themselves in our language : *reynard*, for the fox, and *chanticleer*, for the cock. *Isegrim*, 'the wolf,' is lost in English, and *Bruin*, 'the bear,' entered our language from a Dutch form of the epic at a comparatively late period. *Dame Partlet* for the hen (and figuratively for a bustling or fussy woman) has been traced no farther back than Chaucer's tale of the Cock and the Fox (The Nonne Prestes Tale).

In taking leave of the interesting category of words and

phrases derived from the names of animals, we must once more emphasize the distinctly 'popular' character of this part of our vocabulary. Even such of them as owe their presence in it to literary treatment are derived, in the last analysis, from primitive man's naïve conception of the world about him. So modern a word as the colloquial *foxy*, 'sly,' leads us straight back, by an unbroken clew, to the infancy of the race. Here is the explanation of the pertinacity with which animal symbolism has held its ground in the most cultivated tongues. The *fox* is a synonym for 'craft' with thousands of persons who have never seen reynard *in propria persona*, — to whom, indeed, the fox is as literary a character as the behemoth or the leviathan.

CHAPTER XXVI

WORDS FROM PLACES OR PERSONS

ONE of the most entertaining chapters in the history of our vocabulary deals with words from proper names. These are of every conceivable kind. Some are mere nicknames, originating in slang or the humors of the hour, and perpetuated either because they seem to fill a gap in the language or because they suggest allusions or anecdotes which it tickles our fancy to remember; others are serious technical terms, coined in honor of an inventor or a discoverer. They may come from history or from literature, indifferently. Sometimes their origin is obscure, because the story or the incident to which they allude, though striking enough to attract attention at the moment and thus to give rise to a new word or phrase, has not proved of sufficient importance to be put on record.

The process that we are considering may go no farther than to transfer the name of a well-known personage to some one who resembles him. Thus, we may call a great orator 'a Demosthenes' or 'a Burke' or 'a Webster,' a great general 'a Wellington' or 'a Marlborough,' a cruel tyrant 'a Nero,' the assertor of his country's liberties 'a Washington.' This happens every day and calls for no remark. A further step is taken when the name of such a character is used for *all* who resemble him. It is then a pure common noun, and, if our coinage passes current, the language has gained a word. Perhaps the most impressive example is *Cæsar* which, originally the name of a Roman family of no great distinction, has become a synonym for 'emperor' in languages so widely different as German (*Kaiser*) and Russian (*Tsar*).[1]

Examples of such nouns are: *hector*, 'a bully,' from a wrong conception of the great Trojan's character; *mentor*, 'a wise counsellor,' from the sage adviser of Telemachus in the Odyssey; *Nestor*, 'a veteran,' from the aged hero in the Iliad, who had ruled three generations of men; *Solon*, from the Athenian lawgiver (one of the Seven Wise Men), 'a sage,' often used jocosely of a person who has an habitual air of sagacity; *Shylock*, 'a merciless usurer,' or, in general, 'a grasping money-getter'; *Judas*, 'a traitor,' or, in particular, 'a false friend' (cf. 'a Judas kiss'); *pandar* (or *pander*), from the part played by *Pandarus* (*Pandare*) in Chaucer's romance of Troilus and in Shakspere's Troilus and Cressida;[2] *Bayard*, 'a knight without fear and without reproach,' then, generally, 'a high-minded and chivalrous gentleman'; *Braggadocio* (from a character in Spenser's *Faerie Queene*), formed from *brag* and a quasi-Italian termination, 'a cowardly boaster'; *Drawcansir*, 'a swashbuckler,' from a character in The Rehearsal, the famous burlesque play written to caricature Dryden; *Mæcenas*, 'a patron of literature,' from one of Augustus's ministers, who favored literary men; *dunce* (from *Duns Scotus*, a celebrated scholastic philosopher), 'a stupid

---

[1] The Anglo-Saxons had the word in the form *cāsere*, whence *kaser* in Middle English, but *kaiser*, another Middle English form, shows High German influence. Spenser's *kesar* is an intentional archaism.

[2] Pandarus is a Trojan hero in the Iliad, but his activity as a go-between dates from the Middle Ages. Chaucer's *Pandare* is a development from Boccaccio's *Pandaro*, but is very different from his prototype, being, indeed, the most remarkable character-study in our literature before the Elizabethan age. Shakspere's *Pandar* is Chaucer's, utterly debased.

person,' first applied in contempt to the schoolmen who opposed the new or humanistic learning; *Timon*, 'a misanthrope,' from a celebrated Athenian whose life was written by Plutarch and dramatized by Shakspere; *Lucretia*, 'a virtuous woman,' from Collatinus's wife, whose tragic fate forms a part of the legendary history of Rome; *Benedick* or *Benedict*, 'a newly married man,' from a character in Much Ado About Nothing, who rails against wedlock, but finally succumbs to the charms of Beatrice;[1] *Satan*, 'a person of diabolical wickedness' (cf. *devil*), or, jocosely, 'a little Satan,' 'a mischievous child'; *Termagant*, 'a scold,' from a supposed god of the Saracens, whom the Middle Ages regarded as idolaters.[2]

The Bible has given us a number of similar terms: as, — a *Joseph*, a *Job*, a *Samson*, a *Solomon*, a *Methusalah*, an *Ishmael*, a 'doubting *Thomas*,' a 'Good *Samaritan*,' a *Dives*, a *lazar* (from *Lazarus*), 'to raise *Cain*.' *Jezebel* has contributed her name to our vocabulary in two senses. In accordance with the wicked queen's true character, every haughty woman may be called a *Jezebel*, and it is with this in mind that Sir Andrew Aguecheek applies the name, with fine disregard of gender, to the strutting Malvolio. But *Jezebel* more commonly means 'a flaunting jade,' — especially in the phrase 'a painted *Jezebel*,' from the passage in which we read that 'Jezebel painted her face, and tired her head, and looked out at a window' (II Kings ix. 30).

A *pasquinade* is a lampoon, such as used to be attached to a mutilated statue in Rome called *Pasquin*, from *Pas*-

[1] The word is used with particular allusion to a passage in which Benedick is jeeringly greeted by Don Pedro as 'Benedick, the married man.'

[2] Hence *Saracen* in Middle English is frequently 'pagan,' and sometimes is substituted for 'heathen Dane' (as in one version of the romance of King Horn).

quino, a cobbler celebrated for his wit, who lived and worked near the place where it was exhumed. A *lovelace* is a person like the rake in Richardson's Clarissa Harlowe; a *gay Lothario* gets his name from a similar character in Rowe's Fair Penitent; *Don Juan* was a Spanish libertine, whose adventures were traditionally current in Seville before they received literary and musical treatment at the hands of Tellez, Molière, Goldoni, Glück, and Byron. *Paul Pry* is a character in a comedy by John Poole. *Simon Pure* is a Quaker in Mrs. Centlivre's Bold Stroke for a Wife. *Tartuffe* for 'hypocrite' is from Molière. *Squire of Dames* is a character in Spenser's Faerie Queene (iii, 7, 51). *Fidus Achates* is Æneas's friend in Virgil. A *Mrs. Harris* for a 'non-existent person,' a 'myth,' is from Mrs. Gamp's fictitious patron in Martin Chuzzlewit, and practical *Gradgrind* is in Hard Times. *Mrs. Grundy* is often referred to as a standard of propriety by Dame Ashfield in Morton's Speed the Plow. *Dulcinea* was Don Quixote's ladylove. The *Rev. Dr. Dryasdust* is a device of Sir Walter Scott's. *Roorback*, 'a campaign lie,' is named after The Travels of Baron Roorback, a fiction intended to injure Polk when he was a candidate for the presidency in 1844. *Rip Van Winkle* needs no interpreter.

'The driving is like the driving of Jehu, the son of Nimshi, for he driveth furiously' has given us *jehu*, 'coachman.' As for Nimshi, his father, his name is still used in New England for a mischievous child — 'a regular little *Nimshi*.'[1] *Nimrod* was 'a mighty hunter before the Lord'; *Achitophel* led Absolom astray by evil counsel; 'a *Daniel* come to judgment' is Shylock's allusion to the story of Susannah.

There are also an abundance of classical proper names

---

[1] A similar use of *Jebusite* is more intelligible.

that are used in the same manner: as, — an *amazon*, a *Juno*, a *Circe* (cf. ' *Circean* wiles '), ' a perfect *Adonis*,' ' an out-and-out *Xanthippe*.'

Now and then the name of a town or the like is used in the same way: as, — ' a *babel* of sounds,' from the confusion of tongues at the Tower of Babel ; *Mecca*, for a place of pilgrimage, or, even the goal of one's aspirations ; ' one's *Capua*,' for an easy position which tempts to neglect of duty, from the enervating effect of Hannibal's winter quarters in this luxurious town. The *Land of Nod*, for ' slumber-land,' is a pretty pun (see Genesis iv. 16). The constellation Ursa Minor was called ' Dog's Tail,' κυνός οὐρά (*kunós ourá*), by the Greeks. It was a guide to mariners (like the Pole Star), and this has given us *cynosure*, for ' the observed of all observers.' A passage in Milton's L'Allegro has done much to keep the word alive. *Palace* is *palatium*, the house of Augustus on the *Palatine* Hill.

The adjective *maudlin*, ' ridiculously tearful or sentimental,' comes, through the French, from *Magdalen*. This was the surname of Mary *of Magdala* (a town in Palestine), one of the early disciples of Christ. She was identified (without good grounds) with the ' woman who was a sinner ' (Luke vii. 36), whence *Magdalen*, ' penitent.' The adjective use of *maudlin* was doubtless suggested by pictures of the weeping Magdalen.

Some of the words that we have mentioned have had a further development of meaning. *Judas* is applied to a peep-hole in a gate or door. *Braggadocio* has been transferred from the person to the quality, and usually signifies ' empty boasting.' So *chimera*, the name of a fabulous monster composed of different parts of incongruous animals, has become a synonym for a ' wild fancy '

WORDS FROM PLACES OR PERSONS 377

or 'grotesque idea.' *Mahomet* has had a strange history. In the Middle Ages it was thought that the Mohammedans worshipped idols. Thus, the name of their prophet, in the form *Maumet*, became a synonym for 'idol,'[1] and then for 'image' in general, and hence we have *mammet* for a child's 'doll,' or even for a 'baby.' Old Capulet upbraids Juliet as a 'whining *mammet*.' An interesting transference has taken place in *Frankenstein*. In Mrs. Shelley's novel, Frankenstein is a young German physiologist who manufactures a human being out of fragments, endows it with life by some mysterious process, and is forever haunted by the creature, who finally causes his death. Hence, a Frankenstein is properly one who is 'hoist with his own petard.' Yet one hears the term used for 'a creature that torments his creator,' as if it had been the name of the monster that Frankenstein made.

Tawdry, 'vulgarly fine,' is a corruption of *Saint Audrey*, that is, Saint *Ethelreda*, and was first applied to what was called a 'tawdry lace,' that is, a kind of lace bought at Saint Audrey's Fair. The initial *t* is all that is left of the adjective *Saint*. Compare *Brummagem* (from *Birmingham*) and *pinchbeck* (a man's name).

Now and then a proper name is used as a verb.[2] Thus, to *hector* is 'to play the bully,' or, in a slightly generalized sense, 'to torment' or 'tease.' The verb *pander* is commoner than the substantive. It is figuratively used of almost any kind of base subserviency. Thus, one may pander to the vices of another or to his prejudices or to his love of flattery. From one *Burke*, an Edinburgh

[1] 'What difference is bitwixe an ydolastre,' asks Chaucer's Parson, 'and an avaricious man, but that an ydolastre, per aventure, hath but o (*i.e.* one) *mawmet* or two, and the avaricious man hath manye? For certes, every florin in his cofre is his *mawmet*.' The Persones Tale, § 64.

[2] As may be the case with almost any English noun (see p. 192).

criminal, who murdered many persons in order to sell their bodies to surgeons for dissection, comes the verb *to burke* (always figuratively used), 'to smother,' 'to pass over in silence': as, — 'His book was *burked* by the critics.' Burke and his gang used to smother their victims in order that the bodies might show no marks of violence. To '*out-Herod* Herod' is from Hamlet's description of a ranting player. It alludes to the furious demeanor of the Herod of the old religious drama, whose raging was not confined to the scaffold on which such plays were presented, but extended to the street as well. 'Here Herod rages,' says an old stage direction, 'in this pageant, and in the street also.' To *boycott* is said to be from Captain Boycott, who was the first boycotted landlord in Ireland. The term has extended far beyond the limits of its original application. A *guy*, for a 'queer-looking person' (especially one who is badly dressed), and the verb *to guy*, 'to make fun of,' come from the effigy of Guy Fawkes, carried in procession on the fifth of November, the anniversary of the Gunpowder Plot. To *meander* comes from the winding course of the river *Mœander* in Phrygia.

To *lynch* is something of a mystery. '*Lynch* law' has the air of being named after a person, and there have been various claimants, but the original Judge Lynch is still unidentified. The phrase is singularly parallel to the English 'Lydford law,' which is mentioned by William Browne as already proverbial in the seventeenth century: —

> I oft have heard of *Lydford law*,
> How in the morn they hang and draw,
>   And sit in judgment after.

The reference is to the stannary courts at Lydford in Devonshire, which were extremely arbitrary in their action.

But the phrase 'law of Lydford,' for summary justice,[1] has been traced as far back as the fourteenth century, which seems to be too early for the tinners, but may refer to the severity of the forestry laws; for Lydford was the seat of government for the ancient Forest of Dartmoor.

The ending *-ize* (or *-ise*) is sometimes used to make a verb from a proper name. It is an adaptation of the Greek *-izō*, which had a similar function (as $\mu\eta\delta\ell\zeta\omega$, *mēdízō*, 'to Medize,' 'to favor the *Medes*'). Thus we have *tantalize*, from *Tantalus*, — now commonest in the adjective use, as 'a *tantalizing* sight.' So *bowdlerize*, 'to expurgate' (always with a contemptuous suggestion of prudery), from Dr. *Bowdler*, who published a 'family Shakspere' in 1818. Two years before, J. L. *Macadam* had introduced the plan of *macadamizing* roads.[2] To *harvey* or *harveyize* steel is an American invention; the process is named after the discoverer, H. A. *Harvey*. Maud's lover in Tennyson was *gorgonized* 'with a stony British stare.'

Names of tribes or nations have often become common nouns, usually in a sense according with supposed national characteristics. Thus *Goth* may designate a rude or barbarous man; *Vandal* (whence *vandalism*), a wanton destroyer; *Turk*, a ferocious person; *Jew*, a usurer or one who drives a sharp bargain; *Yankee*, a keen or tricky trader. 'The *myrmidons* of the law' preserve the name of the ferocious tribe that followed Achilles to Troy. *Tartar*, for a 'peppery person' or 'tough customer,' still carries a faint suggestion of the terror inspired by the Tartar invasion of Europe in the thirteenth century. The change from *Tatar* (the native name) to *Tartar*

[1] Cf. the American phrase 'Jersey (*i.e.* New Jersey) justice.'
[2] The noun *macadam*, for the 'surface' of such a road, is a back-formation from the verb *macadamize*.

(from *Tartarus*) is more impressive testimony. *Ogre* is 'Hungarian,'—through a confusion of the Magyars with the Huns, and of both with the dreaded Tartars.[1] *Gypsy* is *Egyptian*, and is used in half a dozen derived senses. *Bohemian* was often substituted for 'Gypsy' (by an easy ethnological mistake); hence the modern social *Bohemian*, —a coinage of Thackeray's. *Street Arab* is also a recent term for a particular variety of nomad. *Slave* is *Slav*, since the Germans reduced many of this race to servitude. We have the word from the French, which borrowed it from the German; but it is the national name of the Slavonian people. A *blackamoor* is a 'black Moor,' that is, by another blunder in ethnology, an 'Ethiopian' or negro. The *Assassins* were a fanatical Eastern sect who, like the Thugs, committed murder for the glory of their divinity. The name is an Arabic derivative of *hashish*,—to the use of which the Assassins were addicted. The *Zouaves* are a tribe of Algerian mountaineers (cf. *Croat* for any 'irregular' soldier).

Derivatives from personal, national, or local names have also become common in special senses. The boasting Gascons have given us *gasconade* and *gasconading*. Compare '*Roman* firmness,' '*Punic* faith' (for 'perfidy,' L. *Punica fides;* cf. the Frenchman's 'perfidious Albion'), '*Attic* salt' (for 'wit,' L. *sal Atticum*), and Thackeray's version of *Persicos odi puer apparatus*, — 'I hate all your *Frenchified* stuff.' A '*Parthian* shot' was very literal to Crassus, who found to his cost that the flight of the Parthians was more to be dreaded than their onset; to us it is only an elegant and pointed synonym for one method of 'having the last word.' *Romance* is an Old French word for the 'vernacular' (the *lingua Romanica*, or vulgar Latin, as opposed to

[1] Wiener, in Anglia, XXIII, 107.

the learned tradition of the schools), and was easily transferred to a 'tale' or 'story' in the vernacular. Most of the Middle English *romances* are translations from the French. The development of the word has been of the multifarious kind. Observe the variety of suggestion in 'a romantic girl,' 'nineteenth-century romanticism,' 'the Romance languages,' 'he gave a romancing account of his journey.'

Sir Thomas More's *Utopia*,[1] a fanciful sketch of the ideal commonwealth, has given us the adjective *Utopian*. *Atlantis* was a fabled continent in the Atlantic Ocean, which Plato and others mention. Bacon's *New Atlantis* supplied Milton with *Atlantean*, in the same sense, but this has never got into general use, perhaps because we already had *atlas* (from the giant's name). The Earthly Paradise was often sought in mediæval times. The Spaniards of the sixteenth century believed that a golden country existed somewhere in South America, and Raleigh thought he could find it in Guiana. This is *El Dorado*, 'the gilded' (Spanish, from L. *de-aurare*, 'to gild,' from *aurum*, 'gold'), — a kind of romantic equivalent of 'the Promised Land' of the Israelites.

Castles in the air tells its own story. *Castles in Spain*, however, we should not understand, if we did not know that it is a mere translation of *châteaux en Espagne*. 'Across the Pyrenees' is a natural outlook for a Frenchman, but not for a native of England. When the translated 'castles in Spain' crosses the sea, and is used by Americans or Australians, its *rationale* seems still less obvious. In other words, the whole phrase has become a

---

[1] That is, 'the land of Nowhere,' from Gr. οὐ, 'not' and τόπος, 'place' (as in *topography, topical*). Compare Carlyle's *Weissnichtwo* ('I know not where'), the city where Teufelsdröckh was professor of 'science in general' (*Allerley-Wissenschaft*).

mere symbol, and we do not think of analyzing it any more than if it were a single word.

From persons, real or fictitious, we have *thrasonical*, 'boastful,' from *Thraso*, the braggart in Terence's Eunuchus; *quixotic*, from *Don Quixote*; 'in a *Pickwickian* sense,' from an amusing passage in the records of the Pickwick Club; *magic*, from the Persian *Magi* or 'wise men'; *stoical* and *stoicism* for 'unruffled fortitude,' 'insensibility to pain' (see p. 39); *epicurean*, from Epicurus; *cynical*, from the Cynic (*i.e.* 'currish')[1] philosophers, especially Diogenes; '*platonic* love,' from an attempt to adapt the doctrine of Plato to modern social life; *machiavellian*, in a sense of unscrupulous craft that Machiavelli would certainly have repudiated; *mosaic*, from the *Muses*, but perhaps confused with *Mosaic* from *Moses* (cf. *Jews' work* for *arabesque*[2]); *simony*, from Simon Magus, who offered money for a share in the apostles' mysterious powers (Acts viii.); *jeremiad*, 'a mournful or denunciatory speech,' from the Lamentations of the prophet Jeremiah; *panic*, for 'panic fear,' literally such unreasoning terror as the god *Pan* was supposed to inspire by his sudden appearance to a solitary wanderer; *stentorian*, from Stentor, the herald of the Greeks before Troy; *morris* dance, from the Spanish *morisco*, 'Moorish.'

Frequently the name of a person is applied to a *thing*, because he invented, discovered, or introduced it, or because the inventor named it after him. Thus boots may be *Wellingtons*,[3] or *Bluchers*; a *mackintosh* is a kind of waterproof cloak; *broughams* and *victorias* are carriages;

---

[1] Greek κυνικός, from κύων, κυνός, 'dog' (as in *cynosure*, see p. 376).

[2] Chaucer, Sir Thopas, v. 153.

[3] For the omission of the general term (as *boots*, *coat*, etc.) in such cases, see p. 255.

shrapnel was invented by General Shrapnel of the British army; a *phaeton* is so called from the unlucky son of Phœbus, who drove a chariot so disastrously; a *roquelaure* (eighteenth century) was named after a French duke of the time of Louis XIV. Every rank in life is represented. Thus we have *orrery*, 'a machine to represent the motions of the solar system,' from the Earl of Orrery; and *derrick*, for 'a hoisting apparatus,' from *Derrick* the hangman. Derrick 'flourished' about 1600, at Tyburn. His name is an anglicised form of *Dierryk* or *Diederik*, which is the Dutch for *Theoderic*, — the great king of the Ostrogoths. *Theoderic* is, being interpreted, 'mighty among the people.' This brings us to the conundrum of the gravedigger in Hamlet, who insisted that the hangman 'builds stronger than the mason or the carpenter.' Nothing is more democratic than language, or conducts one to more preposterous conclusions.

A *sandwich* is so called from the Earl of Sandwich, a passionate gambler, who is said once to have saved time at a game by stratifying the bread and meat which his servant brought to the card-table. An amusing instance of this kind of derivation is the word *spencer*. The Earl of Spencer, a celebrated dandy about 1800, once made a bet that he could introduce the fashion of wearing an overcoat so short that the tails of his coat would appear beneath it. He won his bet, and the name *spencer* was given to short coats of this style, and has since been transferred to a woman's garment.

The language of science is full of similar terms, which sometimes get into common use. Naturalists like to ticket new species of plants and animals with queer Latin designations formed from the names of the persons whom they delight to honor, — their patrons or predecessors, their colleagues or personal friends, or, perhaps, the explorer who brought home the specimen. Thus we have *dahlia* (from *Dahl*), *fuchsia* (from *Fuchs*), *wistaria* (from *Wistar*), — all three well-known flowers ; *cinchona*, from the Countess *Chinchon*, who introduced Peruvian bark into Europe; and so on *ad infinitum*. Modern electrical science has applied to particular units of measurement the names of *ohm, volt* (from Volta; cf. *voltaic*), *ampère, watt*, thus celebrating the services of a German, an Italian, a French, and a Scotch investigator. *St. Vitus' dance* and *St. Anthony's fire* ('erysipelas') are named from the saints invoked to cure them; cf. *king's evil* for 'scrofula.' '*Hermetically* sealed' celebrates the fame of Hermes Trismegistus, the supposed founder of alchemical (or *hermetic*) philosophy, — Milton's 'thrice great Hermes,' the fabled Egyptian prophet, priest, and king.

Articles of commerce are often named after the place from which they come or are supposed to come: as, — *java, mocha, oolong, champagne, sauterne, sherry* (older *sherris*, from *Xeres*, in Spain); *cambric* (from *Kamerik*, i.e. *Cambrai*); *gin* (from *Geneva*); *china, japan; cashmere, madras, tweed, muslin* (from the Mesopotamian town of *Massoul* or *Mausil*); *damask* (from *Damascus*); *fustian* (from *Fustāt*, i.e. *Cairo*); *morocco; cordovan* or *cordwain* (from *Cordova*); *landau, berlin, surrey; arras*, 'tapestry hangings' (from *Arras*, in France); *fez* (from *Fez*, in Morocco); *macassar* (from a district in the Celebes Islands).[1] Compare *basque, polonaise, jersey, newmarket, italics*.

Latakia is a kind of tobacco, from a town of that name;

[1] Byron's 'thy incomparable oil, Macassar.' Compare *antimacassar*, a word redolent of a bygone age. *Tidy*, the usual term in America, is surely a 'nicer' word. The knotting of antimacassars replaced the 'plying of samplers' and, to some extent, 'the teasing of the housewife's wool.

WORDS FROM PLACES OR PERSONS

a *Laodicean* is a lukewarm person, from the reproof of the Revelation to the Church of the Laodiceans, who were 'neither cold nor hot.' *Latakia*, however, is only the Turkish form of the ancient *Laodicea*.

Most of the words just noted are obviously place-names and still recognizable as such. But there are many other similar terms whose origin is seldom thought of. Thus *spaniel* is a 'Spanish dog' (O. Fr. *espagnol*); *pistol* is from *Pistoja* (*Pistola*, through Fr. *pistole*); *milliner* is *Milaner*, one who imported fal-lals from *Milan*; *jet* is from *Gagas*, an ancient town in Asia Minor; *pheasant* is from the river *Phasis* in Pontus; *copper* (L. *cuprum*) was *aes Cyprium*, 'bronze from *Cyprus*'; *finnan haddie* (*haddock*) is from the Scotch village of *Findon* or the river *Findhorn*, or, more likely, from both together; *currants* are 'raisins de *Corinthe*'; a *canter* is a clipped form of '*Canterbury* gallop,' an easy pace such as pilgrims rode on their way to Saint Thomas's shrine.

Magnet is '*Magnesian* stone,' from the district of *Magnesia* in Thessaly (whence also the chemical names *magnesia* and *manganese*[1]). The mystery of the loadstone has been a constant temptation to theorists of one school or another, and thus *magnetic* and *magnetism* have not only renounced their Thessalian connections, but have turned their backs on mineralogy. The modern figurative uses of the words — as in 'a magnetic personality,' 'he lacks magnetism' — might easily have come straight from the *magnet*. In fact, however, they are derived from Mesmer's speculations on 'animal magnetism' (about 1775). As Mesmer's theory of a physical force akin to that of the magnet became discredited, the phrase was

---

[1] *Manganese* is a doubtful form, but is thought to be a corruption of L. *magnes*, 'magnet.'

replaced by *mesmerism*, which was popular until very recently. But Mesmer was felt to be something of a charlatan. At all events, investigators repudiated his views with unanimous enthusiasm. It was not tolerable, then, that his name should remain attached to a great class of psychic phenomena. *Hypnotism* was accordingly coined and has become rapidly popular. Perhaps this will hold the field, for, coming as it does from Gr. ὕπνος (*húpnos*), 'sleep,' it is vague enough to cover any discoveries that may be made in the future.

Sometimes a common 'Christian name,' in a diminutive form, is jocosely given to a tool or other implement, apparently because the tool is looked upon as a pet or fellow-workman. Thus we have the *spinning-jenny; jimmy* and *betty* for burglars' implements; *billy* for a policeman's club, or (in Australia) a bushman's kettle. The habit is essentially the same as that of using diminutives for the names of tools (see p. 60), and is near akin to the trick of personifying inanimate objects by calling them *he* or *she*. A ship is always *she*, and the same pronoun is often applied to a locomotive by the engineer ('driver') who has it in charge. A miller may also use *she* of his mill.[1] A gardener has been known to call his favorite ivy *he*. The word *jack*, which means 'fellow' as being the commonest of masculine diminutives, has received a very wide extension. Sometimes, as in *jackass*, it simply implies the masculine gender ; usually, however, it carries the meaning of strength, size, or coarseness.

---

[1] Cf. Phillips Brooks in a familiar letter to a friend describing the fire in which Trinity Church, Boston, was destroyed in 1872 : 'Old Trinity seemed safe all night, but towards morning the fire swept into her rear, and there was no chance. She went at four in the morning. I saw her well afire inside and out, carried off some books and robes, and left her.' A. V. G. Allen, Life and Letters of Phillips Brooks, 1900, II, 67.

Thus we have *jack-knife* for a large pocket-knife, bigger than a pen-knife; *jackscrew* for a very strong screw used to raise buildings and the like; *jackstraws*, originally large straws used in playing a game which is known by the same name. Compare such terms as *jack-in-the-box*, *jack-in-the-pulpit*, *jackanapes*.[1] The word *jack* is also used alone for certain kinds of implements and utensils, in particular for a device to raise the wheels of a carriage from the ground (cf. *boot-jack*), for a leather coat, and for a kind of bottle (*black jack;* cf. *demijohn*).[2]

Demijohn is a corruption (by popular etymology) of the French *Dame Jeanne*, apparently a jocose name for a big bottle, like *Toby* for a kind of beer-mug shaped like a stout man. *Dame Jeanne* itself looks like a popular etymology of something else; but all efforts to settle the question have been fruitless. The Arabic *damajāna*, which appears to conduct us to the Persian glassworks at *Damaghan*, is thought to be a modern borrowing from the Romance.

Here may be mentioned such jocose names as *jack* for 'fellow'; *Jeames* for 'footman'; *'Arry* for 'a London rough'; *Jack Tar* or *jacky*, for 'a seaman'; *Bridget* or *Biddy* for 'an Irish maidservant'; *zany* (It. *zanni*, for *Giovanni*, 'John') for 'a buffoon' or 'merry-andrew.'

The words that we have studied in this chapter illustrate a considerable variety of linguistic processes.[3] But they are even more significant as documents in the history of civilization. They cover the map of the world with

[1] With the discussion of this word in the Oxford Dictionary should be compared the remarks of Dr. Scott, in Trans. Amer. Philol. Assoc., XXIII, 189 ff.

[2] See p. 61, note 1.

[3] In particular, they enforce what was said of the identity between slang and ordinary language in all essentials of linguistic behavior.

well-marked dots and boundary lines. They pervade the tables of the chronologist from the earliest times to the instant of writing. A single word, like *bedlam*, has stood for thousands of years and thousands of miles. *Bedlam* (a clipped form of *Bethlehem*) is now jocosely used for any great confusion : as, — 'It was a perfect *bedlam* of discordant opinions.' The generalizing process in this word is curiously connected with religious history. There was in Palestine a religious establishment dedicated to Saint Mary of Bethlehem, that is, the Virgin. In early times, a branch of this establishment existed in London. Attached to the church was a hospice or house of entertainment, meant, in the first instance, for the use of members of the fraternity who might be temporarily residing in that city. Gradually the ecclesiastics of this house gave their attention to a special form of charity, — the reception and treatment of lunatics, and *Bedlam*, that is, 'the London hospice of Saint Mary of Bethlehem,' became an insane asylum. When the violent measures of Henry VIII abolished so many monastic houses, this particular hospice was given to the city of London and continued to be used as a refuge for the insane under the name of *Bethlehem Hospital* or *Bedlam*. Hence the word *bedlam* was applied to any insane asylum, and from this use its modern employment for any kind of tumultuous assembly or any great disturbance was easy. It is interesting to observe that in the history of this word we have involved the founding of the Christian religion, the passing of the Holy Land into the control of the Saracens, the Crusades, which restored it to Christianity, the continued relations between the Latin Orient and Western Europe, the whole theory and practice of monastic institutions and fraternities, with their labors in behalf of the poor and sick, the

Reformation in general, and, in particular, the Reformation in England under Henry VIII, with its confusion of religious and secular motives. Incidentally, this involves the personal history of Henry VIII, and, in particular, his quarrel with the Pope over the question of his divorce from Katharine of Aragon and his marriage to Anne Boleyn. In other words, the history of the single word *bedlam* cannot be completely understood without some knowledge of the history of Europe and Asia for more than fifteen hundred years. It would be hard to find a more striking instance of the absurdity of regarding the study of words as a narrow and trivial diversion of pedants. Words are the signs of thoughts and thoughts make history.

APPENDIX

P. 6. We have said that the origin of language is undiscoverable. If, however, philologists ever do solve the great problem, we may conjecture that natural cries (natural in the same sense in which kicking and working the fingers are natural), common alike to men and the higher animals, each after its kind, will be found to be the *material*, and that the alternate building-up and breaking-down of words (the eternal systole and diastole of speech) will be found to be the *means*, of the growth which has produced as well the root-system of the Indo-European (with its puzzling determinatives), as the Semitic triliteralism, the elements of aggregative languages, and the extreme complexity of Chinese monosyllables. Such a theory would probably be nicknamed the 'goo-goo theory.' All that is requisite for the beginning of language proper is that any one sound should come to be purposely uttered, however vaguely, and actually understood, and we have the promise and potentiality of the most cultivated human speech. The initial understanding, indeed, may perhaps come from the listener and be reflected back to the person who utters the sound. When the first step has been taken, the processes which we see going on around us every day will do the rest. The 'goo-goo theory' includes all that can be true in the 'ding-dong theory'; for it is only in such natural cries, produced by the mere purposeless activity of the vocal organs, that it can justly be said that 'everything that is struck, rings.' It covers the ground of the 'bow-wow theory,' since it admits the possibility of imitation, holding, indeed, that the natural cries referred to are the only sounds in language that are *not* imitative. It also includes the 'pooh-pooh theory,' since the cries in question are the only interjections that are actually spontaneous and do not like *pooh!* and *bah!* require to be *learned*, like other words. The 'goo-goo theory' meets alike the views of a Sayce, who finds in language a progress of decay, and a Brugmann, who finds in it a progress of growth.

A readable account of various theories of the origin of language may be found in A. H. Sayce, Introduction to the Science of Language (2 vols., Lond., 1880), Chap. I. See also Max Müller, Lectures on the Science of Language (2 vols., Lond., 1861–4; revised edition, N.Y., 1891); Whitney, Language and the Study of Language (5th ed., N.Y. [1875]); Whitney, The Science of Language, in his Oriental and Linguistic Studies (N.Y., 1873); Whitney, Max Müller and the Science of Language (N.Y., 1892). On language in general see H. Paul, Principien der Sprachgeschichte (3d ed., Halle, 1898), translated from the 2d edition by H. A. Strong, Principles of the History of Language (N.Y., 1889); Strong, Logeman, and Wheeler, Introduction to the Study of the History of Language (Lond., 1891).

Pp. 34 ff. A useful handbook of philosophical terms is R. Eisler's Wörterbuch der Philosophischen Begriffe und Ausdrücke, quellenmässig bearbeitet (Berlin, 1899).

P. 48. For biblical words see J. Eastwood and W. Aldis Wright, The Bible Word-Book (Lond., 1866).

P. 54. On women's languages see Crawley, Journal of the Anthropological Institute, XXIV, 233–5.

Pp. 55 ff. Among collections of English slang may be mentioned John Camden Hotten's Slang Dictionary (new ed., Lond. [1874]); Barrère and Leland's Dictionary of Slang, Jargon, and Cant (2 vols., 1889–90); Farmer and Henley's Slang and its Analogues (4 vols., A–MYZ, Lond., 1890–6); H. Baumann's Londonismen, Slang und Cant (Berlin, 1887). The ordinary large dictionaries also contain a considerable number of slang words.

P. 80. On the development of the literary language see Lounsbury, History of the English Language (revised ed., N.Y., 1894); O. F. Emerson, History of the English Language (N.Y., 1894); Skeat, Principles of English Etymology, First Series (Oxford, 1887); Kluge, Geschichte der englischen Sprache, in Paul's Grundriss der germanischen Philologie, Vol. I.

On dialects see the publications of the English Dialect Society, and the great English Dialect Dictionary, edited by Joseph Wright. Cf. Sheldon, 'What is a Dialect?' in Dialect Notes, published by the American Dialect Society, I, 286 ff. The modern English dialects have been classified by A. J. Ellis in Part V of his Early English Pronunciation (Lond., 1889). A minute study of a single dialect is Joseph Wright's Grammar of the Dialect of Windhill in the West Riding of Yorkshire (Lond., 1892). For Scottish see Murray, Dialect of the Southern Counties of Scotland (Lond., 1873); Jamieson, Dictionary of the Scottish Language (5 vols., Paisley, 1879–87).

P. 81. There is no satisfactory treatment of 'American English.' Material may be found in Bartlett, Dictionary of Americanisms (N.Y., 1848; 4th ed., Boston, 1877); Schele de Vere, Americanisms, the English of the New World (2d ed., N.Y., 1872); J. S. Farmer, Americanisms Old and New (Lond., 1889); the publications of the American Dialect Society and the Modern Language Association of America. For bibliography, see Dialect Notes (published by the American Dialect Society), Vol. I. On the history of American pronunciation, see especially Grandgent, From Franklin to Lowell, a Century of New England Pronunciation, in the Publications of the Modern Language Association of America, XIV, 207 ff. On Australian English, see E. E. Morris, Austral English: a Dictionary of Australasian Words, Phrases, and Usages (Lond., 1898), and J. Lake, Dictionary of Australasian Words and Phrases (in the Australasian Supplement to Webster's International Dictionary). On Anglo-Indian, see Colonel Henry Yule and A. C. Burnell, Hobson-Jobson: being a glossary of Anglo-Indian Colloquial Words and Phrases (Lond., 1886).

Pp. 93 ff. The Latin contingent in Anglo-Saxon has been studied by A. Pogatscher in a very distinguished monograph: Zur Lautlehre der griechischen, lateinischen und romanischen Lehnworte im Altenglischen (Strassburg, 1888), Quellen und Forschungen, No. 64. See also Sievers, Zum angelsächsischen Vocalismus (Leipzig, 1900), where different grades of 'popularity' in words are discriminated with great subtlety.

P. 107. For Old Norse words in English, see Kluge in Paul's Grundriss der germanischen Philologie, I, 785 ff.; Skeat, Principles of English Etymology, I, 453 ff.; E. Björkman, Scandinavian Loan-Words in Middle English (Halle, 1900).

Pp. 108–9. On these miscellaneous borrowings, see Skeat's Principles of English Etymology, II, 342 ff., and compare the lists in the revised edition of the same scholar's Concise Etymological Dictionary (Oxford, 1901).

P. 114, note. See also Kellner, Abwechslung und Tautologie: zwei Eigenthümlichkeiten des alt- und mittelenglischen Stiles, in Englische Studien, XX, 1 ff. (1894).

P. 116. Love allegory. See W. A. Neilson, The Origins and Sources of the Court of Love, in Studies and Notes in Philology and Literature, V (Boston, 1899).

P. 117. On Euphuism, see Landmann's edition of Lyly's Euphues (Heilbronn, 1887); the same author's Shakspere and Euphuism, in the Transactions of the New Shakspere Society for 1880–5, Pt. II, pp. 241 ff.; and especially C. G. Child's monograph, John Lyly and Euphuism (Erlangen, 1894).

P. 123. Romantic revival. See W. L. Phelps, The Beginnings of the English Romantic Movement (Boston, 1893).

Pp. 183–4. On decay of inflection as an improvement, see O. Jespersen, Progress in Language, with Especial Reference to English (Lond., 1894).

Pp. 185 ff. For details with regard to prefixes and suffixes, see Haldeman, Affixes in their Origin and Application (Phila., 1871); Skeat, Principles of English Etymology; Sweet, New English Grammar, Pt. I (Oxford, 1892).

P. 219. On the conventional character of words, see especially Whitney's Language and the Study of Language.

Pp. 219 ff. On semasiology or 'the science of meanings,' see A. Darmesteter, La Vie des Mots, 2d ed. (Paris, 1887), and M. Bréal, Essai de Sémantique (Paris, 1897). Bréal's book has been translated by Mrs. Henry Cust, Semantics, Studies in the Science of Meaning (Lond., 1900). Cf. also Hey, Die Semasiologie, in Archiv für lateinische Lexicographie, IX, 193 ff.

P. 228. On the magic power of the *name*, see Child, English and Scottish Popular Ballads, Index of Matters, under 'Naming'; K. Nyrop, Navnets Magt (Copenhagen, 1887).

P. 297. National nicknames. There is an interesting list in Notes and Queries, 9th series, IV, 212-4.

P. 301. Australian aborigines. See W. E. Roth, Ethnological Studies among the North-West-Central Queensland Aborigines (Brisbane, 1897), p. 184.

P. 304. On disguised and distorted oaths, see A. E. H. Swaen, Figures of Imprecation, in Englische Studien, XXIV, 16 ff., 195 ff.

P. 330. On folk-etymology, see K. G. Andresen, Ueber deutsche Volksetymologie (6th ed., Leipzig, 1899). Much valuable material for English is collected by the Rev. A. Smythe Palmer in his Folk-Etymology (Lond., 1882), but the author's derivations are not always to be trusted.

P. 345. Doublets are treated by Skeat, Principles of English Etymology, I, 414 ff. The largest collection is Sheldon's, in his etymologies in Webster's International Dictionary.

P. 357. There is a long list of homonyms in Skeat's Etymological Dictionary.

P. 361. On primitive ideas with regard to animals, see Tylor's chapter on Animism, in his Primitive Culture, Vol. I.

P. 370. On fables, etc., see Jacobs, History of the Æsopic Fable, Vol. I of his edition of Caxton's Æsop (Lond., 1889); Kittredge, Beast-Fables, in Johnson's Universal Cyclopædia, I, 545–8.

P. 378. On Lydford Law, see S. Rowe, Perambulation of Dartmoor, 3d ed. (1896), pp. 423 ff.

INDEX OF MATTERS

Abbreviations, Latin, 104 f., 140.

Ablative absolute, 104 n.; degree of difference, 202.

Abrasion, 180 ff.

Abstract and concrete, 256 ff.

Abusive language, 364.

Academic terms, 287.

Accent, variable, 355 f.; of dissyllabic adjectives, 356.

Accountants' terms, 102.

Accusative as adverb, 195.

Address, terms of, 322 ff.

Adjective stem-forms, 174 f.

Adjectives, 185 f.; in -*ly*, 15; in slang, 73; adverbs from, 179, 198 f.; as adverbs, 199; become nouns, 253 ff., 382 n., 384 f.; transference of meaning 274 ff., 282 f.; participles in -*en* as, 203; of material in -*en*, 203; dissyllabic, accent of, 356; from names of animals, 365; from proper names, 376 f., 379, 382; ellipsis of, 252 f., 265 ff. *See* Degree, words of; Comparison.

Adverbs, in -*es*, 196 ff.; in -*e*, 198 ff.; in -*a*, 198; without ending, 198 ff.; in -*ly*, 199; case-forms as, 182, 195 ff.; as prefixes, 188; with copula, 238 n. *See* Words of Degree.

Ælian, 368.

Æsopic fable, 370.

Affirmation, words of, 310 f.

Alaska, 79 n.

Alchemical terms, 108, 350, 384.

Alfred, King, 83.

Allegory of love, 116.

Allusion, literary, 111.

Amber, 294.

Americanisms and American usage, 13 n., 58, 61 n., 65, 66, 71, 130, 134, 136, 138 f., 140 f., 144, 165 f., 207, 214, 244, 255, 268 n., 271, 289, 297, 299, 310, 318 ff., 321 f., 331, 340, 347, 351, 355, 356 f., 362 n., 365, 366, 374, 378 f.

Analogy, 343 f.

Andrewes, Bishop, 104 n.

Angles, 82.

Anglo-Saxon, its relations, dialects, and development, 81 ff., 163; borrowings from Latin, 43 ff., 93 ff.; ecclesiastical words, 43 ff.; inflection, 182 f., 195 ff., 201 f., 343 f.; words replaced by foreign words, 25; style, 82, 84, 113 f.; poetry, 82, 84; culture, 84, 137.

Anglo-Saxon Chronicle, 145, 341.

Anglo-Saxon Conquest, 81 f., 145.

Anglo-Saxons, conversion of, 43, 349 f.

Animal names, 336, 339, 352; used figuratively for human qualities, etc., 361 ff.; beliefs of savages with regard to animals, 361 f.; nursery tales and fables, 362; popular comparisons, 362; metaphors, 362 f.; surnames, 363; verbs of this class, 365; tools, etc., 366 f.; idiomatic phrases, 367 f.; fantastic science, 368 ff.; Physiologus, 368; Uncle Remus, 370; Æsopic fable, 370; primitive nature of these conceptions, 371.

Animals, speech of, 3; reason ascribed to, 362; words from the names of (Chap. XXIV), 361 ff.

Anjou, Counts of, 86.

Antithesis, 16.

Antonomasia, 16.

Aphetic forms, 63 f.

Approval and disapproval, terms of, 313 f.

Arabic, in medicine, etc., 45, 108; other words, 57, 108, 128, 380, 387.

INDEX OF MATTERS

Archaisms, in poetry, 26; mistaken, in Spenser and elsewhere, 118 f.; mistaken or manufactured, 118 f. See Obsolete.

Architecture, 244, 350.

Areopagus, 118 n.

Argot, 55 n.

Arians, 156 f.

Aristotle, 34 ff., 46 f., 368.

Armor, 153.

Art, dialect of, 42 ff., 51 f.; Italian in, 51 f., 242.

Article, confused with following word, 197 f.; Arabic in English, 108.

Aryans, home of, 161.

Ascent of words, 295 f.

Ascham, Roger, 57, 100.

Ash, lexicographer, 338.

Assimilation of sounds, 132.

Associations of words, 224 ff.; constantly shifting, 225. See Degeneration; Euphemism; Hyperbole.

Astrology, words from, 31, 33 f., 282.

Astronomy, 376.

Athens, 37.

Augural terms, 359.

Aulus Gellius, 232.

Australian words, 49, 50, 76, 109, 141, 305, 331, 332 n., 386; aborigines, 109, 301.

Baboo English, 226.

Baby talk, 44 (*papa*), 61, 63, 298. See Pet names; Diminutives.

Bacon, Lord, 115, 244, 381.

Ball, John, 89.

Ball play, 56 f., 59.

Banking, from Italy, 351 f.

Base-ball, 59.

Basque, 59.

Beast epic, 370.

Beast tales, 362, 370.

Becoming, words for, 233.

Bede, Venerable, 83, 113.

Beresarks, 228.

Bible, 44, 48, 57, 108, 152, 237, 258, 311, 317, 351, 369 f., 374 f., 376, 385.

Birds, names of, 129 f., 346 f.; as synonyms for stupidity, 363 f.

Black Death, 88.

Boccaccio, 89, 363 n.

Body, parts of, 304 f.

Boers, 112, 347.

Book of Common Prayer, 114.

Borrowed words distinguished from cognates (Chap. XII), 159 ff.

Borrowing, 9; learned words, 21 ff.; from French and Latin, 22 ff., 29 ff., 43 ff., 85 ff., 93 ff., 117 f.; from Greek, 23 ff., 29 ff., 44 ff.; from Celtic, 106 f.; from Scandinavian, 107; from Arabic, 45, 108; from Hebrew, 108; from Italian, 51 f.; from Spanish, 58, 107 f., 112; from miscellaneous sources, 108 f.; from Dutch and Low German, 108 f., 112; complexity of our vocabulary, 128 ff.; unity of our vocabulary, 147 ff.; cognates and borrowed words, 159 ff.; successive, of same word, 350.

Botany, 384. See Plants, names of.

Bowling, 56.

Bow-wow theory. See Origin of language.

Britain, Anglo-Saxon conquest of, 81 f.

Brooks, Phillips, 386 n.

Browne, William, 378.

Building, figures from, 56.

Burns, 58.

Business terms, 13, 42 ff., 59, 66 n., 102, 287, 351 f.

Butler, Samuel, 36, 147.

Byron, 375, 384 n.

Cabal, the, 68.

Cædmon, 83.

Cæsar, 227, 372 f.

Campion, Thomas, 333 n.

Canada, 68 n.

Card playing, 347.

Carlyle, Thomas, 127, 381 n.

Cases, names of, 13; and prepositions, subjective and objective, 274.

Catachresis, 16.

Catechism, 69 n.

Causative verbs, 281.

Celtic, 106 f., 142 n., 153, 161.

Celts, 130, 142; Latin words adopted by, 83.

Centlivre, Mrs., 375.
Central French, its relations to English, 86 f.
Charles II, 68.
Charms and incantations, 228 f.
Chaucer, 22, 27, 65, 94, 96, 118, 150, 189, 196, 206, 214, 253, 267, 288, 292 n., 297, 313 n., 327, 342, 348, 349, 364 n., 368, 369 n., 370, 373, 377; his relations to English, 88 ff.; character of his century, 88 ff.; his career, 90; his dialect 88 ff., 92 n., 203; his inflections, 182 f., 198, 202.
Chaucerisms in the Elizabethans, 118.
Chemistry, 108, 350; Arabic in, 108.
Child, F. J., 119 n.
Children's language, 29, 44, 61, 63, 243.
Chinese, 109.
Choice of words, 27, 52, 76 ff., 328; neologisms, 78.
Christianity, 71, 244, 349 ff., 388 f.; conversion of the Germans, 156 ff.; of the Anglo-Saxons, 43, 349. *See* Bible; Religious.
Church. *See* Arians; Christianity; Religious.
Cicero, 36 f., 39, 232.
Civilization and language, 41, 93 ff., 108 f., 128 ff., 144 ff., 147 ff., 156 ff., 183 f., 230 ff., 242, 246, 286, 287, 290 f., 295 f., 300 ff., 304, 317 ff., 348 ff., 357 ff., 360 ff., 372 ff., 387 ff.; and inflection, 183 f.
Class dialects (Chap. V), 42 ff., 53 f.
Clerical language. *See* Religious.
Clipped words in slang and in legitimate speech, 61 ff., 385; phrases, 70 ff., 252 ff.
Clothing, 44, 152, 153, 190, 304 f., 338, 383.
Cnut, 144.
Coaching, 271.
Cock-fighting, 57.
Cognates and borrowed words (Chap. XII), 159 ff., 345.
Coinage, 49, 89, 140 f.
Coleridge, 320.
Colloquial language, 25 n., 28, 62 ff., 74, 99, 102, 111 f., 149, 189, 202, 225, 238 n., 297, 304, 306, 362 ff.; ironical, 221 f. See Slang; Fashion; Hyperbole.
Colonization, 108 f.
Comedy of humors, 33.
Commerce, 287. *See* Business.
Comparative grammar, 159 ff., 165 f.; its limitations, 165 f.
Comparison of adjectives and adverbs, 199 ff.; double comparison, 17, 200 f.; terminations multiplied, 17 n.; folk-etymology in, 200, 342 f.
Comparisons, popular, to animals, 362.
Complexity of the English vocabulary (Chap. X), 128 ff.
Composition, 168 ff.; of roots and stems, 168 ff.; of words, 177, 179 f., 185 ff., 294; endings, derivation of, 185 ff.; origin and history of, 185 ff.; living suffixes, 186; prefixes, 187; adverbial prefixes in verbs, 188; vague syntax of composition, 126, 172 ff. *See* Phrase-composition.
Compound words, 177 ff.; disguised, 152, 210; hybrid, 154; obsolete words in, 210 ff.; obscured compounds felt as simple words, 210 f.; variety of meaning, 274; Elizabethan, 274.
Congregationalism in New England, 121.
Connotations of words, 224 ff. *See* Degeneration; Euphemism; Hyperbole.
Conservatism in language, 77 f.
Constructions, old, survival in a few phrases, 204 ff.
Contempt, words of, 284 ff.
Conventional character of language (Chap. XVI), 219 ff., 73.
Cooper, F. T., 61 n.
Copula, 238.
Correctness of style and grammar, 122 f.
Corruption by folk-etymology, 330 ff. *See* Analogy.
Cotgrave, 67.
Courtesy, mediæval conception of, 284, 327; in language, 310 f.; euphemism in, 304 ff.; in titles, 322 ff.; hyperbole in, 311, 317 ff., 322 ff.
Covent Garden, 244.

Creech, 67.
Criticism, literary, 14 ff., 40 f., 76. *See* Choice of words; Literature.
Cromwell, 100.
Cross influences, 194, 360.
Crusades, 388.
Currency. *See* Money.

Danes in England, 107, 144 f.
Darmesteter, A., 260 n., 265 n.
Dartmoor, stannary and forestry courts, 378 f.
Dative, singular, 195, 201; plural, 195; as adverb, 195.
Death, euphemisms for, 300, 302.
Decay of inflections, 85, 181 ff., 195, 201, 205.
Declension, Anglo-Saxon, 195 ff., 201, 343 f.
Degeneration of meaning (Chap. XX), 284 ff.; due to euphemism, 307 f. *See* Hyperbole.
Degree, words of, 312 ff.
Democracy in language, 322 ff.
Demons, 152.
Derivation and composition (Chap. XIV), 185 ff.
Derivative endings, 174 ff., 185 ff., 201 f. *See* Composition; Inflection; Comparison; Diminutives.
Development of words, I. Roots, stems, and inflections (Chap. XIII), 168 ff.; II. derivation and composition (Chap. XIV), 185 ff.
Dialect, distinguished from literary language, 80 f.; of Chaucer, 88 ff., 203; of modern English, 92, 203; dialectic variations in English, 354; dialect and provincial words, 13 n., 61 n., 128, 132, 139 n., 149, 188 n., 203, 364; in slang, 58. *See* Americanisms; Australian.
Dickens, 375, 382.
Digest, the Roman, 222.
Dignity of words, 354. *See* Associations.
Diminutives, 136 n., 137; as names of familiar objects or tools, 60 f., 386 f.
Ding-dong theory. *See* Origin of language.
Diseases, 31, 384.

Disguised oaths, 34 n., 304.
Diversity of the English vocabulary, 128 ff.
Divinity. *See* Religious.
Docked words. *See* Clipped forms.
Dog-Latin, 51.
Double comparison, 17.
Double negative, 220, 312.
Doublets and homonyms (Chap. XXIV), 345 ff., 44.
Dutch, 81, 83, 109, 149, 153 ff., 160, 163, 227, 348, 350, 360, 370, 383; in South Africa, 112, 347.
Dwelling places, 142 ff., 319 f.

Eastern question, 89.
East Germanic tribes, 156.
Ecclesiastical words in Anglo-Saxon, 42 ff., 93. *See* Religious.
Edward III, 89.
Electrical terms, 384.
Electricity, 293 f.
Elizabeth, Queen, 100.
Elizabethan style and language, 116 ff. *See* Euphemism; Shakspere; Spenser.
Ellipsis, in thought or expression, 252 ff.
Emerson, O. F., 114 n.
Empedocles, his four elements, 36.
Endings, derivative. *See* Derivative.
English, Old. *See* Anglo-Saxon.
English language, history of, 80 ff.; its place in the Indo-European family, 163. *See* Language.
English vocabulary, extent and variety of, 7 ff., 108 f., 128 ff.; learned and popular words in, 19 ff.; technical, 42 ff.; place of slang and colloquialism in, 55 ff.; sources of, 80 ff., 93 ff., 128 ff., 147 ff.; fashion, 110 ff.; unity of, 147 ff.; fossils in, 193 ff.; euphemism, 300 ff.; hyperbole, 309 ff.; doublets, 345 ff.; homonyms, 357 ff.; words from names of animals, 361 ff.; from proper names, 372 ff. *See* Words; Meaning.
Epithets, transference of, 275 ff.; indiscriminate, 314 f.

INDEX OF MATTERS

Etymology, false, its effect on words, 227; Stoic etymological doctrines, 229 f. *See* Folk-etymology.

Etymon, Stoic, 230.

Euphemism (Chap. XXI), 300 ff.; decency and propriety, 300 f.; origins of decency in language, 300; found among savages, 301; avoidance of ill-omened words, 301 ff.; death and disaster, 302 f.; profane language, 304; courteous euphemisms, 305; scientific terms used euphemistically, 306; degeneration of words from euphemism, 307 f.; litotes, 17.

Euphuism, 117; animal similes, 361, 369.

Evocation, formula of, 229.

Exaggeration. *See* Hyperbole.

Execution of criminals, 293.

Existence, verbs of, 237 ff.

Fables and beast-tales, 362, 370.

Fading of meaning, 235 ff.; because of hyperbole, 309 ff.

Falstaff, 67, 210.

Family names, 361; from obsolete nouns, 209 ff.

Farming, language of, 42, 284 f.

Fashion, in language (Chap. IX), 110 ff.; in literature and common talk, 110 f.; literary allusion and quotation, 111; school, university, and profession, 112; influenced by special events, 112; by discovery, invention, etc., 112 f.; Anglo-Saxon tautology, 113 f.; similar double phrases in more modern English, 114 f.; allegory of love, 116; mannerism in the Elizabethan age, 116 ff.; Euphuism, 117; ink-horn terms, 117 f.; archaisms, 118 f.; punning, 119 f.; freedom of the Elizabethan age, 120; Puritanism, 120 f.; eighteenth century, 121 f.; Romantic Revival, 123; nineteenth century, 124; permanent element in language, 124 ff.

Fawkes, Guy, 378.

Feminine terminations, 204.

Fencing, 56.

Figurative language, 9 ff.; negative, 311 f.

Figures of speech, 14 ff.

Finance, 89, 139.

Fire-arms, 244.

Fishery, language of, 42.

Flemish, 81.

Fletcher, J. B., 118 n.

Folk-etymology (Chap. XXIII), 330 ff.; 69, 150, 207, 246 n., 254 n., 346, 347, 365.

Foreign words, attempts to expel them from the vocabulary, 26 f. *See* Cognates; Native words; Borrowing.

Forestry, terms, 339; courts, 379.

Fossils (Chap. XV), 193 ff.

Fourteenth century, character of, 88 ff.

Frankish, Old, 81, 163.

Frankish kings, 152.

French, Germanic element in, 130, 151, 296; French words in music, 52; French and Latin, their relation to each other and to English, 94 ff.; Sprachgefühl, 126. *See* Norman French; Central French; Law French.

Frisian, 81, 163.

Fruits. *See* Plants, names of.

Gallic Latin, 96 f.

Gambling terms, 57.

Garter, Order of the, 34.

Gems, names of, 136 f.; properties of, 137.

Gender, 386.

Generalization and specialization of meaning (Chap. XVII), 234 ff.; special processes (Chap. XVIII), 259 ff.

Genitive, 274, 343; as adverb, 195 ff.

Genius of a language, 125, 147 f.

Gentility as defined by Chaucer, 327.

German, its relation to English, 81, 159; words, 51, 64, 66 f., 70, 107, 119, 129 f., 132, 136, 140, 142 f., 151 f., 160, 189, 197, 199, 204, 208, 210, 214, 236 f., 243, 249, 253, 270 n., 276 n., 280, 286, 289, 290 n., 296, 306, 310, 313, 320, 323, 326 n., 331 f., 337, 342, 347, 358, 360, 367, 373.

Germanic languages, 160 f., 163; element in French, *see* French.

Gerry, Elbridge, 68.

Gerund, Latin, in English, 102, 103 f.

Gods, heathen, become demons under Christianity, 152.

Goldsmith, 64.

Goodell, A. C., 121 n.

Goo-goo theory. *See* Origin of Language.

Gothic, 156 f., 161, 182 ff.

Gower, John, 91, 95.

Grandiloquence. *See* Magniloquence.

Greek, slang in, 60, 67 n.; English words from, 21 ff., etc.; in the language of science, 23; in philosophy, 34 ff.; in medicine, 45; Arabic words from, 108; idiom ('might of Hercules') in English, 257 f.; middle voice, 279 f.; religious ceremonial, euphemism in, 301.

Greek Church, 156 ff.

Greenough, J. B., 60 n.

Guevara, 118.

Gunpowder Plot, 378.

Gypsies, 380.

Hall, Fitzedward, 206 n.

Hamann on language, 5.

Hart, J. M., 114 n.

Hastings, Battle of, 83.

Haytian, 136, 138.

Hebrew, thought to be the primitive tongue, 3; words in English, 68, 108, 133, 137, 156.

Henry VIII, 388 f.

Henry of Huntingdon, 341 n.

Herder, on the origin of language, 3; on language as poetry, 5.

High German. *See* German.

Hindoo, 59.

History, words illustrative of, 68 f., 71 f., 93 ff., 112, 120 f., 128 ff., 144 ff., 152 f.; 156 ff., 288, 348 ff., 358, 372 ff., 387 ff.; of English language, *see* English language.

Hoccleve, Thomas, 91.

Homer, 61, 190, 373, 377.

Homonyms, 139, 345 ff., 357 ff.

Horace, 37, 67 n., 258.

Horn, Romance of King, 374.

Horsemanship, 56, 59, 75, 111, 210 f.

Houses, names applied to, 143 f., 319 f.

Hudibras, 36, 147.

Humor in language, 16 f., 34, 35 n., 40, 48 f., 51, 55 ff., 68 f., 102, 119 ff., 135, 141, 211, 224, 230, 255, 298, 302 n., 304, 311, 313, 331 f., 332, 339, 349, 354, 362 ff., 373 ff., 378, 386 f. *See* Colloquialisms; Slang.

Hungarian, 109.

Hunting terms, 57, 62, 75, 111, 288.

Huss, John, 89.

Hybrid words, 68 f., 105, 108, 129, 133, 135, 153 f., 166, 293 f., 331 ff.

Hyperbole or exaggeration (Chap. XXII), 309 ff.; natural tendency of speech, 16, 309; its causes, 309 ff.; in words affirmative and negative, 310 f.; figurative negative, 311 f.; double negative, 312; exaggeration in slang, 312 f.; schoolgirl dialect, 312 f.; words and phrases of degree, 312 ff.; terms of disapproval, 314; grandiloquence, 317 ff.; in local names, 318; in courtesy, 322 ff.; terms of courteous address, 322 ff.

Iberian, 153.

Icelandic. *See* Old Norse.

Idioms, English, 16, 17, 35 n., 49, 51 ff., 114 f., 173, 180, 190, 197, 204 ff., 220 ff., 227, 235, 237 ff.; 257 f., 274 f., 311 f., 315 f., 349, 369 f., 381; euphemistic, 301 ff.; from quotations, 216 f.; irony in, 222; French, 103, 150, 173, 312, 381; Greek, 257 f.; Italian, 173; Latin, 13, 102 ff., 173, 230, 302, 303, 316.

Imitation of the sounds of nature, 3.

Imitative words, 16, 155.

Imperialism, 89.

India, 76.

Indians, North American, 66.

Indo-European family of languages, 161 ff.; inflection, 181 ff.; parent-speech, 345.

Indo-European migration, 162.

INDEX OF MATTERS

Infinitive as noun, 173 n.; active and passive, 274 f.

Inflection, development of, 180 ff.; English, 182 ff.; Gothic, 182 ff.; Greek, 279 f. See Anglo-Saxon; Verb.

Ink-horn terms, 117 f.

Insanity, inspiration and, 290; effect of moon on, 364; care of, 388 f.

Inspiration and madness, 290.

Instrumental case, 202.

Interjectional theory of language, 3 f.

Interjections, 3 f., 234 f.

Invocations, 228 f.

Irish missionaries, 349.

Irony, 16, 221 f., 312.

Isolation, 195.

Italian, 58, 64, 70, 131, 154 f., 160, 173, 189, 239, 242, 244, 323 ff., 340, 351 f., 355, 366, 374, 387; literature, 22, 107; words in art and music, 51 f.; effect on Elizabethan style, 118.

Jacquerie, 89.

Jargon, 42 ff., 75.

Jocose words and phrases. See Humor.

John of Gaunt, 89.

Johnson, Dr., 238, 338.

Jonson, Ben, 337.

Jutes, 82.

Kentish dialect, 82.

Labor question, 29, 88 f.

Language, origin of, 1 ff., 391; natural rhythm of, 5; is poetry, 4 ff., 11 ff., 264; cultivated and uncultivated, 19 ff.; technical and class dialects, 42 ff., 111; women's, 54; slang, 55 ff.; secret, 55 n.; conservatism and innovation, 76 ff.; literary language and dialect, 80 ff.; fashions in speech, 110 ff.; families of languages, 159 ff.; language and race, 162; language of a people given up, 162; machinery of, 168 ff.; variety and consistency, 128 ff., 147 ff., 192 f.; petrifaction, 195 ff., conventional character, 72 f., 219 ff.; Stoic theory of, 229 ff.; euphemism, 300 ff.; hyperbole, 309 ff.; confusion in language, 330 ff. See also Table of Contents; Choice of words; Comparative grammar; English; Literary language; Magic; Meaning; Sprachgefühl; Words, etc.

Latin, slang in, 57, 60; Sprachgefühl, 126.

Latin in English (Chap. VIII), 93 ff.; before the Saxon Conquest, 93; in the Anglo-Saxon period, 93 f.; in the Middle English period, 94 ff.; a second vernacular, 94, 100 f.; French and Latin borrowings distinguished, 96 f.; vulgar, 96 f.; learned borrowings, 98 f.; Latin words and phrases adopted without change, 99 ff.; Latin abbreviations, 104 f.; Roman numerals, 105. See French.

Latinization of English, revolt against, 27.

Latin literature, 22.

Latin Orient, 388.

Law, Roman, 222.

Law French, 45 f., 348.

Law Latin, 45 f., 102 f.

Law terms, 45 f., 64, 71, 75, 102 f., 154, 208 f., 212 f., 214, 217 n., 222, 247, 353.

Laws of sound change, 163 ff.

Learned words and popular words (Chap. III), 19 ff.; learned words often of foreign origin, 21; sometimes native, 23 ff.; learned words become popular (Chap. IV), 29 ff., 157; scientific and technical, 30 ff.; old physiology, 30 ff.; astrology, 33 ff.; philosophy, 34 ff.; technical or class dialects, 42 ff.; learned and popular words in French and English, 96 ff.; learned and popular terms affected by euphemism, 306.

Length of words, 175 n.

Letters, formulæ in, 221.

Literary language (Chap. VII), 80 ff.; distinguished from dialects, 80 f.; developed from a dialect, 80 f.; history of the development, 81 ff. See Choice of words; Colloquialism; Slang.

Literature, poetry precedes prose,

4 f., 82; study of, 14; figures of, 14 ff.; vocabulary of, 19 ff.; criticism of, 40; slang gets into, 55 ff.; technique of, 76 ff.; oral, 82, 370; Anglo-Saxon, 82 ff.; Middle English, 84 ff.; Chaucer and his contemporaries and successors, 88 ff.; fashion in literature, 110 ff.; tendencies of Anglo-Saxon, 113; of Middle Ages, 116; of Elizabethan time, 116 ff.; of seventeenth century, 120 ff.; of eighteenth century, 121 ff.; of romanticism, 123; of nineteenth century, 124; beast-epic, 370; fables, 370. See Learned words; Literary language; Poetry.

Lithuanian, 61.
Litotes, 17.
Local names, hyperbole in, 318.
London, 65 f., 88.
Louis XIV, 155.
Love, allegory of, 116.
Low German, 81, 109, 140, 163.
Lumbering, 56, 214 n.
Lydford, 378 f.
Lydgate, John, 91.
Lyly, John, 117.

Machinery of language, 9, 168 ff., 192.
Macrobius, 229 n.
Magic, 119, 141 f., 313; power of words, 228 f.
Magnetism, animal, 385.
Magniloquence in language, 134, 317 ff.
Mandrake, superstition about, 340 f.
Mathematics, Arabic words, 108.
Matthews, Albert, 244 n., 299 n.
Meaning, conventional, 219 ff.; Stoic theory, 229 ff.; root-meaning, 232 f.; generalization and specialization, 234 ff.; radiation, 259 ff.; the $a+b$ process, 265 ff.; new applications, 269 ff.; transference, 272 ff.; degeneration, 284 ff.; euphemism, 300 ff.; hyperbole, 309 ff.; affected by supposed etymology, 336 ff.
Medical terms, 13, 31, 101, 128 f., 153, 213, 266, 352 f., 367, 384; Greek, 45; Arabic, 45.

Mercantile words. See Business.
Mercian dialect, 82 ff.
Mesmer, 385.
Metamorphosis, 361 f.
Metaphor, 9 ff., 14; in slang, 55.
Metonymy, 15.
Middle English, 84 ff., 116, 182 f., 195 ff. See Chaucer.
Middle voice, 279 f.
Midland dialect, 87 ff.
Military terms, 56, 58 f., 60, 61, 63 n., 99, 112, 154, 155, 189, 227, 296, 350, 360, 366 f., 380.
Milton, 100, 130, 141, 143, 229 n., 258, 283, 376, 381, 384.
Mining, figures from, 56.
Miracle plays, 67.
Misfortune, euphemisms for, 302 f.
Molière, 71, 375.
Monasticism, 44, 245, 388 f.
Money, 49, 89, 139 ff.
Moon, effect on insanity, 364.
Moore, Thomas, 355.
More, Sir Thomas, 381.
Morton, John, 375.
Müller, Max, on origin of language, 3.
Municipal government, 146.
Musical terms, 51 f., 57 n.
Mythology, 222, 326 n.; animals in, 362.

Name, of person, used as common noun, 16, 129 f., 141, 372 ff.; of dead, avoided, 300; of persons or places applied to things, 154, 255 f.; magic power of, 228 f.; of God, distorted in oaths, 34 n., 304.
Names, family. See Family names.
Names of animals, birds, etc. See Animals; Birds, etc.
Nashe, Thomas, 67.
Native and foreign words contrasted as to popularity, 21 ff.; native words driven out, 25 ff.; attempt to oust foreign words, 26 ff.; learned words become popular, 29 ff.; native words in technical dialects, 42 f., 48, 49, 51; borrowing, 85 ff., 93 ff.; cognates and borrowed words, 159 ff.

INDEX OF MATTERS 405

Natural history, fantastic, 117, 361, 368 ff. *See* Animals; Birds; Plant names.

Negation, words of, 306 f., 311 f.; affected by hyperbole, 311; double negative, 220, 312; figurative negative, 311 f.

Neologisms, 78.

New England dialect, 165 f. *See* Dialect.

New England Puritanism, 121.

New York, 293 f.

Nicknames, 65 f., 297.

Nineteenth Century, style and language, 124.

Nobility, titles of, 144 ff., 258, 317 ff., 322 ff., 348.

Nobles, coinage of, by Edward III, 89.

Nominal stems, 172 ff.

Norman Conquest, 22, 83 ff., 145.

Norman French, in the law, 45; its relations to English, 85 ff., 94, 353.

Norse. *See* Scandinavian.

North American Indian, 109, 139.

Northern dialect of English, 87, 149.

Northumbrian, 82 ff.; the first literary English, 83; succeeded by West Saxon, 83; Scottish language, 92; influence of Norman French, 85 ff; influence of Central French, 86; relations of English and French in England, 84 ff.; East Midland becomes the literary dialect, 88 ff.; decadence of French, 86 ff.; characteristics of Chaucer's age, 88 ff.

Noun-stems. *See* Nominal.

Numerals, 196 ; Roman, 105.

Nursery tales, animals in, 362.

Oaths, 240; disguised, 34 n., 304.

Obsolete, native words made so by borrowing, 25, 28 ; words in poetry, 26; archaisms revived, 26, 78 f., 118 f., 123; surviving as fossils, 195 ff.; in a few phrases, 209 ff.; meanings surviving, 212 ff.

Obsolete science, 30 ff.

Occleve. *See* Hoccleve.

Occupations, names of, 133 f.; as proper names, 209.

Offices, names of, 144 ff., 222, 295 f. 353.

Old English. *See* Anglo-Saxon.

Old Frankish, 81, 163.

Old French. *See* French.

Old High German and French. *See* French.

Old Norse in English, 107, 144 f., 202, 345.

Old Saxon, 81, 163.

Omens, 232, 302.

Onomatopœia, 3, 16, 155.

Oral literature, 82, 370.

Orient, names of spices from, 133; of gems, 137 ; Latin Orient, 388.

Origin of language, 1 ff.; bow-wow theory, 3, 6 ; ding-dong theory, 3, 6 ; pooh-pooh theory, 3, 6 ; goo-goo theory, 6 n., 391 ; Stoic theory, 229 f.

Oxford, 88.

Oxymoron, 16.

Parisian dialect, 132.

Parisian French. *See* Central French.

Parliamentary formula, 229.

Parsing as a test of correctness, 206.

Participles in -*en*, 203.

Patriarchal institutions, 146.

Payne, John Howard, 143.

Peddlers' French, 55 n.

Percy, Bishop, 119.

Peripatetic philosophy, 34 ff.

Periphrasis, 17. *See* Euphemism.

Persian, 109.

Personal endings, 180 f., 182 f.

Personal pronouns, 180, 202 f., 204.

Personification, 257.

Persons, names of. *See* Names.

Peterborough Chronicle, 145, 341.

Pet names, 60 f., 63, 135, 298 f., 386 f. *See* Diminutives.

Petrarch, 89.

Petrifaction in language, 180. *See* Fossils.

Philosophy, 34 ff., 46 ff., 382.

Phrase-composition, 35 n., 50, 70 f.,

103, 187 ff., 201, 292 n., 301, 310, 332, 350, 352, 367.
Physiologus, 368.
Physiology, 30 ff., 129, 213, 295.
Piracy, 81, 291.
Place-names, 60, 61, 71, 93, 129, 131, 136 f., 140 f., 142 n., 338; hyperbole in, 140.
Places and persons, words from (Chap. XXVI), 372 ff.; nicknames or serious technical terms, 372; names of persons used figuratively, 372 ff.; from the Bible, 374 f.; from the classics, 375 f.; names of places similarly used, 376; corruptions of such names, 377; verbs from proper names, 377 ff.; verbs in *-ize*, 379; names of tribes or nations as common nouns, 379 f.; derivatives of, in special senses, 380 f.; fanciful names, 381; adjectives from proper names, 382; names of persons applied to things, 382 f.; in common talk, 383 f.; in science, 383 f.; articles named from places from which they come, 384 ff.; diminutives applied to tools, 386 f.; significance of such terms in the history of civilization, 387 f.
Plants, names of, 138 f., 210 n., 337, 340 f., 360, 364 f.
Plattdeutsch, 81, 109, 163.
Pleiade, 118 n.
Pleonasm, a universal tendency of speech, 17. *See* Comparison; Tautology.
Pliny, Natural History, 368.
Pliny the Younger, 54 n.
Plural, singular in *s* mistaken for, 132 f., 139, 343; irregular, 201 f.; in verbs, 343.
Plutarch, 374.
Poetical and unpoetical words, 295. *See* Slang, 55 ff.
Poetic faculty, 7 ff., 176.
Poetry, language is, 4 ff., 7 ff., 176; figures of, compared with ordinary language, 9 ff., 14 ff.; archaisms in, 26, 118 f., 123; precedes prose, 4, 82; pathos, 40; bathos, 40 f.; doggerel, 65; bombast, 67.
Polish, 109.

Political economy, 112 f.
Political slang, 68 f., 112, 362 n., 365.
Polynesian in English, 109, 360.
Pooh-pooh theory. *See* Origin of language.
Poole, John, 375.
Pope, 40.
Popular etymology. *See* Folk-etymology.
Popular origin of figures from animals, 361, 371.
Popular words and learned words, 19 ff. *See* Learned words.
Portuguese, 108, 160, 325, 346, 348, 350, 363 f.
Prefixes, 151, 187 f.
Prepositions, compounded with verbs, 187 ff.; subjective and objective use, 273 f.
Primitive man. *See* Savages.
Printers' language, 214.
Prize-fighting, 56, 75, 353.
Procrastination in language, 292 f.
Profanity. *See* Oaths.
Professional dialects (Chap. V), 42 ff. *See* Law; Medicine, etc.
Progress of language, 183 f., 344.
Pronominal roots, 169 f.
Pronoun, demonstrative, 202; personal, 202 f.; dative and nominative confused, 204.
Pronunciation, various, 355 f.
Proper names as common nouns. *See* Names.
Propriety in language, 300 f. *See* Choice of words.
Provençal, 248 n., 339.
Proverbs and proverbial phrases, 71, 214, 216, 367 f.
Provincial English. *See* Dialect.
Psychology of primitive man, 361.
Puns, 49, 68 f., 141, 264, 288 n., 302 n., 332; Elizabethan, 119 ff. *See* Humor.
Purism, 77.
Puritanism, 120 f.
Purity in language, 76 ff. *See* Choice of words.

Quotation as a means of introducing words into the language, 70 f., 75 f.; idioms from, 216 ff.

R, vocalic, 356.
Race and language, 162.
Radiation of meaning, 259 ff.
Railroading, 130 f.; vocabulary in England and America, 271.
Reduplication, 132, 173, 346.
Reflexive verbs, 279 f.
Reformation, 89, 388 f.
Rehabilitation of words, 287.
Religious establishments abolished by Henry VIII, 388.
Religious words, clerical language, etc., 33 n., 43 ff., 45 ff., 71, 72, 76, 93, 116, 120 f., 152, 212, 268 f., 290, 297, 326, 349 f., 351, 353, 388. *See* Bible.
Repetition of synonyms, 113 ff.
Reproach, terms of, 284 ff.
Restoration of Charles II, 121.
Revival of Learning, 23, 98.
Reynard the Fox, 370.
Rhetoric, function of, 76 f.; figures, 14 ff.
Rhythm of language, 5 f.
Richard II, 89.
Richardson, Samuel, 375.
Roman de la Rose, 327 n.
Roman formula for evocation, 229; for silence at sacrifice, 302.
Roman law, 222.
Roman slavery, 323 ff.
Romance languages, 160.
Romances, 381.
Romans in Britain, 93.
Romantic revival, 123.
Rome, name kept secret, 229.
Root, growth of words from a single, 12 ff.
Root-meanings, 220, 232 f.
Roots, meanings of, 12 ff.; 171; verbal, 169 ff.; pronominal, 169 ff.; examples, 12 f., 170 ff., 175, 177, 223, 231 n., 238 f., 359; reduplicated, 173.
Roots and stems, 168 ff.
Rowe, Nicholas, 375.
Rowlands, Samuel, 117 f.
Russian, 161.

Sacrifice, 302.
Sailors' terms. *See* Sea-terms.
St. Dominic, 348.
St. Isidore, 325.
St. Martin, 152.
St. Paul, 57 n., 317.
San Domingo, 79.
Sandwich, Earl of, 256.
Sanskrit, 161 f., 286, 339.
Saracens, 129, 374, 377.
Satire, 333 n.
Savages, eighteenth-century idea of, 5; superstition as to language, 228; euphemism, 300 ff.; subject to religious restrictions, 301; belief as to animals, 361 f.
Saxon. *See* Anglo-Saxon; Old Saxon.
Scandinavian, languages, 81, 160, 163; words, 107, 140 n., 144 f., 150 f., 160, 202, 207, 209, 236, 287 n., 291, 311, 326 n., 337, 342, 345, 347, 349, 354, 359.
Scholastic philosophy, 35 ff., 46 f.
Schoolgirl dialect, 16, 312 ff.
Schoolmen's Latin, 35 ff., 46 f.
Science, terms of, 29 ff., 49 ff., 112 f., 203 n., 234, 294, 383 f.
Scott, C. P. G., 66 n., 198 n., 387.
Scott, Sir Walter, 238, 375.
Scottish, language, 92; words, 58, 149, 353, 364.
Scriptural language. *See* Bible.
Sea-terms, 48 f., 103, 108 f., 150, 153, 154 f., 291, 335.
Secret languages, 55 n.
Semitic languages in English, 108.
Sense and sound, 331 ff.; sense affected by supposed etymology, 336.
Sentiment of words, 143 f.
Separative compounds, 190.
Serfs in England, 89, 284.
Shakspere, 10 f., 34 n., 36, 46, 57, 67, 69, 119 n., 135, 151, 155, 204, 207, 208, 210, 212, 216 ff., 226, 234, 238 n., 250, 257, 258, 263, 274 ff., 279, 285 n., 289, 295, 296, 298, 302, 312, 313 n., 323, 337, 349, 362 f., 364, 365, 366, 373, 374, 375, 377, 378.
Sheldon, E. S., 137 n.
Shelley, Mrs., 377.

INDEX OF MATTERS

Shortened forms. *See* Clipped words.

Sidonius, 278.

Simile, 15; adjectives comparable with, 365.

Singular in *s* mistaken for plural, 132 f., 139, 214 n., 343.

Skeat, Professor, 341 n.

Slang (Chap. VI), 55 ff.; phenomena parallel to those of legitimate speech, 55 ff.; how made, 55 ff.; from games and sports, 56 ff.; from provincialisms or foreign words, 58 f.; ancient slang, 56, 59 ff.; use of diminutives and the like, 60 f.; clipped words, 61 ff.; Swift on clipped words, 62 f.; clipping process natural in our language, 63 f.; fantastic coinages and distortions, 64 ff.; substitutions and variety in slang, 69 f.; phrase-composition in slang, 70; fragments of phrases, 70 ff.; reasons for avoiding slang, 72 ff.; all slang not on the same level, 74; use of slang under special circumstances, 74 ff.; elaboration of, 362 n.

Slang words, 99, 102, 111 f., 119 n., 141, 155 n., 189, 192, 207, 211, 255, 304, 306, 307, 312 ff., 332, 349, 351, 353, 354, 356 f. *See* Words from the names of animals (361 ff.), and from places or persons (373 ff.); Colloquial language; Hyperbole; Fashion.

Slavery, 89, 284 ff., 322 f.

Smith, C. A., 237 n.

Society, jargon of, 53 f.; phrases from French, 99; conventional phrases, 220 f.

Soldiers' slang. *See* Military terms.

Song and language, 5.

Sophocles, 238.

Sound, similarity of, 331; effect, 331 ff.

Sound and sense, 4, 194, 226.

Sound-change, laws of, 164 ff.

South African Dutch, 112; War, 112.

Southern dialect of English, 87.

Spanish, 58 f., 66, 107 f., 136, 138, 160, 164, 207, 323, 339, 346, 348, 350 f., 381 f.; effect on Elizabethans, 118.

Spanish War, 112.

Specialization, 247 ff.; cause of, 248 ff.; slight change, 250; every man his own specializer, 251 f.; results from ellipsis, 252 ff.; names of articles, 254 ff.; in proper names, 255 f.; abstract to concrete, 256 ff.; radiation, 259 ff.; the $a+b$ process, 265 ff. *See* Generalization.

Spelling, affected by etymology, true or false, 149, 331 ff.

Spencer, Earl, 256, 383.

Spenser, 118, 295, 354, 363 n., 375.

Spices, 133, 337 n.

Sport, words from, 56 ff.

Sprachgefühl, 126 f., 147 f., 181, 233.

Stage-terms, 58, 223, 246, 251, 268 f.

Stem-composition, 176 ff., 185 ff.

Stem-endings, 174 ff.

Stem-formations, vagueness of, 175 f.

Stems, reduplicated root as, 173.

Stems and roots, 168 ff.

Stoic philosophy, 37 ff.; theory of the etymon, 229 ff., 301.

Straw, Jack, 89.

Style, as affected by the rejection of foreign words, 26; artistic, 70; tendencies of, 110. *See* Choice of words; Fashion.

Subjunctive, 204 ff.

Sublime, bathos the opposite of, 40 f.

Substantive verb, 238.

Suetonius, 302 n.

Suffixes, 135, 141 n., 174 ff., 185 ff., 201 f.; confused, 187, 294. *See* Comparison; Inflection; Diminutives.

Suggestion in language, 264.

Sumner, Charles, 78 f.

Superlatives, 315, 342 f. *See* Comparison.

Superstitious opinions about words, 228 f., 300 ff.

Surgery, 13.

Surnames, from animals, 363. *See* Family names.

Swearing. *See* Oaths.

Swift, on slang, 62 f., 65.

Symbols, 105.

Synecdoche, 15.

INDEX OF MATTERS 409

Synonyms, 8; learned and popular, 20; in slang, 69 f.

Syntax, 172, 178; of composition, 172 ff., 177; English, regularity of modern, 122. *See* Dative; Infinitive; Subjunctive; Inflection; Idioms; Phrase-composition.

Syriac, 44.

Tamerlane, 89.
Tartars, 254, 358, 379 f.
Tatler, The, on slang, 62 f., 65.
Tautological compounds, 153, 348.
Tautology, 209, 212 f.; in Anglo-Saxon, 113 f.; in the Book of Common Prayer, 114; in Bacon, 115, 209. *See* Pleonasm.

Technical dialects (Chap. V), 42 ff.; their relation to ordinary speech, 52 f., 75; technical words become popular, 29 ff., 42 ff. *See* Law; Medicine; Science, etc.

Tennyson, 4 n., 9, 283, 284 n., 368, 379.
Tense-endings, 180 f., 182 f.
Terence, 382.
Terminations. *See* Derivation; Inflection.
Thackeray, 380.
Theatrical language. *See* Stage.
Theology. *See* Religious.
Thieves' slang, 55 n.
Titles of honor, 134, 144 ff., 258, 317 ff., 322 ff., 348.
Tmesis, 191.
Tools, etc., 60 f., 366 f., 386 f.
Tournaments, 57 f.
Trade, dialect of, 42 ff. *See* Business.
Trades, names of, 133 f., 209.
Transference of meaning, subjective and objective (Chap. XIX), 272 ff.; from persons to things, 276 ff., 297; from things to persons, 278 f.; in verbs, 151, 279 ff.; in names of objects, 269 ff.

Transitive and intransitive verbs, 190, 279 ff.

Translation, Greek words into Latin, 34 ff., 242; Latin into English, 48, 251; of foreign phrases, 103 ff.; difficulty of rendering English into French, 148.

Trapping, figures from, 56.
Travel and colonization, 108 f.
Turkish, 17, 66.
Turko-Russian War, 71.
Turks in Europe, 89.
Twain, Mark, 148 n.
Tyler, Wat, 89.
Tyndale, 72 n.

Umlaut in English, 136 n., 199 f., 204.
Uncle Remus, 370.
Understatement or litotes, 17.
Uniformity of language, 124 ff.
Unity of the English vocabulary (Chap. XI), 147 ff.
Universities founded, 89.
University slang, 64, 67.
Usage, standard of, 77, 217 f., 233. *See* Americanisms; Dialect.

Vague words, 235 ff.
Van Helmont, 51.
Vehicles, 130 f.
Verbal roots, 169 ff.; stems, 176 f.
Verbs, inflection, 92 n., 180 f., 182 ff., 204 ff.; separative, 190 f.; interchangeable with nouns, 191 f., 363; transference of meaning in, 279 ff.; transitive and intransitive, 279 ff.; causative, 281; from names of animals, 365 f.; from proper names, 377 ff.; in *-ize* (*-ise*), 379.

Vine culture, 13.
Virgil, 238, 325, 375.
Vocabulary. *See* English vocabulary.
Vocalic *r*, 356.
Volksetymologie, 331 n. *See* Folk-etymology.
Vulgarity in language, 72.
Vulgar Latin, 96 f.

Ward, Artemas, 239.
Ware, W. R., 69 n.
Ways, names of, 318 ff.
Werewolves, 228.
West Germanic, 83, 93, 156.
Wiener, Leo, 358 n., 380 n.

Wit. *See* Humor.
Witchcraft, 313 n.
Women's language, 54.
Words, learned and popular, 19 ff.; conventional character of, 72 f.; development of (Chaps. XIII, XIV), 168 ff., 185 ff.; essential or root meanings of, 220; connotations or associations, 224 ff.; magic power of, 228 f., 301; words are not formulæ, 234; fading in particular phrases, 239 f.; transformed by folk-etymology, 330 ff.; doublets, 345 ff.; homonyms, 357 ff.; two words developing from one by variety of pronunciation, 213 f., 355 ff.; from names of animals, 361 ff.; from places or persons, 372 ff. *See* Language; Learned; Meaning; Native.

Wordsworth, 9 f.
Wotton, Sir Henry, 289.
Wrestling, 57.
Writing, words connected with, 136, 230.

Wyclif, 88 f.

Zeno, the Stoic, 37.

INDEX OF WORDS

A 1, 59.
aback, 49, 64.
abalienate, 46.
abandoned, 307.
abbot, 44.
abed, 201.
ab(h)ominable, 342.
-able, 187.
aboard, 49.
absit omen, 302.
absolutely, 315.
absurd, 364.
abuse, 213.
accident, 303.
ace, 57.
Achitophel, 375.
across, 349.
acute, 289.
adamant, 137.
ad captandum, 71.
adder, 198, 369 f.
adjust, 214.
admiral, 108.
admiration, 257.
admonish, 139.
Adonis, 376.
adown, 63.
adventure, 249.
affection, 248.
affidavit, 46, 99.
against, 197.
agate, 137.
age, 152.
ageynes, 197.
agitation, 10 n.
ago, 199.
agone, 199.
aid, 212 f.
aid and abet, 216.
aid-de-camp, 189.
air, castles in the, 381.

-al, 214 n., 343.
alack, 188 n.
alack-a-day, 188.
alamodeness, 188.
alarm, 70, 189.
alb, 44.
alderman, 144 ff.
alembic, 108.
algates, 197 n.
algebra, 108.
alias, 46.
alibi, 46, 99.
alive, 201.
alkali, 108.
allegro, 51.
alley, 319, 321.
all-fired, 304.
All Hallows, 207.
allspice, 133.
aloft, 107.
alonges, 197.
alongst, 197.
alphabet, 136.
always, 197 n.
am, 238.
amanuensis, 230, 239.
amaze, 309 f., 328.
amazon, 376.
ambassador, 63 n., 296.
amber-de-grece, 346.
ambergrease, 346.
ambergris, 346.
amiddes, 196.
amidst, 196.
amonges, 196.
amongst, 196.
ampère, 384.
ampersand, 105.
Amphitryon, 71.
ampulla, -or, *L.*, 58 n., 67 n.

amputation, 13.
ancient, 'ensign,' 359.
ancient, 'old,' 359.
andante, 51.
anger, 151.
angle, 'corner,' 359.
angle, 'fish-hook,' 359.
angry, 237.
animadversion, 59.
animal, 99.
animal spirits, 33.
annexion, 78, 79.
-ant, 187.
ante up, 56.
antic, 356.
antimacassar, 384 n.
antique, 356.
-anus, *L.*, 194 n.
anxious, 282, 307.
anyhow, 240.
apathy, 39, 246.
ape, 365.
apish, 365.
appetite, 13.
apple, 138.
appose, 64.
apron, 198.
Arab, 380.
arabesque, 382.
arbitrate, 29.
arbitration, 29.
arc, 352.
arch, 352.
-ard, -art, 141, 365, 368 n.
argol, 358.
armiger, 172.
army, 25.
arrange, 103.
arras, 384.
'Arry, 387.
artichoke, 340.

INDEX OF WORDS

article, 103.
as, as now, etc., 215.
ascendant, 34.
ashman, 178.
asparagus, 334.
aspect, 33.
assail, 59.
assassin, 246, 380.
assault, 59.
assize, 64.
assurance, 278.
aster, 33, 352.
asteroid, 33, 352.
astonish, 309, 328.
astrology, 33, 352.
astronomy, 352.
-ate, -ation, 193.
at fault, 75.
athwart, 349.
Atlantean, 381.
Atlantis, 381.
atlas, 381.
atrocious, 314.
attach, 153.
attack, 153.
attend to, 59.
Attic salt, 380.
auceps, *L.*, 177.
auction, 248.
augur, 142.
auncien, 359.
auto, 61.
avails, 64.
avenue, 318, 320.
awayward, 64.
awe, 151.
awful(ly), 276, 314 f.

babel, 376.
back, *adv.*, 64.
badger, *n.*, 362.
badger, *v.*, 366.
badly, 316.
bah, 3.
balcony, 355.
ballad, 248.
bam, 65.
bamboozle, 63, 65.
banco, 351.
bandy, 56.

bang-up, 313.
bank, 351.
banke rota, 352.
bankrout, 352.
bankrupt, 352.
bannock, 107.
banter, 63, 65.
bard, 107.
barouche, 132.
base, 288, 307.
Basil, 368.
basilica, 368.
basilisk, 367 f.
basket, 107 n.
basque, 255, 384.
bas-relief, 189.
bat, 362.
bate, 63.
Bath chair, 121.
bathos, 40, 67 n.
battalion, 63 n.
battering ram, 366.
battle, 339.
bawcock, 299.
baxter, 209.
Bayard, 368, 373.
bazar, 109.
be, 239.
bead, 151.
bear, 362 f.
bearable, 187.
bearish, 365.
beastly, 314.
beautiful, 135, 313.
beauty, 135.
beaver, 362.
become, 237.
bedlam, 388 f.
bed rock, 56.
bee-line, 368.
beet, 138.
belfrey, 337.
bell, 337.
Bellerophon, 335.
belles lettres, 189.
belt, below the, 56.
bench, 351 f.
Benedict, 374.
benigne, *L.*, 222.
berlin, 131, 384.

berry, 138.
beside(s), 188, 197 n.
bestead, 207.
betimes, 188, 197 n.
better, 153.
better world, 302.
bettor, 153.
betty, 61 n., 386.
bewitching, 313 n.
bi-, 132.
bias, 56, 59.
bibble-babble, 332.
bicycle, 132.
bid, 151.
Biddy, 387.
big story, 306.
bilboes, 15.
bile, 30.
bilious, 31.
-bilis, *L.*, 187.
bill, 141.
billy, 61 n., 386.
bind, 347.
binnacle, 108.
bird's-eye view, 368.
bishop, 44, 93.
bishopric, 207.
bit, 331.
biz, 61.
bizarre, 58.
blab, 225.
black, 330.
black jack, 387.
blackamoor, 66, 380.
blackball, 192.
blackguard, 66.
blackish, 330.
blackleg, 66.
blench, 281.
blind, 362, 364, 368.
block, 319.
blockhead, 285 n.
blood, 30.
blow, 283.
blubber, 295.
Bluchers, 255, 382.
blue, 62.
blues, 62.
bob, 141.
bobolink, 16.

INDEX OF WORDS

bodkin, 107 n.
body, 246 f.
body politic, 247.
Boer, 347.
bog, 107.
Bohemian, 380.
bombast, 67.
bona fide, 102, 104.
bonus, 99, 102.
boodle, 74.
book, 136.
booking office, 271.
bookworm, 363.
boomerang, 109.
boor, 108, 285, 347.
boorish, 307.
booth, 347.
bootjack, 61 n., 387.
boss, 252.
bottle, 342.
boughten, 203.
boulevard, 318, 320.
boun, 347.
bound, 347.
bow-wow, 3.
bowdlerize, 379.
bower, 347.
bower (card term), 347.
bowl over, 56.
bowyer, 209.
box, 71.
boycott, 378.
boyish, 365.
bracelets, 69.
brackish, 108.
brag, 225, 373.
braggadocio, 373, 376.
braggart, 141, 368 n.
brass, 69.
brasses, 255.
bravado, 58.
brazen, 69, 203.
bread, 330.
breakfast, 330.
break ground, 56.
breathe one's last, 302.
breeches, 305.
Bridget, 387.
bridle, 227.
brine, 295.

brock, 107.
brogue, 107.
broker, 253, 296.
brother, 159.
brougham, 255, 382.
Bruin, 370.
brummagem, 377.
bubble, 63.
bug, 51.
bull, 363, 364.
bully, 63, 66.
Bully Ruffian, 335.
bunco, 351.
buncombe, 71.
bunko, 351.
burgh, 69.
burial, 139 n., 214 n., 343.
buriels, 343.
burke, 377 f.
'bus, 61.
busk, 347.
butt, n., 342.
butt, v., 338.
butter, 342.
butterball, 177.
butterfingers, 178.
butterfly, 177.
buttermilk, 178.
buttertub, 178.
butterwoman, 178.
buttery, 342.
buzz, 16.
by-and-by, 188, 292 f.

cab, 61, 131.
cabal, 68.
cabbala, 68.
cabriolet, 131.
cad, 61.
cadence, 57 n.
Cæsar, 373.
caitiff, 287, 307.
calash, 131.
calèche, 131.
calf love, 368.
calico, 255.
call, 107.
camber, 350.
cambric, 384.
camera, 350, 356.

cancel, 353.
cancer, 352 f., 367.
candelabrum, 270, 294 n.
candidate, 265 f.
candy, 128, 225.
canker, 353.
can't, 62.
cantankerous, 149.
canter, 385.
canting dogs, 367.
cap, 152 f.
cape, 152.
Cape Cod turkey, 331.
caper, 'antic,' 366.
caper sauce, 366.
caprice, 366.
capriole, 366.
captain, 155.
Capua, 376.
car, 130, 134, 271.
caravan, 109.
carcinoma, 353.
careless, 276.
cargo, 49.
carnival, 59.
carouse, 70, 189.
carpenter, 134.
carriage, 130.
cart, 130.
cart-wheel, 141.
case, 13, 240.
cash, 69.
cashmere, 338, 384.
cassimere, 338.
cast, 107, 243.
castaway, 49.
-caster, 93.
castle, 94.
castles in Spain, in the air, 381 f.
casual, 343.
casualty, 303.
cat, 62, 363, 368.
cataract, 252.
catchbasin, 190.
catchpoll, 190.
category, 47.
caterpillar, 363.
cathedral, 132.
Catoun, 96.

414 INDEX OF WORDS

cattish, 365.
caustic, 136.
cela va sans dire, 103.
cent, 140.
cerecloth, 333 n.
certainly, 311.
chaff, 71.
chaise, 132.
chalk, 93.
challenge, 282.
chamber, 350, 356.
chamberlain, 222, 295.
chameleon, 369 f.
champagne, 384.
champerty, 45.
chance, 57.
chancel, 353.
chancellor, 353.
chancery, 353.
chandelier, 270, 294 n.
change, 69.
chant, 142.
chanticleer, 370.
chaos, 51, 249.
chap, 62, 287.
chape, 152.
chapel, 152.
chapelet, 153.
chaperon, 153.
chaplain, 153.
chaplet, 153.
chapman, 62, 209, 287.
character, 8.
charm, 248.
charming, 313.
chasm, 249.
chaw, 354.
chawbacon, 354.
cheap, 198.
cheater, 366.
cheator, 288.
cheek, 69.
chemise, 305.
cherub, 108.
-chester, 93.
cheveaux-de-frise, 367.
chevy, 71.
Chevy Chace, 71.
chew, 354.
chickadee, 16.

chieftain, 155.
childish, 365.
childlike, 15.
chimera, 369 f., 376.
chimney, 270.
china, 255, 384.
chivy, 71.
choir, 152.
choke, 340.
chouse, 17, 66.
Christian, 297.
chuck, 298.
chum, 67.
church, 157.
churl, 284 f.
cicycle, 132.
cinchona, 384.
cinnamon, 133.
cipher, 108.
Circe, 376.
Circean, 376.
circle, 319.
circumstances, 236.
circumvallation, 63 n.
circus, 59.
cit, 61.
citizen, 194.
city, 142 f.
clark, 268 n.
clean, 14.
clear the decks, 49.
cleave, 25.
clench, 119 n., 354.
clergy, 44 f.
clergyman, 178 f.
clerical, 44 f.
clerk, 44 f., 268.
clever, 289.
clinch, 119 n., 354.
cloak, 152.
clod, 285 n.
clodhopper, 285 n.
clodpoll, 285 n.
clotpoll, 285 n.
clove, 337.
clown, 285.
coach, 131, 271.
coast, 49, 249.
coat, 382 n.
cock, 56, 366 f.

cock (for God), 34 n., 304.
cockney, 65, 66 n.
cockpit, 49.
Cœur de Lion, 363.
coiner, 290.
colonial goose, 331 f.
comfort, 212 f.
common, 54.
communication, 63 n.
companion, 154, 287.
companion-way, 154.
competition, 13.
complete, 356.
complexion, 31 f.
compulsion, on, 215.
computation, 13.
concerto, 51.
conclusion, foregone, 216.
Concord wagon, 131, 256.
condition, 212, 235.
conduct, 245.
conductor, 271.
confab, 62.
confound, 212.
congregation, 256, 265.
cónjure, 142, 356.
conjúre, 356.
conjurer, 142.
connection, 216.
considering, 104 n.
consols, 62.
constable, 295 f.
constellation, 352.
continence, 150.
contort, 46.
contradict, 29, 215 f.
convey, 45.
conveyance, 45.
conveyancer, 45.
convoy, 45.
coon, 62.
Cooper's cow, 368.
cope, 152.
copper, 385.
copperas, 350 f.
copperbottom, 192.
cordovan, 134, 254, 384.
corduroys, 255.
cordwain, 134, 254, 384.
cordwainer, 134.

INDEX OF WORDS

corking, 313.
corn, 135 f.
corp, 132, 139, 343.
corps, 343.
corpse, 132, 139, 343.
corpus juris, 247.
corsage, 305.
cosmos, 247.
cottage, 319 f.
cottager, 319 f.
couch, 191.
cough, 332.
count, 144 f.
countenance, 150 f.
counter, 57, 289 n.
counterfeit, 289.
counterpart, 289 n.
countess, 94, 144.
country put, 63.
county, 144.
court, 94, 282 n.
courteous, 282, 327.
courtesy, 284.
courtly, 282.
cousin, 67.
cousining, to go a-, 68.
coverchef, 270.
cow, 365.
coward, 241, 360, 365.
cowish, 365.
cowl, 44.
coxcomb, 66.
Cox my passion, 304.
cozen, 67 f.
crab, 337.
crack, 295.
cradle, 107 n.
craft, 289.
craftsman, 289.
crafty, 289.
cramp, 138.
crate, 130.
crawfish, 336 f., 366.
crayfish, 336 f.
crazy, 307.
cream of tartar, 358.
crestfallen, 57.
crevis, 336.
crime, 249.
Croat, 380.

crock, 107 n.
crocodile tears, 369.
crois, 350.
croon, 58, 149 n.
cropper, 56.
cross, 129, 349 f.
cross swords, 56.
crow, 367, 368.
crowbar, 367.
crown, 141.
crow over, 57, 366.
crucial, 350.
crucifix, 350.
cruciform, 350.
cruise, 350.
crusade, 350.
crusado, 350.
crux, 350.
cryptograph, 30.
cry wolf, 370.
cuckoo, 366.
cui bono? 217 n.
culverin, 367.
cunning, 135, 289.
cur, 338, 363.
curfew, 270.
curious, 277.
curmudgeon, 338.
currants, 385.
currency, 141.
currish, 365.
curst, 129.
curves, 56, 59.
cut, 63, 334.
cute, 62, 289, 293 f.
cutlash, 335.
cutlass, 334 f.
cycle, 62, 132.
cynic, 382.
cynical, 382.
cynosure, 376, 382 n.

d., 104, 140.
dago, 66.
dahlia, 384.
dainty, 345.
dale, 140.
damask, 384.
dame, 322 f., 348, 370.
damn, 212, 216.

damnation, 257.
dan, 348.
dander, 153.
dandruff, 153.
danger, 349.
dangerous, 307, 349.
Daniel, 155, 375.
daredevil, 190.
darkling, 342.
darn, 304.
daw, 363.
Day, 209.
days, 196.
dead-eye, deadman's eye, 49.
deaf, 369.
dear, 314.
death-marked, 274.
death-practised, 274.
debased, 288.
decease, 302.
deceased, 300.
deceitful, 307.
deceivable, 276.
deceive, 96.
deck, 49.
deem, 249.
deemster, 249.
deer, 249, 342.
defaulter, 305.
degraded, 288.
deliberate, 140.
delightful, 313.
demesne, 348.
demijohn, 387.
demon, 152, 158.
Dempster, 249.
denizen, 194.
depart, 302.
depend, 11.
depraved, 307.
deputation, 14.
derrick, 383.
derring-do, 118.
desire, 60.
detach, 153.
devil, 156 ff., 252, **374.**
devil-may-care, 188.
devotee, 290.
diagnosis, 101.

diamond, 137.
dictum, 99.
dignity, 345.
diplomacy, 289.
dipsomaniac, 306.
directly, 292 f.
Dirne, *Ger.*, 286.
dirty, 306.
disabuse, 213.
disappear, 303.
disaster, 33, 282, 303, 352.
disease, 248, 303, 307.
disgusting, 314 f.
dispensation, 216.
dissolute, 307.
dissolution, 302.
distemper, 31 f.
distort, 46, 151, 306.
distressful, 276.
distressing, 314.
disturb, 10 n.
Dives, 374.
divide, 25.
dividers, 102 f.
divine, 313.
divisor, 102 f.
divorce, 46.
doc, 63.
doctor, 134.
doctrine, 249.
dodo, 108, 363.
do for, 303.
dog, 363.
dogged, 365.
doggerel, 65.
dog-grass, 334.
dog-Latin, 65.
dog-logic, 65.
dog-rose, 364.
dogs, 367.
dogwhip, 330.
dold, 364.
dollar, 140.
dolt, 364.
-dom, 179, 187.
domain, 348.
domestic, 299.
dominant, 348.
dominate, 348.
domination, 348.

domine, 324, 348.
domineer, 348.
Dominican, 348 f.
dominie, 348.
dominion, 348.
domino, 348.
dominos, 349.
don, 322 f., 348.
donjon, 348.
donjon-keep, 348.
Don Juan, 375.
do-nothing, 190.
don't-ee, 203.
don't speak of it, 302.
doom, 179, 187, 249.
doomsman, 249.
door, 339.
dote, 250, 363.
dotterel, 363.
double a cape, 216.
doubtful, 276.
doubting Thomas, 374.
dough, 210.
dove, 130, 346, 369.
down, *adv.*, 63, 64, 107.
down, *n.*, 64.
downright, 279.
dragon, 340.
drake, 64, 340 f.
dramatis personae, 269.
Drawcansir, 373.
drawers, 305.
draw the long bow, 306.
dray, 131.
dreadful, 276, 314.
dreadnaught, 190.
dredge, 131.
drench, 281.
drill, 12.
drink like a fish, 362.
driver, 271.
drone, 363.
druid, 142.
drunkard, 141, 360, 368 n.
drunken, 277, 307.
drunkenness, 306.
Dryasdust, 375.
duck, 363.
dudgeon, 208.
duet, 52.

duke, 145.
Dulcinea, 375.
dum, 304.
dumb as an oyster, 362.
dumbfounded, 310.
dump, 141.
dun, 107.
dunce, 373 f.
dungeon, 348.
durance, 216.
dust in one's eyes, to throw, 335.
dustman, 178.
duties, 253.

-e, 201.
eagle, 130.
earl, 144 f.
earn . . . salt, 60.
earthen, 203.
eat, 173 n., 281.
eatable, 187.
eccentric, 32.
eculeus, *L.*, 367.
-ed (-d, -t), 182.
Edda, 107.
edible, 187.
editorial, 254.
education, 231 f., 239.
effect, 236.
effluvium, 306.
eft, 198.
e.g., 105.
egregious, 11.
-el, 136 n.
elder, -est, 199, 200.
El Dorado, 381.
electric, 293 f.
electricity, 294.
electro-, 294.
electrocute, 293 f.
electrocution, 294.
electrolier, 294 n.
electrolysis, 294.
electro-physics, 294.
elegant, 277.
element, 36.
elemental, 37.
elementary, 36.
elephantine, 365.

INDEX OF WORDS 417

elevator, 271.
elixir, 108.
-els, 214 n.
'em, 202.
emancipist, 305.
embankment, 318.
embonpoint, 189.
emerald, 137.
emotion, 10 n.
emporium, 134.
empty, *v.*, 279.
-en, *adj.*, 203.
-en, *causative*, 281.
-en, *fem.*, 204.
-en, *participial*, 182, 203.
-en, *plural*, 182.
enchant, 248.
enchanter, 142.
enchanting, 313.
enchantment, 257.
end, 302, 342.
endlong, 342.
energy, 8.
engage, 280.
engine, 131, 223, 251.
engineer, 271, 294 n., 296.
England, 83 n.
English, 83.
English walnut, 340.
enkindle, 10 f.
enrolled, 60.
ensign, 359.
entail, 45.
enthusiasm, 290.
enthusiastic, 290.
entrancing, 313.
envy, 156.
ephthianura, 50.
epic, 249.
epicurean, 382.
episcopal, 44.
epos, 249.
equanimity, 38.
-er, *comparative*, 179, 201.
-er, *n.*, 153, 293.
erm, 358.
errata, 99.
erring, 291.
erus, *L.*, 323.

-es, *genitive* and *adv.*, 182, 196 ff., 343.
-es, *plural*, 182, 202.
-es, 3. *personai ending*, 182.
-es, 2. *pers'l ending*, 180.
escheator, 288.
essen, *Ger.*, 276 n., 354.
essence, 37.
-est, *superlative*, 179, 200.
-est, 2. *pers'l ending*, 180.
estate, 235.
etc., 105.
etymology, 230.
euphemism, 117 n., 301 f.
euphony, 117 n.
event, 240.
ever so, 316.
everybody, 188.
evet, 198.
exactly so, 310.
exam, 61.
ex cathedra, 103.
excellency, 258.
excesses, 305.
exclusive, 104.
execute, 293, 305.
execution, 293.
executioner, 293.
executive, 293.
executor, 293.
exempli gratia, 105.
exercised, 216.
exist, 239.
exorcise, 156.
exorcist, 142.
ex parte, 102.
expedite, 60.
expedition, 60.
expire, 302.
expiree, 305.
explode, 223.
expression, 150.
extempore, 189.
extravagantly, 315.
extremely, 315.
ey, 65, 66 n.

fable, 62, 249.
fact, 236 f., 253.

factor, 134.
factory, 134.
factotum, 71.
fain, 210.
fair play, 57.
fairy tale, 306.
falcon, 164, 362.
fall, *n.*, 253.
fall, *v.*, 302.
falsehood, 306.
falsetto, 51.
familiar, 175.
familiarity, 175.
fanatic, 290.
far, 200.
farmer, 285.
farmstead, 207.
farther, 17 n., 200.
farthing, 140.
fast, *adj.* and *adv.*, 198, 307 f., 336.
-fast, 336.
faste, 308.
fatal, 303.
fate, 249.
father, 163, 227.
fault, 305.
favete linguis, 302.
favor, 214.
feather, in high, 57.
feather, white, 57.
feature, 151.
fee, 165.
feed, 225.
feeling, 275.
fell, *v. trans.*, 281.
fellow, 287, 299 n., 327
fellowship, 287.
felo de se, 303.
fence, 56, 61.
'fess, 63.
fetching, 313 n.
feu, 'late,' *Fr.*, 302.
fez, 384.
fiasco, 58.
fib, 62, 306.
fibble-fabble, 62.
fidus Achates, 375.
figure, 8, 52, 95.
figurine, 52.

2 E

418   INDEX OF WORDS

filius, *L.*, 160.
finale, 51.
fine, 313, 315.
fine, in, 206 f.
finely, 315.
finish, 303.
finnan haddie, 385.
fire, *v.*, 11, 60, 243.
fire-dogs, 367.
first, 200.
first-rate, 313.
fish, 163, 165, 336, 362.
fisherman, 178 f., 330.
fish story, 306.
fisnomy, 62.
fist, 224.
flabbergast, 74, 310.
flannels, 305.
flatlong, 342.
flea in his ear, 368.
fletcher, 209.
flexure, 96.
float, 281.
floor, *v.*, 74.
florin, 141.
flotilla, 107.
fly, *n.*, 51, 367.
fly, *v.*, 281.
focus, 249.
foliage, 338.
folio, 99, 102.
folk-etymology, 331.
folk(s), 25.
follow-me-lads, 190.
folly-fallen, 274.
fond, 250.
fonned, 250.
fonnen, 250.
fool, 298, 306.
foolish, 307.
foolish-compounded, 274.
foot, 202.
fop, 66 n.
for-, 151.
forbid, 151.
force, 113, 259.
foregone conclusion, 216.
foremost, 342 f.
forget-me-not, 190.
forlorn hope, 227.

forms, 290.
forth, 200.
forthright, 188.
fortune, 249.
foul play, 57.
founder, 49.
fourth, 140.
fox, 129, 204, 362, 371.
foxy, 175, 365, 371.
Frankenstein, 377.
fraternal, 159.
frau, 326 n.
free rein, 306.
Frenchified, 380.
French of Norfolk, 60, 332.
fressen, *Ger.*, 276, 354.
fret, ' adorn,' 276 n.
fret, ' consume,' 11, 276.
fretful, 276.
fret-saw, 276 n.
fret-work, 276 n.
Freyja, 326 n.
Freyr, 326 n.
friend, 330.
friendship, 330.
frightful, 314.
fro, 199.
front, 11.
froward, 154.
fry, 225, 295.
fuchsia, 384.
-ful, 276.
full, *adv.*, 199.
full-acorned, 274.
full tilt, 58.
further, 18 n., 200.
fustian, 67, 384.

Gad, 34 n., 304.
gage, 280 n.
gainsay, 29, 215.
gait, 207.
gala, 355.
gale, 355.
gallant, 355.
gallop, 281.
game, 282.
gargle, 173 n.
gargoyle, 173 n.
garlic, 210.

gar-pike, 210.
gas, 51, 252.
gasconade, 380.
gate, 207.
gawk, 366.
gear, 236.
geewhillikens, 304.
geewhiz, 304.
gem, 137.
general, 254.
generally speaking, 103 f.
generate, 223.
generous, 327.
genteel, 350.
gentile, 350.
gentle, 326 f., 350, 362.
gentleman, 322, 325 ff.
genus, 223.
gerrymander, 68 f.
gesture, 150.
get, 237.
get-at-able, 189.
ghost, 248.
ghostly, 212.
gill, 61.
Gillian, 61.
gillyflower, 338.
gin, 61, 384.
ginger, 133.
gingiver, 133.
gladsome, 135.
glass, 153, 255.
glasses, 254.
glaze, 153.
glen, 107.
gloaming, 149.
glome, 149.
gloom, 149, 153.
gloomy, 149.
glorious, 313.
glow, 149, 153.
go, 237 ; go at, 59.
go-ahead-itive-ness, 189.
go-between, 190.
goat, 165.
Godfrey, 304.
gold, 136 n.
golden, 203.
golly, 304.
gone, 300.

INDEX OF WORDS 419

good and ready, 315.
good-for-nothing, 298 n.
good-natured, 288 n.
goodness, 304.
Good Samaritan, 374.
goods, 249.
goody goody, 173.
goose, 363.
gore, 'triangular piece,' 210.
gore, 'blood,' 210.
gore, v., 210.
gorge, Fr., 305.
gorgeous, 313.
gorgonize, 368, 379.
gorry, 304.
gosh, 34 n., 304.
Goth, 379.
Gothamite, 66.
grab, 138.
Gradgrind, 375.
grain, 135.
gramarye, 119.
grampus, 362.
grand, 313.
grandee, 107.
grape, 138.
-graph, 30.
grapple, 138.
grass, 334.
grease, 346.
greenhorn, 65.
grief, 94.
gris amber, 346.
grit, 69 f.
grocer, 133, 293.
grow, 237, 281.
Grundy, Mrs., 375.
guard, 60, 271.
guest, 163, 345.
guileless, 288.
guinea, 141.
gull, 363, 365.
gums, 255.
gurgulio, L., 173 n.
guy, 378.
gypsy, 380.

habeas corpus, 46.
habitable, 187.

hack, 61.
had, *inflection*, 183 f.
had better, etc., 198, 205 f.
haddock, 385.
hag, 331, 360.
haggard, 'gaunt,' 360.
haggard, 'hawk,' 360.
hagged, 360.
haggle, 331.
half-, 187.
hallelujah, 108.
hallow, 207.
Hallowe'en, 207.
hamlet, 143.
hand, 211, 230, 239.
handicraft, 211.
handiwork, 211.
handkerchief, 270 f.
handsome, 135.
hang, hanged, hung, 357.
hangdog, 190.
hansom, 131.
harbor, 49.
hard, 141 n., 368 n.
hard-favored, 214.
hardly, 311.
Harpies, 154.
harpoon, 154.
Harris, Mrs., 375.
harvey, 379.
harveyize, 379.
hateful, 276, 314.
hath, 206.
hatred, 207.
hautboy, 52.
have, 182 ff., 205 f. See had, hath.
hawk, n., 331.
hawk, v., 366.
hawker, 331.
hazard, 57.
he, 62, 202, 386.
head, 261 ff.
head-flaw, 49.
headlong, 342.
head man, 274.
headsman, 274.
headway, 49.
heap, 227.
heart-struck, 277.

heart-whole, 274.
heart-wished, 274.
heave, heaved, hove, 357.
heavenly, 313.
heavenward, 180.
hector, n. and v., 373.
hedge, 360.
hell-hated, 274.
helm, 49.
help, 299.
hem, *pron.*, 202.
hemiptera, 51.
hen, 311.
hence, 197.
henceforth, 188.
hennes, 197.
henpeck, 366.
hent, 250.
here, *pron.*, 202.
hereabouts, 197 n.
hermetically, 384.
he's, 62.
hiccough, 332.
hicket, 332.
hickup, 332.
hicock, 332.
hideous, 151.
higgledy-piggledy, 74.
high, 198.
highness, 258.
himself, 188.
hint, 250.
hipps, 62.
hire, *pron.*, 202.
his, 61.
hit or miss, 74, 190.
hoax, 51, 70, 189.
hocus, 189.
hocus pocus, 51, 70, 189.
hodman, 178.
hoggish, 365.
holdback, 190.
holdfast, 190.
holey, 49.
Holiness, his, 258.
hollow, 282.
holocaust, 136.
holy dollar, 49, 141.
Holy Ghost, 212.
holystones, 49.

420 INDEX OF WORDS

home, 143 f., 227.
homelike, 185.
homely, 186.
homestead, 207.
hominy, 109.
honesty, 252.
honey, 298.
honor, 273.
honorable, 273.
-hood, 187.
hook or crook, 74.
Hoosier, 297.
horoscope, 34.
horrible, 314.
horrid, 314 f.
horridly, 314.
horse, 331, 364 f., 367.
horse-car, 271.
hostile, 345.
hostler, 331.
hound, 363.
hound, v., 365.
hove, 357.
hue and cry, 209, 216.
hug the shore, 216.
hug-me-tight, 190.
human, 356.
humane, 356.
humor, 30 ff., 129, 248 n.
humorous, 32.
hung, 357.
hussar, 109.
hussy, 286.
hustle, 108.
Hyde Park, 318.
hyena, 352.
hypnotism, 386.
hypo, 62.
hyps. *See* hipps.

i-, 211.
-ic, 187.
-ical, 187.
I'd, 62, 205.
idea, 156.
idiot, 306.
idol, 156.
i.e., 105.
ignoramus, 58.
ill, 129, 303.

ill-conditioned, 212.
ill-favored, 214.
ill-humored, 129.
illicit, 291.
ill-tempered, 129.
imaginary, 275.
immediately, 293.
immense, 313.
immoral, 242.
immorality, 305.
impassibility, 40.
impassive, 39 f.
impeachment, 216.
impetus, 13.
impolite, 307.
imprimis, 102 n.
improbity, 59.
imputation, 14.
inaccurate, 307.
in articulo mortis, 103.
in bank, 351.
incantation, 142, 248.
incentive, 11.
inclusive, 104.
incog, 63.
India rubber, 255.
indigestion, 306.
indiscretion, 307.
indomitable, 137.
inertia, 99.
infinite, 315.
infinitely, 315.
influence, 33 f.
-ing, 173, 180, 182, 187, 192.
injunction, 46.
injury, 245, 303.
ink, 136.
ink eraser, 274.
ink stain, 274.
innocent, 288.
innuendo, 99, 102.
insane, 307.
insect, 363.
inside out, 188.
insides, 306.
insignia, 359.
insincere, 307.
insinuate, 365.
instantly, 293.

instead of, 207.
instigation, 11.
insult, 59.
insurance, 178.
intemperate, 307.
intenible, 275.
interim, 99.
intestines, 306.
intoxication, 306.
invidious, 156.
inwards, 306.
iota, 311.
irons, 254.
is, 238, 240.
-ise, 379.
Isegrim, 370.
-ish, 186 f., 365.
Ishmael, 374.
isinglass, 108.
it, 170.
italics, 384.
item, 99, 102.
iteration, 170.
itinerary, 170.
iwis, 119.
-ize, 379.

jack, 61 n., 154, 386 f.
jackanapes, 387.
jackass, 386.
jacket, 153 f.
jack-in-the-box, 387.
jack-in-the-pulpit, 387.
jackknife, 387.
jack-of-all-trades, 71.
jackscrew, 387.
jackstraws, 387.
Jack Tar, 387.
jacky, 387.
jade, 137.
Jamestown weed, 256.
Japan, 255, 384.
java, 255, 384.
jay, 362.
Jeames, 387.
Jebusite, 375 n.
jehu, 375.
jenny, 61 n., 386.
jeopardize, 189.
jeopardy, 70, 189.

INDEX OF WORDS

jeremiad, 382.
jersey, 255, 384.
Jersey justice, 379 n.
Jerusalem, 304.
Jerusalem artichoke, 340.
Jerusalem crickets, 304.
jet, 137, 385.
Jew, 379.
jewel, 137.
Jew's work, 382.
Jezebel, 374.
jimmy, 61 n., 386.
jimson weed, 256.
jingo, 71.
Job, 374.
Johnny-jump-up, 190.
Joseph, 374.
jot, 311.
jovial, 31.
Judas, 373, 376.
Judas kiss, 373.
juggler, 142.
jump on, 59.
juncture, 216.
Jungles, 66 n.
Juno, 376.
junta, 107.
jupartie, 189.
just, 214.
just so, 310.
justicer, 46.
justiciar, 46.
justiciary, 46.
justify, 214.

Kaffirs, 66 n.
kaiser, 373 n.
kangaroo, 109.
kaser, 373 n.
keen, 289.
kerchief, 270.
kernel, 135.
kersey, 338.
kerseymere, 338.
kesar, 373 n.
kicker, 59.
kickshaws, 189.
kidney, 63.
kill, 302.
killjoy, 190.

kilo, 61.
kind, 330.
kindly, 330.
kindness, 330.
kindred, 207.
kingdom, 179.
king's evil, 384.
kink, 108.
kiss-me-quick, 190.
knapsack, 108.
knave, 285 f., 299.
knee, 163.
knickerbockers, 305.
knifeblade, 330.
knight errant, 291.
knock-out, 56.
knowing, 289.
kyrie, 72.
Kyrie eleison, 72.

lackadaisical, 188.
lack-a-day, 188.
lady, 210, 317, 322, 324 f., 327 f.
lamb, 363.
lame, 364.
landau, 131, 384.
Land of Nod, 376.
landscape, 109.
lane, 319, 321.
language, 2.
lanyard, 335.
Laodicean, 385.
lapse, 305.
large, 25.
last, 302.
latakia, 384 f.
late, 209 n., 300.
Latimer, 209.
law, 104.
lay, 151, 281.
layman, 245.
lazar, 374.
lazaret, 48.
leaden, 203.
lead pencil, 270.
league, 347.
leal, 353.
lee shore, 49.
leek, 210 n., 311.

leeway, 49.
leg, 61, 304.
legal, 353.
legion, 256.
lenger, -est, 200.
lesson, 249.
let, *n.*, 213.
let, 'hinder,' 209.
let, 'permit,' 209; to let, 275; let's, 180.
level, 140.
lewd, 290.
liard, 368 n.
liberal, 215.
lick, 370.
lie, 151, 281.
lie, *mentiri*, 254, 305 f.
lief, 196.
lien, 347.
-lier, 294 n.
lieu, 207, 339.
lieutenant, 189.
lifeless, 302.
lift, *v.*, 58.
lift, *n.*, 271.
ligament, 347.
like, 15, 179, 185 f.
like, *v.*, 204.
lily, 226.
limb, 304.
linen, 305.
-ling, 187, 342.
lingerie, 305.
lionlike, 365.
lion's share, 370.
liqueur, 248.
liquor, 248.
list, 214.
listless, 214.
lists, 58.
litter-egg, 65.
little, 61.
livelong, 216.
lively, 20, 307.
liver, 225, 295.
livery, 154.
lives, 196.
loaf, 210.
loathsome, 314.
loch, 107.

INDEX OF WORDS

locomotive, 131.
locum tenens, 189.
logic, 46.
loiter, 109.
long, 200.
-long, 342.
long bow, 306.
loo, 61.
look, 151.
loon, 364.
loony, 61, 364.
loosen, 281.
loot, 59.
lord, 210, 325 f.
lordship, 258.
lorimer, 209.
lose, lost, 302.
Lothario, 375.
louis, 141.
loun, 364.
love, 135.
lovelace, 375.
lovelock, 274.
lovely, 135, 313.
lovesick, 274.
low, 198, 288.
lown, 364.
loyal, 353.
lucifer, 177.
Lucretia, 374.
ludi magister, 44 n., 324.
lunatic, 31, 364.
lupus, 367.
lust, 214, 290.
lust-dieted, 279.
lustring, 335.
lutestring, 335.
-ly, 15, 179, 186 f., 199.
Lydford law, 378 f.
lynch, 378.
lyric, 254.

'm, 202.
macadam, 379 n.
macadamize, 379.
macassar, 384.
machiavellian, 382.
machine, 251.
mackintosh, 255, 382.
macrocosm, 247.

mad, 307.
madam, 323.
madding crowd, 216.
madman, 306.
madras, 255, 384.
madrigal, 52.
Mæcenas, 373.
Magdalen, 376.
magic, 141, 382.
magnesia, 385.
magnet, 385.
magnetic, 385.
magnetism, 385.
magnificent, 313.
magpie, 362.
mahogany, 69.
main, 216, 254.
mainland, 254.
maintenant, *Fr.*, 292 n.
maize, 136.
Majesty, his, 258.
makeshift, 190.
make way with, 302.
mammet, 377.
man, 327, 341.
-man, 178 f.
mandrake, 340 f.
manganese, 385 n.
maniac, 306.
manna, 108.
mannish, 365.
mansion, 249.
manual, 343.
mar, 211.
marching order, 60.
mare, 296.
mariage de convenance, 103.
mark, God save the, 302.
mark, to hit the, 57.
marline, 109.
marquess, 145.
marsh, 211.
marshal, 295 f., 320.
martinet, 155.
mass play, 56.
master, 324.
mastheaded, 192.
masticate, 354.
mate, 287.

mater, *L.*, 160.
matter, 236.
matter-of-fact, 188.
mattock, 107 n.
maudlin, 376.
maumet, 377.
meander, 378.
meantime, 188.
meanwhile, 188.
meat, 216, 249.
Mecca, 376.
Mediterranean, 254.
medium, 252.
meerschaum, 254.
melancholia, 31 n.
melancholy, 30 f.
mellifluous, 128.
memorandum, 99, 102.
ménage, 191.
mentor, 373.
mercenary, 307.
merchant, 287.
merci, *Fr.*, 222.
mercurial, 31.
meridian, 254.
mermaid, 211.
mesel, 364 n.
mesmerism, 386.
Messiah, 108.
-mest, 200, 343.
metal, 355 f.
metaphysical, 46.
metaphysics, 46.
mete, 209.
Methusaleh, 374.
mettle, 355 f.
mew up, 216.
microcosm, 247.
mid, 61.
middy, 61.
might and main, 216.
mile, 202.
milkman, 178.
mill, 140.
milliner, 385.
milord, 326 n.
minimum, 99.
minister, 248, 296.
minster, 44.
mint, 139 f.

INDEX OF WORDS 423

mischance, 303.
misconduct, 305.
miscreant, 245.
misdemeanor, 305.
miserable, 314.
misfortune, 303.
misguided, 305.
mishmash, 332.
misrepresentation, 306.
miss, 61.
Miss, 322, 325.
missing, 302.
misstatement, 306.
Mister, 322, 324.
mistress, 324.
mite, 311.
mob, 61 ff.
moccasin, 109.
mocha, 255, 384.
molasses, 128.
mole, 363.
Moll, 63.
monarchy, 44.
monastery, 44.
money, 139 f.
moneyer, 293.
monitor, 139.
monk, 'monachus,' 44, 93.
monk, 'monkey,' 61.
monkey, 363.
monkey with, 365.
monologue, 44.
monotone, 44.
monstrous, 314.
moo, 3.
moor, 212.
mop, 107 n.
mope, 225.
moral, 242.
morass, 211.
morbid, 39 n.
morocco, 384.
morris dance, 382.
mortal, 303.
mortgage, 45.
mortmain, 45.
Mosaic, 382.
mosaic, 382.
most, 201.

-most, 343.
mother, 161, 227.
motoneer, 294 n.
motorman, 178.
mountebank, 352.
mousing, 366.
Mr., 324 f.
Mrs., 324 f.
Mrs. Grundy, 375.
Mrs. Harris, 375.
much, 312.
mule, 362, 367.
mulish, 365.
murmur, 173, 346.
muslin, 384.
mutande, *Ital.*, 304.
myrmidons, 379.
myth, 249.

nadder, 198.
nagent, 197.
nankeen, 109.
napoleon, 141.
napple, 197.
napron, 198.
nasty, 314.
natural, 254.
natural spirits, 33.
naturally, 149.
naught, 298, 311.
naughty, 298.
nauseous, 315.
navy, 25, 311.
near, -er, 17 n., 200.
neck, 305.
necromancer, 141.
nedes, needes, 196.
ne'er-do-well, 190.
neger, 357 n.
negro, 149, 356 f.
neighbor-stained, 274.
nephew, 166.
nequam, *L.*, 298 n.
nerve, 213.
nervous, 213.
-ness, 186 f.
nest, 200.
Nestor, 373.
nethermost, 17 n., 200 f., 342 f.

never, 311.
never so, 316.
newmarket, 384.
newspaper, 253.
newt, 197.
next, 200.
ney, 66 n.
nice, 54, 277, 297 f., 314 f.
nick of time, 292 n.
nig, 207.
nigger, 357 n.
nigger, 66, 356 f.
nigh, 200.
night-horse, 211.
nightmare, 211.
nights, 196.
nil, 204.
Nimrod, 375.
Nimshi, 375.
nincompoop, 51, 67, 70.
nip and tuck, 74.
no, 311.
no end, 315.
no kind (sort) of, 298 n.
no more, 302.
noble, 327.
nobody, 188, 298 n.
nonce, 197.
non compos mentis, 51, 67, 70.
non-con, 62.
non obstante, 104 n.
nonplus, 103.
noon, 44.
Norn, 107.
nosethril, 12.
nostril, 12.
nostrum, 99, 101.
not, 311 f.
note, 141.
notemuge, 133.
notwithstanding, 104 n.
nowheres, 197 n.
nun, 44, 93.
nut, 133.
nutmeg, 133.

ob., 104.
obiit, *L.*, 303.
obituary, 303.

INDEX OF WORDS

oboe, 52.
Odd's, 304.
Odd's bodkins, 304.
Odd's my life, 304.
Odd's pitikins, 304.
odium, 273.
of course, 311.
offence, 305.
offhand, 188.
officious, 253.
oftentimes, 188.
ogre, 380.
oh, 3.
ohm, 384.
old, -er, -est, 152, 199.
old hand, 305.
old man, 325.
omen, 282.
on, 215.
once, 196 f.
ones, 196.
oolong, 255, 384.
opera, 51.
operations, 63 n.
operetta, 51.
opinion, 272 f.
opposal, 64.
oppose, 64.
-or, 153.
orphan, 211.
orrery, 383.
-osity, 193.
oust, 197.
out, 347 f.
out-, 187.
outdoor, 188.
outer, 347.
out-Herod, 378.
outlaw, 188.
outrageous, 314.
outrance, 347 f.
outskirts, 318.
overcrow, 57, 366.
overlord, 188.
owlish, 365.
oyster, 311.

pad, 61.
Paddy, 66.
pain, 245.

painful, 276.
painter, 340.
palace, 376.
pall, 63.
pallisadoes, 63 n.
palming, 63.
pan-, 342.
pandar, 373.
pander, 373, 377.
panic, 382.
pantere, 340.
panther, 339 f.
pantry, 342.
papa, 44.
paper, 136, 245, 253.
par, 74.
paralyze, 310.
parchment, 136.
parfet, -fit, 333.
parish council, 271.
park, 319.
parole, 71.
paroquet, 129 f.
parrot, 129, 363.
parry, 56.
parsley, 138.
parson, 268 f.
part, 236.
Parthian shot, 380.
pas, *Fr.*, 312.
pasquinade, 374 f.
pass away, 300, 302.
passion, 39, 41, 47.
passionately, 315.
passive, 39 f.
pasteboard, 69.
past master, 324.
pate, 225.
patent, 39.
pathetic, 40.
pathos, 40.
patriarch, 318.
patron, 318.
Paul Pry, 375.
pauper, 155.
pawn, 296 n.
pay the scot, or shot, 140.
pea, 132, 139.
pea-jacket, 153.
peach, 138.

pear, 138.
pearl, 137.
pearline, 203 n.
peculiar, 175.
peculiarity, 175.
pedagogue, 44 n.
peevish, 149, 155.
pelican, 369.
pen, 13, 136, 269 f.
pencil, 270.
penny, 140.
pennyroyal, 340.
penthouse, 337.
pentis, 337.
pepper, 133.
per cent, 61, 140.
perfect, 313, 315, 333.
perfectly, 315.
perfidious, 307.
perfidious Albion, 380.
periwinkle, plant, 360.
periwinkle, shell, 360.
perpendicular, 69.
persely, 138.
persil, 138.
person, 54, 268 f., 326.
perspiration, 306.
pert, 61.
pese, 139.
Peter, 138.
peter out, 56.
petition, 13.
petrel, 130.
petrified, 310.
petticoat, 305.
petulant, 13.
phaeton, 222 f., 383.
pheasant, 129, 385.
phiz, 62.
phlegm, 30.
phlegmatic, 31.
phœnix, 369.
'phone, 62.
phonograph, 30 n.
phosphorus, 30.
photo-, 30.
photograph, 29 f.
phthisis, 50.
physical, 239.
physician, 117 n.

INDEX OF WORDS

physics, 117 n.
physiology, 117 n., 239.
piano, 51, 61.
piazza, 244.
piccolo, 51.
pickers and stealers, 69.
Pickwickian, 382.
picture, 244.
pig, 362.
pigeon, 130, 363.
piggish, 365.
pike, 62.
pillar, 295.
pilot, 149.
pincers, 342.
pinchbeck, 377.
pinchers, 342.
pin-money, 60.
pion, 290.
pioneer, 296.
pipe, 252.
piracy, 289.
pirate, 291.
piratical, 49.
piscatorial, 165.
pistol, 385.
pitiful, 276.
place, 94, 239, 244, 319.
planet, 254.
platonic, 382.
platypus, 49.
plausible, 291.
play, 250 f.
please, 204.
plenipo, 63.
plight, 253.
pluck, 363.
plum, 138.
pocket, 249.
pocket handkerchief, 270.
pocket pistol, 69.
poet, 248.
point, 96, 312.
poison, 96.
poke, 249.
polite, 282.
polka, 109.
polonaise, 255, 384.
pompous, 278.
ponder, 140.

poor, 155.
pope, 44, 93.
pore-blind, 342.
port, 93.
port duties, 253.
portly, 225.
pose, 64.
poser, 64.
position, 235.
possum, 62.
post, 295.
post mortem, 102, 303.
post obit, 303.
posture, 235.
potato, 138.
pother, 225.
pound, *n.*, 140, 202.
pound, *v.*, 119 n.
power, 259 ff.
powerful, 314.
pozz, 62.
pp., 104.
practice, 253.
practise, 274.
præmunire, 71.
precious, 222.
precocious, 11.
predicament, 47, 253.
predominant, 34.
preliminaries, 63 n.
premium, 102.
presbyter, 44.
presently, 292 f.
pretty, 135.
priest, 44.
priestcraft, 290.
prime of life, 337.
primerole, 337.
primrose, 337.
prince, 317 f.
prison, 94.
prithee, 203.
private, 254.
privateering, 289.
probity, 59.
prof, 63.
professor, 318.
profound, 356.
profoundly, 310.
Promised Land, 381.

pronunciamento, 107.
propaganda, 71.
property, 8.
prophet, 142.
prophylaxis, 101.
propriety, 252.
pros and cons, 62.
prove, 280 f.
provisions, 256.
pruning hook, 274.
pshaw, 4.
pub, 62.
publican, 288.
puliall royal, 340.
pump, 251.
pun, 119.
Punic faith, 380.
puppy, 363.
purblind, 341 f., 364.
Puritan, 297.
purlieu, 339.
purpose, on, 215.
put, *n.*, 63.
put away, 303.
putative, 14.
puzzle, 64.
pyro, 62.

quaint, 277 f.
Quaker, 297.
quality, 35.
quantity, 35.
quartet(te), 52.
quean, 286.
queen, 286.
quench, 281.
quibble, 35 n.
quick, 198.
quiddity, 35.
quillet, 35 n.
quinine, 203 n.
quinsy, 64.
quintessence, 37.
quip, 35 n., 119 n.
Quirites, *L.*, 227.
quirk, 119 n.
quite so, 310.
quixotic, 382.

raccoon, 62.
rag, 67.

INDEX OF WORDS

ragamuffin, 67.
railroad, v., 187.
raise, 156.
raise Cain, 374.
rake, n. and v., 337.
rakehell, 337.
rakel, 337.
ram, 366 f.
ramrod, 190.
range, 251.
rapid, 308.
rarebit, 331.
rascaille, 288.
rascal, 288, 298.
rash, 291.
rat, v., 365 f.
rate, 240.
ratio, 350.
ration, 350.
rat-tail file, 367.
rattling, 313.
raven, 331.
ravening, 331.
ravishingly, 314.
re-, 187.
read, 214.
reason, 350.
rebel, 253 n.
recalcitrant, 59.
recipe, 99, 101.
reckless, 291, 307.
recognizance, 216.
regard, 14, 232.
regarding, 104 n.
register, 251.
reindeer, 342.
religion, 231 f., 239, 244 f., 252.
religious, 245, 290.
remove, 303.
renegade, 107, 207.
renege, 207.
renig, 207.
rep, 62.
repeat, 13.
reputation, 14, 272 f.
residence, 319.
Residenz, Ger., 249.
respect, 14.
respectable, 292.

restive, 194.
restless, 194.
revel, 253, 291.
Reverence, his, 258.
reverend, 276.
reverent, 276.
revise, 156.
reynard, 370.
rhododendron, 350.
rhyme, 332 f.
rhythm, 333.
rickshaw, 62.
riddance, 216.
riddle, 214.
rien, Fr., 312.
right, 199.
rill, 319.
rime, 332 f.
Rip Van Winkle, 375.
rival, 222.
river, 222.
rivulet, 222, 319.
road, 165, 318, 320.
roadstead, 207.
roar, 156.
robin, 130.
rogue, 298.
romance, 306, 380 f.
Roman firmness, 380.
romantic, 381.
rook, n. and v., 363.
roorback, 375.
root, v., 359.
roquelaure, 383.
rose, 350.
rosemary, 339.
rosmarine, 339.
rotten, 314.
rough-and-ready, 74, 188.
rubber-neck, 255.
rubbers, 255.
ruby, 137.
rude, 307.
rug, 67.
ruin, 303.
rum, 61, 128 f.
rumbullion, 128.
ruminate, 354 f.
run, 207, 281.
run aground, 49.

run counter, 57.
runagate, 207.
rush, 154.
rush the growler, 75.

s., 104, 140.
-s, in nouns, 182.
-s, in verbs, 92 n., 182.
sack, 59.
sackbut, 338.
sage, 38.
sail, 246.
saint, 290, 377.
St. Anthony's fire, 384.
St. Vitus's dance, 384.
sal Atticum, 380.
salaam, 108.
salamander, 69, 369.
salary, 60.
saleable, 187.
saleslady, 318, 322.
salvage, 150.
salvages, 149.
Samson, 374.
sanctified, 290.
sanctimonious, 290.
sand, 70, 335.
sandblind, 335.
sandwich, 256, 383.
sanguine, 31.
sapphire, 137.
Saracen, 374 n.
sardonic, 60.
Satan, 374.
satire, 333 n.
Saturnalia, 59.
saturnine, 31.
satyr, 333 n.
satyr(e), 333 n.
sauterne, 384.
savage, 149.
savvy, 58.
sawhorse, 367.
Sawney, 66.
scald, 364.
scales, 270.
scape, 63.
scarcely, 311.
scene, 246.
school, 44.

INDEX OF WORDS

schoolboy, 330.
scilicet, 105.
scissors, 333 n.
scold, 129.
score, 266.
scorpion, 369.
scot, 140.
scratch, come to the, 56.
scuttle, v., 49.
'sdeath, 304.
searcloth, 333 n.
secure, 278.
security, 97.
sedan chair, 131.
seer, 142.
seigneur, 325.
seisin, 154.
seize, 154.
selectmen, 271.
self-slaughter, 303.
sely, 288 n.
semi-, 187, 335.
seneschal, 295 f., 320.
senior, 322, 325, 353.
señor, 325.
sent up, 305.
separable, 275.
sequelae, 101.
seraph, 108.
sere, 359.
serious, 303.
serpent, 363.
servant, 25, 286, 299.
set, 151, 154, 200, 281.
settle, 303.
seven, 163.
sever, 97.
Shaker, 297.
sham, 63, 65.
shame, 273, 336.
shamefaced, 235 f.
shamefast, 335 f.
shameful, 273, 314.
shamrock, 107.
shan't, 62, 204.
sharp, 289.
sharpen, 281.
shay, 132.
she, 386.
sheep, 363.

sheepish, 365.
shekel, 108.
sherbet, 108.
sherris, 384.
sherry, 384.
shift, 304 f.
shilling, 140.
shilly-shally, 204.
ship, v., 49.
shipman, 178.
shipwreck, 49.
shirt, 305, 345.
shop, 134.
shoplifter, 58 n.
short, 305.
shot, 140.
shrapnel, 383.
shrew, 129.
shrewd, 129.
shuffling, 63.
shut . . . to, 360.
Shylock, 373.
sick, 303 n.
sick bay, 49.
sidelong, 342.
siesta, 108.
signor, 322, 325.
silent majority, 302.
silly, 288.
Simon Pure, 375.
simony, 382.
simple, 288.
simple-answered, 274.
simply, 315.
since, 197.
sine die, 103.
sinew, 213 n.
singe, 281.
singsong, 190.
sink or swim, 74.
sir, 322, 325, 331, 353.
sire, 323, 325, 353.
sirloin, 331.
sirrah, 354.
sir-ree, 354.
sit, 151, 200, 281.
sithenes, sithence, 197.
situation, 235.
six, 163 f.
sizar, 64.

size, 64.
skald, 107.
skirt, n., 305, 345.
skirt, v., 216.
skunk, 363.
sky, 107.
sky-pilot, 69.
slantin', 69.
slantindicular, 69.
slave, 380.
sleepy, 277.
slender, 109.
'slife, 304.
sling, 243.
slip, 305.
slogan, 107.
slough, 107 n.
slow, 198, 332.
slowworm, 332.
slubber, 225.
slug, 141.
sluggard, 141.
sly, 289, 362.
smallclothes, 305.
smalls, 62.
smart, 289.
smock, 304.
smug, 225.
snake, 298, 363.
sneaking fondness, 216.
snow, 164.
so, 310.
sofa, 108.
soft impeachment, 216.
soldier, 140.
sole, 12.
solecism, 60.
solemn, 278.
solemnity, 278.
solemnize, 278.
Solomon, 155, 374.
Solon, 155, 373.
-some, 135.
some-place, 188 n.
somewhat, 188.
somewhere, 188.
somewheres, 197 n.
son, 160.
soon, 198, 292.
sooth, 142.

428 INDEX OF WORDS

soothsayer, 142.
sophist, 289.
soprano, 51.
sorehead, 362 n.
sorrel, *adj.*, 359.
sorrel, *n.*, 359.
sortilege, 141.
sot, 66 n., 306.
sound, *adv.*, 198.
sound in, 214.
sour, 359.
sovereign, 141.
sow, 352.
sow-thistle, 364.
space, 153.
Spain, castles in, 381 f.
span, 153.
spaniel, 385.
sparrow grass, 334.
spasm, 153.
spasmodic, 153.
spatter, 279.
specie, 133.
species, 133.
specs, 62.
speculations, 63 n.
speed, 214.
spencer, 256, 383.
spendthrift, 190.
spice, 133.
spider, 367.
spill, 249.
spin, 153.
spinning jenny, 61 n., 386.
spirit, 33 n.
spiritual wickedness in high places, 258.
spit, 279.
splendid, 313.
spoil, 11.
sport, 62, 307.
spot, 292 n.
spout, 295.
spread-eagle, 368.
sprinkle, 279.
spur, 11.
square, 319.
squash, *n.*, 139, 360.
squash, *v.*, 139, 360.
squaw, 109.

squeeze, 342.
squinancy, 64.
squire, 63, 266.
squire of dames, 375.
-st (-est), 200 f.
stand, 207, 239 f., 281, 341.
standard, 341.
stanza, 51.
star, 352.
stars and garters, 34.
start in, 56.
starvation, 192.
state, 235.
status, 235.
stead, *n.* and *v.*, 207.
steer clear of, 49.
stellar, 352.
stellate, 352.
stellify, 352.
stench, 306.
Stentor, 382.
stentorian, 382.
step-, 211.
stepchild, 211.
stepfather, 211.
stepmother, 211.
stepson, 211.
-ster, 209.
steward, 296.
Stewart, 296.
stick, 249.
stien, 211.
still, 198.
stimulus, 99.
stirrup, 210.
stocks, on the, 56.
Stoic, 37.
stoical, 39, 382.
stoicism, 39, 382.
stone, *n.*, 252, 330.
stone, *pl.*, 202.
stool pigeon, 363.
store, 134.
stove, 109.
straightforward, 279.
Stratford French, 60.
straw, 71.
street, 93, 246, 318, 321.
street Arab, 380.

strenger, -est, 200.
strengthen, 281.
strong, 200.
stunning, 313.
stupefied, 310.
stupendous, 313.
sty, *n.* and *v.*, 211.
style, 15, 333 n.
sublime, 313.
Sublime Porte, 71.
suborn, 208.
subpœna, 46, 103.
success, 253.
sugar, 128.
suggestion, 253.
suicide, 303.
sullen, 12.
summer beam, 367.
Sumner, 209.
sumpter, 367.
superb, 277, 313.
superfluous, 279.
superior, 99.
superlatively, 314 f.
support, 295.
supreme, 356.
sur-, 331.
sur le champ, 292 n.
sure, 278, 311.
surely, 311.
surety, 97, 278.
surfeit, 306.
surloin, 331.
surprise, 310.
surrey, 256, 384.
sweat, 306.
sweet, 314.
sweetmeat, 249.
sweets, 62.
swift, 308.
swine, 352.
swing, 69.
syllable, 343.
sylvan, 149.
Sylvanus, 149.

tabernacle, 351.
taboo, 109.
tack, 153.
tailor, 45.

INDEX OF WORDS

take, 107, 281, 313 n.
taken aback, 49.
taking, 313 n.
tally, 45, 266.
tame, 137.
tanner, 141.
tantalize, 379.
tar, 153.
taradiddle, 306.
tarantula, 339.
tarnal, 61 n.
tart, 153.
tartar, 358.
Tartar, 358, 379 f.
Tartuffe, 375.
Tatar, 358, 379.
tatter, 153.
tattoo, 'drum-beat,' 360.
tattoo (of the flesh), 360.
tavern, 351.
tawdry, 377.
tea, 109.
tear, 153.
tea-totaller, 332.
tea-tree, 332 n.
teche, 338.
techy, 338.
teetotal, 332.
teetotaller, 332.
teetotum, 332.
telegraph, 30 n., 50.
telephone, 30 n.
telltale, 190.
temper, 32, 129.
temperament, 31 f.
temple, 'part of the head,' 358 f.
temple, 'place of worship,' 358 f.
tenner, 141.
tense, 359.
termagant, 129, 374.
terrace, 319.
terra cotta, 51.
terrible, 282.
terrier, 254.
terror, 151.
Tervagant, 129.
tetter, 153.
texture, 95.

-th, *comparative*, 200 f.
-th, *personal ending*, 92 n.
thank'ee, 203.
that, 202.
the, 202.
thee, 203.
their, 202 f.
them, 202 f.
then, 197.
thence, 197.
thereabouts, 197 n.
thereby, 182.
therefrom, 182.
therein, 188.
thief, 298, 305.
thing, 235 f.
thorough, 213.
thoroughfare, 214.
thorough-lighted, 214.
thoroughly, 213.
thorough-shot, 214.
thoroughwort, 359.
thou, 180.
thrasonical, 382.
thrice, 196 f.
thrill, 11, 314.
throstle, 130.
through, 213.
through and through, 188, 214.
throughout, 188.
throw, 153, 241, 243.
thrush, 130.
thryes, 196.
thug, 246.
thunderstruck, 310.
tick, on, 62.
ticket, 62.
ticket-office, 271.
tide, *v.*, 150.
tidings, 150.
tidy, 384 n.
tighten, 281.
tilt at, 57 f.
times, the, 152.
Timon, 374.
tip-top, 313.
ti-tree, 332 n.
ti-tri, 332 n.
tittle, 311.

tittle-tattle, 332.
to-, 154.
to, 360.
to and fro, 199.
to be let, 275.
to be sure, 311.
to let, 209, 275.
to wit, 156.
toad, 298.
toby, 387.
toe the mark, 56.
Tom, 63.
tomahawk, 109.
tooth and nail, 74, 188.
topical, 381 n.
topography, 381 n.
torsion, 46.
torso, 51.
tort, 46, 151.
tortoise, 347.
Tortugas, 346.
tortuous, 151.
torture, 46, 151.
total, 332.
touch, 338.
touch of nature, 217.
touchy, 338.
toward, 154.
towards, 188, 197 n.
tower, 94.
town, 142 f.
trace, 57.
track, 57.
tram, 271.
transgression, 305, 307.
traps, pack up one's, 56.
treacle, 128, 266 f.
tree, 153.
tremendous, 313.
triantelope, 339.
trice, 216.
trio, 51.
trip up, 57.
trouble, 305.
trough, 153.
trow, 119.
true, tru-th, tru-ly, etc., 9, 315.
truss up your trinkets, 56 n.

INDEX OF WORDS

trusty, 277.
tsar, 373.
tuber, 339.
tuberose, 338 f.
tuberous, 339.
tug, 306.
tuneable, 275.
Turk, 129, 379.
turkey, 129.
turn, 280.
turncoat, 190.
turnstile, 190.
turtle, 'dove,' 346.
turtle, 'tortoise,' 346 f.
tweed, 384.
tweeze, 342.
tweezers, 342.
twice, 196 f.
twicet, 197.
twit, 156.
twitch, 153.
-ty, 187.
tyke, 298, 363.
typo, 62.
tyrant, 248 f.

um, 202.
umbrage, 208.
umpire, 198.
un-, 187, 306.
uncivil, 307.
unclean, 307.
uncomprehensive, 275.
underclothes, 305.
undershot, 188.
undertaker, 252 f.
under way, 49.
underwear, 305.
uneasy, 307.
unexpressive, 275.
unfaithful, 307.
unlicked cub, 370.
unsafe, 307.
unship, 49.
unsophisticated, 289.
untidy, 251.
untoward, 154.
untruthful, 307.
unutterably, 310.
unwelcome, 150.

unwise, 307.
uppermost, 17 n.
up to you, it is, 56.
upwards, 197 n.
Utopian, 381.
utter, 347.
utterance, 347 f.
utterly, 310, 315.

V, 141.
vacuum, 99.
vails, 64.
valet, 286.
valkyrie, 107.
vamoose, 58.
van, 61.
Vandal, 379.
vandalism, 379.
varlet, 286.
varsal, 61 n.
'varsity, 61.
vasa colligere, 56.
vaseline, 203 n.
vassal, 286, 325.
vassalage, 286.
vastly, 314.
vaticination, 290 n.
vehicle, 130.
velocipede, 132 n.
venge, 96.
venison, 282.
ver-, *Ger.*, 151.
veranda, 244.
verdigris, 346.
vernacular, 239.
verse, 44.
very, 25, 315.
veto, 99.
via, 99.
vice, 'fault,' 242, 291, 307, 358.
vice, 'instrument,' 358.
vice-, 358.
vice-president, 358.
vicinity, 318.
victoria, 256, 382.
victory, 25.
vie, 156.
vigorously, 308.
viking, 107, 291.

vile, 291, 307.
villa, 143 n., 319, 321 f.
village, 143.
villain, 284 ff.
villany, 284 f.
vim, 99.
violence, 10 n.
violin, 51 f.
viper, 363.
virago, 129.
virtù, 51, 242.
virtue, 241 f.
visage, 156.
vision, 156.
visnamy, 62.
visor, 153, 156.
vital spirits, 33.
vivacious, 20.
vixen, 129, 204, 362.
viz., 105.
volt, 384.
voltaic, 384.
voyage, 96.
vulpine, 365.

wag, 61.
wage, 280 n.
wager, 45, 280 n.
wages, 45, 280 n.
wag(g)on, 130.
wain, 130.
waist, 305.
walking stick, 274.
wall, 93, 246, 340.
walnut, 340.
Waltham calf, 368.
wan-, 306.
wanted, 305.
wanton, 253, 306 f.
-ward, -wards, 180, 197 n.
warlock, 339.
warp, 243.
was, 239.
washerlady, 322, 326 n.
washerwoman, 326 n.
wassail, 189.
watch and ward, 216.
waterfly, 363.
watt, 384.
wax, 237 n., 305.

INDEX OF WORDS

way, 130, 154, 321.
wayward, 64.
weaken, 281.
wear, 274 f.
weasand, 207.
weather, *v.*, 49.
webster, 209.
wedlock, 207, 248.
weed, 'garment,' 358.
weed, 'plant,' 358.
Weib, *Ger.*, 287, 326 n.
welcome, 150.
welkin, 208.
well-favored, 214.
well-groomed, 56.
Wellingtons, 255 f., 382.
well-to-do, 188.
Welsh, 340.
Welsh rabbit (rarebit), 331.
wench, 286.
were, 239.
werewolf, 152.
whale, 51.
what, 202.
what's what, 35.
wheedle, 67.
wheel, 251.
wherewith, 188.
wherewithal, the, 216.
Whig, 297.
while, 195.
whiles, 196.
whilom, 195.
whilst, 196.
whip, 62.
whit, 346.
white-livered, 295.
whiz, 16.
who, 202.
whopper, 306.

why, 202.
wight, 346.
wigwam, 109.
wildcat financiering, 368.
wild-goose chase, 368.
will, 204.
Will, 63.
willy nilly, 190, 204.
wink, 214 f., 225.
winsome, 135.
winters, 196 n.
Wirrwarr, *Ger.*, 332.
wise, 141, 156.
wist, 156.
wistaria, 384.
wit, wits, 141, 156, 289.
witch, 141.
with, 215.
withers, 215 n.
withhold, 215.
withsay, 29, 215.
withstand, 215.
wizard, 141.
wol, 204.
wolf, 363 f., 370.
wolfish, 365.
wolt, 204.
woman, 287, 326.
womanish, 365.
woman-tired, 366.
wonderful, 313.
won't, 204.
woodcock, 364.
wooden, 203.
woodland glade, 319.
woo't, 204.
workman, 179.
world, 152.
worm, *n.*, 51, 363, 367.
worm, *v.*, 365.
worship, 292.

worshipful, 292.
wort, 359.
worth, *adj.*, 292.
worth, *v.*, 237.
worthless, 307.
worthy, 292.
wot, 156.
would better, 206.
would rather, 206.
wreak, 288 n.
wreck, 288 n.
wren, 130.
wrestle, 57.
wretch, 288, 298.
write, 136.
wrong, 107, 306.
wroot, 359.

Xanthippe, 376.

-y, 186 f.
yacht, 109.
Yankee, 66, 297, 379.
yard, 335.
yea, 310 f.
year, 201 f.
yearn, 'desire,' 358.
yearn, 'mourn,' 358.
Yengees, 66.
yes, 310 f.
yoke, 163.
yokefellow, 287.
yon, 310.
yore, 198.
you, 204.

zany, 387.
zealot, 290.
zoo, 61.
zouave, 380.
zounds, 304.

Printed in the United States of America.

Date Due

APR 1 0 1944			
OCT 2 2 1957			
FEB 6 1958			
MAY 1 2 1960			
FEB 4 1961			
APR 23 '78			
MAR 1 '84			
APR 2 0 '89			